BY GARDINER HARRIS

No More Tears: The Dark Secrets of Johnson & Johnson

Hazard: A Mystery

NO MORE TEARS

No More Tears

THE DARK SECRETS OF JOHNSON & JOHNSON

Gardiner Harris

RANDOM HOUSE • NEW YORK

Published in the United States by Random House, an imprint and division of Penguin Random House LLC, New York.

RANDOM HOUSE and the HOUSE colophon are registered trademarks of Penguin Random House LLC.

Hardback ISBN 9780593229866
Ebook ISBN 9780593229880

Printed in the United States of America on acid-free paper

randomhousebooks.com

9 8 7 6 5 4 3 2 1

First Edition

Contents

A Quintessentially American Company

IN LATE MARCH 2004, I WAS RETURNING FROM A SPRING SKIING TRIP and had a couple of hours to kill at Chicago's O'Hare Airport. Nothing in that cavernous place looked nearly as inviting as an open stool at a burger joint in front of a March Madness men's college basketball game. I dropped my bag under the bar and sat down to watch.

Next to me was a woman wearing a maroon Mississippi State baseball cap with a blond ponytail pulled out the back. She had a beer and half a hamburger on the bar and didn't seem to care that some of her fellow patrons might not appreciate her screaming at the TV in the middle of the afternoon.

The second half had just started, and Mississippi State had a commanding lead over Xavier, the tournament's Cinderella story. We exchanged a few words during commercial breaks, but I'd spent most of the 1990s in Kentucky and knew enough rabid college basketball fans to know I should keep my trap shut while the game was on.

Keeping mum, I watched as Mississippi State collapsed. When the buzzer sounded, the woman with the ponytail groaned audibly, ordered another beer, and turned a rueful smile on me.

She told me her first name and said she was a pharmaceutical sales rep for Janssen, Johnson & Johnson's biggest drug unit. I laughed and told her that I was a drug reporter for *The New York Times*.

She made a face, and I shrugged. "You should probably leave right now," I said.

"I was here first!" she blurted and gave a terrific laugh.

We spoke about our lives and families in ways you only do with a stranger you're all but certain never to see again. And then she told me a story that would drive my reporting for years.

She said her sister had a ten-year-old son who, a year earlier, had gotten into a fight on a school playground. The principal insisted the boy see a shrink. My bar mate's job was selling Risperdal, a drug used to treat schizophrenia, so she offered to get her nephew an immediate appointment with one of her favorite psychiatrists, a specialist who would otherwise require months to see. Her sister gratefully accepted.

Convinced her nephew was perfectly normal, she expected the psychiatrist would admonish him not to fight again and then send him on his way. Instead, the doctor provided her sister with free samples of Risperdal—samples she had dropped off just days before. My bar mate was shocked and told her sister "to think a minute before giving him that medicine."

But it was too late. Over the following year, her nephew gained twenty-five pounds and, embarrassed about his size, stopped visiting the neighborhood pool with his favorite aunt. My bar mate tried without success to persuade her sister to stop the medication. Her brother-in-law, who didn't want the boy on Risperdal either, stopped speaking to her.

Around that time, word got out that the FDA would soon demand that every drug in Risperdal's class of medicines carry new warnings noting that they could cause diabetes and other metabolic problems. Insisting this wasn't true, Johnson & Johnson provided her with talking points to reassure doctors that Risperdal, unlike competing pills, didn't increase the risks of diabetes. But watching her nephew, she knew those reassurances were false. Three weeks after our meeting, the FDA sent the company a warning letter stating that its claims about Risperdal and diabetes were false. A few months later, the company sent doctors across the country a letter admitting that it had mistakenly minimized the risk of diabetes and had made misleading claims that Risperdal was safer than similar drugs—confessions that came too late for many.

Before her nephew became one of the psychiatrist's patients, she was thrilled that his Risperdal prescription numbers continued to climb and loved that his drug sample closet needed frequent restocking. He was one of her "whales," a term drug sales reps use to describe doctors whose many prescriptions fund their bonuses. She'd showered him with gifts as recompense. J & J had paid him to give frequent marketing talks about Risperdal to other doctors, allowing him to build a robust referral network. Now the psychiatrist's numbers made her sick, and she had a hard time even looking at him.

In fact, since Risperdal wasn't approved by federal drug authorities for use in children, she'd been vaguely aware that parts of her job were a bit shady, including pitching Risperdal to child psychiatrists, dropping off drug samples to their offices, and paying these psychiatrists to tell other doctors how to prescribe Risperdal to children. But it hadn't *not* been approved, so . . .

Now she suspected what she'd been doing was just plain wrong and told me she was about to quit. I asked for her last name and phone number and told her that, once she left J & J, she'd be the perfect source for a story about all this.

She shook her head. "Can't do that," she said in a southern drawl that had gotten thicker with her second beer. "I'm only talking to you now 'cause I'm stuck in this dang airport, drank two beers, and the Bulldogs—God bless 'em—freakin' lost. Seeded number two and they lost!"

I sighed. "First of all, let's be clear about one thing," I said. "The Bulldogs didn't just lose, they got crushed. Had to be some kind of historic collapse. I mean, mother of God. Just painful to watch."

We both started laughing. I was never good at keeping a straight face when the moment demanded it.

"Oh Lordy," she said and breathed deeply. "And you think I'm going to talk to you now?"

I slid my business card across the bar. "Look," I said, "you know this is an important story. How many other kids are out there just like your nephew? I can't do this unless folks like you agree to talk."

Shaking that blond ponytail from side to side, she got up and gathered her luggage. She left my card untouched on the bar. "Take care of yourself, Mr. *New York Times.*"

I never saw or heard from her again.

EIGHTEEN YEARS LATER, IN FEBRUARY 2023, *Fortune* MAGAZINE RANKED Johnson & Johnson among the most admired corporations in the world for the twenty-first consecutive year and ranked the company number one on the pharmaceutical industry list for the tenth consecutive year.

"If there is a more American—quintessentially American—company than Johnson & Johnson, I do not know what it is," Tyler Mathisen, a longtime CNBC anchor, said at a network healthcare conference in May 2019. "And in fact, I can't think of another company in the world with the possible, *possible* exception of Coca-Cola, that touches a billion people a day with its products and services as Johnson & Johnson does."

It's true: Johnson & Johnson has been beloved for generations, and many Americans use its products daily. These have included Johnson's Baby Shampoo, Johnson's Baby Oil, and dozens of other baby lotions, conditioners, and sprays; Aveeno and Neutrogena skin moisturizers and cleansers; Tylenol and Motrin for headaches and fever; antihistamines Zyrtec and Benadryl; medicines like Pepcid, Sudafed, and Imodium; Listerine mouthwash and Nicorette gum.

Many of the company's products are lifesavers, including medicines to treat HIV, cancer, and rheumatoid arthritis. Seven in ten patients globally who undergo surgery are stitched up with Johnson

& Johnson sutures. J & J sells catheters and stents for the heart and implants for hips, knees, ankles, shoulders, and breasts.

Beyond its commercial success, Johnson & Johnson has long been seen as a paragon of ethics. First written in 1943, its credo—among the first and most prominent of corporate mission statements—promises that J & J will never put profits before people: "We believe our first responsibility is," it begins, not to shareholders, not to owners, not the profit principle itself but to the patients, doctors, nurses, parents, and others who use Johnson & Johnson's products and services.

Etched in stone at Johnson & Johnson's New Brunswick, New Jersey, headquarters, the J & J credo is discussed at every major corporate meeting and consulted before significant strategic moves. When a maniac tested the credo in 1982 by packing Tylenol capsules with cyanide and killing at least seven people, Johnson & Johnson responded by withdrawing hundreds of millions of bottles from store shelves and relaunching with tamper-proof seals, an effort that cost $100 million.

A Harvard Business School case study of that episode has been used to teach thousands of executives in training that if they do the right thing even at considerable expense, customers will reward them—one of many Harvard case studies that collectively describe J & J as a capitalist's nirvana where doing well and doing good are synonymous.

And it has done well. Johnson & Johnson is the largest healthcare conglomerate in the world, and one of only two corporations on the planet with a AAA credit rating, something not even the United States government can boast.

I spent my early teens in Princeton, New Jersey, where Johnson & Johnson is revered. Robert Wood Johnson II lived his final decades in Princeton, and his namesake foundation—the fifth largest charitable organization in the world—is headquartered there. The region is dotted with mansions owned by Johnson family members and top company executives who send their children to private academies like Princeton Day School and Lawrenceville.

To me, my family, and everyone I knew, Johnson & Johnson was the ideal American corporation. It was mother, medicine, and money all rolled into one. The kids I knew whose parents worked at J & J mentioned the association with pride, and the company's distinctive red cursive logo was featured on T-shirts, jackets, and hats along the poolsides and sidelines of my swim meets and football games.

That image slowly began to change when I was assigned to cover the pharmaceutical industry in 1999 at *The Wall Street Journal* and then at *The New York Times*. My requests for even basic information were often unanswered. I was puzzled. What could Johnson & Johnson—of all companies—possibly have to hide? But bit by bit, I kept discovering things that transformed my confusion to disbelief. For example, I found that J & J was the *only* major manufacturer of HIV/AIDS medicines that refused to share its patents with a United Nations program that has saved millions of African lives. How was that possible? What about the credo?

Around the time of my encounter at O'Hare, I began to suspect that the company's culture and its apple-pie image might be entirely at odds. But I couldn't figure out when this change could have occurred, or why. And even as the company pleaded guilty to multiple crimes, paid huge fines, and was identified as a prime contributor to the nation's opioid crisis, nothing seemed to dent its pristine reputation.

How could that be?

These questions haunted me for years. And though I moved off the healthcare beat and became a foreign, White House, and diplomatic correspondent for the *Times,* I kept thinking about J & J. Finally, my curiosity won out, and I turned again to the company that was simultaneously ever present and invisible. This book is the product of five years gathering tens of thousands of documents, reading through hundreds of thousands of pages of trial transcripts, and contacting hundreds of executives and employees. Among the records I uncovered are secret grand jury files. Providing such documents to a reporter is a criminal offense, but my sources put themselves at considerable risk because they found the company's conduct so singular.

As a many-tentacled conglomerate, Johnson & Johnson's history is exceedingly complicated and difficult to tell. Rather than bouncing between different products with their own discrete narratives inside one continuous chronology, I settled on recounting the separate histories of nine distinctive J & J products. The first section details the story of the company's two most iconic consumer products—Johnson's Baby Powder and Tylenol. The second looks at several important prescription medicines. The third tackles the company's medical device business. The final section describes the path of the company's Covid vaccine effort.

Johnson & Johnson is American healthcare's central player, a colossus standing astride every part of a system that represents 20 percent of the nation's gross domestic product, more than any other sector. Its story is the defining narrative of American healthcare and among the most important in all of American capitalism, but it has a very dark side. As we'll see, its involvement with the rise of the opioid epidemic is horrifying. ("The Sacklers are pikers compared to Johnson & Johnson," a former J & J executive told me.)

A crucial actor in this drama is the Food and Drug Administration, which has regulatory authority over that 20 percent of the American economy. Like Johnson & Johnson, the FDA has a reputation that is often at odds with its deeds.

The American media is also an important player. Much of what is written and broadcast about Johnson & Johnson and its partners is wrong. Because of my years working for them, *The Wall Street Journal* and *The New York Times* come in for particularly sharp censure. Their failings—and by extension my own—have been crucial to Johnson & Johnson's mythmaking.

Perhaps most upsetting is that J & J could not have undertaken many of its most important and problematic sales efforts without the participation of doctors, researchers, academics, and educators. The

American professional class is supposed to have independent self-policing mechanisms to ensure that its members don't engage in unethical or criminal activity. J & J's story offers significant reasons to be skeptical of the effectiveness of this self-policing infrastructure.

The vast disconnect between the mythology and reality of Johnson & Johnson should cast doubt on common fairy tales about the equity and rightness of the American systems of healthcare, government, and economy. Because CNBC's Mathisen was right: J & J's is the quintessential American story.

PART I

Consumer Products

CHAPTER I

An Emotional Bond

JOHNSON'S BABY POWDER AND TYLENOL ARE AMONG THE MOST BE-loved and iconic consumer products ever sold. They largely define Johnson & Johnson's image and have long provided the company with a protective halo of affection from consumers, professionals, and government officials.

While Tylenol is a juggernaut, Johnson's Baby Powder is among the most potent branding instruments ever. The product's fragrance resulted from a lengthy effort to concoct just the right bouquet. After multiple experiments, the company created a complex and distinctive floral scent with more than two hundred ingredients—natural oils, extracts, and aromatic compounds—from all over the world. The fragrance has a sweet, vanilla-like base but also contains overtones of jasmine, lilac, rose, musk, and citrus.

Company surveys found this distinctive mixture of ingredients to be the most recognized fragrance in the world, and for much of the American adult population it conjured the most pleasant memories and associations. Talc products were the cornerstone of the company's baby products, which, despite sales that have in recent years represented less than 1 percent of the company's revenues, were collectively the company's "most precious asset" and "crown jewel," according to a 2008 company slide deck titled "Our Baby History."

"The association of the Johnson's name with both the mother-infant bond and mother's touch as she uses the baby products is known as Johnson & Johnson's Golden Egg," the 2008 slide deck stated.

Surveys showed that the Johnson & Johnson brand is associated most strongly with baby products, and that this association creates an unmatched level of trust—invaluable for a healthcare company.

"Many companies have rational trust," a 1999 corporate slide deck stated. It listed Merck, Bristol-Myers Squibb, GlaxoSmithKline, Procter & Gamble, and Colgate as among the companies with rational trust. At the time, pharmaceutical companies topped surveys of the most admired companies in the world. "Only Johnson & Johnson also has real emotional trust."

"Johnson & Johnson's unique trust results in real business gains for the company," the presentation stated. Among the important benefits, the presentation claimed, is that consumers will forgive missteps and brand crises.

The most powerful of human emotional bonds is between a mother and her baby, the presentation stated. In the slides, the value of this bond is pictured as a piggy bank with coins dropping into its slot on the back, with the words "Mother-Baby Bond" on its side.

"Johnson's baby is 50% heart and 50% mind," concluded the slide deck, which is titled "Trust Is Our Product."

A crucial way that Baby Powder engenders and sustains emotional trust is through its fragrance. Smells feed directly into the brain's limbic system, the ancient seat of human emotion.

"Olfactory learning occurs before birth and helps develop social capacities," another 2009 deck said. "Infants attach meaning to familiar smells within first hours after birth" and "Odor is important in human mother-infant bonding."

So, for generations, much of the American population was implanted in the womb and throughout infancy with a brain worm that associates Johnson & Johnson with love, happiness, trust, and intimacy—a public relations contrivance of unrivaled power and perseverance. Those who attend graduate classes in business, communications, or medicine are still taught that Johnson & Johnson executives wrote the book on crisis response with their honesty and unselfishness in responding to an infamous Tylenol poisoning scare in 1982.

Internally, the positive associations with both products has been vital in creating and sustaining unusually strong beliefs amongst the company's employees that J & J is uniquely ethical and an abiding force for good in the world, faith that paradoxically gives license to lapses that might not otherwise be accepted. Since the 1980s, every new J & J employee has been told soon after their hiring about the company's response to the 1982 Tylenol poisoning case. The official story is repeated so often within the company that it has become something of a prayer.

Johnson's Baby Powder and Tylenol have not contributed significantly to J & J's profits in decades. But their histories remain the company's defining narratives.

CHAPTER 2

Three Brothers Go to New Brunswick, 1860–1968

W HEN THE CIVIL WAR BEGAN, SYLVESTER AND FRANCES LOUISA Wood Johnson saw two of their eleven children immediately enlist in the Union Army. The next boy in line was Robert Wood Johnson, who was sixteen when the war started.

To protect Robert, his parents sent him from their home near Crystal Lake in northeastern Pennsylvania to Poughkeepsie, New York, to serve as an apprentice in an apothecary shop owned by his mother's cousin, James G. Wood. Wood taught the young boy the laborious and mysterious art of medicinal plasters, an early combination of bandage, cast, and medicated patch made by cooking plaster and herbs such as mustard seed, belladonna, and capsaicin together, and then spreading the mixture over cloth and adhesive.

After finishing his apprenticeship in Poughkeepsie in 1864, Robert moved to New York City, where he took a job at a wholesale drug firm. Two years later he struck out on his own, setting up as a broker and importer of chemicals and drugs. He soon met George J. Seabury, another New York drug broker, who had dropped out of medical school to fight in the war. In 1873, the two men started Seabury & Johnson, renting three floors at 30 Platt Street in what is now New York City's cavernous financial district to manufacture medicinal plasters and other products. The older of the two, Seabury served as the company's president while Johnson took the titles of corporate secretary and sales manager.

In 1876, the two brought their plasters to the Centennial Exhibition in Philadelphia, the first official world's fair in the United States, which lasted six months, attracting eight million visitors. Also displaying their wares that year was the German firm Paul Hartmann, which produced a line of antiseptic surgical dressings infused with creosote that had been popularized by Joseph Lister, an English surgeon whose success sterilizing surgical wounds had gained him international fame. In a vast and varied exhibition that featured the first look at Alexander Graham Bell's telephone, the first typewriter, and the first electric lamp, Lister had top billing. At the closing banquet, he was seated at the right hand of President Ulysses S. Grant.

Johnson took careful notes on Hartmann's products and attended Lister's lecture at the fair. Finding himself among the believers in Lister's findings, Johnson soon began experimenting with antiseptic postsurgical dressings. Lister's products were tempting. "The difficulties in manufacture of plasters," Johnson later explained, "were that we could make plasters that would stick but wouldn't keep, and we could make ones that would keep but wouldn't stick." An 1879 Seabury & Johnson catalog had thirty pages of medicated plasters and also included "Lister's Antiseptic Gauze"—a sign of things to come.

Around the time of the fair, Johnson brought Edward Mead Johnson, one of his younger brothers, into the business. Two years later, he offered a job to James Wood Johnson, another younger brother.

An inveterate tinkerer, James became intrigued with the challenges of plaster manufacturing. Hoping that rubber could solve both the stickiness and preservation issues, he created a machine to wash and crush crude rubber and another to grind, stretch, and roll it into thin sheets. These sheets were then coated with various medicines and sandwiched by protective cotton fabrics. These plasters, a yard wide and 120 yards in length, could be rolled onto spools from which hospitals and doctors could cut specific lengths for patients.

After expensive and time-consuming trials, James made what he, his brothers, and the wider medical community came to see as a true breakthrough: consistently achieving the right rubber consistency to make the plasters both effective and long-lasting. Sales surged, but as they did so, Johnson's partnership with Seabury became strained. On July 18, 1885, not long after a contentious board meeting in which Seabury believed his partner was lying, Johnson resigned from the company, signed a ten-year noncompete agreement, and sold his shares to Seabury for $250,000, worth about $8 million today. His brothers resigned the same day.

Six months later, James Wood Johnson was on a westbound train going through New Jersey when he spotted a TO LET sign on a four-story red brick building in New Brunswick. He promptly disembarked and inspected the space, which was on the top floor of an abandoned wallpaper factory.

He and Edward Mead Johnson decided to get back into the medicinal plasters business. They rented the space, lured away fourteen employees—eight of them women—from Seabury & Johnson, and were off.

Robert's noncompete agreement prevented him from joining his brothers. But Seabury soon missed some of his promised payments, and the two renegotiated their agreement. In exchange for canceling $120,000 in promissory notes, the noncompete was voided. On October 28, 1887, he took over his brothers' nascent business, which had been incorporated as Johnson & Johnson. Robert got 40 percent of the shares and his brothers 30 percent each.

Over the course of the next months, two crucial things ensured the company's success. First, Johnson retained the services of James Walter Thompson, who had just started a self-named advertising firm that would eventually become a global giant. The other was that Johnson met Dr. Fred B. Kilmer, the owner of the Opera House Pharmacy on Spring Street in New York City.

A folksy and engaging writer, Kilmer was widely respected in the pharmacy business. In 1888, he authored *Modern Methods of Antisep-*

tic Wound Treatment, a cross between a book and a catalog that included a listing of Johnson & Johnson products along with instructions about their use. The advertorial was a wild success and became a model for the company's marketing efforts for decades in which engaging tutorials were paired with company products. The next year Kilmer sold his pharmacy and joined J & J as director of scientific affairs, a job he would hold for forty-five years.

Johnson & Johnson soon began mass-producing cotton and gauze bandages, constantly innovating new ways to clean, bleach (to sterilize), and comb cotton to produce soft, absorbent dressings. By 1894, the company had four hundred employees working in fourteen buildings, mostly along New Jersey's Raritan River. Every morning, a steamship pulled up to a company dock to load four thousand pounds of cotton and fifteen thousand pounds of plaster dressings.

While the company's supplies to doctors and hospitals formed the foundation of their business, Johnson and Kilmer had a knack for developing consumer spin-offs. One such creation was a small blue carton with a red cross on the label that contained absorbent cotton—a product that soon became one of the most recognized in the United States. Today, it's almost impossible to imagine that simple sheets of cotton could be seen as so attractive to consumers. But up until then, they'd had to staunch cuts and wounds with whatever cloth they had around, no matter how dirty, or race to the doctor's office or hospital.

In 1890, a doctor wrote Kilmer to report that one of his patients had complained of irritated skin after using one of the company's medicated plasters. Some of the ingredients in the company's plasters were known to have this effect, and Kilmer responded by sending the doctor a small tin of Italian talc, which he said would soothe the patient's skin. The company soon decided to include small containers of talc with every order of certain plasters, and the powder became so popular that customers started asking just for talc refills. Some mothers reported that talc was an especially effective remedy for diaper rash.

Sensing an opportunity, in 1894 the company introduced Johnson's Baby Powder, packaging it in a square metal container to prevent it from rolling away during diaper changes. The first toothpaste (called Zonweiss and soon sold in collapsible metal tubes inspired by those for paints) and smaller-sized consumer bandages followed, popular products in which Johnson & Johnson's executives still take great pride.

Pfizer's first big product was morphine. Merck's early blockbuster was cocaine. Both companies conveniently tend to begin their corporate stories around World War II, when they became vital to the war effort by successfully ramping up production of penicillin. But Johnson & Johnson's signature efforts to aid the country launched much earlier. After Congress declared war on Spain in 1898 following the mysterious explosion on the USS *Maine* in Havana harbor, Johnson & Johnson made and quickly delivered to the army and navy three hundred thousand packets of a newly developed compressed surgical dressing. When American troops landed in Cuba, they brought with them a new cloth stretcher that had been rapidly designed and manufactured at J & J—in the words of Fred Kilmer as told to reporters, "Millions of pounds of cotton, millions of yards of gauze, miles upon miles of bandages, plasters enough to encircle the Earth. They are yours, Uncle Sam, if you need them."

Similar pledges were made two years later when a hurricane struck Galveston, Texas. In 1901, Kilmer authored a book with simple instructions and clear illustrations on bandaging and treating injuries. *Johnson's First Aid Manual* was an instant hit and widely adopted in first-aid training programs around the country. When an earthquake leveled much of San Francisco in 1906, railroad cars filled with company products were moving toward the city within hours.

As the company moved into the twentieth century, business boomed. In 1911, J & J marked its twenty-fifth anniversary by touting the fact that it was producing 90 percent of the sterile cotton, gauze, and bandages sold in the world. A factory building near the railroad tracks linking New York City and Philadelphia sported a giant, iconic sign, 20 feet high and 102 feet across, of the Johnson & Johnson logo lit up in white lights with red crosses on either side. The company owned its own fleet of steamships. Its advertising campaigns highlighted its global reach with photos of Red Cross–branded products being carried by camel in India, hot-air balloon in Germany, and dogsled in the Arctic.

Robert Wood Johnson II was the oldest boy of his father's four children and from his earliest days was the company's heir apparent, often accompanying his father to business meetings. At the age of six, he was given a tuxedo with short pants so he could attend fancy social functions.

Raised largely by a governess, Robert attended Rutgers Prep, a private school a block from his palatial home in New Brunswick. Robert's father decided to send his son away from home for his junior year in high school, and he was enrolled in the Lawrenceville School in Mercer County, one of the top private schools in the country. Unhappy, Robert ran away several times. Each time, he made his way to the Trenton, New Jersey, train station, where he waited to be picked up by his father or a member of the household staff. His father finally allowed him to return to Rutgers Prep, where he repeated his junior year.

Robert Wood Johnson II often spoke about his prep school years as wild, fun, and deeply educational. Robert's wildness may have grown out of grief. In 1910, R. W. Johnson died of kidney failure. Soon after his father's funeral, Robert's mother moved to New York City with her two youngest children while Robert was left behind to live with his half sister and her husband.

"Father died at the wrong time for Bob's development," his sister Evangeline later said. "He was just going into adolescence."

Since Robert Wood Johnson II was just sixteen at the time, R. W.'s younger brother James Johnson became the company's president. That summer, Robert Wood Johnson II took a job at one of the company's factories. When he graduated high school the next year, he decided that instead of attending college like so many of his friends, he would join the company full-time. His mother and his uncle, the company president, thought this a bad idea. A compromise was reached in which Johnson promised to attend postgraduate classes at Rutgers Prep while working part-time.

But Johnson soon began skipping classes and begging various foremen to hire him full-time. But with clear instructions from James Johnson that the young man was not allowed to work full-time, none would. Finally, the foreman of the power plant relented, and Robert Wood Johnson II started working there. He would later fondly recall his years working in the lowest rungs of the company's operations but admitted that his drinking and late-night carousing got worse and started to seriously worry his uncle.

Finally, he reached a turning point—one that he recounted many times in his later years. Just before his twenty-first birthday, he arrived at the company offices blind drunk. He promptly passed out on the floor outside the room where the board of directors was meeting. The meeting over, the directors had to step over his body on their way out. Robert Wood Johnson II's uncle was livid.

"Uncle Jimmy told him that if he didn't stop fooling around, he would sell the business," Walter Metts, Robert Wood Johnson II's power plant boss, later recalled. "He stopped that kind of behavior almost overnight and became a very serious-minded young man."

The transformation was so profound that Johnson was soon elected to the board of directors. Over the following years, Johnson was given more and more responsibility over a business that, with the outbreak of World War I, couldn't keep up with demand. Factories began running twenty-four hours a day, seven days a week. Johnson & Johnson became the major supplier of medical products for Allied forces, and the company was soon launching new products and improving older ones based on discoveries made by army surgeons near the battlefield. Hundreds of temporary workers were hired, many of them women who saw working at J & J as a patriotic duty.

For the 1918 flu pandemic, J & J churned out millions more gauze masks, and millions more in profits. But by the summer of 1918, the company's management team realized that, with the war nearing an end and the Spanish flu likely to peak soon, business as it had flourished would collapse. Consumer products, however, wouldn't depend on crises, and the company's Baby Powder seemed the most promising.

In 1918, Johnson & Johnson launched the largest advertising campaign in its history for Baby Powder. Hugely successful, it would forever link the J & J brand with proper infant care—so much so that a shelf of companion products followed. J & J began to refer to itself as "the baby company," a moniker it would use through the first decades of the twenty-first century.

The next breakthrough came in 1920. After his wife kept cutting herself in the kitchen, a cotton mill employee created a long strip of surgical tape with gauze at intervals so she could quickly cut off a bandage to stem the blood. Thus was born J & J's Band-Aid bandages—to this day the most trusted individual product brand in the world.

In addition to consumer products, Robert Wood Johnson II persuaded the company's board of directors to let him and his younger brother take a seven-month trip around the now more settled world, a voyage that generated contacts and insights that would spur the company's foreign expansion for years.

As Robert Wood Johnson II gained in confidence, his uncle began to recede from day-to-day management, and the company's policies and operations began to reflect Johnson's personal traits. At Rutgers Prep, he had delighted in being part of the school's military drill team and became a punctilious dresser. As the corporate flag bearer for the antiseptic movement, the company had always insisted that its factory workers wear white uniforms that resembled those of hospital nurses and orderlies. But the young Johnson took cleanliness to another level, demanding that every corner and window of the company's plants sparkle, office desktops always be free of paperwork, and executives dress sharply. His focus on appearance could be extreme; for example, he used a special scale to measure daily changes in his weight to within a fraction of an ounce.

Johnson was especially appalled at the sorry state of many industrial plants in the United States, particularly in the South, and he wanted to prove to the world that there was a better way. In 1926, as the beginning of Johnson's "Factories Can Be Beautiful" effort, he commissioned a new and beautiful model of a textile-company village within Gainesville, Georgia. Next to a glistening single-story mill he built two hundred employee homes, a grade school, a medical facility, and several churches. Power lines were buried so as not to be visible, and the homes were among the first in northeastern Georgia to have indoor plumbing, electricity, and hot water.

Johnson eventually moved to a vast estate in Princeton but continued to commute to corporate headquarters in New Brunswick. The Route 1 corridor between the two towns became dotted with company plants that Johnson routinely visited to make sure they gleamed, varying his route so that no one could predict which plant he might inspect next. Sometimes he even appeared on Saturdays, surprising a few maintenance workers with a barrage of questions about operations.

Johnson insisted that factory floors and stairwells be painted white so dirt could not go undetected. Plant managers often received follow-up memorandums detailing myriad changes they needed to make, including trimming or replacing specific trees.

"A disorderly plant is a symptom of confused management," he once wrote. "I cannot look into a man's mind, but I can look into his plant." Once, he drove by a plant and noticed that the building's perfect symmetry was marred by a misaligned Venetian blind in one of its windows. He stopped, marched inside, and made sure the blind got straightened. During another inspection, Johnson spotted a dirty window over a stairwell landing and asked a foreman to have it cleaned. When he returned days later and found the window still dirty, he got a stick and carefully smashed out all of its panes. "Perhaps," he reportedly said, "now we will have a clean window."

Johnson decided early in his tenure that J & J would become a conglomerate of largely independent subsidiaries. Legend has it that he called a meeting to discuss problems bedeviling a new product and seventeen people showed up. "I now know what the problem is," he told the assemblage. "Too many people are involved. This meeting is over."

From that moment onward, he was a passionate advocate of decentralization, creating a conglomerate that became known as the Johnson & Johnson Family of Companies. When he expanded overseas, he did so by establishing separate companies operated by locals.

Johnson was as tough an auditor of ethical conduct as he was of dirty windows. Perhaps as a result, Johnson for decades resisted executives' entreaties to enter the pharmaceutical business, which had long been tainted by hucksterism and poisoning scandals. In the 1950s, however, he finally relented, telling colleagues that he would agree to a drug acquisition if it was the right fit. In 1959, the team landed on McNeil Laboratories, a family-owned, Philadelphia-based drug firm founded in 1879 that specialized in sedation and muscle-relaxant drugs. Among McNeil's most promising products was a prescription medicine for pain called Tylenol.

Just months after the McNeil acquisition, Johnson & Johnson purchased Janssen Pharmaceutica, a small drug development firm based in Belgium and run by Paul Janssen, who would prove to be one of history's great medicinal chemists. While Janssen's science was remarkable, the company lacked marketing and sales prowess, which Johnson & Johnson had in abundance.

Both the McNeil and Janssen purchases were spectacular successes. Two years after J & J bought McNeil, the FDA approved over-the-counter sales of Tylenol, and one of the greatest consumer franchises in history was born. Paul Janssen synthesized Haldol, which would become a huge-selling antipsychotic drug. And months before closing the deal with Johnson & Johnson, he developed a synthetic opioid that he would call "fentanyl." Janssen eventually birthed seventy compounds that became commercial drugs, five of which were added to the World Health Organization's list of essential drugs.

With astonishing speed, pharmaceuticals quickly became the

company's fastest-growing business. As J & J's drug sales soared, Johnson named his son, Bobby Johnson, the company's president. The bond between father and son was complicated and strained, in part because Johnson had divorced Bobby's mother when Bobby was just eight. (Bobby told acquaintances that, in multiple instances, it was the family chauffeur who played what should have been his father's role.)

Still, Bobby was eager to follow in his father's professional footsteps and spent four summers working various jobs at the company. After he graduated from Millbrook School, an exclusive private school, Bobby attended Hamilton College for two years before joining the company as an hourly worker in the plaster mill, figuring his birthright was ultimately much more advantageous than a bachelor's degree.

During World War II, Bobby enlisted in the army and served in Europe, rising to the rank of sergeant. When he returned, he got married, started having children, and quietly began to forge his own identity in the company. Pushing to make the company somewhat more democratic, he hired a series of hotshot marketing executives. At one point, Johnson suggested to his son that Bobby's secretary wasn't an appropriate guest in the executive dining room, but Bobby insisted otherwise.

It was just one of many examples of the father and his son's inability to mesh. Rail thin and invariably well-dressed, Johnson couldn't hide his disapproval of his son's excessive weight and more casual outfits. In 1963, with his health beginning to fail him, Johnson appointed Philip B. Hoffmann, who had started at the company as a shipping clerk, to succeed him as chief executive and chairman, bypassing Bobby, who was appointed a co-vice-chairman of the company's executive committee.

After being told of the new arrangement (Johnson instructed others to break the news), Bobby responded with a letter in which he wrote that while he disagreed with "some of these changes," he pledged to remain loyal to his father and the company.

A year later, Johnson insisted that Bobby seek medical help for his excessive weight and other health problems. Bobby took a five-month leave, lost thirty pounds, cured his ulcer, and got the rest of his health back in shape. But Johnson made clear to other executives that even this improved Bobby wasn't welcome back and demoted him. In a bitter letter dated May 12, 1964, Bobby resigned. He was forty-five. No family member would ever again reach the top rungs of the company's hierarchy, and the Johnson family would be visited by a series of tragedies and scandals that would keep them in the society pages for decades.

Johnson died on January 30, 1968, of liver cancer. He bequeathed much of his wealth—his personal fortune was immense—to the Robert Wood Johnson Foundation, among the world's largest charitable organizations. By the time of his death, Johnson & Johnson was the biggest healthcare conglomerate in the world, a position it retains to this day.

CHAPTER 3

Mineral Twins

FOUND IN NATURAL DEPOSITS ON ALMOST EVERY CONTINENT, TALC in blocks is known as soapstone and is used to make stoves, sinks, laboratory countertops, and electric switchboards. Finely ground, talcum powder is used in paint, paper, electric cables, ceramics, and on inner tubes and rubber gloves to keep them from sticking. But its most intriguing and controversial use is in cosmetics.

Indeed, there is no softer mineral on earth than talc. Powdered talc feels cool and almost oily to the touch. The ancient Egyptians used it as a cosmetic, and thousands of years later, it is still found in eye shadow and blush. In places like India, where the biggest-selling cosmetics are skin lighteners, talcum powder has for millennia served as a low-tech way to make skin whiter. Often sold with strong fragrances, talcum powder is also sometimes used by women in their crotch to cover normal vaginal smells.

The weakness of bonds between talc's microscopic platelets, which allows them to slide easily past each other, creates the smooth, greasy feel. It's also why talcum powder creates such a cloud when sprinkled and can remain suspended in room air for more than an hour after a powdering. Since mothers change diapers of young children six to twelve times a day, such powdering can lead to talcum powder being suspended in a changing room's air for much of the day.

The first reports documenting dangers specific to talcum powder were published in 1922. Researchers noticed that babies sometimes grabbed the distinctive white bottle of Johnson's Baby Powder and showered powder on their faces. Because of its small particle size and water insolubility, talc can block the alveoli in a baby's lungs—the tiny air sacs where oxygen is passed into the blood—which is exactly what it did in some infants, fatally asphyxiating them.

In 1969 and again in 1981, *Pediatrics*, the official journal of the American Academy of Pediatrics, carried items warning against using talcum powder during diaper changing because so many babies were being injured this way.

The authors of the 1981 alert wrote that the national Poison Control Center was surprised to discover that it had received forty calls in the six months between January 1, 1980, and June 30, 1980, about children under five years old who had inhaled excessive talcum powder. Nine of the calls originated from emergency rooms, five from doctors' offices, and twenty-six from mothers at home, and together they represented about one in every hundred calls to poison control centers involving young children.

Johnson & Johnson placed a warning on bottles about these risks. "Keep powder away from children's nose and mouth," it stated. "Inhalation can cause breathing problems." But while the company made several changes over a century to the bottle's spout to reduce chances that babies would die this way, the risk never disappeared.

A deeper question was whether chronic inhalation of powders might be dangerous. When the century dawned, underground miners had been pulling coal and other kinds of rock from the earth mostly using picks and shovels. Industrialization led to the use of dynamite, drills, and continuous mining machines that vastly increased the amount of rock and dust produced. Concurrently, hundreds of thousands of miners died from lung disease.

In one terrible example, Union Carbide hired from 1930 to 1935 nearly three thousand workers—mostly African Americans—to dig a tunnel through a mountain of quartz at Hawk's Nest in West Virginia to divert a river for hydroelectric power. The workers drilled through quartz, creating clouds of silica dust, but weren't given masks or respirators, although the white engineers and managers who inspected the work always wore protection.

As many as one thousand of the tunnelers died of silicosis, the lung disease that results from breathing too much silica. The intake was so severe that some miners died on their feet; others were dead within a few weeks of starting work. Even after the death toll rose to shocking levels, Union Carbide did nothing to protect its employees. To conceal the scope of the tragedy, the company buried many of the bodies in secret cemeteries nearby.

The worst industrial disaster in American history, Hawk's Nest demonstrated for the first time that intense exposure to some kinds of rock dust can kill within days. Those who worked with talc—including tire workers and millers—got sick, too. Studies published in 1942 and 1955 documented high levels of this disabling and fatal lung disease—talcosis—among talc workers.

Still, for much of the twentieth century, consumers had few reasons to suspect that regular and appropriate use of talcum powder would endanger them. There were hints, though. In 1956, 1963, and 1968, researchers and industry officials wrote that asbestos was a common talc contaminant. These findings suddenly cast the risks of talc-based powders in a far more concerning light, as research had already strongly suggested that asbestos powder might be the most dangerous rock dust on the planet.

ASBESTOS HAS MUCH GOING FOR IT. THE ODDEST OF MINERALS, IT looks like wool or cotton, not stone. It can be spun into a thread and woven into a cloth. Clothes, couches, oven mitts, and a slew of other soft products can be made from asbestos. No other rock is nearly as pliable. It's lightweight, easy to mine and process, abundant, almost indestructible, long-lasting, electrically nonconductive, and heat resistant. It can be blended with a host of other materials, like resins and plastics, to make almost anything. As a bonus, rats and mice hate it.

Archaeologists in Finland unearthed ceramic utensils and pots made from a mixture of clay and asbestos that appear to have been made around 2500 B.C., the earliest confirmed use. Textiles made from asbestos have been found in digs in Greece and China dating to as early as 1500 B.C. The Egyptians sometimes used asbestos cloth to protect the embalmed bodies of pharaohs, and the Romans used it to collect the ashes of emperors. Charlemagne, a Roman emperor who ruled from 800 to 814, had an asbestos tablecloth that was cleaned after meals by being tossed into a fire, such was its imperishable nature.

Countless early historians mentioned the qualities of asbestos and its cloth with amazement, including Marco Polo, Saint Augustine, and Benjamin Franklin. But asbestos was little more than a novelty until the second Industrial Revolution of the late nineteenth century. A material that resists heat, fire, motion, and electricity represented the perfect companion to the internal combustion engine. Between 1890 and 1968, global asbestos production rose 800,000 percent, from five hundred tons to four million tons annually.

By mid-twentieth century in America, there was not a car, airplane, ship, train, building, factory, or home that did not contain asbestos. It was present in drywall, fireproofing sprays, pipe insulation, oven mitts, and brake pads. Steel ships were filled with the stuff. The snow that washed away the poison in the field of poppies in the 1939 movie *The Wizard of Oz* was asbestos, as were the snow-like sprinkles used on home Christmas trees.

But over the course of the twentieth century, asbestos was eventually found to be the cause of at least four fatal illnesses: asbestosis, lung cancer, ovarian cancer, and mesothelioma. Asbestos's crystalline needles—the source of its extraordinary pliability—are so microscopic that they spear DNA itself, causing genetic changes that lead to cancer growth. (By comparison, one linear inch of asbestos contains nearly 1,000,000 fibrils lying side by side, compared to 3,800 fibrils for fiberglass.) The tiniest exposures can kill, which is why asbestos has been banished from modern life. In March 2024, the Biden Administration finalized a ban on chrysotile asbestos, the last type still imported and used in the United States.

Hints of asbestos's deadly effects date back to the first century A.D., when the Greek geographer Strabo and the Roman naturalist Pliny the Elder both mentioned a sickness of the lungs in slaves who wove asbestos. More evidence emerged in the United Kingdom and France in the early twentieth century as doctors and labor inspectors noted the horrific lung damage and exceptional death rates among those who worked with asbestos. In a *British Medical Journal* paper on the death of a thirty-three-year-old woman who had worked in an asbestos textile factory near Manchester, England, Dr. W. E. Cooke declared, "We have never seen anything parallel" to the yellowish-brown "curious bodies" in her lungs, and that there was no reasonable doubt that they were anything other than "the heavy, brittle, iron-containing fragments of asbestos fibre."

Following up, between 1928 and 1929, Edward R. A. Merewether, a medical inspector based in Glasgow, examined one-sixth of Britain's total asbestos textile workforce. About one quarter showed signs of lung scarring. Among those who had worked in the factories for at least twenty years, 81 percent were affected. In 1931, the British government enacted regulations to control asbestos dust levels, and acute asbestosis cases declined.

This was certainly not the first time lung disease had been discovered among industrial workers. Black lung among coal miners had been known for a century, and dust from cotton fibers had long been known to cause a disabling lung condition known as byssinosis. But continued research began to show that asbestos was also a carcinogen, with autopsies revealing lung cancers that could be of "huge" size and appear in workers at ten times the normal background rate of lung cancer.

In 1960, South African researchers published a seminal paper pointing out that mesothelioma, a rare cancer of the lining of the lung and abdominal cavity, occurred almost exclusively in the country's asbestos-mining region. Beyond their regional concentration, the most striking thing about most of the victims was how *little* contact they'd had with asbestos. One was a fifty-six-year-old woman whose husband had once owned an asbestos mine. Another was a forty-two-year-old housewife who lived near an asbestos mine.

The 1960 Wagner paper was the first clear signal that tiny amounts of asbestos could kill, sometimes decades after exposure. Researchers around the world began expressing alarm. Another team of South African researchers decided to check for asbestos in the lungs of five hundred people who underwent consecutive autopsies in the city of Cape Town. More than a quarter were found to have asbestos deep in their lung tissue.

"The half-life of strontium 90 is 28 years, but the half-life of the asbestos fibre is an infinity of years," the researchers wrote. Strontium 90 is a radioactive waste product from nuclear reactors. "The 2,400,000 tons of asbestos used each year are added to the millions of tons used in previous years, and even if a small proportion becomes available as an air-contaminant in towns, the actual amount will increase, as more asbestos accumulates on the surface of the earth." Subsequent autopsy studies in Pittsburgh, Finland, Miami, Montreal, New York, and Belfast found asbestos in the lungs of between 25 percent and 50 percent of adults. In 1965, a study of eighty-three mesothelioma patients at a London hospital found that many had no documented exposure to asbestos other than living within a half mile of an asbestos plant. Other studies reinforced the fatal results of minimal exposure.

Around the same time as the South African studies, Dr. Irving J. Selikoff, an internist who operated a clinic in Paterson, New Jersey, decided to follow up on seventeen patients who had worked at a nearby, now-shuttered asbestos textile factory. Selikoff found that six years after the plant had closed, six of the seventeen were dead.

Alarmed, Selikoff started writing to asbestos companies and asking if he could examine their workers or employment records. None agreed. He asked for a government grant from the U.S. Public Health Service and was denied. Finally, he asked a union of insulation workers whether he could examine the group's employment and health histories. The union consented. In 1964, his study of 632 insulation workers was published in the *Journal of the American Medical Association*.

"Building trades insulation workers have relatively light, intermittent, exposure to asbestos," he and two co-authors wrote. Nonetheless, forty-five had died of cancer of the lung or its lining. In a normal population, fewer than seven such deaths would be expected.

By then, researchers had started to link asbestos with cancers beyond the lungs and their lining. In 1953, a doctor at the London Hospital started noticing that women with asbestosis seemed to suffer abdominal cancer at exceedingly high rates. In a study published in 1960, he wrote that of the twenty-three women with asbestosis treated at the hospital, nine had died of what may have been ovarian cancer. How could inhaled asbestos migrate to the ovaries and cause cancer there?

In 1968, *The New Yorker* published the first in a series of articles by Paul Brodeur about the hazards of tiny amounts of asbestos. The piece placed the dangers of asbestos firmly in the public consciousness and made a star of Selikoff, who by then was leading a team of thirty asbestos researchers at Mount Sinai School of Medicine on Manhattan's Upper East Side.

Selikoff and his team were in the midst of studying the lung tissues of three thousand consecutive autopsies performed at three different New York City hospitals, and Brodeur wrote that early results suggested half contained asbestos fibers. Brodeur also quoted Selikoff as saying the growing ubiquity of asbestos in modern America was a serious health threat. Even children's products were contaminated, Selikoff told Brodeur.

Selikoff may have been referring to tests done that year by Dr. Arthur M. Langer, one of his researchers. Having studied under a famous mineralogist at Columbia University, Langer had, early in his training, tried to grow asbestos in the lab. But, like a soufflé that falls into a gelatinous mess, Langer's first batch had not come out as asbestos but . . . talc. The chemical ingredients to make both minerals are the same. They just require a different mix of temperature and pressure.

Selikoff had recruited Langer in 1965 to join his group at Mount Sinai and help them try to explain why half of New Yorkers had asbestos in their lungs. The real puzzle was the asbestos particles in women. Why were so many homemakers suffering from what had long been deemed an industrial illness?

Selikoff's team had asked relatives of the deceased to complete detailed surveys. Langer noticed that 80 percent of the women were regular users of talcum powder. With his early experience of the mineralogical similarities between talc and asbestos, Langer thought he might have found the culprit.

In 1968, to test his theory, Langer went to a local pharmacy, purchased a brace of popular talcum powders including Johnson's Baby Powder, and ran them through the lab's electron microscope. He found that all were contaminated with asbestos.

A consistent theme throughout this book is how unsurprising so many findings were, given previous research—and that the earlier research had been ignored or essentially suppressed by those whose business interests would be impacted by awareness and regulation. In April 1968, about the time Langer was shopping at his local pharmacy, a paper presented at the American Industrial Hygiene Conference in St. Louis, Missouri, confirmed that all talcum powder products contained asbestos, which "may create an unsuspected problem," the authors wrote. A year later, a researcher wrote in the *American Review of Respiratory Disease*, "It is difficult to conceive of a better way of having fibers inhaled than the use of cosmetic talcum powders."

For Johnson & Johnson, virtually none of this was new. In 1958, when it was looking for ways to make its baby powder even less abrasive, J & J sent several tons of talc to the Battelle Memorial Institute in Columbus, Ohio. A private laboratory, Battelle advised J & J that the best way to improve the appearance, feel, and purity of the powder was to remove as many impurities as possible. Those impurities, Battelle noted, were "less than 1 percent to about 3 percent of contaminants," and these were mostly asbestos.

In 1964, Johnson & Johnson—worried about the political stability of Italy, according to internal documents—decided to transition from importing Italian talc and purchased a set of talc mines in Vermont with names like Argonaut, Rainbow, Frostbite, and Black Bear. (Bottles of Johnson's Baby Powder sold abroad still generally used Italian talc. But those sold in the United States contained exclusively Vermont talc.) As Italy remained sufficiently stable, J & J now had far more talc than it needed for Baby Powder and its other talc-based cosmetics, so it sold much of its mines' production for industrial uses like roofing, flooring, and tires.

One of the new talc mines was located in Johnson, Vermont, a few hundred yards from an asbestos mine owned by the Vermont Asbestos Group and three miles from what was once the largest chrysotile asbestos mine in the United States. That colocation was no accident; talc and asbestos are so chemically, geologically, and structurally similar that veins of one are often sandwiched between or ribboned with the other.

While the Johnson mine was deep underground, most talc mines are close to the surface. Miners drill holes, place charges in them, blow up huge areas, and scoop up the resulting rubble with shovels that can be as big as a house. Once intermingled, talc and asbestos are impossible to completely separate.

Predictably, Johnson & Johnson's tests of its Vermont talc were problematic. A memorandum dated November 1, 1967, from William Ashton, a top J & J talc executive, contained a table of impurities that included trace quantities of two kinds of asbestos, including tremolite.

About a year and a half later, Ashton wrote a memo to Dr. Gavin Hildick-Smith, a J & J scientist, stating that he was worried tremolite's "needle type crystals" could penetrate and irritate the skin. He wrote that some of the world's environmental health agencies had severe objections to tremolite's presence in talcum powders, and a lot of attention had lately been paid to the risks of inhaling such particles.

"The question is," Ashton concluded, "how bad is Tremolite medically, and how much of it can safely be in a talc base we might develop?"

Hildick-Smith passed Ashton's letter to Dr. T. M. Thompson, Johnson & Johnson's associate director of clinical research, who replied six days later in a lengthy memorandum that he had no information about how tremolite might irritate the skin. The real worry, he wrote, was inhalation.

Over the years, the recently deceased Robert Wood Johnson II had expressed concerns about whether talcum powder adversely impacted the lungs of babies or mothers, Thompson explained. So, too, had pediatricians. However, the company had always offered reassurances that Baby Powder had minimal amounts of tremolite, Thompson wrote. Making sure that those reassurances were true was important, he insisted.

"Since the usage of these products is so widespread, and the existence of pulmonary disease is increasing, it is not inconceivable that we could become involved in litigation in which pulmonary fibrosis or other changes might be rightfully or wrongfully attributed to inhalation of our powder formulations," Thompson wrote. "It might be that someone in the Law Department should be consulted with regard to the defensibility of our position in the event that such a situation should ever arise."

In 1971, the Tenovus Cancer Research Institute in Cardiff, Wales, published a study titled "Talc and Carcinoma of the Ovary and Cervix." Two years before, the Tenovus researchers had developed a new "extraction-replication" technique to try to find asbestos in ovarian and cervical tumors. They failed. Instead, the Tenovus team found talc—lots of it. Worse, the talc particles seemed to be located at the very core of the tumors, suggesting they were the primary irritant that led to the development of the ovarian cancer itself.

If this idea became widely accepted, talc-based Johnson's Baby Powder was doomed. With Baby Powder profits being too important to the company, J & J executives developed a plan to discredit the study. One aspect of that plan was to hire Selikoff to (hopefully unsuccessfully) try to replicate the Tenovus work. Tenovus agreed to send Selikoff its actual tissues samples, and Selikoff gave the job of peering into the cells to the young Langer. J & J sent one of its own employees to watch Langer work.

With his company monitor beside him, Langer prepared slides of the Tenovus tissues and peered through his microscope. The Johnson & Johnson employee observing all this wrote a memo to his superiors describing how Langer found fibrous particles whose density and diameters proved that they were asbestos. In a letter that Langer sent J & J on November 10, 1971, he affirmed that he had indeed found talc in the Tenovus tissues. "We also got a few surprises in that we observed some chrysotile asbestos to be present in the tissue as well," Langer wrote.

The Tenovus team had gone looking for asbestos but had instead found only talc. Langer found both, something he considered important enough to publish, which he also told J & J. But Langer did more than just look at the Tenovus tissue samples. With the J & J monitor watching, he prepared slides of Johnson's Baby Powder—and found a similar mixture of talc and asbestos.

"We also observed trace amounts of chrysotile asbestos," he wrote. Perhaps to ease the blow, he said that "J & J baby talc is of quite high quality and as a matter of fact, in relation to the number of samples we have examined thus far, it is the 'purest.'"

Johnson & Johnson hadn't asked Langer to examine Baby Powder and certainly didn't want him finding asbestos in it. The company had no interest in Langer publishing any of these findings and seriously discouraged such a step, according to company documents and later statements in court.

So instead of publishing against the wishes of their funders, Langer and Selikoff shared their results with Jerome Kretchmer, New York City's top environmental protection official. On June 29, 1971, Kretchmer called a press conference to announce that two unidentified brands of cosmetic talc appeared to contain asbestos. He asked New Yorkers to stop using talc-based powders.

At the time, sales of Johnson's Baby Powder exceeded the sales of all other talcum powders combined. Johnson & Johnson promptly issued a statement falsely reassuring its customers: "Our fifty years of research knowledge in this area indicates that there is no asbestos contained in the powder manufactured by Johnson & Johnson."

Nevertheless, the FDA opened an investigation. On July 8, 1971, a delegation of J & J scientists met face-to-face with agency officials. The private meeting, which took place at the longtime headquarters of the Department of Health and Human Services just downhill from the U.S. Capitol building in Washington, D.C., began with Wilson Nashed, a J & J scientist, telling agency officials that his team was going to be sharing documents and information that the company deemed to be trade secrets. He warned the FDA officials that they could not make the information public without the company's explicit permission.

The J & J team then told FDA officials that company tests showed that J & J's talc contained "only minor amounts (below 1%) of tremolite and actinolite, or in other words less than 1%, if any, asbestos particles," according to a contemporaneous FDA memo summarizing the meeting.

This, of course, contradicted the company's public avowal that Johnson's Baby Powder was asbestos-free. J & J's private communications acknowledging asbestos contamination continued for decades.

The most sympathetic explanation is that executives truly believed that asbestos concentrations were so low and had such negligible health effects that declaring Baby Powder as asbestos-free was justified. But as evidence mounted, these false declarations became more difficult to explain in a sympathetic way. Years later, a company representative would acknowledge in court testimony that statements made under oath by a top company executive—statements identical to those made by other company executives and lawyers—that asbestos has never been found in Baby Powder were false.

CHAPTER 4

The FDA Conducts a Survey

FOR YEARS, THE FDA HELD INFORMAL MEETINGS WITH TALC MANU-
facturers to discuss the industry's asbestos problem. But as public attention grew, agency officials decided that quiet persuasion wasn't
enough.

In August 1971, the agency invited a range of manufacturers, scientists, and officials from other government agencies to come to
Washington for a formal conclave. Among the invitees were representatives from Johnson & Johnson and Pfizer, officials from the
FDA, the Bureau of Mines, the National Institute for Occupational
Safety and Health, and the U.S. Geological Survey, as well as Langer
and some of his colleagues from Mount Sinai.

The meeting's stated goal was to "discuss in detail analytical methods for the determination of minor amounts of 'asbestos like' material in talc with particular reference to cosmetic grade talcs." The
technology to measure asbestos concentrations was evolving rapidly,
and the FDA wanted a consensus on what machines to use and how.
Regulators also hoped for a decision on how much asbestos was too
much.

No firm decisions were reached on any of the crucial issues, but
FDA officials came out of the conference deciding that they needed

to understand the true extent of the problem. So, in December 1971, the FDA hired Professor Seymour Z. Lewin of New York University to analyze consumer talc. In September 1972, Lewin began sharing his results with the FDA: Of the 102 samples of consumer products containing talcum powder, about 40 percent were contaminated with asbestos, including J & J's Baby Powder and Shower to Shower products.

Around that time, the National Institute for Occupational Safety and Health released its own test results of nine popular baby powders using electron microscopy. Its study indicated "possible asbestos fiber contamination of commercial baby powders."

The FDA privately shared Lewin's results with J & J and other talc manufacturers but didn't announce them publicly. Nashed, the J & J scientist who had visited the FDA previously, responded by writing to the FDA that removing asbestos entirely from talcum powder was impossible, and he argued that there was no evidence that small amounts of asbestos hurt people.

Whether Nashed actually believed this can't be known, since he died in 1988. In fact, though, research conducted over the previous twelve years had already demonstrated that even small amounts of asbestos could sicken and kill.

J & J hired Dr. Albert M. Kligman, a professor of dermatology at the University of Pennsylvania School of Medicine, to find out what would happen both to rabbits and to human beings if they were injected with talc and asbestos.

Kligman was a problematic researcher, to say the least. For many years, he had conducted tests of Johnson's Baby Powder, as well as Band-Aids, shampoos, and other drugs, on African American prisoners and mentally disabled children. These experiments were often exquisitely painful for his vulnerable subjects.

Kligman wrote a letter dated December 10, 1971, to Hildick-Smith describing his results. First, Kligman injected the rabbits and discovered that the chrysotile sample "produced an intensely granu-

lomatous reaction associated with necrosis and later by cyst formation." Necrosis means cell or tissue death.

Despite this response, Kligman then proceeded to inject chrysotile samples into the lower backs of ten of the Black prisoners. He
noted that the injection sites showed considerable swelling at ten and
twenty days, but by thirty days the obvious irritation had lessened.
No one tracked whether the prisoners later developed cancer.

(In 2021, J & J finally expressed remorse for sponsoring such experimentation, explaining: "In no way do they reflect the values or
practices we employ today.")

ON AND ON IT WENT AS THE FDA'S INVESTIGATION CONTINUED.
A private lab in Chicago got samples of Johnson's Baby Powder
from the same lots as Lewin. The lab declared the samples free of
chrysotile, contradicting Lewin. But it did find small amounts of
tremolite—0.5 percent in one batch and 0.2 percent to 0.3 percent in
others. When J & J forwarded the Chicago report to the FDA, however, the lab's line about the tremolite content had been eliminated.
("DO NOT USE THIS REPORT," someone at J & J wrote by hand
on the original report's cover.) In the cover letter that accompanied
the doctored Chicago report, J & J stated that the results clearly
showed that the tested samples "contain no chrysotile asbestos."

In June of 1972, Kretchmer, New York City's Environmental Protection Administrator, decided that in the year since his first warning,
not enough had been done to eliminate asbestos from common baby
products. Calling reporters back to his office, he named names.

"Two brands of talcum powder have been named by the city's
Environmental Protection Administration as having heavy asbestos
fiber levels that might contribute to lung cancer years after a person
inhaled their dust," read *The New York Times* story that followed:

"The environment agency's concern about asbestos in baby
powder surfaced almost a year ago, when Jerome Kretchmer, the

Environmental Protection Administrator, advised consumers to stop using talcum until suspicions about its asbestos content were cleared up."

At the time, Mr. Kretchmer said two brands tested showed from 5 to 25 percent asbestos fibers in them but declined to name them until tests on other brands were made.

After repeated inquiries from newsmen, the agency released a letter dated June 8 from James R. Marshall, director of public information, to a consumer, naming Landers and Johnson & Johnson as the brands. He said the agency was still awaiting results of tests on other brands, since it suspected that "virtually every talcum powder contains some asbestos."

KRETCHMER'S CLAIM THAT J & J'S TALCUM POWDERS CONTAINED UP TO 25 percent asbestos was wrong—the amounts were far lower. Outraged, Nashed called an FDA official, Dr. Robert M. Schaffner, and stated that the latest report that J & J had forwarded to the agency from the Chicago lab and other testing sites "prove conclusively the absence of asbestos in our powder." That was true to an extent—but only because J & J had redacted the tremolite result from the Chicago test. Schaffner got on the phone with the *Times*, as did Langer, who corrected Kretchmer's figures.

The next day, the *Times* published a corrected story titled "Talc Warning Is Labeled False." Langer was quoted as saying that more recent and detailed analyses had found only trace amounts of asbestos in Johnson & Johnson's Baby Powder. And "Dr. Robert M. Schaffner, director of the Office of Product Technology for the F.D.A., said that out of 40 talcum samples recently tested by the Federal agency, 39 contained only 1 per cent or less of asbestos," the *Times* story stated. "Dr. Schaffner said that in light of this research, 'we would not agree with the warning on talc.'"

Still, the controversy over the presence of tremolite in talcum powders continued to build, and J & J executives continued their whack-a-mole strategy of discrediting any scientist or report that publicly revealed Baby Powder's contamination while debating internally whether this plan of action was sustainable. They hired Dr. Fred D. Pooley, a professor at the Department of Mineral Exploitation at Cardiff University in Wales, along with two of his colleagues at the university, to analyze the Italian talc the company was still using in the baby powder it sold abroad. The analysis found "very minor amounts" of tremolite, among other impurities.

A few months later, Tom Shelley, director of J & J's Central Research Laboratories in New Jersey wrote a memo to Ashton, Nashed, Hildick-Smith, and others noting that "it is quite possible that eventually tremolite will be prohibited in all talc," and therefore it was imperative that they figure out a way to rid talc of tremolite. Assuming that Pooley could come up with an effective separation technique, the invention should be patented as quickly as possible, Shelley wrote. That sort of invention might have to be employed by every talc producer in the United States, making it potentially lucrative in its own right.

A month later, Shelley changed his mind in another memo to a J & J lawyer, pointing out that this patent would in effect be a public acknowledgment by the company that talc was routinely contaminated with asbestos. (Pooley designed a method to assess talc's contaminants and found asbestos in J & J's Vermont talc, prompting J & J to declare the technique "too sensitive.")

Meanwhile, DeWitt Petterson, Johnson & Johnson's research director, toured the Vermont mining operations with several top company executives. J & J was claiming that Johnson's Baby Powder was free of asbestos because its talc mines were asbestos-free. Petterson wanted to know if making such claims represented a viable long-term strategy. As it turned out, it was not. In an April 26, 1973, memorandum Petterson sent to D. D. Johnston, the president of J & J's baby division, he noted that "We believe this mine to be very clean; however, we are also confident that fiber forming or fiber type minerals could be found. The usefulness of the 'Clean Mine' approach for asbestos is over."

Petterson said that analytical techniques to identify asbestos were improving rapidly and would soon allow almost any good laboratory to spot asbestos in just about any sample of talc. He proposed several solutions to Baby Powder's increasingly obvious contamination problem, including a switch to corn starch, which "by its very nature does not contain fibers" and "is assimilated into the body." He recommended that the switch to corn starch be made a priority.

It wasn't, and a year later, yet another mole popped its head up. The Val Chisone mine outside of Turin had been the exclusive source for Johnson's Baby Powder during much of the early twentieth century. Gianfranco Villa, the son of the mine's owner, believed that his family's talcum powder was the best in the world and wished to prove that by publicizing test results showing its relatively low level of impurities. Villa created a pamphlet, Practical Guide to Recognition of Impurities in Talc, which noted that talc contained a variety of impurities including various metals and "very hard silicates, as chrysotile and tremolites, of amphibolitic derivation, namely with strict asbestos content." He pointed out that the asbestos content of some talcs was as high as 10 percent. But he claimed that his own talc, by contrast, had only trace quantities of asbestos—making it the cleanest in the world.

What Villa failed to understand was that, while admitting to trace quantities of asbestos had been acceptable in the 1960s, it was no longer so in 1974. Ashton wrote that the pamphlet "calls undue attention to a host of trace metals in talcs and brands them as harmful elements." The J & J team emphatically explained to Villa the risks involved with publishing his pamphlet in English. The group drank a bunch of wine, and finally Villa relented.

CHAPTER 5

Birth of the Modern FDA

THE FOOD AND DRUG ADMINISTRATION WAS BORN IN 1906 WITH the passage of the Pure Food and Drugs Act, which gave some oversight powers to a small laboratory previously known as the U.S. Department of Agriculture's Bureau of Chemistry.

For the next three decades, the FDA was mostly a toothless reference agency, allowed to crack down on patent medicines and snake-oil cures only when the products' listed ingredients weren't present. But if the medicines were toxic or promised cures they couldn't deliver, the FDA was powerless to intervene.

In the 1930s, women's groups, public health leagues, government officials, and a few members of Congress began to push for legislation that would give the FDA the power to ban unsafe medicines. But the 1936 elections strengthened the hands of opponents, and by the summer of 1937, reform advocates quietly admitted defeat.

Then on October 11, 1937, Dr. James Stevenson, the president of the Tulsa Medical Society in Oklahoma, sent a telegram to the headquarters of the American Medical Association reporting that six people had died after taking a proprietary anti-infective medicine called Elixir Sulfanilamide made by S. E. Massengill, a patent medicine company based in Bristol, Tennessee.

The AMA's chemical laboratory tested the drug and determined that S. E. Massengill's medicine included diethylene glycol, a key ingredient in antifreeze and a potentially lethal industrial solvent.

Tulsa medical authorities soon alerted the FDA, which discovered that similar deaths were occurring across the country. Panic gripped the nation. By late October, reporters began following FDA agents as they seized Elixir bottles in towns far and wide. Stories noted that if not for agents' quick work, thousands more would have died.

At least seventy-three deaths were conclusively linked to the elixir, with dozens more suspected. Among the dead was six-year-old Joan Nidiffer of Tulsa, Oklahoma, whose mother sent a letter to President Roosevelt along with a photo of her child. Little Joan's adorable and smiling face was just the heartbreaking exhibit that women's groups and public health associations needed. They pointed out that Joan would be alive if their earlier proposals to strengthen the FDA had become law.

In 1938, Congress passed the Food, Drug, and Cosmetics Act, which required drugmakers to seek FDA approval before selling new medicines. The FDA was tasked only with testing whether a drug was safe, not whether it was effective.

Over the next twenty-five years, however, FDA medical reviewers realized that they couldn't properly assess a medicine's safety without some information about its efficacy. Blindness might be an acceptable side effect for a lifesaving drug, but no one would risk their sight to cure toenail fungus. So, even without explicit legislative authority, some FDA reviewers began quietly insisting that drugmakers provide evidence about how well products worked. But the requests were spotty, and schlock cures still got through.

In September 1960, the William S. Merrell Company of Cincinnati, Ohio, submitted an application to sell a sedative with antinausea properties. The company named the drug Kevadon and claimed that it was safer than the barbiturates widely used at the time. While the FDA considered the application, Merrell's German partner quickly won approval for general sales in Europe, where the medicine became a popular remedy for morning sickness in expectant mothers. Kevadon's chemical name was *thalidomide*.

At the FDA, Merrell's application was assigned to Frances Kelsey, a junior medical officer who soon grew suspicious about both the safety of Kevadon and the truthfulness of Merrell's executives. Kelsey sat on the application for months.

In the meantime, an epidemic of congenital birth abnormalities struck West Germany, Great Britain, and Australia. Affected babies were born with flippers instead of arms and legs, or with no limbs whatsoever. In late 1961, a doctor in West Germany and another in Australia independently identified thalidomide as the culprit.

For months, Merrell executives insisted to Kelsey that the reports were false and that Kevadon was safe. In March 1962, with the link to thalidomide unequivocal, Merrell quietly withdrew its application. That summer, *The Washington Post* revealed that Kelsey had saved thousands of American families from horror and despair, and she instantly became a national heroine.

In the wake of the story, Congress passed the 1962 Kefauver-Harris Amendments requiring that drugmakers prove that their medicines were effective—finally giving the FDA the official authority some of its medical officers had already adopted.

One of the most important effects of the law was the mandate it gave the FDA to reassess the effectiveness of thousands of older remedies. The United States had long been overrun with over-the-counter quack cures, and the agency eventually examined more than 3,400 drugs. A third of them were deemed ineffective and forced off the market.

Since many of these products were popular sellers, drugmakers marshalled doctors and patients to testify on the products' behalf, and companies sued again and again. In 1973, the Supreme Court issued a pair of landmark rulings confirming the FDA's authority. Polls in the 1960s and early 1970s showed that the FDA was not only among the most respected agencies in government but one of the most admired institutions of any kind. But by the mid-1970s, the agency's critics were increasingly pointing out that the FDA's lengthy reviews often meant that life-savings medicines were sometimes available in Europe months or even years before patients in the United States could access them. The country's "drug lag" became a rallying cry for the industry and probusiness conservative politicians.

Cosmetics were a wild card in all of this. Though the 1938 Food, Drug, and Cosmetic Act was a whopping 345 pages long, only two of those pages were specifically devoted to cosmetics. Blush, hair tonics, shampoos, and baby powders never needed FDA approval before being sold, and the agency never had the resources to regulate or analyze them anyway.

Peter Barton Hutt, a Washington lawyer who represented cosmetic manufacturers before becoming the FDA's top lawyer from 1971 to 1975, said the FDA never cared about cosmetics anyway. He was told, "Drugs can kill, food can kill, and medical devices can kill. Nobody dies from cosmetics." The very idea of seriously investigating the safety of a product as beloved and widely used as Johnson's Baby Powder likely struck agency officials as crazy. They had bigger fish to fry.

Nonetheless, officials in the agency's small cosmetics office spent years quietly prodding the talc industry to create an adequate testing process to ensure the absence of asbestos. After much back-and-forth, the cosmetics office in 1973 formally proposed a fairly rigorous testing method that would ensure talc products were 99.99 percent free of asbestos.

The FDA estimated that at least a third of talc-based cosmetics then being sold would flunk the new test. Unsurprisingly, the Cosmetic, Toiletry, and Fragrance Association (CTFA), an industry trade group (now known as the Personal Care Products Council), pitched a fit and threatened legal action. J & J's Wilson Nashed wrote the FDA's Dr. Robert M. Schaffner a letter on September 6, 1974, stating that "methods capable of determining less than 1% asbestos in talc are not necessary to assure the safety of cosmetic talc," adding that a 1 percent limit offered consumers a "substantial safety factor."

In February 1975, J & J executives met personally with FDA officials and reiterated their argument that a 1 percent limit rather than the 0.01 percent one that the FDA wanted offered adequate protection. But an FDA official scoffed that the industry's push for a 1 percent standard was "foolish."

"No mother was going to powder her baby with 1% of a known carcinogen irregardless [sic] of the large safety factor," the official said.

Yet, with almost no legal authority and little support within the agency, the FDA's cosmetics office quietly withdrew its proposal.

But that wasn't the end, because the drug side of the FDA—which had far more legal authority and a greater willingness to confront industry—began to make noises about completely banning talc. Prodded by their drug counterparts, FDA cosmetics officials not only revived their consideration of an asbestos testing standard but considered one even more stringent than their 1973 proposal. One proposal involved concentration methods, in which talc is placed in a centrifuge, making asbestos far easier to find. J & J executives had long known that such methods were the best way to detect asbestos, good enough to find concentrations as low as 0.05 percent.

What the industry needed was a talc testing standard that would be widely perceived as stringent but wouldn't actually find asbestos when it was present at concerning levels. And it needed one right away, "before the art advances to more sophisticated techniques with higher levels of sensitization," as one CTFA memo put it.

So the industry created the J4-1 method, which used fancy-sounding techniques that—like using a bathroom scale to weigh a pin—were incapable of detecting even substantial levels of asbestos. Instead of using relatively large quantities of talc and concentrating them to ensure that even trace quantities of asbestos were found, J4-1 used microscopic quantities. One of the most common talc contaminants is chrysotile asbestos, which is known as white asbestos and is the only type of asbestos still used to this day in the United States.

J4-1 wasn't designed to detect chrysotile. The CTFA sent talc to seven different labs and asked them to examine the products using only J4-1 and included fourteen samples that had been deliberately spiked with tremolite and anthophyllite. No lab detected more than three of the fourteen. Four of the labs failed to detect a single spiked sample.

John Schelz, a J & J executive who chaired the CTFA talc committee, said at a meeting held on May 17, 1977, that the committee's goal was to make sure that the J4-1 testing method was "accurate, reliable and practical." But the failure of the labs to detect the spiked samples meant that "these objectives have not yet been achieved," Schelz told the meeting, according to its minutes.

In fact, the actual objectives had been achieved. The CTFA adopted J4-1 unchanged.

Satisfied that the industry had finally and fully dealt with its asbestos problem, the FDA largely ended its oversight of talcum powder. There were, after all, never enough resources available to the cosmetics office to do anything other than rely on J & J and other cosmetics manufacturers to test their products themselves.

If tests conducted by J & J revealed asbestos contamination, J & J didn't notify the FDA or suggest in any way that its testing program was inadequate. But it was worse than that: In a 2019 deposition, Dr. Susan Nicholson, a J & J talc safety executive, admitted that the company hadn't sent the agency a single talc test result since 1973.

CHAPTER 6

The Power of Pressure

As the battle over the safety of Johnson's baby powder intensified, J & J began to view many of the scientists and regulators involved with suspicion and hostility. On November 29, 1972, Hildick-Smith wrote a memo to the president of J & J's baby division titled "Antagonistic Personalities in the Talc Story in the U.S.A." Hildick-Smith's rant began with the Tenovus Research Institute study, which was bad but not itself the problem. That problem was that the Tenovus study was being promoted in the United States by a series of others who together posed a huge risk to the well-being of J & J. The first person listed was Selikoff, who was described as having a full-time press agent who got him considerable media exposure. Kretchmer, whom Hildick-Smith described as a politician who wanted to become mayor, was also listed, as were an FDA official and Lewin of New York University.

Then there was Langer. "Dr. Langer," the memo stated, beginning a line of attack, "is a microscopist who visually identifies chrysotile in most samples of talc that he examines, although, he seldom confirms any identity by chemical means."

Only four labs in the world were closely analyzing the effects of inorganic particles on lungs and other tissues, and Langer knew he was lucky to be employed at one of them. He was also keenly aware that much of his and Selikoff's work made some very rich men and companies deeply unhappy. Among the researchers collaborating with Selikoff in those years was Dr. E. Cuyler Hammond, a biologist and epidemiologist at the American Cancer Society whose work was among the first to show a causal link between cigarette smoking and lung cancer. Hammond regaled Langer with stories about the many threats he had received from tobacco interests, ultimatums Hammond told Langer he always defied. But as the pressure from J & J built, Langer's personal life fell apart. His first wife, Betty Langer, learned she had ovarian cancer soon after the birth of their second child in 1971.

Devoted to his work, Langer nonetheless drove his Dodge Dart every day from the couple's suburban Westchester home to Mount Sinai. Years later in an interview, Langer allowed that he was "a little selfish" in his continuing devotion to his work during those dark years. Betty died on March 5, 1975, leaving Langer in charge of two young children whom he often left in the care of a housekeeper.

Langer's last stand on talcum powder began a few months after Betty's death. For years, he and others from the Mount Sinai lab had attended various symposia to discuss the possible risks of talcum powders. That summer, Langer decided he should co-author a scientific paper documenting these risks and present it at the British Occupational Hygiene Society's meeting in Edinburgh. So he bought thirty-three consumer talcum powders, including those made by Johnson & Johnson. As he'd been doing since 1968, he put them on slides and went looking for asbestos.

As his collaborator, Langer chose Fred D. Pooley, the British mineralogist from University College, Cardiff, Wales, who had by the time of the Edinburgh conference developed a considerable side business consulting for J & J. Pooley had previously found asbestos in J & J's talc from both its Italian supplier and its Vermont mines.

As soon as Pooley received Langer's manuscript describing the results of his tests, he told Bob Dean, a J & J executive, that he was "very concerned." Langer had examined thirty-three talcum powders, seventeen of which were sold in Britain and sixteen in the United States. Pooley said that Langer's results were different from his own. "Langer is claiming that he has detected chrysotile and amphiboles," Pooley's September 1975 memo stated, referring to asbestos. "He has identified the products by name and claims that he has detected tremolite and anthophyllite in Johnson's Baby Powder." Both minerals are types of asbestos.

Ten days later, Pooley met personally with J & J executives and told them that he had yet to discuss with Langer or Langer's colleagues at Mount Sinai his unease about Langer's findings. Although Pooley had told J & J executives that he did not intend to present the shared findings at the conference, J & J discovered that preprints of the paper Pooley and Langer co-authored had already been compiled and assembled for distribution to Edinburgh conferees upon their arrival.

DeWitt Petterson persuaded Pooley to insist to conference officials that they remove the paper from the conference packet. When Pooley arrived at the Edinburgh conference, he met with Langer and other researchers from Mount Sinai and told them that their shared paper should be withdrawn from the conference—and that they shouldn't present their data about the asbestos content of consumer talcum powders.

In a memo, Langer wrote that Pooley asked the Mount Sinai team to agree to the withdrawal of their shared paper because "he was subjected to personal and professional pressures and industry harassment. We respected Dr. Pooley's wishes at the time of the conference and allowed him to withdraw it." Instead of co-authoring with Pooley, Langer and his colleagues decided to rewrite the paper and submit it to a journal later, without Pooley.

Before the journal could publish the results, though, they were leaked to Marian Burros at *The Washington Post*.

Burros called the manufacturers listed in the piece as selling contaminated talcum powders, including representatives from J & J,

Colgate, and the industry's trade association, CTFA. All told Burros that the talcum powders Langer had analyzed were "old" and not representative of talcum powders being sold at the time.

Burros's story created international headlines.

Johnson & Johnson's top executives soon demanded a meeting with Mount Sinai's top administrators, including Dr. Thomas C. Chalmers, the school's president. The objective was to get Mount Sinai to issue a public statement declaring that Johnson's Baby Powder was safe, that the product samples that Langer and his colleagues had analyzed were at least three years old, and that the contaminants they had identified weren't hazardous.

Medical schools and their administrators almost never issue statements correcting, retracting, or otherwise undermining the research findings of faculty. The rare exceptions are when schools conclude, after exhaustive internal reviews, that results were unethically or fraudulently obtained. But J & J executives also reached out to members of the school's board of trustees, according to Langer. And that kind of pressure was hard to resist.

Chalmers initially told the J & J executives that a public retraction issued by the school was a bad idea. J & J executives reiterated their strong preference for a repudiation.

Chalmers then told the executives that in the aftermath of Burros's story, Langer and his co-authors had analyzed another six samples of the company's talcum powders, all of them of more recent vintage. They found asbestos in all six. The age of the samples was a red herring.

Given those findings, the J & J executives decided the best strategy was to trash Langer personally. They told Chalmers that in 1971, Langer had publicized the results of his talc analyses only to suffer a later retraction. (The executives may have been referring to Kretchmer's incorrect announcement in 1972 that Johnson's Baby Powder contained as much as 25 percent asbestos; but in that instance, the error was Kretchmer's, not Langer's.) They also told Chalmers that Langer had co-authored a paper that was supposed to be presented at the Edinburgh conference six months earlier, but that the paper was pulled from the conference after Pooley, Langer's co-author, expressed doubts about Langer's findings. Predictably, they said nothing of the pressure they'd put on Pooley to make sure the findings were buried, or Pooley's pleadings with Langer to facilitate the paper's withdrawal.

Chalmers expressed his surprise and claimed to have been un-aware of any differences between Pooley and Langer. At that point, feeling that he hadn't been leveled with by Langer, Chalmers agreed that a retraction was in order, and the group began negotiating the statement's language.

An initial draft of the correction Chalmers sent to J & J defended Langer's work as being "of the highest technical quality and a major contribution to the field," adding that "the contamination was news-worthy because prolonged exposure to asbestos can cause cancer." In the final statement, both lines were cut, as was another that reported that "six recently purchased talcs have revealed minimal contamina-tion by particles that are probably asbestos." Langer had been sold out.

Langer was, unsurprisingly, upset. He couldn't believe that Chalmers—the head of one of the country's most prestigious medical schools—had adopted the views of industry executives over those of public health professionals on his own staff.

"Tom Chalmers liked his job. He was well paid. He had prestige. He had a chauffeur-driven car. He considered himself a fancy guy in terms of clinical analyses of studies," Langer said years later. "And I was a junior faculty member making his job tougher."

Newspapers around the country, including *The New York Times*, wrote stories about the correction and reassured readers that John-son's Baby Powder was safe. Chalmers reinforced the claim in an in-terview on WCBS radio, declaring, "It is the opinion of Mount Sinai's Department of Pediatrics that baby talc is a useful and safe product."

But Marian Burros refused to go along.

Burros was a food writer at *The Washington Post* who joined *The*

New York Times's Washington bureau in 1982. Within a year, she'd become a fixture after the paper published her spectacular plum torte recipe. An instant fall classic, the recipe was republished every September until 1989, when her editors announced that year's republication would be its last. The paper was inundated with angry letters of protest.

Burros did far more than dream up tasty recipes. For years, she covered the food side of the FDA, which included cosmetics (the cosmetics office is tucked into the agency's main food center). Burros's writing had bite. When restaurants started claiming their salmon was caught in the wild, Burros sent samples to labs, often discovering the telltale orange dye of farmed fish. She asked tough questions and she never backed down.

Internal J & J files reveal that she was the lone snag in the company's otherwise successful campaign to hide the Baby Powder evidence. She dutifully reported Mount Sinai's clarification that the tested samples were several years old and that more recent tests by the FDA "have not revealed appreciable amounts of asbestos" in talcum powder. But unlike her counterparts at the *Times* and other outlets, she insisted upon speaking to Selikoff, and that made all the difference.

Selikoff explained that the FDA's testing techniques were not sensitive enough to detect small amounts of asbestos, which was not only true in 1976 but would remain so for decades. He acknowledged that the cosmetics industry had in recent years quietly improved the quality of its talcum powders.

"But there is a huge chink in their armor," Selikoff told Burros. "They were dusting people with asbestos all these years before, so what was put in the lungs before is still there."

He continued: "I certainly wouldn't want to be dusted with any asbestos. There is no safe level of asbestos known."

Asbestos particles take years and sometimes decades to engender the genetic changes that lead to lung, ovarian, and other cancers. And by 1976, the medical literature was filled with reports of women who died of mesothelioma after washing their husbands' asbestos-contaminated clothing. Such "domestic exposure" cases compellingly demonstrated that tiny amounts of asbestos could kill, and that long periods sometimes passed between exposure and illness.

Selikoff's remark was an invitation for anyone with mesothelioma, lung cancer, or ovarian cancer to sue J & J. If J & J admitted that Johnson's Baby Powder was contaminated with asbestos for most of its history, patients suffering from any of those diseases could claim at any time that they were sickened by the product.

The same day Burros's story was published, D. D. Johnston sent a blistering letter to Chalmers, with the story attached.

Dear Dr. Chalmers:

Attached is a copy of the Washington Post's treatment of your press release in this morning's paper. It also was carried in its entirety by the Washington Post Wire Service, which goes to 340 newspapers nationally.

The article falls far short of our mutual goal of reassuring consumers about the safety of present day talcum powders. In fact, statements attributed to Dr. Selikoff and his staff, allegedly commenting on your press release, served only to perpetuate and increase public anxiety.

Dr. Selikoff's inflammatory remarks have once again been "supported" with references to data not published or reviewed with other experts. (Once again there is confusion about simple facts, like whether there are 6 or 10 recently purchased samples, and whether some of the original 19 samples were purchased more recently than 1973.) Dr. Selikoff and staff continue to treat their findings as facts, ignoring Dr. Pooley's results, dismissing FDA results, promulgating the no dose-response thesis, implicitly attributing the effects of chrysotile to tremolite, etc.

I am particularly disturbed by Dr. Selikoff's "chink in their armor" remark. If the chink exists in fact, it clearly has potential for alarming the consumer, embarrassing the industry, and publicizing Dr. Selikoff, but its potential for any constructive effect appears nil.

Very truly yours,
D. D. Johnston
President

Langer's data on twenty consumer talcum powders was published later that year in the *Journal of Toxicology and Environmental Health*. The piece noted that half of the tested powders had "detectable amounts of tremolite and anthophyllite," with amounts ranging from tenths of a percent to over 14 percent by weight. Other mineral contaminants were also found. But the table listing the brand names of contaminated talcum powders—information Burros had found so newsworthy—was not published.

The study got almost no attention. J & J's scorched-earth public relations campaign accomplished its goal of tarnishing the Mount Sinai work, muddying the record on asbestos lurking in Johnson's Baby Powder, and persuading Selikoff and Langer to get out of the talc testing business altogether.

J & J's success in persuading Chalmers to insist upon a retraction led a generation of food and drug reporters to treat claims of asbestos in baby powder with great care, knowing retractions and corrections might follow—every journalist's nightmare.

And with the Mount Sinai team finally out of the picture, concerns about the safety of Johnson's Baby Powder gradually dissipated, as outlined in an internal assessment written at J & J in August 1977 titled "Defense of Talc Safety."

"We attribute this growing opinion," the memo asserted, in part to "favorable data from the various J & J sponsored studies that have been disseminated effectively to the scientific and medical communities in the U.K. and U.S."

· · ·

FOR JAMES E. BURKE, WHO ON NOVEMBER 1, 1976, WAS ANNOUNCED AS Johnson & Johnson's next chief executive, the entire episode was instructive. Burke joined J & J in 1953 as a product director for the Band-Aid brand. He quit a year later to start his own consumer products business. One of his products was a tablet that, when dropped into a bath, made bubbles. The venture failed, and he returned to J & J.

With a degree from Harvard Business School, Burke was among a cadre of young, well-educated marketing executives that Bobby Johnson admired and promoted. In 1961, Burke was promoted to head a new division of the company that included its baby products and Tylenol. Three years later, just as Bobby Johnson was losing his place in the company, Burke made a blunder.

"I had helped develop a new product that was a failure, and it cost the company a substantial amount of money," Burke later recalled. "General Johnson sent for me, and I was convinced I was going to be fired."

Burke entered the great man's office as Johnson was dictating memos.

"He looked up and said, 'Mr. Burke, I understand that you made a decision that has cost this company a great deal of money. Is that true?' 'Yes, sir,' I replied, and with that he stood up and shook my hand and said: 'Congratulations! Making decisions is what business is all about, and you don't make decisions without making mistakes. Don't ever make that mistake again, Mr. Burke, but please be sure you make other mistakes.'"

The encounter instilled in Burke a fierce loyalty to the old man. But in one area, he definitely did not follow his lead.

Several of Johnson's closest friends were influential newspaper columnists, and Johnson took great personal pride in the rare occasions when he was paid to author pieces in local and national publications. But Burke, with few exceptions, ended the company's openness with reporters—a strategy that largely remained in place for another forty years. In subsequent interviews, Burke claimed that his experience with inaccurate newspaper stories about asbestos lurking in Johnson's Baby Powder was the reason for his about-face in press tactics.

Burke's brother, Daniel Burke, co-founded the TV conglomerate Capital Cities, which in 1986 merged with ABC in one of the boldest media deals of the decade. J & J executives thus continued to talk on TV, where the company had much more control over the message. But newspapers and writers were out—a decision that would later have major repercussions for the public.

Burke's major strategic contribution to J & J was to continue the company's push into medicines. He supported the aggressive marketing of Extra Strength Tylenol, launched just as he took the reins. It quickly became the company's most profitable product. To support the Tylenol franchise, for which a combination with codeine was an important spin-off, the company under his guidance purchased an Australian opioid maker that would soon become the dominant opioid supplier in the United States.

Near the end of his tenure, he supported a deal with a small California biotech called Amgen to co-market EPO, a blood thickener that displaced Tylenol to become the company's most profitable product. The Amgen arrangement and others helped transform J & J from being a hospital supply wholesaler and consumer products giant to being a prescription drug behemoth. All of those deals—and the scandals associated with many of them—were to come. (As was J & J finally selling its Vermont talc mines, which happened just as he was leaving.)

Burke was widely seen as being among the most ethical corporate chieftains ever. He was president of the Business Enterprise Trust, an organization that honored acts of integrity and social conscience in business. He was elected to the National Business Hall of Fame, and *Fortune* magazine named him as one of the ten greatest chief executives of all time. When he retired from J & J, he served as the chairman of the Partnership for a Drug-Free America, a nonprofit that ran ads discouraging teens from illegal drug use. President Bill Clinton awarded him the Presidential Medal of Freedom, the nation's highest civilian honor.

Langer, meanwhile, mostly succeeded in putting the talc controversy out of his mind. He was engaged in what he saw as some of the most important research of the era, including the design of safe respirators, the exploration of airborne asbestos particles through the examination of ice cores in Greenland, and tracing the lung disease and cancer rates of workers in multiple industries. And unlike his talcum powder research, this work was well funded by government grants, corporate clients, and labor unions.

He soon met a young and idealistic epidemiologist. The two started dating and, in 1977, married. Cathy Langer moved into her husband's Westchester home, where she helped raise Betty's two children and had two more of her own. On her husband's advice, Cathy never used Johnson's Baby Powder on herself or any of the children.

Langer said that none of the withdrawals and corrections done at J & J's behest ever overturned or seriously questioned his findings. He stood by the results. He remained proud of the piece in the *Journal of Toxicology and Environmental Health* and said he continued decades later to get calls about it from other researchers, many in foreign countries. But the media at the time saw the piece as hopelessly compromised, a fact that Langer acknowledged.

"Have these bastards hurt me in the past?" he asked. "Sure, but you can't dwell on the personal side of things. Because they hurt humanity."

Nearly five decades would pass before lawyers and journalists reassessed Langer's work. "It wasn't our responsibility to keep following it," he declared. "The government agencies had all this information. What the hell were they doing? That's the point. We could not keep reproducing all of the laboratory work required for the continuing monitoring of the marketplace. Others had to do that."

CHAPTER 7

A Meeting at a Harvard Hospital

THEY MET IN A DREARY CONFERENCE ROOM AT BRIGHAM AND Women's Hospital in Boston. The weather outside was typical for Boston in August—muggy with temperatures in the mid-eighties. But Dr. Daniel W. Cramer, a professor of obstetrics, gynecology, and reproductive biology at Harvard Medical School, felt a distinct chill from his two guests.

Three weeks earlier on July 15, 1982, Cramer published a study in *Cancer*, a major medical journal, which concluded that women who dusted their crotch with talc had a 92 percent increased risk of ovarian cancer. Johnson & Johnson representatives described Cramer's research as "inconclusive" in the press and said that the issue needed more study. Privately, executives were furious.

Dr. Bruce Semple, a company executive, had come to Boston to persuade Cramer that he'd made mistakes in his research and should stop talking about it. Cramer in turn tried to persuade Semple that women should be informed that there was a possible risk in using the company's talc products. The two sides argued about Cramer's methodology and Cramer conceded some mistakes. Still, as an internal J & J memo stated, he "stood by his conclusion that talc usage may be associated with ovarian cancer." However, "He agreed not to make further public statements or grant interviews on this study." The same memo noted that half of American women reported frequent use of talc in their crotch area.

Cramer was distinct from some of his cohorts in his belief that talcum powder is dangerous not because it is contaminated with asbestos but because it is full of talc. He said that research demonstrates that talc particles enter the vaginal canals of women who dust themselves and then migrate to the ovaries, which respond by attacking the dust particles in a way that can precipitate cancer.

Other scientists are skeptical of his talc particles theory and argue that talc's association with ovarian cancer results from the inhalation of small amounts of asbestos. The evidence that inhaled asbestos can cause ovarian cancer is robust enough to be accepted even by Johnson & Johnson. And eighteen other studies of Cramer's supposition were mixed.

Nonetheless, when in the early 2000s a working group at the World Health Organization's International Agency for Research on Cancer (IARC) examined the issue, it concluded that women who regularly dusted their vaginal areas with talc (known as "perineal use") had a 30 percent to 60 percent greater risk of ovarian cancer than those who didn't. IARC is widely regarded as the last word on carcinogenicity, so these findings carried enormous weight in the medical community.

Roberta Ness, former dean of the University of Texas School of Public Health and former president of the American Epidemiological Society, has testified that a middle ground among these many studies suggests that Johnson's Baby Powder contributes to about 2,500 women in the United States being diagnosed with ovarian cancer every year and 1,500 dying.

And as Cramer pointed out, whether talcum powder is dangerous because it contains small amounts of asbestos or because it contains large amounts of talc ultimately shouldn't make a difference in women's decision to use it as a cosmetic. Given that talc has no medical benefit, even a hint of risk is unacceptable.

At Johnson & Johnson, the Cramer study led to the realization that the battle to defend Johnson's Baby Powder—something many hoped had ended with the defeat of the Mount Sinai group in 1976 and the FDA's acceptance in 1977 of the J4-1 testing standard—would likely continue for years. The result was the creation of a Talc Steering Committee "to prepare and enforce Johnson & Johnson's positions and policies related to the sources' quality, manufacture, labeling, packaging and sale of talc." The committee's members included lawyers, technical personnel, and the company's baby franchise director.

Only a few months after its creation, the committee faced one of Baby Powder's gravest threats.

Engelhard was a major mining company that in 1966 bought from Johnson & Johnson a talc mine located in Johnson, Vermont. In some ways, Engelhard's purchase was ideally timed. Concerns about asbestos's dangers were growing. Companies making wallboard, insulation, and other products were looking for asbestos alternatives. For many, talc was an obvious and cheap substitute. Engelhard's talc sales climbed smartly.

"When we bought the mine in 1966, we had no inkling at all, never even thought about the fact that there might be an asbestos-related mineral in the talc," Glenn A. Hemstock, Engelhard's research director, said in a sworn deposition taken in May 2012, nearly a half century after the purchase.

Among Engelhard's customers was National Latex, a rubber manufacturer. One of National Latex's products was children's balloons, which were often dusted with talcum powder both inside and out to ensure that the rubber didn't stick together.

In 1977, National Latex became aware that its children's balloons had trace amounts of tremolite, a form of asbestos. It undertook a search for its source. About two hundred National Latex balloons were sent to Engelhard's headquarters in Menlo Park, New Jersey, where Engelhard's research staff measured the amount of talc present inside each one. An Englehard executive wrote in a memo dated December 2, 1977, that even if the talc contained small amounts of asbestos, the exposure levels for the balloons once they were inflated would be so tiny that they would not represent a health threat. As a result, more tests with more sophisticated testing equipment didn't make sense, "since there is no suspicion of our material."

Actually, Engelhard had by then been informed many times over many years that the talcum powder and mine environment at the former Johnson & Johnson talc mine had worrisome levels of asbestos. Langer speculated that the probable reason was that talc deposits in northern Vermont are more thoroughly penetrated by asbestos than those at the southern end of the state. If considerable asbestos contamination was the reason that J & J sold its mine in Johnson, the mine's buyers were unaware of it. Nor, among thousands of internal J & J memos, is there any mention of why it sold the Johnson mine just three years after purchasing it but held on to its other talc mines in southern Vermont.

In sworn depositions, Hemstock, Engelhard's research director, explained that the men pulling talc out of the company's Johnson mine were experiencing lung problems. Indeed, a study co-sponsored by Harvard University and the National Institute for Occupational Safety and Health found that between 1970 and 1978, Engelhard's miners lost significant lung function well beyond what would have been expected from the effects of cigarette smoking and age-related decline.

Hemstock could have gamed the system by choosing the insensitive testing equipment or industry-friendly labs that J & J relied on. He didn't. Beginning in late January 1979, Engelhard sent weekly talc samples to the Georgia Institute of Technology, which had one of the most sensitive labs in the country. Initial results were worrisome enough that the company kept sending samples to Georgia Tech for fifteen weeks straight. Every single one was positive for asbestos.

Engelhard was in a bind. Its talc sales were soaring so fast that the facility had outgrown its mill, which needed to be replaced. But much of the reason for that success was Engelhard's guarantees that its products were asbestos-free. Among the companies that received such faithless promises were Uniroyal Tire, United States Gypsum Company, Stoller Chemical, and General Electric. And continuing to cover up the problem was getting harder. Indeed, in July, federal mine safety regulators gave Engelhard two citations because dust monitors carried by a dozen men working in the mine showed excessive levels of fibers. But that warning sign turned out to be nothing compared to what came next: Thomas Howard Westfall, a worker at Uniroyal Tire's plant in Providence, Rhode Island, hired a local attorney to sue for the deadly mesothelioma that he believed resulted from the clouds of talc at his plant that had all been sourced from the Johnson mine.

Two months before Westfall's death on July 10, 1979, his lawyer filed suit against Windsor Minerals, Johnson & Johnson's talc subsidiary. In turn, Windsor Minerals filed a third-party complaint against Engelhard, making the companies partners in fighting Westfall and everything that might result from his suit.

Westfall's lawyer hired a geology professor from the University of Vermont to conduct independent tests of the talc being taken out of the Johnson mine. Engelhard refused to allow the geologist to enter the premises, so the professor took samples from its exterior. He found significant asbestos contamination.

And then the lawyer subpoenaed Hemstock.

CHAPTER 8

Secrecy Is a Top Priority

THE FIRST DAY OF HEMSTOCK'S DEPOSITION TOOK PLACE ON A COLD day in January 1983 in a lawyer's office in Manhattan's financial district, and it continued six weeks later in an office in Providence. Lawyers from Johnson & Johnson, Engelhard, and other talc companies were in attendance, watching.

In the deposition, Westfall's lawyer carefully walked through fifty-one separate documents, many clearly demonstrating that the company's talc had far more than trace quantities of asbestos. Hemstock grudgingly but repeatedly confirmed that asbestos had been found in the Johnson mine. When pressed, he fell back on what he said was a poor memory of crucial events. Other times, he conceded he had no expertise in health and thus could not offer a professional opinion.

For Engelhard and J & J, the deposition was devastating. The documents and Hemstock's sworn statements proved that talc from a mine J & J had once owned and that Engelhard still used was thoroughly contaminated, that Engelhard knew about this contamination, and that both companies had lied about it repeatedly and consistently to their industrial customers.

A year earlier, the Manville Corporation—the nation's largest asbestos company—had filed for bankruptcy protection after a jury awarded nearly $4 million to a retired boilermaker who had contracted mesothelioma. Facing sixteen thousand similar lawsuits, Manville claimed it couldn't pay.

Thousands of tire workers would eventually follow Westfall's lead and file suit against Engelhard, J & J, and other talc companies. If Hemstock's deposition and the documents he reviewed ever became public, that avalanche of litigation might seriously damage or even destroy the companies. Manville's downfall was the opening salvo in the largest mass tort litigation in American history, which would eventually ensnare nearly eight thousand companies.

The largest company ever to file for bankruptcy, Manville had $2.2 billion in revenues in 1982 and was 181st on the Fortune 500 list. Johnson & Johnson had $5.4 billion in revenue that same year and was 68th on the size chart. Engelhard and J & J settled the Westfall case by paying an undisclosed sum. The attorneys demanded confidentiality and the return of all evidence proving asbestos contamination. Even the University of Vermont geologist turned over his original notes, photomicrographs, and samples of talc. Engelhard stopped selling talc and closed its Vermont mine, which filled up with water, making subsequent testing impossible.

Engelhard issued the first document-purge memorandum in its history, instructing Hemstock and his employees to carefully comb through their files, retrieve anything involving talc, and give them to the company's legal department. "It is the policy of Engelhard Corporation to avoid the undue accumulation of documents that are no longer likely to be needed in our business operations," the purge memo stated. Pages in bound laboratory notebooks that mentioned talc had to be carefully and painstakingly ripped or sliced out. The documents were collected by Engelhard's lawyers, who sent them to a secret storage facility where they would remain largely forgotten for decades.

Johnson & Johnson then helped Engelhard replace its real records with false ones, creating affidavits swearing that asbestos had never been found in the Johnson or any other talc mine owned by them.

Among those who signed such false affidavits was Roger N. Miller, president of J & J's talc subsidiary.

Following this, Engelhard's and J & J's lawyers sent letters to lawyers for tire workers and other plaintiffs falsely declaring that all of the talc from the companies' mines had always proven to be asbestos-free and that there was no evidence suggesting otherwise. The letters insisted that the workers and other plaintiffs drop what would surely be losing litigation. John Beidler, J & J's in-house lawyer, who was in the room for the first day of Hemstock's deposition in 1983, signed similar letters. Plaintiffs' attorneys who persisted were threatened with sanctions.

Many years later, in testimony at trial on July 23, 2019, John Hopkins, a former J & J talc executive who for years served as Johnson & Johnson's designated representative in talc litigation, acknowledged that the company's top talc executive's sworn testimonial was a lie.

"And that is—you understand that is perjury, do you not?" the lawyer asked.

"I do," Hopkins responded.

IN 1989, J & J SOLD ITS TALC SUBSIDIARY. INSTEAD OF TAKING THE OP-portunity to transition Johnson's Baby Powder entirely to corn starch as other giants like Pfizer were doing, the company kept buying and using talc. There is no easy answer as to why. In the 1960s and early 1970s, Johnson's Baby Powder was one of many common products contaminated with asbestos. By 1989, it was almost unique. By then, asbestos (and rock dust inhalation of any kind) had become radioactive in American life, and no American mother would sprinkle her baby with anything that had even the remotest chance of containing it.

Still, Baby Powder was just one of several J & J products that used talc. In 2004, Imerys, J & J's talc supplier, began placing a cancer warning on every sack of talc delivered to Johnson & Johnson and its other customers after the World Health Organization's International Agency for Research on Cancer announced that it had placed talc on its list of possible carcinogens. Concurrently, Imerys executives quietly put together a formal proposal that the industry voluntarily phase out talc-based baby powders, body powders, and dusting powders that women use on their genitals. Imerys intended to ask the FDA to require a cancer warning on any talc powders that remained on the market. The company never followed through on the proposal.

Material Safety Data Sheets, or MSDS, are required by law to list ingredients that are potentially hazardous to human health. A few months later, a J & J executive wrote an internal email dated January 19, 2005, announcing that the shipping label for Shower to Shower, a cousin of Johnson's Baby Powder that was half talc and half cornstarch, would have to include a cancer warning.

A top company executive responded four days later: "Do NOT send out any MSDS with this statement on it!!!!!!!!!!!!!!!!!!!!!!!!!!!!!!!!!!!!!" The executive said they would come back with more information after speaking with colleagues. The company ignored the law.

J & J had still not abandoned efforts to improve the safety of Baby Powder altogether, having launched a corn starch version to accompany its original formulation. In 2008, J & J's Global Design Strategy Team tested whether the company should change for good its iconic Baby Powder formulations and packaging to highlight differences between old and new. They hired Research International, a huge branding and market research company, to survey women, and particularly mothers, about their preferences among four possible versions of Johnson's Baby Powder, including Johnson's Classic Powder, Johnson's Talc Powder, and Johnson's Baby and Talc Powder.

Sales analyses showed that mothers were already shifting away from talc. The more Todd True, a member of the design team, learned, the more uneasy he became. In an April 18, 2008, email headlined "Baby Powder—not for babies," he wrote that, "I admit that Powder has not been a priority for me but the more I think about it, the more

our proposition makes me uncomfortable. The reality that talc is unsafe for use on/around babies is disturbing. I don't mind selling talc,
I just don't think we can continue to call it Baby Powder and keep it
in the baby aisle."

He continued: "Using Our Credo as our guide, I'd like to develop
a strategy with you to eliminate the use of talc under Johnson's Baby."

In another email with a headline "Johnson's Baby Powder—
unsafe for babies?!" True acknowledged that his proposal was controversial and that the team would have to work hard to justify "the cost
implications" of his idea. But he wrote that almost every other baby
powder manufacturer had long since abandoned talcum powder and
moved to cornstarch.

In response, other team members noted that trying to educate
women about the differences between talc and cornstarch might
open a can of worms for Johnson & Johnson. Yes, the company had
a safe substitute for talcum powder that to many users is indistin-
guishable from the original. But could the company suddenly admit
that talc was problematic around babies?

True's proposals were shelved.

TO THIS DAY, ASBESTOS IS LINKED TO ABOUT FORTY-THOUSAND CAN-
cer deaths in the United States every year, or about the same toll as
breast cancer. With every passing year, Johnson & Johnson's deceit
not only killed and sickened more people but promised an ever
greater shock when revealed. Doing anything that might reveal this
fact may have seemed unthinkable.

Another puzzle is why the FDA didn't take a stand. Following the
1982 publication of Cramer's study linking talcum powder with ovarian cancer, a sizable number of subsequent studies confirmed the association.

In 1994, the Cancer Prevention Coalition sent a letter to Ralph
Larsen, Johnson & Johnson's chief executive and chairman, asking

the company to stop selling talc. The coalition simultaneously filed a citizen petition with the FDA asking that all talcum powder products contain a cancer warning. As justification, the coalition cited a growing number of studies showing that "talc is a carcinogen, with or without the presence of asbestos-like fibers."

The coalition noted that this was the third such petition received by the FDA. Relying on false reassurances from J & J, the FDA had rejected the first two out of hand.

In response to the third, the FDA co-sponsored a conference titled "Talc: Consumer Uses and Health Perspectives." The other co-sponsor was the International Society of Regulatory Toxicology and Pharmacology (ISRTP), which received grants from J & J and CTFA, to hold the workshop. The journal of the ISRTP, *Regulatory Toxicology and Pharmacology*, was financed in part by the tobacco, pharmaceutical, and chemical industries.

The CTFA sent the ISRTP names of participants the association wanted to attend the talc symposium. Most came from industry, and nine of the fourteen academics invited served as talc industry consultants but did not disclose these financial ties. In 2018, the FDA held another such conference, and again the participants were mostly those with industry ties. Experts not associated with industry who asked the FDA if they could attend were told they could not.

In the end, the FDA told the Cancer Prevention Coalition in July 1995 that it couldn't respond to its petition "because of the limited availability of resources and other agency priorities." This wasn't just a smokescreen: Nothing had changed over the decades in terms of the FDA's cosmetics office being perennially starved of resources.

But the entire process was too much for Dr. Alfred Wehner, a Johnson & Johnson consultant who, in a letter to a top company executive, described multiple statements made in defense of talc to be "outright false" and inaccurate.

"At [the] time there had been about 9 studies (more by now) published in the open literature that did show a statistically significant association between hygienic talc use and ovarian cancer," Wehner wrote. "Anybody who denies this risks that the talc industry will be perceived by the public like it perceives the cigarette industry: denying the obvious in the face of all evidence to the contrary."

In 2008, the Cancer Prevention Coalition filed the fourth citizen petition asking the FDA to require a warning. After a lot of back-and-forth with J & J and the industry trade association—outreach the agency never made to consumer groups—the FDA again said it didn't have the resources to respond. And again, that was true.

But then things at the agency got (to use a technical term) icky. In late 2013, J & J lost its first Baby Powder cancer lawsuit ever. The trial took place in federal court in South Dakota, and with the verdict, J & J's defense of Johnson's Baby Powder was suddenly vulnerable. A surge of women began filing lawsuits.

What J & J needed now—perhaps more than ever—was a whole-hearted endorsement of the safety of its product from the most trusted agency in the federal government. But by 2014, the evidence linking talcum powder and cancer was persuasive, so their chances were minimal at best.

But this was Johnson & Johnson. Six months after the South Dakota verdict, the FDA, seemingly out of the blue, issued denials for both the 1994 and 2008 petitions. The agency said that the growing mountain of epidemiological data couldn't be used to prove a link between talc and ovarian cancer because none of the published studies had focused *exclusively* on women who had begun using talc only after 1976, when the FDA said that manufacturers began eliminating asbestos from their products.

"Thus, while it has been reported in the past that cosmetic talc has been contaminated with asbestos, it has been also reported that asbestos-free talc deposits do exist," the FDA wrote without specifying where such deposits could be found, how the agency knew they were asbestos-free, and how the agency was sure that talc-containing products were exclusively sourced from such deposits.

Republican administrations are often accused of being too cozy with corporate interests. But the FDA's petition denials took place during the administration of President Barack Obama, a Democrat.

The FDA's 2014 talc statements were part of a long pattern that would continue for years in which the FDA issued statements that were tailor-made to help J & J fend off legal claims. (Several came after 2012, when J & J's chief executive used his industry and political connections to save hundreds of FDA jobs, a story discussed later in the book.) Bolstered by the FDA's endorsement, J & J's Baby Powder business continued to flourish—but not for long.

CHAPTER 9

A Sacred Cow

In 2009, Donna Paduano sued Engelhard, claiming that Engelhard caused her mesothelioma because she sometimes did her homework in her father's lab. Engelhard (now owned by German chemical giant BASF) responded to Paduano's suit the same way it had responded to thousands of previous claims: It falsely claimed that asbestos had never been found in its laboratories, mines, or talc and cited the false affidavits and sworn statements that Engelhard's and J & J's lawyers and executives had created following the settlement of the Westfall case in 1983.

But Paduano wasn't just any plaintiff. Her father had worked for Glenn Hemstock, whose research into Engelhard's decades-long efforts to conceal the presence of asbestos in its talc had been hidden or destroyed when the Westfall case was settled. And as it turned out, Hemstock's decades-old deposition had survived earlier efforts to make it disappear. Not only that, but Hemstock himself was still alive.

For a second time, Hemstock sat for a deposition about the asbestos he had found lurking in talc from a mine J & J had once owned. The eighty-six-year-old not only confirmed everything he'd said

nearly forty years before but expressed outrage that J & J and Engelhard executives had been lying about it ever since.

More legal wrangling ensued until a federal appeals court in 2014
pointed out that the attorneys working for Engelhard and J & J
might have committed crimes. With this blistering ruling in hand,
plaintiffs' attorneys began forcing J & J's lawyers to sit for depositions
and answer how the company's lawyers and executives had sworn for
so many years that asbestos had never been found in Johnson's Baby
Powder and J & J's other talc products when that was so clearly untrue. One top New York law firm that had worked for Engelhard resolved claims that it had lied on the company's behalf by contributing
to a nearly $75 million settlement.

Soon after the 2014 appeals court ruling, a plaintiffs' lawyer
named Mark Lanier began to demand documents from J & J that
mentioned asbestos—the same documents plaintiffs' lawyers had
been demanding for years but had been told didn't exist. Thanks to
the Paduano trial, it was clear beyond a reasonable doubt that some
such documents existed. For the first time, the company's lawyers—in
this case, working for an outside law firm—began producing them.
One document led Lanier to ask for others, and a decades-old secret
finally unraveled.

"THIS CASE BOILS DOWN TO SOMETHING AS SIMPLE AS A, B, C," MARK
Lanier, a plaintiffs' attorney representing twenty-two women with
ovarian cancer, said at the start of his opening remarks on June 6,
2018, in a courtroom in St. Louis. Lanier showed the three letters on
a slide.

He pointed to the letter A. "Asbestos," he said, and then pointed
at the letter B. "Breathed or internalized." And then he moved to the
letter C: "becomes cancer.

"That's the entire case," Lanier continued. "If I prove that asbestos
is in that Baby Powder, you're going to know why these women had
ovarian cancer, at least what a cause of the cancer was.

"The big fight, really, is whether or not asbestos is in the powder. And I think you're going to see quite readily that it's in the Baby Powder, the Shower to Shower powder, and the other things as well."

This was the beginning of a trial known as the Ingham case, named for one of twenty-two plaintiffs. Lanier gave folksy and endearing descriptions of their lives and families, making clear the emotional power of the case jurors were about to hear. His clients had different educational, ethnic, racial, and class backgrounds. "But all of these women have something in common. All of them used regularly and extensively Johnson & Johnson Baby Powder and had to listen when a doctor said to them: 'You've got cancer,'" he said. "'And not just any cancer. You've got ovarian cancer. A cancer that has a mortality rate of almost 50 percent.'"

Lanier reminded anyone who didn't know that J & J was a massive conglomerate that sold myriad products; but, he pointed out, its most beloved product was Johnson's Baby Powder—which had long been contaminated with asbestos. The company knew of this contamination, Lanier claimed, and in response created a testing scheme that prevented detection of this dangerous mineral. But even with such an insensitive testing program, the company still found asbestos.

Lanier then walked through a few of the many documents he would eventually show the jury proving J & J's malfeasance. He described the witnesses he intended to bring before them, and he warned the jury not to believe much of what was going to be said by his rival, Peter Bicks, J & J's lead defense attorney.

Seventy-three minutes after he began, Lanier sat down, and the judge gave the jury a break. During the recess, Bicks made the first of many requests for a mistrial, saying that a study that Lanier referenced had prejudiced the jury. The temperature both inside and outside the courtroom was rising—reaching ninety degrees outside by the time the judge denied Bicks's mistrial motion—the jury returned to the courtroom, and Bicks rose for his opening remarks at 11:19 A.M.

Bicks began by thanking the jury on behalf of himself, his team, "and most importantly on behalf of the men and women of Johnson & Johnson." He said that the claims Lanier had made were not only false but so inflammatory that he likened them to shouting "fire" in a crowded theater. And he said that Lanier had understated his profound burden of proof.

"They must prove to you that not only was there asbestos in a mine that Johnson & Johnson used, but it somehow made its way into a bottle of Baby Powder, and that bottle of Baby Powder was a bottle that a plaintiff used, and that whatever was in there, in whatever baby bottle there was, somehow made it to a point in somebody's body where it caused their disease," Bicks said. "That's a lot of steps that plaintiffs' counsel didn't talk about. The burden of proof is on the plaintiff to prove that. We don't have to prove anything. But we will."

Bicks said that science was on J & J's side, and he mentioned witnesses who would show that. And then he outlined three basic points that he intended to demonstrate: "That Johnson & Johnson acted responsibly in selling its products. That decades of testing confirm that Johnson & Johnson products do not contain asbestos. And that talcum powder use does not cause ovarian cancer."

Bicks said that while Johnson & Johnson never made much money on Johnson's Baby Powder, the product was important to the company because it signified trust. He listed the many testers, organizations, and agencies that for decades had determined that talcum powder was safe. But he focused on the FDA, mentioning the agency twenty times in his opening remarks.

"The FDA, in 1986, evaluating the test results and all of the information, says that there's no need to require a warning label on cosmetic talc," Bicks said. "This is from the FDA. This isn't from Johnson & Johnson."

Bicks expressed sympathy for the plaintiffs, all of whom had suffered a terrible illness. But he told the jury not to be blinded by emotion.

"So, at the end, the question is: Is there asbestos in Johnson &

Johnson's products? We believe and have always believed that there isn't," which was why Johnson & Johnson's own experts and employees continued to use it on themselves and their family members, Bicks said.

Bicks asked the jury to maintain an open mind during the plaintiffs' case. And then he sat down exactly seventy-five minutes after he began. The judge sent the jury to lunch.

When the trial resumed, Lanier called his first witness, Dr. Alice Blount. A mineralogy professor at Rutgers University, Blount testified that during the 1990s, she bought multiple bottles of Johnson's Baby Powder and, for the sake of class projects, tested them. She found asbestos in all of them, published her findings, and wrote a letter to Johnson & Johnson describing her results. On cross-examination, J & J's attorney suggested that Blount might have mixed up her samples. Blount disagreed.

Lanier's next witness was William E. Longo, the president of Materials Analytical Services, a testing lab in Suwanee, Georgia. Lanier's law firm had collected thirty-seven bottles of Johnson's Baby Powder sold over decades. One from 1978 was retrieved by subpoena from Johnson & Johnson's own museum at its headquarters. Others were purchased on eBay. Over the course of two years, all were sent to Longo, who found asbestos in twenty of the thirty-seven bottles, including the one from J & J's museum.

Myriad experts told J & J over the years that concentration methods involving liquids and a centrifuge to separate asbestos from talc were the only reliable way to test for asbestos, Longo testified. Because he used a concentration method, Longo said, in two years he tested one hundred times more Johnson's Baby Powder by weight than J & J had tested in its entire history.

And then Lanier put his many clients on the stand. One of the twenty-two plaintiffs was Toni Roberts of Virginia, who was diagnosed with ovarian cancer when she was fifty-eight.

The mother of two boys, Roberts spent a lifetime using considerable quantities of Johnson's Baby Powder. Every time she showered, sometimes twice a day, she would sprinkle powder into her hands and then rub it under her breast line and across her breasts. Then she would sprinkle more onto her hands and rub powder on her inner thighs and legs. Before putting on her bra and panties, she often sprinkled powder into them as well.

Her two boys were serious hockey players, and their equipment—shoulder pads, elbow pads, chest pads, knee pads, and skates—were foul smelling.

"I mean, it would knock you out, their hockey equipment," Roberts testified.

She sprinkled Baby Powder on all of it, she said. The owner of three dogs, she also routinely sprinkled it on her carpeting to get out the smell of dog. Johnson's Baby Powder made much of her life sweet smelling.

The day of her diagnosis, she called her two sons and asked them to meet her at a Panera for lunch. She told them, "And my son Zach, the older one, he said, 'Mom, we got this. Don't worry. We got this. You're strong. You can fight this.' And my younger son, Jake, I've always thought that that day, it took his joy away from him. He was never the same after that in so many ways."

On November 28, 2014, the day after Thanksgiving, Roberts underwent a full hysterectomy. Told the surgery would last two hours, she was on the table for nine because the cancer had spread so widely. Surgeons removed not only her uterus and ovaries but her spleen, appendix, stomach lining, and parts of her diaphragm and bowel. A series of infections kept her in the hospital for another two weeks.

Round after round of chemotherapy over more than three years slowed the progression of the disease but never stopped it. Lawyers took her deposition by video because they feared she wouldn't live to see the trial, but she did.

"I'm a fighter and a thriver," she told the jury. "I can't say I'm a survivor yet, but I'm a thriver. But they said we can try another chemo that will slow your death process down. To be honest, that's exactly what it is. To slow down the symptoms so I have a little bit more time. And so I go for that now. It has slowed things down some. I've gotten better, a little better, in terms of being able to keep food down and get out a little bit and do things. And I'm here. I'm so happy to be able to come here today and share."

Roberts described her symptoms: constant nausea, fatigue, diarrhea followed by constipation, loss of sensation in her fingertips and toes, the loss of her fingernails, pain.

Lanier asked if she was prepared to die.

"Some days, I think I've prepared well to do that. And then something will happen, like your son and daughter-in-law telling you they're going to have a baby, and you wonder if you're going to get to meet them and you know you're probably not. At least here. I'm probably not going to get to meet them here."

Fourteen weeks after testifying, on October 4, 2018, Roberts died quietly in her sleep at her home in Shawsville, Virginia, at the age of sixty-two.

All the plaintiffs' testimonies were equally heartbreaking, but the most surprising part of the Ingham trial ended up being Lanier's deconstruction of Johnson & Johnson's expert witnesses. Lanier showed Dr. Joanne Waldstreicher, J & J's chief medical officer, the company's official statement about the controversy, "Johnson's Baby Powder does not contain asbestos, has never been found in the baby powder and never will."

"Ma'am," Lanier said, always the southern gentleman, "for lack of a polite way of saying it, that's a bald-face lie, isn't it?"

"I don't agree with you," Waldstreicher answered.

"Okay. So, if I show you where Johnson & Johnson's Baby Powder has been found to have asbestos in it and has been found to contain asbestos, you would be stunned, wouldn't you?" Lanier asked. He then did just that, walking Waldstreicher through some of the many documents showing that testing had found asbestos. Waldstreicher answered that she had never seen those documents.

And then Bicks began the company's defense. In many ways, the most remarkable aspect of Johnson & Johnson's case was the things its lawyer didn't offer the jury. Not a single academic asbestos expert appeared on behalf of the company. J & J has paid consultants in nearly every major academic medical center in the country. That not a single one could adequately defend J & J under threat of perjury was telling.

The only asbestos expert the company produced was a geologist from RJ Lee, a for-profit testing and consulting firm whose business, then and now, largely revolves around litigation defense for asbestos companies. He declared that his own testing had failed to find any asbestos in the many jars of Baby Powder that had been examined and declared contaminated by Lanier's expert.

RJ Lee's expert claimed that asbestos fibers must be a certain shape—very long and very thin—to be considered real asbestos, which is why the company is so popular with asbestos makers, since the shape definition RJ Lee used was so incredibly exclusionary. It would be like defining a car as only Arthur Langer's old Dodge Dart, and saying that any other model, from any other manufacturer, from any other year, could not be called a car. Anything that was not this precise shape, the RJ Lee expert declared, is "non-asbestiform," although he admitted that he couldn't declare these non-asbestiform particles to be nonhazardous. However, the RJ Lee expert did admit under cross-examination that when J & J's lawyer had declared that the company's mines had always proven to be free of asbestos, that claim was false.

"Looking at every talc deposit, all areas of a talc mine, that would be false, yes," the expert said.

J & J's lawyer then called to the stand the company's talc safety expert, Dr. Susan Nicholson. With close-cropped white hair and large, black-framed glasses, Nicholson was a picture of competent earnestness. She expressed outrage that anyone would even suggest that J & J would knowingly poison tens of millions of mothers and babies over many decades.

"And tell the jury how you personally feel when someone accuses you and the people who work for you of putting profits over health to possibly hurt somebody," J & J's attorney asked.

"I get pissed off. You know, I get pissed off," Nicholson said. "Because the people that work on my team, myself, we've been doing this for decades, and people commit their lives to helping others. . . . Saying that we don't care or we're putting profits ahead of people's safety and good will? Absolutely not."

Lanier objected and asked to speak with the judge outside of the jury's hearing. During this sidebar, Lanier pointed out that J & J has on multiple occasions pleaded guilty to criminal charges of putting profits over patients' health. The company had even pleaded guilty to bribing the regime of Iraqi president Saddam Hussein, he noted.

"They paint the company out to be a collection of nuns, for lack of a better way of saying it," Lanier fulminated, "not wanting the jury to see that they're working at night as prostitutes, and I ought to get to show the other side of that coin."

But the judge cautioned that any references to other cases might be prejudicial, meaning that mentioning them would unfairly paint J & J in a bad light.

Such moments are repeated in nearly every legal case against Johnson & Johnson. Trading on the conglomerate's glowing reputation, defense lawyers invariably portray the company as a beacon of ethics. These portraits largely go unchallenged, since plaintiffs' attorneys are not allowed to reference the company's many missteps.

Nicholson testified that she personally used Johnson's Baby Powder and had grown up with it in her house. This led Lanier to ask whether Nicholson's mother was still okay.

It was a trick. Like all good lawyers, Lanier never asked questions to which he didn't already know the answer. Nicholson grudgingly admitted that her mother had died at the age of sixty-three of what might have been ovarian cancer. Nicholson's mother was just like Lanier's twenty-two plaintiffs—longtime users of Johnson's Baby Powder who contracted ovarian cancer.

The revelation seemed to have a profound effect on the jury. And it got worse from there. The company's remaining experts were clinical doctors who declared that the women suing the company didn't get their cancers from Johnson's Baby Powder. This was a thoroughly credible argument, since the causal insult for long-gestating cancers is often mysterious. But the doctors' profound ignorance about the basics of asbestos—three in a row couldn't name the six types of asbestos when Lanier quizzed them, something a first-year graduate student in the field could easily recite—undermined their credibility.

One of the company's clinical experts declared that asbestos doesn't cause ovarian cancer. Two others said that only heavy occupational exposure can lead to ovarian cancer. Both claims had been contradicted by decades of research.

One of the company's experts made so many misstatements that Lanier, fearing his cross-examination bordered on being cruel, finally softened.

"We'll look at them together," Lanier said gently of studies the expert didn't know. "You got selected—and this just wasn't your area of research before you got hired to do this, was it?"

"No," the expert admitted.

At the end of a monthlong trial, J & J's attorney filed the last of his mistrial motions, saying the trial should be restarted because the jury had seen evidence that it shouldn't have. The judge dismissed the motion and instructed the lawyers to give their closing arguments.

Lanier went first and explained that J & J kept selling talcum powder long after rivals had stopped because Johnson's Baby Powder was the company's "sacred cow" and "golden egg," a cherished and iconic brand that instilled trust in every other product.

He noted that J & J didn't bring before the jury a single medical expert who studied the health effects of asbestos, even though there are thousands of such experts. And he highlighted the shifting and often incorrect explanations by J & J's own witnesses.

"They went from opening, 'No asbestos, no asbestos in talc mines, never have been, all of our mines are clean' to, now, 'Okay, well, there may be asbestos, but that's industrial talc, not cosmetic talc,'" Lanier said. "Where did that come from? They mix at the same place and they're just making that up."

After speaking for seventy-five minutes, Lanier sat down. The judge gave the jury a break. When they returned, J & J's attorney rose for his own closing statement. He noted that the plaintiffs in the case had to meet a high burden of proof, something he said they hadn't come close to achieving.

"They cannot do so because the evidence has shown that Johnson & Johnson's Baby Powder does not contain asbestos, and that Johnson & Johnson's Baby Powder did not cause the ovarian cancer in this case," he said.

He noted that not one plaintiff in the case had been told by her treating physician that Johnson's Baby Powder caused her illness, and all had filed suit only after seeing lawyers' advertisements seeking clients.

He said that in the 1970s, the president of Mount Sinai Hospital declared Johnson's Baby Powder to be safe and free of asbestos. And he pointed out that the FDA had made the same determination again and again.

J & J's lawyer dismissed as absurd the very idea that a company like Johnson & Johnson would deliberately endanger babies.

"And so, with all this independent testing, there's some massive conspiracy going on by Johnson & Johnson to expose babies to asbestos?" he asked. "Does that make common sense when Johnson & Johnson is doing all this testing? That people like Dr. Hopkins and Dr. Nicholson are using the product themselves? That doesn't make any sense."

J & J's attorney sat down, and Lanier got one last shot to make his case. He said that the protein bar that he'd been eating had a warning that it might contain trace amounts of wheat and soy. Not because either is an ingredient but because the facility in which they were made might be contaminated. So why didn't J & J make a similar warning about asbestos?

Because of money, he said.

"Talcum powder works no better than cornstarch. Their documents say it. Their studies say it," Lanier said. "The profit margin just isn't as high."

When he was done with his argument, Lanier sat down, and the judge sent the jury away to deliberate. It was 1:15 P.M. on Wednesday, July 11, 2018.

The case had taken a month, and the lawyers were expecting the jury to deliberate for days. But at 2:28 P.M., the judge called the courtroom back into session because the jury had asked to see a chart that Lanier had shown estimating the number of asbestos fibers to which each plaintiff had been exposed as a result of Johnson's Baby Powder.

Questions from juries are common, and lawyers always try to guess how such questions might signal a jury's intent. In this case, Lanier's side was cheered that the jury wanted to see something he had produced.

The lawyers argued for an hour about how to respond to the jury's question, during which time the judge noticed that J & J's attorney was looking green.

"You're not getting sick now, are you?" the judge asked.

"I am," he said.

Within minutes, the jury asked two more technical questions, and then at 3:30 P.M., they added a fourth: They wanted copies of some of the research cited, much of it by the plaintiffs' side. At 3:50 P.M., the jury asked to see pictures of the plaintiffs.

The lawyers scrambled to gather the requested court exhibits. For J & J, the last question seemed particularly ominous. Pictures of the plaintiffs? How could that be a good thing? A little after 5 P.M., the judge dismissed the lawyers for the day.

At ten the next morning, the jury had a new question: How do they determine monetary damages? For a defendant, no question is more ominous. At 10:35 A.M., the jury asked for Scotch tape, a calculator, ice cream sandwiches, four yellow highlighters, and a smoking break. In an earlier trial with different plaintiffs, a jury found J & J negligent in its sales of Johnson's Baby Powder but didn't offer the plaintiff any compensatory damages. This jury was asking for a calculator.

At 1:20 P.M., the jury room intercom buzzed twice, the signal that they had come to a verdict. The jurors filed back into the courtroom and handed their verdict form to a court clerk.

To win, Lanier needed nine of the twelve jurors to agree that J & J was liable. All twelve decided that J & J had to pay each of the plaintiffs $25 million in compensatory damages, for a total of $550 million. Even more ominously, they ruled that J & J was liable for punitive damages, which are determined separately, after a minitrial in which plaintiffs' and defense attorneys each have ten minutes to speak.

Before the arguments began, the judge told the jury that J & J and its subsidiaries were worth more than $63 billion (the actual number was eight times higher). Huge numbers were being bandied about.

Once again, Lanier went first and last, with J & J's lawyer sandwiched in between.

Lanier began by thanking the jurors. He promised them that the company's board of directors would learn of their verdict within twenty-three seconds. And the board would either celebrate or be forced to do something like pull the company's talc-based Baby Powder off the market.

J & J's lawyer then got up and assured the jury that they had already sent a powerful message. He said that Baby Powder's sales in Missouri were about $300,000 annually, a tiny fraction of the award that the jury had already made. Anything more would jeopardize other products that are widely used, he said.

And he asked the jury to know that the witnesses the company presented "believe in their hearts that what they said is true, even if you concluded that it was wrong."

Lanier got up again and made his final plea:

"This is something where they've deliberately exposed hundreds of millions of Americans and let us do this to our children," he said. "They have marketed this and their company as a baby company so that we would trust the company. They have done things that are outrageous. If you or I ever caused someone to get cancer that was terminal, do you think we'd be able to fall back on, 'Hey, fine me, you know, a few hundred million dollars?' Or if we have a hundred dollars, a dime? No. We'd be in jail."

Lanier sat down at 4:30 P.M., and the jury filed out of the courtroom. An hour later, the jurors alerted the judge that they had reached a decision. By a vote of eleven to one, they awarded $4.14 billion in punitive damages—one of the biggest civil judgments in history.

Such huge awards are routinely set aside entirely or reduced substantially by appellate courts. Sure enough, an appeals court decided that the award was excessive. It cut the award to plaintiffs to $2.1 billion, but ruled that significant punitive damages were warranted because "Plaintiffs proved with convincing clarity that Defendants engaged in outrageous conduct because of an evil motive or reckless indifference."

Johnson & Johnson appealed all the way to the United States Supreme Court, which on June 1, 2021, announced that it wouldn't hear the case. By then, interest charges had brought the total to $2.5 billion, an amount that was increasing by $400,000 each day.

J & J transferred the money to Lanier's account within a day.

FOR MOST OF J & J'S MODERN HISTORY, THE COMPANY HAD RECEIVED overwhelmingly positive press coverage, in part because of the firm's massive advertising budget. Again and again, the company was able to kill critical stories by threatening media outlets with financial ruin. It had done so at the local and national levels.

In 2003, a TV station in Sacramento, California, sponsored its own lab test of Johnson's Baby Powder and found asbestos. The station never aired the story because of fears J & J would retaliate by pulling its ads. In 2018, Lanier offered on the eve of the Ingham trial to give the Fox Business Network an exclusive preview of the lab tests his firm had commissioned that had found asbestos in bottles of Johnson's Baby Powder dating back decades.

Since Lanier was a regular contributor to Fox Business, producers at the network eagerly agreed. But before Lanier's segment, someone at the show called Johnson & Johnson for a response. Just as Lanier was finishing his makeup, one of the show's producers came to his dressing room to report the conglomerate's answer: A top J & J executive had called Fox's corporate headquarters and said that if the show with Lanier went ahead, Johnson & Johnson would pull all its advertising from Fox. Lanier's segment never ran.

But J & J could not do anything about coverage of the Ingham verdict. Five months after the trial, Reuters ran a story describing some of the asbestos documents that Lanier had uncovered. The shock of the revelations can be measured by their effect on the company's share price, which plunged 10 percent that day. Plaintiffs' attorneys, some underwritten by Wall Street hedge funds, began advertising widely for clients. More than sixty thousand people would eventually file suit.

More broadly, the Ingham revelations led many in the cancer community—some of whom had long dismissed worries about talcum powder—to reconsider whether Johnson & Johnson's had knowingly caused thousands of cancer deaths.

Among those who joined the flood of litigation was Dr. Richard Pazdur, who may be history's most influential oncologist. For nearly a quarter of a century, Pazdur has led the FDA's cancer center and, as a result, has seen more confidential cancer-study data than anyone alive. Pazdur is held in such esteem that pharmaceutical executives often rise to their feet when he enters a room. He is among the most well-regarded civil servants in American history.

For most of his adult life, Pazdur was married to Mary Pazdur, a lovely, funny, and dedicated oncology nurse who lavished attention on her husband and their two yappy lap dogs. Almost every day of her adult life, Mary covered herself with Johnson's Baby Powder.

Soon after her sixtieth birthday, Mary was diagnosed with ovarian cancer. She fought the illness with everything she had, even getting her husband to approve a formal application for her to receive experimental treatments. But by the fall of 2015, she knew she'd lost.

"I'm a nurse. I've seen this movie before," Mary told me in October 2015. "I'm going to die from this. And I want to live my last days as best as I can."

She died on the morning of November 24, 2015. She was sixty-three.

Richard Pazdur's attorneys filed suit against Johnson & Johnson on November 13, 2019, days before the fourth anniversary of her death.

In many ways, Pazdur's lawsuit is a telling sign of J & J's peril. He is widely seen as not only one of the knowledgeable and consequential people in cancer history but as sympathetic to drugmakers. That even he believes J & J was responsible for poisoning his wife is remarkable. And Pazdur's lawsuit is clearly not a cynical effort at self-enrichment. A childless and aged ascetic, Pazdur doesn't need the money. The suit is about justice.

Pazdur's suit may have been a tipping point for J & J. Soon after he filed, the company began taking extraordinary measures to ensure that he and tens of thousands of others never see the inside of a courtroom.

THE INGHAM DOCUMENTS AND THEIR REVELATIONS PROMPTED THE FDA to sponsor its own tests of Johnson's Baby Powder and other talc-containing cosmetics, tests that again revealed that Johnson's Baby Powder was contaminated with asbestos. On October 14, 2019, the agency reported the results to J & J but did not immediately announce the danger to the public. At J & J, executives cloistered for days of marathon meetings, with one taking pages of notes that included cryptic references to coercion and blackmail.

Four days later, the agency announced its findings publicly, declaring it had found "chrysotile fibers, a type of asbestos" in Johnson's Baby Powder, and that "Consumers who have Johnson's Baby Powder lot #22318RB should stop using it immediately."

J & J publicly insisted that the FDA had gotten its test wrong and that the lab had been contaminated with asbestos, not the company's Baby Powder. The FDA stood "by the quality of its testing and results."

Seven months later in May 2020, J & J announced that it had stopped selling talc-based Baby Powder in the United States and Canada because of slowing demand "fueled by misinformation around the safety of the product and a constant barrage of litigation advertising." The company later decided to stop selling talc-based Baby Powder globally beginning in 2023.

With the FDA switching sides, Alex Gorsky, the company's chairman and chief executive, took advantage of an unusual Texas law to transfer the company's Baby Powder liabilities into a subsidiary called LTL Management, put a $2 billion trust fund into the company to cover the costs of litigation, and then declared LTL bankrupt. Known as "the Texas two-step," the maneuver depended on a sympathetic bankruptcy judge agreeing up front how much women who had been sickened by Baby Powder could split among themselves in perpetuity—no punitive damages, no outraged juries, no billion-dollar verdicts, just a check in a set amount when a woman got sick or died. And when the $2 billion ran out, maybe nothing at all.

Fewer than a handful of Texas two-step cases had ever been filed, all of which tested the boundaries of acceptable legal practice. But J & J had a long history of pushing and in many cases exceeding legal limits. It had no intent of stopping now. Sometimes its retribution would be petty (in 2019, plaintiffs' attorneys returned to the Heldrich Hotel in New Brunswick to find that their room keys no longer functioned after J & J instructed the hotel manager to evict them) or more substantial (such as issuing subpoenas regarding communications with the press). The company sued doctors who published studies linking talc-based personal care products and cancer. Outside legal experts called the company's tactics all but unprecedented.

Indeed, there may be no more litigious company in the world. Between 2010 and 2021, J & J spent $25 billion on litigation. Hundreds of thousands of people have sued the company in recent years, and J & J has often seemed as if it would fight each case one by one.

In January 2023, a federal appeals court threw out J & J's bankruptcy filing, declaring that the company had no legitimate claim to Chapter 11 protection because it didn't face financial distress. J & J had a market capitalization that exceeded $400 billion. The bankruptcy judge subsequently released his hold on Baby Powder lawsuits.

CHAPTER 10

An Infamous Crime, the Birth of a Myth

WINTER ARRIVES EARLY IN NORTHERN ILLINOIS, AND TWELVE-year-old Mary Kellerman had her first cold of the season when she awoke with a sore throat and a cough at 7 A.M. on a Wednesday morning on September 29, 1982.

Her father, Dennis Kellerman, quickly decided she was too sick to attend school. He went to the bathroom, opened the medicine cabinet, and took out a bottle of Extra Strength Tylenol that his wife had purchased the night before at a nearby Jewel-Osco store in Elk Grove Village, a Chicago suburb.

Carrying a single capsule and a glass of water, he padded back to Mary's bedroom and told her to take the medicine. Just as he was climbing back under the covers in his own bedroom, he heard Mary go into the bathroom and shut the door. Then he heard a heavy object drop to the floor.

Alarmed, Kellerman went to the bathroom's door.

"Mary, are you okay?"

Nothing.

"Mary? Are you okay?"

Still nothing.

He opened the door and saw his daughter lying on the floor.

By the time paramedics arrived, Mary was in full cardiac arrest. Repeated efforts to revive her both at home and at nearby Alexian Brothers Medical Center failed. She was pronounced dead at 10 A.M. from what doctors and her parents assumed was an undiagnosed congenital heart condition or a catastrophic aneurysm. The Tylenol capsule had, for the moment, been completely forgotten.

Just as the Kellermans were watching their world unravel, twenty-seven-year-old Adam Janus was making a quick trip to the Jewel-Osco store on Vail Avenue in nearby Arlington Heights. A postal worker at Elk Grove Village post office, Janus had decided to take the day off.

He bought a steak for dinner, some flowers for his wife, Teresa, and a bottle of Extra Strength Tylenol. After lunch with Teresa, he took two Tylenol capsules—something he often did. He soon told his wife that he wasn't feeling well and went to the bedroom to lie down.

A few minutes later, Teresa, nineteen, found him unconscious and convulsing. He was pronounced dead at Northwest Community Hospital at 3:15 P.M.

Just then, another twenty-seven-year-old was buying a bottle of Tylenol from a different area store. Her name was Mary Magdalene Reiner, but she went by the first name of Lynn. Just five days before, Reiner had given birth to her fourth child, a boy named Joshua. These were the days when new mothers could spend nearly a week recovering in the hospital, and Reiner had checked out of Central DuPage Hospital in nearby Winfield only the day before.

Reiner bought a bottle of Regular Strength Tylenol capsules at Frank's Finer Foods and got home around 3:30 P.M., where her mother-in-law was watching Joshua and his twenty-one-month-old brother, Jacob. Reiner took two Tylenol capsules.

Reiner told her mother-in-law that she was feeling nauseous. Just as her husband, Ed, arrived with their eight-year-old daughter, Reiner pitched to the floor and went into convulsions. Paramedics returned her to Central DuPage Hospital around 5 P.M., her life slipping away.

Moments later, Mary McFarland, fighting a headache at work, took two Extra Strength Tylenol capsules. She'd bought the Tylenol the evening before but had put about a third of the capsules from the fifty-count bottle into a small Dristan bottle she kept in her purse. Sitting in the break room of the Illinois Bell Phone Center in Yorktown Mall, McFarland, a mother of two, walked over to the break room table, told her coworkers, "I don't feel good, guys," and collapsed onto the table. An ambulance took her to Good Samaritan Hospital, where she died.

These four mysterious deaths in four different hospitals would have remained entirely unconnected and unexplored were it not for the fact that after Adam Janus's death, his younger brother and his brother's young bride returned from the hospital to the house with splitting headaches. Stanley Janus, twenty-four, went for the same Tylenol bottle first and popped two of the white-and-red capsules in his mouth while his wife, whose name was also Theresa (spelled with an h) and who was also nineteen, called her parents to tell them that her brother-in-law had just died. After the call ended, Theresa took two of the deadly capsules herself.

When Stanley collapsed on the floor and went into convulsions, Theresa called 911. For the second time that day, the same paramedics from the Arlington Heights Fire Department rushed to the Janus household. While the emergency team tried to revive Stanley, Theresa called her parents again to tell them that now her husband was in crisis. Then Theresa collapsed.

By the time Stanley and Theresa Janus were brought to Northwest Community Hospital, both were in full cardiac arrest. Dr. Thomas Kim, the medical director of the hospital's intensive care unit, had been about to leave for the day. As soon as he heard that the brother and sister-in-law of the man he'd tried to save earlier in the day were on their way, he took off his jacket.

The emergency room staff got Theresa's heart beating again, but her brain activity was gone. Kim tried much the same with Stanley, with no better results.

Kim told staff to call a poison control center to figure out what could have killed three young and healthy adults in such quick succession. An expert in Colorado suggested cyanide.

Meanwhile, two firefighters who had been monitoring the day's emergency calls figured out that Mary Kellerman's death resembled those of the Janus trio, down to the use of Tylenol just before their respective collapses. The bottles that had caused both sets of deaths were collected and sent to the Cook County medical examiner's office, and Kim sent blood samples from Stanley and Theresa Janus to a nearby lab for a cyanide test.

The next morning, Michael Schaffer, the chief toxicologist for the medical examiner, opened the two bottles. The smell of bitter almonds—a telltale sign of cyanide—was unmistakable, he later said. Dr. Edmund Donoghue, the deputy assistant medical examiner for Cook County, held a morning press conference to announce that the deaths of the Januses and Mary Kellerman had all occurred after each had taken Extra Strength Tylenol capsules laced with cyanide. Chicago police went through the streets with bullhorns, warning commuters and residents against taking Tylenol.

It soon became one of the most extensively covered news events since the assassination of President John F. Kennedy almost twenty years earlier. All three national networks made the poisonings the center of their broadcasts for weeks. Almost every newspaper in the country covered it through the fall, with more than one hundred thousand individual stories.

The first anyone at FDA headquarters in Rockville, Maryland, heard about the Tylenol poisonings came from a midmorning call on Thursday from a reporter at the *Chicago Sun-Times*.

Deputy Commissioner Mark Novitch ordered the agency's key personnel to gather in a conference room designated for emergency responses, the FDA's version of the White House Situation Room. The conference room was dark and ominous, with a large conference table and walls decorated with photos of disasters. One showed Mount Saint Helens erupting. Another showed cans of salmon contaminated with botulism, and another showed a rat peeking out of a container of oatmeal. An antique glass-walled cabinet held a grim assortment of agency trophies, including contaminated candy, diet powder, tampons, and infant formula. There was a red phone sitting on a credenza in the corner that, with a dial of "99," connected headquarters with every field office in the country.

Once the poisonings were confirmed, officials sent field personnel to the Johnson & Johnson facilities where the contaminated lots had been manufactured. Inspectors showed up late Thursday afternoon at the plants in Fort Washington, Pennsylvania, and on Friday morning in Round Rock, Texas. Although such inspections can take days and even weeks, officials decided within hours that neither plant could have been responsible for the poisonings.

That Friday evening, Chicago police were called to the North Side apartment of Paula Prince, who had died about the same time on Wednesday as Stanley and Theresa Janus. Since she had Thursday off from work, she wasn't missed by anyone until Friday. When they did find her, she was lying on the bathroom floor near a bottle of Extra Strength Tylenol.

Hours later, Chicago mayor Jane Byrne held a news conference in which she instructed city residents to hand over all bottles of Tylenol to local police stations, along with a note describing where and when the bottle had been purchased.

"Don't take Tylenol," she said, "not even in tablet or liquid form."

FEW AMERICAN CORPORATIONS HAVE EVER FACED SUCH A DISASTER. AT the time, Tylenol was Johnson & Johnson's most important product. Sales in 1982 were expected to approach $500 million and account for nearly 20 percent of its profits.

Now every major media organization on the planet was linking Tylenol with death. The company had to rescue the franchise, but how?

FDA officials faced a similar crisis. The agency's core mission is to ensure the safety of the nation's drug supply, and now America's most popular medicine—more people took Tylenol (generics weren't sold at the time) than any other drug—was killing people.

J & J executives and FDA officials understood that their actions over the ensuing days and weeks would come to define them and their respective organizations for at least a generation.

In the end, Americans gave both high marks. Johnson & Johnson's response has long been seen as the most ethical, honest, and effective crisis reaction in American corporate history—thus the legendary Harvard Business School case, and the use of J & J's decision-making as a model of executive leadership.

J & J executives withdrew every Tylenol capsule on every store shelf—about thirty-one million bottles. It was the largest drug recall in history and cost J & J $100 million to manage. The company undertook a crash program to add protective packaging seals. Glue was added to the flaps on boxes containing pill bottles. A plastic ring was added around the necks of pill bottles. Finally, consumers had to breach foil placed over the bottle's mouth. These measures were soon adopted by every over-the-counter drug manufacturer.

While the new seals can be defeated, and small-scale tamperings have continued to occur, J & J's leadership undoubtedly made mass poisonings far less likely. Scores of deaths have probably been averted as a result of its willingness to put safety first.

This is why most histories of the 1982 case end on an upbeat note: A tragedy causes an entire industry to change for the better. It's a good story, and mostly an accurate one, that leaves J & J covered in plaudits.

But there are a few flaws in this happy narrative, including an account of a stone-cold killer with easy access to J & J's distribution system. Taken together, these footnotes to the oft-told tale about 1982 cast J & J's handling of the episode in a somewhat less commendable light.

CHAPTER 11

Problems with the Narrative

THERE REMAINS A WIDESPREAD ASSUMPTION THAT THE CHICAGO tamperings were a bolt from the blue that couldn't possibly have been anticipated by the company.

In fact, Tylenol had been tampered with many times before. In the previous three years, the company had received three hundred complaints about contaminations. These had become such a problem that Johnson & Johnson had already been seriously considering tamper-resistant packaging, which is why the company was able to relaunch Tylenol with its protective new features so quickly.

History also tends to suggest that Johnson & Johnson announced its nationwide recall immediately to save lives after learning that its product had been a vehicle for murder. But for days, J & J executives agreed only to a limited recall of lots associated with contamination. That was true even though executives received a call on Friday, October 1, from a California physician reporting on a copycat poisoning in Oroville, about seventy miles north of the state capital of Sacramento. The company asked the doctor to forward the suspect Tylenol bottles to the company. By Monday, October 4, company toxicologists had confirmed that the Oroville capsules contained strychnine. Even so, the company resisted widening its recall.

Only after news of the copycat poisoning became public on Tuesday, October 5, and led to even wider panic did J & J announce its nationwide recall. By then, executives realized that a nationwide recall was the only way to prevent an unending series of copycat cases and panics.

There are also reasons to believe that a wholesale customer within the distribution network was compromised, raising a host of questions about just how innocent a victim J & J really was. Almost twenty-nine hours before little Mary Kellerman collapsed on her bathroom floor, two Kane County sheriff's deputies working the night shift pulled into the parking lot of the Howard Johnson's Motor Lodge and Restaurant in Elgin. It was 2:32 A.M. on September 28. As they headed into the restaurant, the duo spotted two big cardboard boxes on the parking lot pavement with the words EXTRA STRENGTH TYLENOL CAPSULES printed outside. The boxes looked as if someone had accidentally let them slip out of a car or truck. One of the boxes was open with at least two dozen bottles still inside.

"They saw two boxes in the parking lot," Sheriff Kramer later told a reporter working for *The New York Times*, "with hundreds of capsules strewn around the ground."

Between the boxes and capsules, all labeled Extra Strength Tylenol, was a substantial amount of white powder. One of the deputies picked up the powder and rubbed it between his fingers. "It looked like hundreds of capsules had been emptied. We looked at them and found a couple capsules had been put together," said Joseph Chavez, one of the deputies.

The men assumed that drug dealers had intended to mix Tylenol with cocaine to give the illegal drug an extra kick. Since Tylenol is not a controlled substance, the officers didn't report the incident, the *Times* noted. "We just blew it off," Chavez said. The two deputies got into their squad cars and drove off, leaving the Tylenol boxes behind.

Minutes later, one of the deputies pulled to the side of the road, suddenly violently ill with vomiting, headache, and dizziness—symptoms of acute cyanide poisoning that can occur by inhalation or absorption through the skin. The other deputy reported similar symptoms later. However, neither linked their symptoms with the Tylenol boxes until after the case exploded into the headlines. By then, the boxes were gone.

These large boxes were used exclusively within Johnson & Johnson's distribution system. There were only a few places in the Chicago area where stock like that was kept.

But many of the investigators working the case somehow missed this vital clue or failed to grasp its significance. Richard Brzeczek, the superintendent of the Chicago Police Department at the time, told me in a phone call from his Florida retirement home that he didn't know about the wholesale boxes of Tylenol until decades later, an extraordinary admission.

Still, Brzeczek dismissed the finding as not terribly relevant, since anyone could have breached J & J's distribution system. But even if Brzeczek was right that the finding didn't substantially change the hunt for the murderer, the fact that Johnson & Johnson's distribution system could be breached "by anyone" changes the narrative about the company's responsibility for the crimes.

In press conferences and interviews, police officials described a system in which boxes of Tylenol were shipped directly from Johnson & Johnson's production facilities to stores, with the boxes sealed in plastic wrap. This is why, they said repeatedly, the contamination could not have occurred in the distribution system: because retailers would have noticed any broken plastic seals.

So, once FDA inspectors determined in the first days of the investigation that the cyanide had not been accidentally dumped into Tylenol capsules at the company's two main factories, J & J was absolved of responsibility, and investigators turned their focus to stores.

In reality, most stores that stocked Tylenol in the 1980s sold only a few bottles a week, so it never made sense for them to accept direct shipments from Johnson & Johnson of dozens of shrink-wrapped bottles. As a result, Johnson & Johnson shipped much of its product to third-party "rack jobbers," or contract warehousing-and-stocking companies that rent shelf space in grocery stores and mini-marts. These are the guys stocking shelves at supermarkets who have no idea where to find the Oreos when asked by shoppers because they don't work for the store.

In press releases and conferences, those who spoke for the Tylenol investigative task force, the FDA, and Johnson & Johnson never mentioned rack jobbers or any other middleman who delivered much of the supplies of Tylenol—not only in Chicago but across the country.

A host of other details similarly didn't fit, including the discovery by the FDA on September 30 of a contaminated bottle of Extra Strength Tylenol in the back-room stock of a drugstore in the Chicago suburb of Schaumburg. Why would a madman risk discovery by slipping a bottle onto a store's publicly inaccessible storage shelf?

The unusual nature of the Janus murders—three people all taking Tylenol from the same bottle within hours of one another—was probably the only reason authorities discovered the contamination. In fact, at least four other deaths around the time of the murders also fit the case profile perfectly. All of the victims had taken Tylenol just before collapsing, and all were later found to have died of cyanide poisoning. The details of some of these cases were kept secret for months. In addition, there was a string of other deaths in which the bodies were never tested for cyanide. Brzeczek concluded that the likely toll from the Tylenol killer was at least eleven, four more than included in the widely accepted narrative.

The final reason the madmen-in-retail-stores theory falls apart upon closer examination is that the biggest rack jobber in the Chicago area was the Jewel company in Melrose Park, which stocked the shelves at many of the stores where contaminated Tylenol was purchased. Among Jewel's many fine employees? The perfect suspect.

ROGER ARNOLD STRUCK FEAR IN MANY OF THOSE WHO KNEW HIM, including most of his coworkers at the Jewel Company.

A forty-eight-year-old dead-ender, Arnold described himself as an amateur chemist, admitted that he had purchased cyanide in bulk six months before the Tylenol murders, had bought a one-way plane ticket to Thailand, owned five unregistered and therefore illegal guns, had an outstanding arrest warrant for aggravated assault, had been overheard on separate occasions by different people bragging that he had killed people using cyanide, had recently gotten divorced, had recently told his supervisor at work that he was "mad at people and wanted to throw acid at them or poison them," and was described by coworkers as a dangerous loner whom they suspected of being the Tylenol killer as soon as the news broke.

To top it off, Arnold's home contained a box of gunpowder and was filled with books and magazines describing do-it-yourself ways of killing people—including *The Anarchist's Cookbook*; *Improvised Explosives and Detonators*; *Boobytraps, Incendiaries, Explosives and Demolitions; Unconventional Warfare Devices*; and *100 Ways to Disappear and Live Free*. (Many of these details come from long-sealed records from the Arlington Heights Police Department, and they collectively confirm that Arnold was a prime suspect.)

Unkempt, with thick glasses and a beard, Arnold spent most of his evenings on barstools in dog-eared establishments around Chicago's periphery. He liked to brag about his years as a military demolitions expert (which was a lie) and often spoke about his fascination with chemistry.

When his marriage fell apart in the summer of 1982, some bartenders noted a decidedly darker turn to Arnold's rants. His parents were dead. He had no children and almost no one who would claim him as a friend. One tavern owner filed a complaint with police in June, saying that Arnold had threatened him with a gun after the man broke up a bar fight.

A week after the Tylenol murders became public, Marty Sinclair, who owned the Oxford Pub on Lincoln Avenue, called police after overhearing a couple of his regulars discuss how Arnold had cyanide in his home. Anyone could use it to kill others, he told other patrons. He said no one would ever know.

"The subject was recently divorced and is despondent," a police report of Sinclair's October 6 call summarized. Arnold "supposedly picked up a quantity of cyanide (two 16 oz. Bottles) six months ago and said that he was working on a project."

Detectives asked Sinclair to call again the next time Arnold showed up, and they canvassed bars in the area and alerted other bartenders to be on the lookout for him. Five nights later, Arnold walked into Lilly's, a Lincoln Avenue dive. Someone called the cops, who picked up Arnold at 7 P.M. and brought him in for questioning.

"Initial interview with Arnold disclosed that he did posess [sic] cyinide [sic] but discarded it three months ago as he was having trouble with his wife (ex) and didn't want the stuff around," an investigation report from the Arlington Heights Police Department dated October 11, 1982, stated. It further pointed out that "Mr. Arnold works for Jewel Foods at their warehouse in Melrose Park and loads and unloads trucks." That meant Arnold loaded and unloaded the same kind of warehouse boxes of Tylenol found by the two Kane County sheriff's deputies.

Arnold was arrested, released, and put under surveillance. Investigators soon found myriad links between him and the killings, but they were circumstantial, not enough to justify an arrest. That would turn out to be yet another tragedy. When his name was mentioned in press reports as a possible suspect, Arnold became consumed with rage and soon blamed Sinclair for his predicament. On June 18, 1983, when a man emerged from Sinclair's bar, Arnold walked up to him, said a few words, and then shot him in the chest. The bullet went straight through the man's heart, and he died in seconds. It wasn't Sinclair but a forty-six-year-old computer consultant and father of three named John Stanisha, who looked uncannily like Sinclair.

Arnold was convicted of murder and sent to prison. While Arnold's name briefly surfaced in a few stories as the Tylenol poisoning suspect, once incarcerated, he essentially disappeared from attention. Released from prison fifteen years later, he spent his last years deeply depressed and finally died of natural causes in 2008.

Although most of the investigators on the case believe the killings were random, Brzeczek believes they were a crime of passion, that the killer tried to cover up a targeted murder by killing a bunch of other random people. A problem with his theory is that the killings that were meant to distract might have gone unnoticed for weeks, or possibly forever. Indeed, the four murders before Mary Kellerman's were in fact missed.

But even for those who believed there had to be some connection between killer and victim, Arnold fit the bill. Lynn Reiner's father also worked at Jewel and was reported to be Arnold's only friend there. At work, they sometimes ate lunch together. They both lived in Villa Park, and they sometimes arrived at work in the same car. Both men had easy access to pallets of Tylenol.

Detectives soon discovered that Arnold was familiar with many of the stores where contaminated Tylenol bottles were sold. Dolores Arnold, Arnold's ex-wife, was once a patient at a psychiatric hospital across the street from the Winfield grocery store where Reiner's Tylenol was from. Dolores Arnold told police that her ex had visited her at the hospital several times.

After his divorce, Arnold moved back to Chicago, having lost the house in the settlement, but he certainly knew the western suburbs where several of the tainted Tylenol bottles had been sold. And the two tainted bottles recovered in Chicago, including the one that killed Prince, were all sold at stores within walking distance of the Lincoln Avenue bars that Arnold frequented.

These and other clues led several Chicago police detectives and Pierce Brooks, a renowned FBI profiler who later created the bureau's National Center for the Analysis of Violent Crime, to conclude that Arnold was the killer.

Brooks suggested that the FBI focus more of its investigation on Arnold. There is no evidence that the federal agency followed the advice. Instead, the FBI focused almost exclusively on James Lewis, a con man living in New York who sent a letter a week after the killings became public to the mailroom of McNeil Laboratories, the J & J subsidiary that makes Tylenol, demanding Johnson & Johnson pay $1 million or more killings would follow.

The FBI had bootstrapped itself into the Tylenol case with the shaky legal claim that the lethal Tylenol bottles—because they contained cyanide—were mislabeled and thus broke federal law. Once J & J was cleared of inserting the cyanide, however, this toehold all but vanished. And if detectives determined that Arnold was their lead suspect, the FBI's role in the investigation became even more untenable, since the perpetrator and victims were all Illinois residents.

But with Lewis as the chief suspect, the FBI's role had a clear legal foundation, since sending an extortion claim through the mail and crossing state lines to commit murder are clear violations of federal law. Brzeczek was among those who didn't believe Lewis was the killer, and he suspected that the FBI wanted to keep the investigation open because it didn't want the public to see files showing just how badly it had botched the case. When the agency closes an investigation, the files become public. With the case unsolved, however, confidentiality reigns.

On October 13, the Tylenol task force distributed a photo of Lewis as their main suspect—which, to the public, he has remained ever since.

After Arnold was convicted of Stanisha's murder, his attorney approached a Chicago police detective and said Arnold might be willing to talk about the Tylenol murders if his appeals were denied. This offer was passed along to a trio of Chicago detectives investigating the Tylenol murders. To them, it suggested that Arnold hoped to trade a possible confession in the Tylenol case for a shorter prison sentence.

"All the pieces, all the tips, all the clues, all the arrows, they all pointed toward him," one of the detectives told the *Chicago Tribune*, which published a story on the fortieth anniversary of the killings that focused on Arnold.

With Arnold as the culprit, much about the Tylenol case changes. Instead of being an entirely innocent victim, Johnson & Johnson may have to share at least some responsibility, given that the killer breached the wholesaler's warehouse, part of a distribution network that the company may have had a responsibility to keep secure.

But a quick poll conducted by Johnson & Johnson showed that 90 percent of respondents believed the company was a blameless victim. The company's confidence that it would emerge stronger from the scandal was demonstrated about a week after the poisonings when, contrary to other J & J scandals where the finger was pointed away from the mothership, executives started adding Johnson & Johnson's name to press releases about the poisoning in addition to that of McNeil Laboratories. Weeks later, McNeil was dropped altogether.

Surveys from before the poisonings revealed that few people knew that Tylenol was made by Johnson & Johnson. Those done afterward found near universal recognition. One benefit, according to executives, was that Tylenol inherited some of the warm feelings associated with Johnson's Baby Powder, which J & J was still lying about.

"It was a bitter irony that the gentle, loving relationship between mother and child should somehow be a factor in the comeback phase of a crime of evil-minded brutality," wrote Lawrence G. Foster, the company's longtime public relations chief. The real irony, of course, is that one contaminated product helped the company recover from another.

CHAPTER 12

Never an Adversarial Relationship

NOT MANY PEOPLE KNOW THAT THE U.S. FOOD AND DRUG ADMIN-istration has a criminal investigative division that includes sworn officers who carry guns and have the power to arrest people. In the extensive files that the FDA still maintains on the 1982 Tylenol killings, there is little sign that the agency's criminal division even became seriously engaged. One reason, according to Scott Bartz, is that J & J deliberately kept the federal drug agency in the dark.

Bartz, a former Johnson & Johnson employee, is no one's idea of a disinterested observer. He filed a secret whistleblower lawsuit against J & J claiming the company defrauded Medicaid and Medicare through price manipulation. After being fired, Bartz wrote several books about the Tylenol case, cheekily describing himself as having "embarked on a career as an independent journalist thanks to the support of Johnson & Johnson's human resources and security personnel who encouraged him to seek a new line of work as they escorted him from the company's premises on the morning he returned from a 'secret' meeting with government prosecutors investigating allegations of Medicaid fraud at J & J."

In his books, Bartz, who settled with the company, persuasively argues that Arnold was the likely killer, and thus, J & J wasn't the innocent victim it claimed to be since the Tylenol distribution was breached far earlier in the chain than suspected at the time and the company was much less cooperative with investigators than it professed. Records that have only recently become available—such as files from the Arlington Heights Police Department—confirm many of his findings.

Bartz's most explosive claim is that Johnson & Johnson executives realized almost immediately that the killer worked for Jewel but kept that knowledge not only from the public but from investigators. For instance, the company and authorities insisted that the poisonings were confined to the Chicago area. But McNeil representatives made repeated and panicked phone calls to drugstores served by Jewel Foods that were far from Chicago. A story in the *Pharos-Tribune*, the local paper in Logansport, Indiana, included an interview with the owner of one drugstore describing multiple calls from McNeil. But drugstores only blocks away that were serviced by different rack jobbers received no such calls.

The one government agency that might have uncovered all of this was the FDA, which has invaluable expertise about how drugs are sold and distributed. But the FDA almost immediately absolved J & J of all responsibility for the poisonings and quickly surrendered its role in the investigation.

Partially, this was due to a lack of proper funding, a chronic problem at the agency but one that was particularly acute in 1982, a year in which Congress failed to pass a budget in time to prevent a shutdown. On October 1, the day after the poisonings were announced, the FDA ran out of money. FDA inspectors and officers had to investigate on their own time and with their own resources.

Even after Congress passed a budget the following week, the agency's resources were still so stretched that it quickly surrendered the role of testing Tylenol bottles for cyanide to Johnson & Johnson, although the company had every motivation to hide the extent of the problem.

The FDA also had little power. Until 1997, the agency had no statutory authority to demand records or inspect documents at plants making over-the-counter medicines (one reason its inspections of Johnson & Johnson's Pennsylvania and Texas plants were so brief). Five months before the Tylenol crisis, the U.S. Government Accountability Office issued a report concluding that the FDA had no ability to evaluate problems with over-the-counter drugs and did not know how many were marketed or whether they were safe or effective. In Congressional testimony following the crisis, officials said that three hundred thousand different over-the-counter drug brands were marketed and billions of packages sold. But officials admitted that both numbers were estimates. That was why the FDA had no clue that the 1982 poisonings were preceded by hundreds of smaller contamination problems.

Investigations into the Tylenol killings continue to this day, and some of the evidence is now being examined with highly sensitive modern equipment in hopes of finding microscopic traces of DNA and fingerprints. Unfortunately, the bottles and poisoned capsules were so thoroughly contaminated by investigators themselves that sorting through the myriad genetic fingerprints has been challenging. Arnold's body was exhumed a year after he died to retrieve a sample of his genetic material, which investigators continue to reference. Few believe the case will ever be solved. The FDA remains so absent from this ongoing probe that, in its extensive fortieth-anniversary series on the case, the *Chicago Tribune* barely mentioned the agency.

The sad truth is that the FDA ignored, enabled, or encouraged every Johnson & Johnson disaster in this book. But the 1982 Tylenol poisonings stand out because of an element not present in the others: the most corrupt FDA commissioner in history.

EVERY FDA COMMISSIONER OF THE MODERN ERA HAS WORKED FOR drugmakers after leaving government service, and many worked for them beforehand. But only Dr. Arthur Hayes, Jr., surreptitiously and illegally took money from drug companies while he led the agency.

Commissioner from 1981 to 1983, Hayes received his medical degree from Cornell University, after which he joined the U.S. Army, where he served as a captain in the Chemical Corps. Among the experiments he oversaw for the military were tests of the effects of nitrogen mustard on the skin of twenty prisoners at Holmesburg State Prison, an experiment overseen by Albert Kligman and partly funded by Johnson & Johnson.

Hayes was brought to the attention of President Ronald Reagan by Donald Rumsfeld, the former defense secretary to President Gerald Ford, who would reprise that role during the administration of President George W. Bush. At the time, Rumsfeld was the chief executive of G. D. Searle, a drug-and-additive company, and he wanted a more industry-friendly commissioner to approve the company's new sweetener, aspartame.

To be fair, Hayes made no bones about his fondness for industry. He believed drug regulation should be a collaborative process, and the Tylenol poisonings allowed him to put that belief into action. He lost little time in publicly exonerating Johnson & Johnson. Hayes told the industry newsletter *The Food & Drug Letter*, "McNeil acted about as responsibly as a company can act under any circumstances, let alone when there are so many unknowns and fears." FDA officials even took pains to tell reporters that the two lots linked to the poisonings were not being termed "recalls," which would imply a manufacturing defect.

The Food & Drug Letter described the relationship between the FDA and J & J as a "love fest." In public statements and testimony before state legislators in California and Massachusetts on October 12, two weeks after the poisonings became public, top agency officials read from an identical script claiming that "the contamination was the result of tampering after the capsules had been shipped to distribution points and, most likely, after they reached retail shelves."

On October 15, the agency put this language into a letter to Johnson & Johnson whose explicit purpose seemed to be to relieve the company of liability for the poisonings. In a notice in the *Federal*

Register, federal officials went even further, officially dismissing even the possibility that the poisonings had occurred anywhere along the company's distribution system.

"The pattern of contamination revealed during subsequent events was inconsistent with the theory that the cyanide had been introduced either at the source of manufacture or at intermediate points in the chain of distribution," the agency's notice stated. "It is believed that one or more persons obtained the Extra Strength Tylenol capsules, contaminated them with cyanide, inserted these capsules into the bottles, returned them to the boxes in which they were sold, and surreptitiously placed the boxes on the shelves of the stores from which the victims purchased them."

Whether Hayes was aware of Arnold's arrest the day before this statement is unclear, but he continued to argue, before Congress and others, that the contamination was not Johnson & Johnson's fault. He also ludicrously defended the FDA's system for reporting drug-related injuries and deaths, which anyone with even a vague awareness of the nation's drug system would know was (and remains) haphazard at best.*

After the health department's inspector general revealed that Hayes was taking money from drugmakers while serving as commissioner, Hayes retired. The Reagan Administration's Department of Justice declined to pursue criminal charges, but the U.S. attorney in Baltimore wrote in a letter that "Dr. Hayes has shown an insensitivity to the principle that government employees must scrupulously avoid the appearance of impropriety in their dealings with the public."

On his way out, Hayes was defiant.

"I think I'm a goddamn good commissioner, I think I am an hon-

---

* To this day, agency officials estimate they learn about somewhere between 0.01 percent and 5 percent of the serious problems that patients and consumers experience with prescription drugs. And that's with products that involve doctors, pharmacists, insurers, and a host of other professionals, and in a system where manufacturers are required to forward to the FDA any reports of serious injuries they receive independently. For over-the-counter remedies like Tylenol, reporting problems are far worse.

est person, I know I'm a clergyman and I'm also a good physician," he said. "I don't think there is a soul in this world that knows me that thinks I am dishonest or trying to make a buck."

It was never clear whether J & J paid Hayes during his time as FDA commissioner, but he spent much of the rest of his life working for a public relations firm owned by a former top J & J executive. Much of the firm's work was for Johnson & Johnson.

The public clearly benefited from one aspect of Hayes's "love fest" with Johnson & Johnson. When J & J was forced to make tamper-resistant packaging, Hayes decided he wanted similar measures for every pill, caplet, and capsule sold in every store and shop. Unsurprisingly, not every company wanted to undertake the expensive and time-consuming manufacturing changes that were needed. But just as it had with the cosmetics association during the talcum powder contamination scandal of the 1970s, J & J held considerable sway with a different trade association of over-the-counter drug manufacturers. Without J & J's full support, Hayes's efforts might have gone for naught, which would have left the FDA with no end of headaches for two reasons.

First, copycat poisonings continued to bedevil the industry for years, including one in 1986, again involving Tylenol. Just as important, state legislatures were considering passing laws to ban over-the-counter medicines lacking tamper-resistant packaging. Such bills were a direct threat to the FDA's authority and might have led to a fracturing of the nation's medicines market.

With J & J's help, Hayes managed to not only bolster protections for all Americans but safeguard his agency's preeminent authority over the regulation of over-the-counter medicines—all because of Johnson & Johnson's enormous size.

These were huge wins. The most popular medicines in the United States have been forever safer and the FDA has maintained its role as the leading drug regulator in the world because of Hayes's partnership with the world's largest healthcare conglomerate.

It is easy to imagine another commissioner making the same

pragmatic compromise that Hayes did: If supporting J & J's less-than-honest narrative and helping it avoid legal liability meant that the entire industry would move in a positive direction and the FDA would be safeguarded, so be it. And so it was: J & J's ability to influence its industry peers would lead the FDA to go easy on the conglomerate again and again in the coming decades—and in one of those instances, Tylenol would again be the focus.

CHAPTER 13

The Cost of Doing Business

Around thanksgiving of 1982, johnson & johnson relaunched Tylenol with tamper-resistant packaging. For many months, Tylenol was the only over-the-counter medicine with this extra measure of safety, providing the product with a halo it never surrendered.

Just as the new bottles were going on sale, the tightly budgeted FDA underwrote a public-service advertising campaign in newspapers nationwide defending the safety of Tylenol and other over-the-counter medicines.

For Anthony Benedi, a scheduler for President George H. W. Bush, Tylenol's apparent safety was a primary reason he reached for a bottle of Extra Strength Tylenol when he got the flu in the first days of February 1993, just after leaving the White House. Benedi, who was thirty-seven, usually drank between two and three glasses of wine a night, the average alcohol consumption for American men. And he took the Tylenol dosage recommended on the bottle.

Several nights after he first got sick, he woke up confused and incoherent. His wife called an ambulance. By the time he arrived at the hospital, he had slipped into a coma. Tests showed signs that his liver was failing and his brain swelling. Doctors drilled a hole in his skull to relieve the pressure.

Three days after becoming comatose, Benedi got a break. A young man taken to Benedi's hospital after a motorcycle accident was declared brain dead, and doctors gave Benedi the man's liver. Two months later, Benedi finally left the hospital with deep scars. He eventually needed a kidney transplant.

Haunted by an injury that occurred even though he'd done everything right, including by not drinking alcohol during his illness, he sued J & J. Eighteen months later, a jury awarded him nearly $9 million in damages. Documents revealed in Benedi's case showed that Johnson & Johnson had known for years that moderate drinkers—a description that applies to most Americans—could suffer catastrophic liver damage from ordinary doses of Tylenol.

Because their purpose is to have an effect that changes the functioning of the body, medicines frequently have trade-offs. Aspirin, Motrin, and similar pain pills can be terrible stomach irritants because they inhibit cyclooxygenase, or COX—an enzyme that has counterbalancing effects on the stomach and heart. Pills that are tougher on the stomach, like aspirin and naproxen (also sold as Aleve), tend to protect the heart, while those that are easiest on the stomach, like ibuprofen (sold as Advil and Motrin) and celecoxib (sold as Celebrex), not only don't protect the heart but may actually encourage heart attacks. (This problematic balance is why Merck withdrew Vioxx in September 2004.)

The outlier is acetaminophen, the medicine found in Tylenol. More than a century after its discovery, scientists still don't know how acetaminophen works, but it seems to have little, or perhaps a very different, effect on COX enzymes than its rivals. What is clear is that acetaminophen has no apparent effect on stomachs and hearts.

The ubiquity of ulcers and gastritis in the 1970s and the sudden realization that Tylenol alone among pain pills had no effect on them led to surging sales, tripling to an annual level of $88 million between 1972 to 1974, and continuing to rise sharply.

But one problem still bedeviled the brand: Surveys showed that Tylenol's greatest strength—its avowed safety—was also its greatest weakness, as consumers deemed it less effective than other brands. To fix this, the company applied to the FDA to sell an "Extra Strength" version that would steeply increase the amount of medicine to 500 milligrams per pill from the 325 milligrams approved in 1960.

The application was made about the same time *The Lancet*, a top British medical journal, stated in a 1975 editorial that if acetaminophen "were discovered today it would not be approved" by British regulators because of its toxic effects on the liver. "It would certainly never be freely available without prescription." Calling the drug's avowed safety "deceptive," the journal pointed out that "not much more than the recommended maximum daily dosage" could cause liver damage and that acetaminophen poisoning was already "one of the commonest causes" of liver failure in Britain.

Nonetheless, the FDA in 1976 approved over-the-counter sales of Extra Strength Tylenol. Lo and behold, deaths and injuries surged.

The next year, an FDA advisory panel released a 1,200-page report on pain relievers with some pointed and urgent advice about Tylenol. While the medicine was generally safe when used as directed, the report stated that some advertising for acetaminophen gave the impression that it was much safer than aspirin, and the committee told the FDA that it must add a strong warning.

The panel's suggested language: "Do not exceed recommended dosage because severe liver damage may occur." With only advisory authority, the panel couldn't mandate anything. But it told FDA officials that it believed the warning should be obligatory.

In September 1977, the *Annals of Internal Medicine* joined the fray, publishing case studies of patients who suffered liver damage after taking acetaminophen for lengthy periods or at slightly elevated doses. The journal emphasized just how narrow the drug's margin of error was for many patients.

Three months later, Johnson & Johnson filed a lengthy response to the advisory committee's recommendation about a liver warning. A liver warning "is unnecessary and serves only to confuse and frighten the vast majority of consumers who use acetaminophen in a rational and appropriate fashion," the company claimed. A warning also wouldn't help, since symptoms of liver damage often appear too late to be reversed. The company claimed that overdoses were exclusively the result of suicide attempts and that they knew of no documented case of anyone harmed while taking the drug for medical reasons, even though the *Annals* had just published a series of case studies of patients who had experienced precisely that.

The FDA considered the issue for a decade, finally deciding a liver warning was unnecessary. The agency said it didn't want people who were contemplating suicide to know the damage the drug could do. And it agreed with J & J that signs of liver toxicity emerged too late for an effective medical response. A generic warning that consumers who overdose should seek prompt medical attention was mandated, nothing more.

Liberated, J & J heavily advertised Extra Strength Tylenol as "the most potent pain reliever you can buy without a prescription," and sales rocketed. By 1979, Tylenol had captured 25 percent of the over-the-counter painkiller market, with the Extra Strength version accounting for 70 percent of the brand's sales. Two years later, Tylenol's share of the analgesics market rose to 35 percent, and sales topped $400 million. Tylenol was so dominant that it outsold the next four leading analgesics combined. By the next year, sales were expected to top $500 million.

Johnson & Johnson's surveys showed that two-thirds of Tylenol customers were taking the drug because of a doctor's recommendation. A quarter had been told to stop taking aspirin to forestall upset stomachs, stomach and intestinal bleeding, or irritated ulcers. With so many people suffering ulcers, Tylenol's risks to the liver seemed less concerning.

Several developments in the 1980s and '90s changed that calculus. The most important was the discovery in 1982 by two Australians that peptic ulcers were mostly caused by *H. pylori* bacteria. A simple course of antibiotics cures most peptic ulcers for good.

And then a raft of cures for excessive stomach acid levels all but eliminated chronic indigestion. First came H$_2$ blockers like Pepcid AC, Zantac, and Tagamet, and then proton-pump inhibitor drugs like Prilosec and Prevacid. The latter drugs are some of the most effective over-the-counter remedies of any kind. Anyone who gets stomach discomfort while taking a lengthy course of ibuprofen can usually solve that problem by taking Prilosec or Nexium as well.

Medicines taken without a prescription are supposed to have wide safety margins—meaning that if someone takes an extra pill or two, no harm will result. That is not the case with Extra Strength Tylenol.

At least 150 Americans die every year and 30,000 are hospitalized from taking too much acetaminophen—and those are just the confirmed cases. The real toll in the United States is likely far higher, and many times that number around the world. By comparison, the death toll from all other over-the-counter pain relievers combined is less than half that of acetaminophen. Acetaminophen has for decades been the nation's leading cause of acute liver failure.

Many of those affected are shocked to learn that Tylenol can be so dangerous. Kate Trunk's twenty-three-year-old son Marcus was working a construction job in Pennsylvania in 1995 when he hurt his wrist. For the next two weeks, he took Tylenol with codeine and Extra Strength Tylenol. Feeling sick, he then started taking Theraflu without realizing that it contained acetaminophen, too. Getting worse, he checked himself into a hospital and soon fell into a coma. After eight days, Kate Trunk and her husband ended life support for their son.

"We stayed with him and held him and talked to him and kissed him and petted him," Trunk said. "He finally just went. It was total shock, walking around in a daze, not knowing, angry at God, angry at everything."

The cause of Marcus Trunk's death remained a mystery until the results of his autopsy showed that it was liver failure from acetaminophen poisoning.

In 2009, more than twenty-seven billion doses of acetaminophen were sold in the United States, most of them over the counter—

making it the most oft-used drug in the country. And even though there are cheaper versions of acetaminophen, Johnson & Johnson's many Tylenol products account for nearly half of all over-the-counter sales because of annual advertising budgets that exceed $100 million.

Despite cases like Marcus Trunk's, the drug's purported safety has long been at the core of Johnson & Johnson's Tylenol marketing strategy, a holdover from the days when a huge share of adults were worried about ulcers. The brand's most iconic advertisement claims that it is the pain reliever "hospitals use most." Another brags that it is "the brand of pain reliever that doctors recommend more than any other." Its packaging promises "safe, fast pain relief."

This messaging is an important reason Tylenol is so deadly. A survey of forty-six patients treated for acetaminophen-related liver damage at the University of Pennsylvania found that the main reason patients hadn't paid close attention to the recommended dose is that they thought the drug was so safe.

Then there's the drug's interaction with alcohol, which put Anthony Benedi in a coma after taking a recommended dose even though he wasn't drinking while taking the medicine. The FDA began considering putting an alcohol warning on Tylenol's label in the 1970s, but an internal J & J memo from 1978 bragged that the company had persuaded agency officials that one wasn't necessary. Aware, however, of growing reports of drinkers being injured, Johnson & Johnson repeatedly test-marketed how consumers would respond to various versions of an alcohol warning. In every case, according to an internal memo from February 1986, most consumers said they were alarmed enough by the language to conclude that drinkers should decrease or discontinue taking Tylenol even at recommended doses.

The next month, the *Annals of Internal Medicine* published a study stating that alcoholics can suffer liver damage after taking only moderate amounts of acetaminophen. A year later, a Swedish medical journal published another study on the dangers of mixing alcohol with acetaminophen.

Alarmed by the growing medical attention to the issue, Thomas Gates, who was McNeil's medical director, sent a memo in September 1987 to J & J's chief executive and other top company officers describing myriad ways the company could keep reporters from focusing on the issue and "limiting the extent and duration of the coverage." Gates noted that the scientific literature included case studies of at least eighteen drinkers who had suffered injuries despite acetaminophen intakes that were "uncomfortably close" to the maximum recommended daily dose. He proposed a potential company letter-writing campaign to medical societies, doctors, pharmacists, and academics, consulting arrangements with favorable academics, and a coordinated public relations effort with the FDA should stories about the risk of alcohol and Tylenol increase.

In 1993, the FDA asked yet another advisory committee to examine the issue of alcohol and acetaminophen. J & J told the panel that a warning wasn't warranted and would unnecessarily frighten consumers. The panel disagreed and called for a warning, which J & J finally added voluntarily in 1994.

Beyond the issue of alcohol, another problem is that some people are simply more susceptible to acetaminophen toxicity, and there is no way to predict who those people may be. In a 2008 report, the FDA acknowledged the dilemma.

"The 4 gram per day recommended dose is also the maximum safe dose, one that must not be exceeded, an unusual situation for any drug, particularly an OTC drug, one placing a large fraction of users close to a toxic doses in the ordinary course of use," the report said.

There's also the absorption issue. A 1997 study of acetaminophen-related deaths found that people who try to kill themselves with large, one-time overdoses are more likely to survive than those who are accidentally poisoned. The reason is that the chemical antidote for acetaminophen poisoning works only if given within eight hours of an overdose. Many of those who attempt suicide soon regret doing so and make it to the hospital within that eight-hour window.

But those with accidental overdoses don't know they've been poisoned. For days, symptoms can resemble the flu, sometimes leading sufferers to take even more Tylenol. By the time they or their doctors realize what's happening, the antidote is often too late.

About the time of Benedi's poisoning, Johnson & Johnson launched a secret program to create a safer version of acetaminophen, forcing outside researchers to sign confidentiality agreements. The work never succeeded, and the company kept the results confidential, refusing even to acknowledge the program to the FDA after the agency specifically asked in 2006 about possible safer versions.

In an email uncovered in litigation, a top company manager wrote that launching an improved product would be difficult since the company would then be acknowledging its existing product "isn't so safe as we've always said before." It was the same reasoning that talc-based Johnson's Baby Powder remained on the market for fifty years longer than it should have.

In an odd twist that reflects both J & J's power and the FDA's weakness, the agency has been far tougher on prescription pills that contain acetaminophen than it has been on the company's big-selling over-the-counter version. In 2011, the agency limited prescription pills to 325 milligrams of acetaminophen and required that they carry a black-box warning, the nation's most serious, stating that "acetaminophen has been associated with cases of acute liver failure, at times resulting in liver transplant and death."

Extra Strength Tylenol has 500 milligrams per pill and its warning is weaker, never mentioning the risks of transplant or death.

Regulators in other developed countries such as Britain, Switzerland, and New Zealand have placed tougher restrictions on how much acetaminophen consumers can buy at one time or required that it only be sold in pharmacies.

The most heart-wrenching Tylenol stories involve babies. McNeil introduced Tylenol in 1955, and, along with pills and capsules for adults, the company sold a liquid version for children. Two years later, the company introduced a more concentrated liquid version for infants.

The medical rationale for having a more concentrated infant version was that parents had to force fewer drops down a fussy infant's throat. There was a commercial rationale as well, since parents often buy both products, depending on the ages of their children.

But many safety experts long decried the risks that the two products invariably carried. Between 2000 and 2009, the FDA got reports of twenty children dying from acetaminophen overdoses, a number that the agency acknowledged was likely a significant underestimate. Three of the deaths resulted from dosing mix-ups involving the two pediatric medicines. Such incorrect instructions from healthcare providers caused half of all infant poisonings, a study found, and a survey of parents of children brought into emergency rooms for acetaminophen poisoning found that two-thirds did not know the difference between the infant formula and other versions of Tylenol. On its label, the infant version of Tylenol didn't offer specific dosing instructions but instead told parents to ask a doctor for the right amount. The FDA and J & J tussled for years over whether this was the right advice, but no change was made.

After their five-month-old daughter Brianna Hutto died after taking the dosage recommended by the nurse at the hospital where they'd brought her, her parents sued. At a trial that began on June 15, 2010, a lawyer asked McNeil's longtime medical director, Anthony Temple, how many babies had died as a result of dosing mix-ups between the infant and child versions of the drug. Over a thirty-year period, he said, "there are maybe a couple of dozen, maybe a little more, where incidents of significant liver injury has occurred, and there's probably a handful of those cases that were fatal."

"And for twenty-five years you've elected to continue to offer infants Tylenol in the concentrated form that has led to the death of babies, correct?" the lawyer asked.

"Yes, we've continued to do it."

The lawyer pressed him: "Rather than pull the products off the shelf, that's sort of the cost of doing business?"

Temple agreed: "McNeil felt that the benefit as— Really, it's the FDA, because it hasn't pulled it off, either— But the benefit to children of having the product available was appropriate to keep it in the marketplace, yes."

Brianna's mother, Christina, said she did everything asked of her. She read the Tylenol label, closely followed its directions, and lost her child. The jury ruled in favor of the Huttos. Johnson & Johnson was ordered to pay the Huttos $1 million. The company appealed the verdict all the way to the U.S. Supreme Court, which two years later declined to hear the case. Finally, the company paid the $1 million judgment.

In 2009, the FDA called together an expert advisory committee to consider restrictions on acetaminophen, including whether to require one concentration for both infants and children. The panel voted 36–1 that the FDA should mandate a single children's dose.

"I've not heard, in the information that we've reviewed, any compelling reason for why there should be these two formulations," said Dr. William Cooper, a professor of pediatrics at Vanderbilt University, who served on the panel.

The FDA once again took no action on its experts' advice.

In 2011, a bill was introduced in Louisiana's legislature that would have mandated that all children's and infants' acetaminophen products only be sold from behind a pharmacist's counter, and that parents had to get written dosing instructions when buying them.

At about the same time, the FDA scheduled yet another advisory committee hearing to consider the safety of children's acetaminophen products. Two weeks before the hearing, Johnson & Johnson and other companies announced a voluntary decision to stop selling different concentrations of kids' products.

The FDA generally follows the instructions of its advisory committees. With Tylenol, the agency ignored its experts' advice almost every time. In this case, however, it didn't matter: The FDA never acted.

PART II

Prescription Drugs

CHAPTER 14

A Valley of Death in Drug Discovery

T HE TRANSFORMATION OF JOHNSON & JOHNSON INTO A PHARMA-
ceutical behemoth coincided with the final flowering of the era of
medicinal chemistry. This epoch began in the 1890s with the discovery of aspirin, accelerated in the 1940s with industrial-scale production of penicillin, and peaked in the 1980s with the arrival of a slew
of blockbuster medications that led the average elderly person to take
nine separate prescription medicines simultaneously.

Antihypertensives like Inderal, Capoten, and Norvasc, blood thin-
ners like Coumadin and Plavix, and cholesterol reducers like Lipitor
and Zocor, became among the most widely used medicines in history
and offered those with cardiovascular disease longer and healthier
lives. Antidyspeptics like Tagamet, Zantac, and Prilosec allowed millions to eat foods they loved. Stimulants like Ritalin and Adderall,
antianxiety drugs like Valium and Xanax, and antidepressants like
Prozac and Zoloft became cultural touchstones and transformed how
Americans viewed mental illness.

Along with these discoveries, the proliferation of private and public health insurance after World War II made prescription medicines
unusually profitable. In the 1960s, Congress passed the Medicare and
Medicaid acts, providing health insurance to the nation's oldest and

poorest citizens. Initially, the programs paid only for drugs prescribed during hospital stays. Private insurers followed suit but soon agreed to pay for all prescriptions medicines.

With insurers picking up the tab, prescription drug prices soared while those of over-the-counter medicines—which patients still must pay for themselves—rose only modestly. Price differences were so stark that drugmakers fought to keep their products as prescription-only, even when the FDA declared them safe enough to be available over the counter. Claritin and Allegra, for instance, were launched as prescription antihistamines even though they were safer than Bena-dryl, an antihistamine available on store shelves.

So, while Tylenol remained the most popular medicine ever sold by anyone, its profits were soon eclipsed by myriad prescription products whose prices were much higher. And companies like Pfizer, Merck, Bristol-Myers, and Glaxo, all of which specialized in produc-ing such expensive prescription drugs, came to be seen as the most innovative, dynamic, and profitable sector in all of business—similar to the way the tech industry is viewed now.

Chasing this gold mine required Johnson & Johnson to shift the focus of its marketing efforts from consumers to doctors. Such a wholesale makeover meant that J & J had to transform itself from the stodgy, button-down organization created by Robert Wood John-son II to one with an army of young and attractive sales representa-tives who strove for ambitious sales targets by offering doctors money, food, gifts, compliments, and favors.

But then, just as optimism in the industry reached its zenith, the era of medicinal chemistry came to a screeching halt. Laboratories that had been churning out one big seller after another suddenly went barren. Across the industry, introductions of new drugs plunged from a peak of fifty-three in 1996 to just seventeen in 2002 despite a near doubling in annual research spending.

In the midst of this crash, researchers announced in 2000 that they had completed the first working draft of the sequence of the human genome, birthing a new era of gene-based drug discoveries.

Now drugmakers mostly focus on turning out medicines intended to correct rare, life-threatening genetic defects. The newest medicines mostly save lives instead of improving them, and they are intended for tiny groups of patients with rare genetic anomalies or rare cancers. Prices have risen into the millions for a single course of treatment.

This transition, however, took years to fully take hold. And since the delay between discovery and FDA approval is often five or more years, Johnson & Johnson and its peers were keenly aware by the mid-1990s that they faced an existential crisis. With their drug cupboards bare, pharmaceutical companies had to rely on medicines approved in the late 1980s and early 1990s to carry much of their growth for a significant period of time.

Without a raft of new products, the industry needed higher prices and more patients taking each drug to grow profits. Of the two, price had always been the easier lever.

For most of the 1980s and early 1990s, pharmaceutical makers had raised prices twice a year to levels that precisely matched profits previously announced to investors. With insurers paying the tab, higher prices did almost nothing to dampen demand. The resulting profit predictability made drugmakers the darlings of Wall Street. But two big changes curtailed the era of easy price increases.

The first was the creation of the generic drug industry in 1984 with the passage of the Hatch-Waxman Act. The law allowed small companies to introduce cheap knockoffs of expensive branded medicines. The only requirements were a few simple chemical tests and the patience to wait for twenty-year patents to expire. No longer would generic drugs need to conduct the same battery of expensive tests in humans as their branded predecessors.

The new law ended the kind of profit perpetuity that companies like J & J had relied on, and it put Big Pharma on a desperate innovation treadmill. Once the patents on big-selling drugs expire, their sales plunge. To keep growing, companies must come up with new drugs.

The second change was related to the rise of the generic drug market. By the mid-1990s, cheap knockoffs had become a serious threat to Big Pharma. The reason was the arrival of managed care.

With managed care contracts, insurers gave themselves the where-withal to push back against large price increases. Drug companies could still increase prices, but if a competing drug—such as a generic—offered the exact same benefit for less, insurers might be able to get some patients to switch. Why pay much more just for a more famous label?

So the industry pushed for more patients to take each medicine. One way they achieved this was by getting Congress in 1987 and then the FDA in 1997 to loosen restrictions on TV advertisements, mak-ing the United States one of only two countries in the world to allow prescription drug ads. (New Zealand is the other.) Soon, most ads that aired during the nightly news urged viewers to "talk to their doc-tor about" some new medicine.

But the amount the industry spends on TV ads has always been a fraction of what it spends wooing doctors, and now that seduction took a dark turn. Laws forbid drugmakers from telling doctors to prescribe medicines in ways that don't help patients or might even endanger them. But harmful prescriptions are just as profitable as helpful ones, and the pool of patients who shouldn't be given medi-cines is often far larger than the ones for whom they have proven beneficial.

So drugmakers began cajoling doctors to use medicines more often and in more patients than was prudent or strictly legal. Even in the early 1980s, J & J was pushing these boundaries. And as the de-cade went on and the company's labs and those of its partners started to stumble, the pressure to push the boundaries of ethical marketing practices increased.

Right around that time, scientists at a small California biotech company discovered a way to manufacture erythropoietin, a break-through hailed at the time as among the most important of the mod-ern era.

CHAPTER 15

The First Great Biotech Franchise Is Born

THE STORY OF ERYTHROPOIETIN BEGINS IN THE LATE NINETEENTH century when scientists discovered that, after two weeks spent at high altitude, they had a measurable increase in red blood cells. Speculation about the cause of this increase eventually settled on a protein that stimulated the bone marrow, where red blood cells are made.

Interest in creating a synthetic form of this protein—called erythropoietin, or EPO—spiked in the 1980s when transfusions of blood from people infected with the HIV/AIDS virus led to thousands of tragic deaths.

Scientists at Amgen eventually found and cloned the gene that coded for the production of EPO and then inserted that DNA strand into the fast-growing cells of a hamster's ovary, which served as the production factory. However, the company burned through so much money in its search that it needed a deep-pocketed partner to complete the final step: getting approval from the Food and Drug Administration.

That partner turned out to be Johnson & Johnson. As part of the deal, Amgen surrendered sales rights outside of the United States, as well as those inside of the United States that weren't related to dialysis, where the main market for the drug was initially thought to be.

Dialysis tends to destroy red blood cells, leading about 16 percent of patients to need transfusions. The hope was that EPO would lessen the strain on the nation's blood supply and lower kidney patients' risks for developing infections like HIV.

FDA's approval for EPO's commercial sale came at the end of 1988, and Amgen and Johnson & Johnson launched a series of products that would eventually earn the two companies more than $100 billion. Johnson & Johnson marketed its versions as Eprex and Procrit. Amgen branded its as Epogen and Aranesp.

Those first years were frustrating for J & J, since sales outside of the dialysis market were low. The company soon came up with a strategy to solve that: Sell to cancer patients. Besides heart disease, cancer is humanity's greatest killer. About 1.6 million Americans are diagnosed with cancer every year, and many are willing to spend their life's savings for a cure or even a brief reprieve. Given that, the market for oncology medicines seemed limitless—which meant the profits could be limitless, too.

The main treatments for cancer are surgery, chemotherapy, and radiation. The first involves slicing away tumors and the second and third poisoning them. All can leave patients weakened and anemic. J & J's idea was that EPO could serve as an all-purpose pick-me-up, giving patients a boost of red blood cells that would treat their anemia, improve their spirits, and make them strong enough for even more intensive chemotherapy or radiation, or for additional surgery.

It was a compelling notion, but there were obvious risks. By stimulating the production of red blood cells, EPO thickens blood. Thicker blood clots more easily and raises blood pressure, both of which increase risks of heart attacks, strokes, and embolisms. For cancer patients, even a slight increase in heart risks is worrisome, since the illness already stresses the heart and most patients are elderly. About half of cancer patients die from heart attacks or strokes well before tumors stop vital organs.

And there was another, more subtle problem. As soon as EPO became widely available, researchers around the world started using it in their own work. A researcher named Athanasius Anagnostou from Brown University added EPO to a petri dish filled with cancer cells and found that the drug supercharged the cells' growth—the opposite of what anyone wanted to happen.

Other scientists found that some types of tumors had EPO receptors and seemed unusually sensitive to the protein. Some tumors even seemed to make their own version of EPO, possibly to spur the production of red blood cells to feed their growth.

These findings dovetailed with an expanding field of cancer research known as antiangiogenesis. The idea behind this work was that tumors need blood to survive, and that some cancers grow and spread by sending signals to the body to stimulate the creation of new blood vessels to feed their growth.

Just as EPO was coming to market, Genentech, a competing biotechnology firm headquartered nearly four hundred miles north of Amgen in South San Francisco, discovered a protein that stimulates the formation of new blood vessels and called it VEGF, for vascular endothelial growth factor. Genentech launched a research program to find out how to block VEGF, thus starving tumors of the blood they needed to grow.

Johnson & Johnson and every other drugmaker were keenly aware of this work. Anagnostou patented a way for EPO to treat blood vessel injuries, an invention J & J soon licensed.

A researcher at Harvard Medical School got a grant from Johnson & Johnson to study EPO's effects on cancer. This researcher confirmed that some types of cancer cells had EPO receptors, and as a result, EPO seemed to stimulate cancer growth.

Along with other grantees, the researcher (who didn't want their name used in this book) traveled to Johnson & Johnson's New Brunswick headquarters to present their findings.

"I was standing there and these two Johnson & Johnson people come up to my poster and start talking to each other," the researcher recalled. "And one of them said to the other: 'We have to kill this work.'"

In the spring and summer of 1987, Genentech sought approval to sell Activase, also known as tissue plasminogen activator, or TPA. Activase was billed as a wonder drug that used a protein naturally found in the lining of blood vessels to dissolve blood clots that cause strokes and heart attacks. The marvel of using genetically altered bacteria to manufacture a human protein that could save tens of thousands of lives enchanted not only the scientific world but the media and Wall Street as well.

Doctors and financial analysts predicted that every ambulance in the country would stock Activase and use it on nearly every heart attack victim. One of the main causes of sudden death seemed about to be defeated. But on Friday, May 29, an FDA advisory committee noted that while Genetech had proven that Activase dissolved clots, the company's trials failed to show that it offered patients any measurable benefit—like saving lives. Even more worrisome, the drug increased the risks of bleeding in the brain.

Before the committee's meeting, Genentech's stock market valuation was $4 billion, accounting for half of the capitalization of the top twenty-five biotech companies. The company's share price dropped by a quarter following the news. On June 15, the FDA rejected Genentech's application—a decision that was greeted with outrage and incomprehension even among agency admirers.

The Wall Street Journal, a frequent agency critic, ran an editorial titled "Human Sacrifice" promising, "Patients will die who would have lived longer." Even those who were not frequent critics were bewildered by the decision. *The Washington Post* published an article titled "TPA Foot-Dragging Costs 30 Lives a Day." And the editor of *Science* wrote, "When a circus clown steps on his toes and falls on his face, it is a cause for laughter. When a regulatory agency that licenses drugs for heart attack stumbles, it may have not only egg on its face but blood on its hands."

In the following years, the FDA's concerns about TPA would become widely shared among doctors and emergency technicians, severely limiting the drug's use. But partly because of the backlash, five months after its rejection, the FDA reversed course and approved TPA, leading one FDA official to remark that "we are all glad that it's going to get on the market and off our backs."

The clear lesson for the agency was that biotechnology products—viewed as natural and less toxic than chemicals—required unusually gentle handling. So when, only a few months later, Johnson & Johnson sought approval to sell EPO to cancer patients, the agency asked for minimal information, which is what they got: J & J had conducted a quick clinical trial involving 131 patients. The study showed that those who got EPO had fewer blood transfusions than those who didn't.

Agency officials still suspected that EPO might cause more heart attacks and even encourage the growth of tumors. But TPA had taught the FDA that it shouldn't ask such basic questions of biotech medicines. Instead, the agency forced J & J to add a mild disclaimer to the drug's label noting that: "The possibility that Procrit can act as a growth factor for any tumor type . . . cannot be excluded."

The agency did mandate that J & J quickly undertake another clinical trial to finally show that this risk and others were indeed ruled out. A new set of EPO trials was particularly necessary because no one knew how much of the stuff patients needed. Red blood cell levels are measured by a hemoglobin test. Healthy patients have hemoglobin levels in the 11 to 14 g/dL (grams per deciliter) range. When the level drops below 8, doctors generally recommend blood transfusions.

A key question that would bedevil government regulators and insurance companies for nearly two decades is what level of hemoglobin should qualify a patient for EPO? Should doctors wait until it falls to 8 g/dL or should they intervene at 10, 11, or even 12? And when should they stop giving EPO? Is 11 g/dL good enough? Wait until it reaches 14, or even 15? What are the risks and benefits at every stage?

A major dose-ranging study—where groups of patients are started at different hemoglobin levels and then treated to differing ranges with different dosages—would have answered such vital questions, and such trials are routine. About the time J & J promised to conduct a major safety study for EPO, Merck launched the Scandinavian Simvastatin Survival Study (4S) to test its new cholesterol-lowering drug Zocor in 4,444 patients who were followed for five years. The study proved that Zocor almost halved the risk of death, an incredible finding that transformed cardiac care. Pfizer conducted a similarly large and long-running study to prove that its cholesterol-lowering drug, Lipitor, was also lifesaving.

But launching such a study, while an ethical and regulatory must, was commercially risky. Companies that undertake such studies must be confident that their drug works or they'll spend millions on a study that costs them billions in sales.

Was J & J confident? The excitement around EPO was certainly real. *Fortune* named EPO Product of the Year in 1989. But hints about EPO's problematic effects on the heart and tumors quickly accumulated—especially among elite athletes hoping that it would increase the amount of oxygen flowing through their blood. The sudden death of thirty-two-year-old Bert Oosterbosch, a Dutch cycling star, was the first public sign of serious trouble. Five days after winning an August 1989 cycling race, he suffered a fatal heart attack. Rumors swirled that in the days before the race, Oosterbosch had used J & J's EPO.

A few months later, twenty-six-year-old Johannes Draaijer, who had helped the Dutch win the previous Tour de France, died in his sleep of what was reported to be heart blockage. His wife told a German magazine that he had taken the J & J medicine in the days leading up to his death, and she blamed the drug for his sudden and extraordinary cardiac event.

Despite these fatalities, cyclists continued to use EPO. Lance Armstrong famously won seven Tour de France titles between 1998 and 2005, in part because of his and his team's secret, banned use of the drug.

In 1993, J & J announced that it had started enrolling four hundred women suffering from cervical cancer into a trial comparing patients who got EPO with those who didn't. Enrollment should have taken weeks or perhaps a few months and follow-up perhaps another year.

But year after year passed with no word about the results. When asked years later, the company said that it was still enrolling patients but that there were no signs that EPO was anything but helpful. J & J kept whatever evidence it had secret.

CHAPTER 16

How Giving Cash to Doctors Became Good Business

DRUG COMPANIES HAVE MADE DOCTORS THE FOCUS OF THEIR marketing efforts since the dawn of modern medicine. For most of that time, the primary tools for currying favor among physicians were gifts, just as they are for many industries.

Merck handed out tens of thousands of copies of its Merck Manuals. Eli Lilly's signature gift was a leather doctor's bag, usually offered upon graduation from medical school. Did the gifts increase sales? Probably, but nobody really knew.

In the 1980s, drug companies got an extraordinary tool from medical information company IMS Health that finally allowed them to measure just how profitable these freebies were. Cofounded by Purdue Pharma's Arthur Sackler, IMS (now known as IQVIA) bought the records of every prescription filled by pharmacists around the country and, using a database sold by the American Medical Association, identified the doctors who wrote them. By the 1980s, cheap computing power allowed drugmakers to buy reports on the weekly prescribing habits of every doctor in the United States.

The results were transformational. Companies soon learned that the best gifts were cash and cash equivalents. Every dollar given to doctors led to between $3.50 and $5.00 in additional drug sales.

No other corporate investment—not in scientists, research labs, manufacturing plants, or anything else—came close to providing that kind of return. So companies rebuilt themselves by prioritizing and transforming sales operations into tools to funnel money to doctors by easing out the pharmacists and drug experts who had previously dominated sales ranks. Instead of hiring people trained in drug chemistry, Johnson & Johnson and its peers started hiring cheerleaders from schools like the University of Kentucky. Equally prized were West Point graduates, who almost always followed orders without question and were admired by doctors and nurses alike.

"There was a time when only persons with a degree in pharmacy science were hired as sales representatives," Winston E. Smith, a fourteen-year veteran sales rep and manager at Eli Lilly, told prosecutors on September 2, 2008, according to secret grand jury files. "As the industry grew, recruitment went away from the classic science degrees to including people with business degrees, and eventually any college degree was accepted."

As a group, sales reps tend to be a rowdy but likable bunch. They drink too much, talk too loudly, sin on Saturday nights, and seek God's forgiveness Sunday mornings. They might tell some off-color jokes, but by and large they're the loyal, friendly kind of people everyone needs in their lives after a bad breakup or divorce. On the other hand, every study done on the effect of drug sales reps shows that they make doctors worse at their jobs.

With payments as the goal, the industry quickly devolved into an arms race of cash, freebies, and pseudo-jobs for doctors. The quid pro quo for freebies was generally unspoken, and doctors often told themselves that they would have prescribed the marketed medicines anyway. Regardless, top restaurants added private rooms that were booked several nights a week by drug companies, who invited not only doctors but their families and friends, too. There were "dine-and-dashes" when doctors picked up free multicourse take-out meals for their families from the best restaurants. "Gas-and-goes" when they filled their gas tanks gratis at designated service stations. Free back-to-school shopping sprees at Staples and other stationery stores. Rounds of golf at expensive courses. Free trips to Disney World and Hawaii. Tickets to the Masters Tournament, the Super Bowl, March Madness, and Bruce Springsteen concerts.

Many doctors' offices refused entry to reps unless they brought enough food for the entire staff, with favorite take-out places often specified by office administrators. Office secretaries began booking caterings weeks in advance, with some large practices having three feedings a day, five days a week. Complex wall calendars listed the food expected each day, with doctors sometimes planning their schedules around favorite offerings. In turn, doctors told prospective secretaries and nurses that jobs came with free food and medicines, allowing doctors to pay lower salaries and reduce staff turnover.

Beyond in-office food offerings, sales reps often brought invitations to dinner meetings in the region or at far-off resorts where doctors could socialize with colleagues, eat a gourmet meal, and briefly participate in a discussion about uses—unapproved or not—of whatever drugs they were currently pushing.

Dinners sometimes got out of hand. "I'd get up to go to the bathroom, and I'd come back and someone would have ordered a three-hundred-dollar bottle of wine," one rep recalled. "It was so crazy that they got so comfortable spending all this money on free meals."

But many of the doctors who ordered the most expensive meals were the ones writing the most prescriptions, and they knew their value to the company. Even after rules were adopted by the Pharmaceutical Research and Manufacturers Association in 2002 to limit the expense of free meals, the rep said she was expected to find a way to pay the tab.

A survey of medical residents found that 61 percent thought gifts from drug sales representatives had no impact on their own prescribing habits but only 16 percent thought other physicians were similarly unaffected. In other words, most doctors think they're immune to the seductions of gifts and money, but few have the same confidence about their colleagues.

Not everyone found a way to consistently balance their Hippocratic oath with free trips to tropical islands. Dr. Stefan Kruszewski, a Harvard-educated psychiatrist who was a speaker for Johnson & Johnson, said that the marketing message diverged so sharply from the science that he could not ethically continue as a part-time drug sales rep.

"When I started speaking for companies in the late 1980s and early '90s, I was allowed to say what I thought I should say consistent with the science," he said. "Then it got to the point where I was no longer allowed to do that. I was given slides and told, 'We'll give you a thousand dollars if you say this for a half hour.' And I said: 'I can't say that. It isn't true.'"

The slides he was told to use made claims that were demonstrably false.

"They made it all up," Kruszewski said. "It was never true."

Marketing lectures delivered during free lunches and dinners were so obviously promotional that many doctors treated them with appropriate skepticism. That is why Johnson & Johnson spent significant resources creating a far more sophisticated disinformation effort using academics at top-flight universities.

Once the company identified a professor with just the right mix of professional acclaim and pliable ethics, J & J hired them to undertake scientifically dubious clinical trials, contracted with ghostwriting firms to write up the results in deceptive ways, and then paid the purported authors to exaggerate or lie about the trials at medical conferences in lectures many doctors were required to attend. Spotting the dishonesty and danger in these lectures was beyond the capabilities of most practicing physicians.

Most doctors were uncomfortable simply taking cash, which was why most drug companies came up with ways to disguise the transactions. Sales reps hired doctors to give speeches, offer marketing advice, and undertake research. That the speeches were often to near-empty rooms, the advice ignored, and the research a joke didn't matter.

Companies paid doctors to enroll patients in fake research studies, midwifed dozens of sketchy medical journals to publish them, hired public relations firms to ghostwrite them, and helped create bespoke specialty medical organizations to disseminate industry talking points. All of this created a fog of disinformation that, along with cash payments, was designed to get doctors to prescribe drugs in sometimes suspect ways while making them feel good about the process.

And in a profession dominated by men, even baser incentives were promoted. To sell its prostate cancer drug Lupron, TAP Pharmaceuticals created a sales force of almost exclusively young female reps dubbed "the lovely ladies of Lupron" to focus mostly on urologists, who were overwhelmingly male. Some companies got caught hiring hookers for doctors. Sales reps occasionally did the job themselves in the dark closets where free drug samples were kept. (In October 2001, TAP pleaded guilty to criminal charges related to its marketing of Lupron.)

The one government agency that might have prevented or policed this was the FDA. But politics made sure that the FDA never really tried.

Overwhelmed by the explosion of new medicines that resulted from the final flowering of medicinal chemistry, and with Congress and Republican administrations refusing to increase the agency's budget, the FDA's review times for new drugs ballooned to an average of twenty-nine months. Such delays cost drugmakers precious patent time, and as generic substitutions became more efficient, the industry realized that such waiting periods were financially catastrophic. And then, in the wake of the HIV/AIDS crisis, patient advocates grasped that approval delays could consign hundreds and even thousands of patients to unnecessary death and suffering. In a widely covered event, AIDS advocates in 1988 laid siege to the agency's headquarters in Rockville to demand quicker approval times.

With rage building among both conservatives and liberals, FDA leaders realized that the agency either had to get faster or risk losing its exclusive control over drug approvals. Proposals to privatize agency functions gained political support. Going after doctors for taking courtside seats and free gas simply was not—and budgetarily could not—be on the agenda.

Indeed, with Congress showing no signs of stepping up with new funding, FDA commissioner David Kessler made common cause with the drug industry, which agreed in 1992 to start paying massive user fees directly to the FDA. It was a fateful decision. The first five-year funding agreement was fairly narrow in scope. The industry's money bought faster approval times. But each subsequent five-year funding agreement chipped away at the FDA's authority and independence.

It was in a 1997 funding deal that the FDA finally allowed un-complicated TV ads for prescription medicines, lowered its approval standards to just one clinical trial instead of two, and authorized drugmakers to provide reprints of "studies" to doctors urging them to use medicines in ways that the FDA hadn't approved. In some cases, the FDA had data showing that these unapproved uses could be dangerous. All three were enormous concessions.

But perhaps an even bigger compromise in the 1997 deal was the agency's unspoken agreement to put a leash on its criminal investigators, who were all transferred from regional offices, where they had independence, to headquarters, where they now needed the approval of supervisors to launch an investigation. And such approvals became almost impossible to get. And while federal prosecutors occasionally took up the charge against industry misdeeds, they had far less expertise than the FDA and were almost as easy for the companies to stonewall.

The person who taught Johnson & Johnson this lesson most forcefully was Dr. Albert Kligman, the University of Pennsylvania dermatologist who'd spent years burning the skin off the backs of Black prisoners in tests of Johnson & Johnson's powders and bandages.

In 1971, the FDA approved Retin-A (the *A* stood for vitamin A) as a treatment for severe cases of acne, making Kligman, its inventor, a very rich man. But a 1974 law limiting medical testing among prisoners and mentally disabled children shut down part of Kligman's lucrative contract research business, so he became increasingly focused on the cosmetic potential of vitamin A drugs.

Kligman's tests showed that in addition to helping resolve acne, Retin-A was also a powerful antiwrinkle cream. But instead of asking the FDA to approve a new kind of use for the drug, as was required by law, Kligman and J & J decided to ignore the agency and start promoting Retin-A's antiaging properties anyway.

That promotion included "$1.6 million to implement a Retin-A educational program" to gain "acceptance by physicians and consumers of Retin-A's benefits for adult skin," according to an October 1985 company planning document, which included paying dermatologists to visit local TV stations to tout the antiwrinkle properties of Retin-A. At the national level, the highlight of this effort was a lavish press conference at the Rainbow Room in Rockefeller Center, New York City, in January 1988 to tout a small study published in the *Journal of the American Medical Association*. The study claimed that the active ingredient in Retin-A had erased fine wrinkles in the skin of thirty patients.

The study's author, Dr. John Voorhees of the University of Michigan, conducted a satellite media tour to discuss the study's findings, for which J & J paid him $25,000 for his time. In the aftermath of the media blitz, Retin-A's sales increased tenfold to more than $500 million a year.

Instead of applying for an antiwrinkle indication for Retin-A, Johnson & Johnson decided to submit an application in 1989 for an entirely new vitamin A–based drug called Renova. Doing so allowed antiwrinkle sales to continue for years longer without generic competition. But in making the application, Kligman got greedy.

While they had given the University of Pennsylvania a portion of Retin-A's royalties, since the drug had been developed in the university's labs, Kligman and Johnson & Johnson excluded Penn from getting anything from Renova. The university sued, and the resulting litigation uncovered company documents detailing J & J's illegal effort to promote Retin-A as an antiwrinkle drug. Such marketing campaigns are known as "off-label," since the marketed benefits of the drug are not on the drug's FDA-approved label.

The FDA requested a grand jury investigation and froze its review of the new-drug application for Renova until the investigation was complete. Agency investigators made unannounced visits to the homes of two Johnson & Johnson executives to try to seize documents. The next day, in a panic, company executives launched a company-wide effort to destroy all documents related to Retin-A's off-label campaign. By the end of the day, thousands of documents had been shredded and myriad videotapes trashed or secreted in the homes of employees.

Outraged by the purge, federal investigators promised to charge the company and its executives with obstruction of justice, a crime that could potentially land executives in jail. Negotiations between the company and prosecutors dragged on for years. Renova's FDA application languished.

In January 1995, Johnson & Johnson agreed to plead guilty and pay $7.5 million for a crime that had brought the company hundreds of millions in additional profits—dollar for dollar, a brilliant investment. A month later, the FDA approved Renova.

Financially dependent on the drug industry after 1992, the FDA would never again launch such an investigation, never again visit the homes of top Big Pharma executives unannounced, and never again delay the approval of a new drug while an investigation continued. In fact, the agency repeatedly approved new uses for J & J drugs based on information given by the company, even in the midst of criminal investigations launched by federal prosecutors that involved allegations that the company was lying to the FDA. Getting tough on drugmakers is simply not part of the agency's mandate anymore.

And for J & J and other drugmakers, the clear lesson of the Retin-A episode was to simply factor the price of possible criminal penalties into their costs of doing business.

Far from declining, payoffs to doctors quickly became commonplace. The money was crucial for doctors and their families, but so, too, was the feeling sales reps gave doctors that they were part of something important—that they had not made a huge mistake by investing so much time and money in medical school.

THE 1960S AND '70S WERE THE HEYDAY OF THE MODERN MEDICAL practice. Although the American Medical Association strongly opposed the creation of Medicare and Medicaid in 1965, the two government programs turned out to provide doctors with a bonanza of new patients and revenue streams. New tools to measure and lower heart risks, check for cancer, and vaccinate against deadly diseases gave patients additional reasons for visits. And with the FDA eliminating many favorite over-the-counter remedies, doctors' prescription pads became the exclusive source for replacement cures.

But this golden era started to fade in the 1980s. The rise of managed care restricted doctors' ability to price their services as they wanted. And insurers' maddening tendency to refuse some charges and slow-walk reimbursement for others forced doctors to hire more clerical staff.

In 1989, the federal Medicare program implemented for the first time a fee schedule for physician services—basically, price controls. No matter if a doctor was talented or terrible, serving rich patients or poor, they were increasingly paid similar rates. For many, these changes were deeply frustrating.

Physicians who wanted the good life had to start adding patients and hours to stay ahead. Some clinicians went from seeing twenty patients a day to forty and then sixty, and patient encounters went from twenty minutes to ten minutes, and then to half that.

Most doctors abandoned making morning rounds at local hospitals because, as with house calls from an earlier era, insurers didn't pay enough to support the practice. But doing so cut doctors off from the most interesting, rewarding, and socially intensive part of their practices. Days that had been filled with laughter and gossip became a bewildering blur of sniffles, charts, and hated insurance forms.

Just as bad, doctors' decisions started to be questioned. The proliferation of specialty publications and eventual rise of the Internet meant patients sometimes knew (or thought they knew) more about their illnesses than doctors. Medical societies and insurers started demanding that doctors follow evidence-based protocols, or what many clinicians derisively referred to as "cookbook medicine." Computerized medical records allowed department chairs and hospital managers to notice patterns in doctors' treatment decisions. Those whose practices diverged from the most profitable would be taken aside in clinic hallways and told to change their ways.

Amidst all these changes, drug sales reps were an oasis that offered not only food and money but respect. Border checkpoints to enter this oasis, however, soon became strict. In the past, doctors could say they had prescribed a lot of a drug without actually doing so. By the 1990s, sales reps could check on a weekly basis whether these claims were true. Doctors who failed to follow through on expected prescriptions were cut off and reinstated only when they reformed. Free rides were over.

While paying kickbacks for prescriptions is illegal, the process wasn't blatantly criminal in many cases because companies were careful not to put sales targets in writing or tie payments directly to specific prescriptions. Sales reps simply told doctors that if they wanted to become a speaker for a drug, they had to prescribe a lot of it so they could talk honestly about their experience. And once they started giving marketing lectures, doctors who increased their prescriptions were invited to give more speeches and attend more advisory meetings, often in lush locales.

Even with this added bonus, many doctors felt increasingly left behind. The spectacular growth of executive salaries in the 1980s and

'90s meant that the football players who had gotten C's in high school chemistry were suddenly making more—much more—than their straight-A pre-med classmates.

For many doctors, part-time marketing gigs for Johnson & Johnson, Pfizer, and other such companies could mean hundreds of thousands of dollars per year in freebies and cash, and a select few got millions—far more than they earned from their practices. For some medical and specialty societies, every doctor who served in leadership positions in the 1990s and 2000s had side gigs as part-time drug sales reps.

And as a result, millions of Americans died from or were injured by dangerous and inappropriate prescriptions.

CHAPTER 17

J & J's Biggest-Selling Drug

By 1998, PROCRIT HAD BECOME J & J'S MOST PROFITABLE PRODUCT ever, with sales growing at such a spectacular rate that by 2001, the biotech drug represented 10.4 percent of the conglomerate's total sales—and a far higher share of its profits. American oncologists were such enthusiastic advocates that Procrit, along with Amgen's identical version, became the federal government's largest individual health-care expense. By then, Procrit's risks to the heart were well known, but its potential to encourage the growth of tumors had largely been dismissed or forgotten.

Perversely, oncologists assumed that the drug's benefits vastly out-weighed its risks—not because J & J had failed to finish its promised safety study, but because the company said that it was still enrolling patients. Surely they would have shut the study down if Procrit was proving to be damaging, right? That was, after all, how these things worked.

Amgen, by contrast, had managed years earlier to enroll 1,233 patients—three times as many as J & J's goal—into a different study comparing how well patients getting dialysis fared on different levels of EPO. In 1996, Amgen announced that the trial had been stopped. Still, even then, the company told the story that it wanted to.

"Nothing in these study results suggests that any changes should be made in the treatment of dialysis patients who are receiving the currently approved treatment," Dr. Allen Nissenson, a professor of medicine at the University of California Los Angeles and a principal investigator in the study, said. "The safety and efficacy of this treatment has been demonstrated in numerous clinical trials and in general clinical practice over the past several years." These reassurances all proved to be false.

Called the Normal Hematocrit Trial (hematocrit is the ratio of the volume of red blood cells to the total volume of blood), the study's objective was to determine whether patients who were only slightly anemic—the vast majority of dialysis users—would benefit from EPO, to get their hemoglobin levels up to a normal range. The study's data-safety monitoring board—a group of independent experts charged with protecting patients—halted the testing because patients receiving more EPO were dying in far greater numbers than those getting lower doses. They also felt no better or healthier than those who got lower doses. In short, the study proved that EPO increased the risks of death while doing nothing to improve patients' quality of life.

When the study was published in 1998 in *The New England Journal of Medicine*, little of this alarming information was included. Although the FDA concluded that the risks of death in the high-EPO group were statistically significant, the authors of the published study—who either worked for or consulted for Amgen—said the higher dose was "not associated with higher mortality." The FDA kept its findings to itself, and the published study never mentioned that those receiving the higher dose felt no better than those in the lower dose group.

Subsequently asked to explain these discrepancies, the authors said they used a different statistical technique than the FDA. They also said that someone—they didn't say who—had edited out a mention of the failure to find any improvement in quality of life in the higher-dose group.

Three years later, the first author of the study paper, Dr. Anatole Besarab, who was then at West Virginia University School of Medicine, cowrote an article in which he recommended that dialysis patients be given high doses of EPO, arguing that patients in the Normal Hematocrit Trial had seen "significant improvements" in quality of life, a claim his own study contradicted.

In 1998, just as the Normal Hematocrit trial was finally published, Johnson & Johnson launched its massive "Strength for Living" advertising campaign for Procrit with a TV ad in which a group of healthy-looking people appeared on screen as a narrator said, "If you are a chemotherapy patient and feel tired and weak, ask your doctor about Procrit."

The narrator continued by claiming that "Procrit is the natural way to regain red blood cells lost during chemotherapy," a remarkable description for a synthetically produced protein. The ad included the disclaimer that "in studies, only diarrhea and edema occurred more often with Procrit than with a placebo."

These claims were all false. Procrit had never been proven to resolve or ameliorate fatigue or weakness. Reviewers in the FDA's beleaguered advertising oversight division complained, without effect. In one letter to the company, a top FDA official wrote that the ads were misleading because Procrit treats "anemia associated with certain chemotherapeutic regimes, not 'tiredness' in general." The company pulled that ad only to launch others with almost identically false claims.

Drugmakers soon learned that they could jawbone the agency for months while a misleading ad campaign continued uninterrupted, and J & J was among the best at this. The back-and-forth allowed the ads to be seen by millions more before they were finally pulled.

In 2001, the administration of President George W. Bush installed as FDA's top lawyer Daniel Troy, a man who had spent years fighting to allow drugmakers to make expansive claims about their drugs because he believed corporations, like people, had almost unabridgeable rights to free speech. The drug industry had donated millions to

Bush's campaign and those of other Republican politicians. Troy's appointment was in part recompense for that support.

Soon after being installed, Troy required that FDA's ad reviewers seek his approval before sending any demand letters to drugmakers. He rarely granted such approvals, which meant the number of attempted FDA enforcement actions for false advertising plunged. When Troy left the FDA in 2004, he became one of J & J's lawyers, continuing in this new role his fight with those very same FDA ad reviewers.

Predictably, Troy's tenure at FDA had done nothing to improve J & J's laboratory rigor. In 2001, the company had started yet another EPO study in cervical cancer patients. After enrolling 109 patients, within two years, the company stopped the trial because patients given EPO were dying at a more rapid clip than those not given EPO. J & J spent the next four years secretly "analyzing" the results. Despite laws that require drugmakers to report worrisome clinical-trial data to the FDA immediately, the company waited until December 2007 before sending the data to the agency. The study was never published.

Unsurprisingly, given the combination of research silence and unsupported hype, average EPO doses given to both dialysis and cancer patients soared during this period. By 2007, more than 80 percent of dialysis patients received EPO doses above what the FDA considered safe. More than three years would pass before the FDA, in response to a Freedom of Information Act request, provided its own interpretation of the Normal trial showing just how concerning the results really were.

CHAPTER 18

A Brave Researcher Breaks the Silence

In OCTOBER 2003, A STUDY IN *THE LANCET* CAME TO A SHOCKING conclusion: EPO may be killing cancer patients.

A follow-up story in *The New York Times* quoted several cancer experts who cautioned that the results should not lead cancer patients to stop taking EPO. Their implication was that the study was an outlier, an aberration. Since by now researchers rarely challenged the financial interests of major pharmaceutical companies that largely funded their work, the main author of the study would normally have ratified this view. But not this time.

"The senior author of the study, Dr. Michael Henke of the University of Freiburg in Germany, disagreed, saying he would not recommend administering the anemia drug to patients undergoing treatment meant to cure their cancer, except perhaps in studies," the *Times* wrote. For the first time, an EPO researcher refused to play along with this deadly game.

That EPO carried risks to the heart had long been known. That it might encourage the growth of tumors was suspected. The vast majority of oncologists assumed that the drug's benefits far outweighed its risks, because J & J and Amgen had for fifteen years kept them in the dark about the growing mountain of data showing otherwise.

Days later, Paul Goldberg, the editor of *The Cancer Letter*, broke the news that despite what the *Times* had suggested, Henke's study was not an outlier. Goldberg uncovered an obscure and easily missed letter that had appeared two months earlier in *The Lancet Oncology* reporting on a breast cancer trial in 939 patients that found forty-one deaths among those who got Procrit versus sixteen in the placebo group—a nearly threefold difference. Like in Henke's study, the Procrit deaths resulted largely because cancers grew.

And then Goldberg had this bomb about major organizations that conduct much of the cancer research in the United States: "In recent weeks, several U.S. cooperative groups suspended clinical trials or made dose adjustments of the J & J epoetin alpha after finding an increased risk of thrombosis among patients receiving erythropoietin intended to increase hemoglobin to the normal range."

By the time of Henke's study, EPO sales in cancer were bigger than any other drug ever before, with profits flowing not only to J & J and Amgen but to almost every oncologist and hospital in the United States. But it was now becoming apparent that Henke's study was part of a pattern, that dozens of researchers working for or on behalf of J & J and Amgen had participated in trials that had found much the same as Henke. But in nearly every case, the results had been kept secret, and none of these researchers had been brave enough to blow the whistle.

The reaction to Henke's study showed why. In comments to reporters, William Sheridan, Amgen's vice president for medical affairs in the United States, was highly critical of Henke. Sheridan said that many of those chosen for the trial did not have serious anemia. And he said that Henke's conclusion that EPO was to blame for poor outcomes was flat wrong.

MICHAEL HENKE WAS BORN IN A SMALL TOWN IN NORTHERN BAVARIA, Germany. His father was a family doctor, but as a boy Henke was far from sure that he wanted to follow him into medicine. Mathematics attracted him but so, too, did the priesthood.

His father finally persuaded him to apply to medical school. He said, "Come on, Michael. It's an area that's interesting. And people will always be ill. You will always have a job and earn money."

He made a few sharp turns in his training: starting in pathology, moving to radiation oncology, and finally finishing in internal medicine. After his studies, in the early 1980s, he was offered a position on a bone marrow transplant team at City of Hope, a well-regarded clinical research center, hospital, and graduate medical school outside of Los Angeles, California.

There, Henke's team treated patients with acute leukemia, a condition for which bone marrow transplants are still used. At the time, bone marrow transplants as a means to treat breast cancer were soaring. Trials would eventually prove that such transplants did nothing for those suffering from the disease other than drain their savings, shorten their lives, and cause intense suffering. The lesson that doctors, even with the best of intentions, can do great harm impressed him deeply.

Michael and Gabby Henke had arrived in California with one child, but soon had two more. Wanting to be near Gabby's parents so they could help with the children, Henke took a substantial pay cut to return to Freiburg, accepting a job as an internist.

In the mid-1990s, Henke switched his specialty from internal medicine to radiation oncology. As a refresher, he attended a radiation oncology conference in Austria, but a bad snowfall made him miss much of the first session. Not wanting to enter the session halfway through, he headed to the bar, where he met another conferee who had also been snow-delayed. The two got to talking and eventually ended up speculating about how EPO might improve outcomes among their patients.

When both returned to their practices, they each noticed that radiation seemed to offer few benefits in anemic patients. "We checked other risk factors like age, sex, size of tumor, metastases," as well as the kind of cancer cells, he said, "but anemia beat them all."

Patients with low blood-oxygen levels also fared poorly. Since anemia is a measure of the level of red blood cells, and red blood cells act as the primary transport mechanism for oxygen, and EPO encourages the growth of red blood cells, "the step to using EPO was a small step."

Henke asked Johnson & Johnson to fund a study in patients undergoing radiotherapy, but the company declined. So he took his proposal to Boehringer Ingelheim, a German pharmaceutical company that was in the process of launching its own version of EPO. Boehringer agreed, and Henke began recruiting patients.

TWO YEARS AFTER HENKE STARTED ENROLLING PATIENTS IN HIS EPO study, Boehringer Ingelheim, the study's sponsor and the manufacturer of the EPO he was using, sold the product to Roche Holdings Ltd. After some initial skepticism, Roche agreed to keep funding Henke's trial. Hans Ulrich Burger, who still works for Roche today, was assigned as the study's statistician.

The last patient was enrolled in April 2001, and since the study was double-blinded—neither Henke, his study collaborators, nor the patients knew who was getting EPO and who got a placebo—nobody had any hint how well the study had gone until the code was broken.

In November, Burger was convalescing at home after a heart scare when the big day arrived.

"My colleague called me up and he said, 'It looks good. It's positive. We're just having an issue with the code. We've mixed it up,'" Burger recalled.

Despite the reassurance, Burger said he "had a sinking feeling." How could they have mixed up the code?

An hour later, his colleague called him back. "It's not the code," the colleague told him. "It's the study. It went in the opposite direction."

EPO use resulted in more deaths, not fewer.

The study's 351 patients had been split into two groups—171 got a placebo and 180 were given EPO. The EPO group experienced a 69 percent increase in cancer progression and a 39 percent rise in deaths. The most damning thing about the trial was that the deaths resulted from cancer, not from heart attacks or strokes that the field already knew were more likely among those taking EPO. In the study, the EPO treatment lasted only seven weeks, while nearly all of the deaths occurred after thirteen weeks. It was a clear and unmistakable signal that cancer patients should not be given Procrit or any other kind of EPO.

These were exactly the kinds of results that Johnson & Johnson and Amgen had repeatedly found in study results the two companies had kept secret for years. The scientists, statisticians, and executives overseeing those trials had all gone along with cover-ups. Now Burger and Roche had to decide whether to follow the same path.

"The team struggled with that question," Burger admitted. "You invest a lot of money in a study. You think you can make a business out of it. And then you get the opposite out of the study. What do you do? It could harm your business." After all, Roche was already making hundreds of millions of dollars annually selling EPO to cancer patients.

Burger finally called Henke on Christmas Day, and Henke burst into tears. His decision to conduct the trial had resulted in the deaths of some of his patients. He was heartsick.

Now the question was what to do with the data.

Burger said he had more statistical work to do. Every month that passed would mean more unnecessary deaths but also more EPO sales for Roche.

Burger finished his analyses in April. The results were formally presented to Henke in July. "I can't say it was fun," Burger said ruefully about the gap and the internal arguments that led to it. When the conclusions finally reached a top Roche executive, instead of ordering the data to be covered up, he said, " 'No, no, no. You have to publish it immediately. You have to do that. We cannot sit on this,'" Burger recalled.

AFTER LEARNING OF HENKE'S STUDY AND PAUL GOLDBERG'S REVELA-tion that there were others with similar results, the FDA called a public hearing of cancer experts. The meeting was held in May 2004 in Rockville, and it was mobbed with reporters, financial analysts, and researchers. During the meeting, a top J & J research executive was forced to admit publicly for the first time that the company had undertaken at least five studies that had to be stopped because patients getting EPO died more often than those getting a placebo. J & J executives dismissed the results of all these studies as uninterpretable or confusing. In the wake of the meeting, J & J put a new note on Procrit's label that the drug might promote tumor growth and increase the risks of death.

There are many moments in the history of American healthcare that are difficult to explain in retrospect. The opioid and antipsychotic disasters in the late 2000s and early 2010s—long after the dangers of these medicines were clear—are among the more well-known. But just as inexplicable was the growth in EPO prescriptions after the FDA advisory committee made the drug's dangers plain.

Both the opioid and EPO disasters resulted in large measure from the financial incentives in the American system. Europe, which does not have the same financial incentives and, where direct payments to doctors from drugmakers are generally banned, experienced neither disaster.

In the EPO case, prosecutors and investigators later expressed shock at how thoroughly corruption infected almost every major institution involved in cancer care.

While partners in making and selling EPO, Amgen and J & J were also fierce competitors who sued each other repeatedly over various aspects of their EPO relationship. J & J executives have said that it is unfair to suggest that they were in any way complicit in Amgen's crimes, for which Amgen eventually pleaded guilty. Johnson & Johnson was indeed never charged for its EPO marketing efforts. But the Amgen investigative files, as well as work done by reporters at *The New York Times* and *The Wall Street Journal*, show that both companies broke the law routinely.

The federal Medicare program began in 1965, and for most of its history it generally paid for hospital care but not routine drug prescriptions. Since cancer treatments were usually administered in hospitals by infusion, the drugs were considered part of hospital care, so Medicare paid the bill.

Drug companies were supposed to report the average wholesale prices, or AWP, of drugs. This was the amount the government reimbursed the hospitals. But companies routinely lied about this number and charged the hospitals less. The larger the gap between the actual price that hospitals paid and the fictitious AWP that drug companies reported to the government, the bigger the amount of money that hospitals could pocket as profit. Given this, drug companies figured out they could boost sales of medicines simply by widening the gap between the real price and the fake AWP price.

In 2005, to crack down on some of this fraud, the Medicare program changed its reimbursement formula to something called the average sales price, or ASP. But the games and the gaps between real and reported prices continue, and as cancer medicine prices soared, the drug markups got bigger and bigger. Again and again over the years, cancer doctors have tended to favor drugs that gave them the most money, whether those drugs worked better than other drugs or not.

Although the vast majority of oncologists are honest and caring, financial incentives can unconsciously nudge even the most honest doctors to change their prescribing habits, studies show. Many patients pay a portion of those costs out of their own pockets. So, as doctors enrich themselves, some also bankrupt their patients and—because their prescribing decisions are based on profits instead of effectiveness—undermine their patients' health. Again, much of this—in some cases, maybe all of it—may be done unconsciously, given the many incentives dangled in front of oncologists. But conscious or unconscious, the results are the same.

This, in a nutshell, is the story of EPO. It is also the grim reality of cancer care in the United States and is among the chief reasons why Americans who get cancer tend to die earlier and poorer than their European counterparts.

At roughly $1,000 a dose during the height of its use, EPO was and remains expensive. Doctors and hospitals often pocket nearly a third of that price themselves—or about $300 per dose in the 2000s. Many patients get dozens of doses. In addition to drug markups, both J & J and Amgen often gave doctors kickbacks in the form of volume discounts that by themselves could add up to millions of dollars.

J & J sales reps have admitted that they, with the full knowledge and support of top J & J executives, even gave doctors free Procrit vials, for which the reps helped them seek full-price reimbursements from Medicare and private insurers. Both Johnson & Johnson and Amgen added 10 percent to 17 percent more medicine to their EPO vials than they listed on the containers. The companies justified the practice by saying the extra product was meant to compensate for spillage. But infusion nurses don't spill expensive cancer drugs. The extra was just another way to give free product to doctors and hospitals, for which they would then bill the government and private insurers as if they had paid full freight. The profits involved were so huge that some hospitals hired compounding pharmacies to repackage EPO into smaller vials.

Other sales representatives told investigators that Johnson & Johnson and Amgen encouraged almost every oncologist and nephrologist in the country to bill Medicare for medicine they got for free because both companies deliberately overfilled vials. Such widespread fraud created huge financial incentives for doctors to use enormous quantities of EPO, resulting in an estimated doubling of oncologists' take-home pay—from about $300,000 a year to about $600,000. A practice manager in Washington State in 2007 was so appalled by the payments that he gave the *Times* financial statements showing that doctors in the practice pocketed $2.7 million after prescribing $9 million worth of J & J's EPO over the course of a year. Looking at a different set of records, reporters at the *Journal* reported the very next day that cancer doctors got back $237,885 for every $1 million of Procrit they prescribed.

According to secret investigative documents, Amgen created a shell company called the International Nephrology Network, or INN, which offered volume discounts on EPO to doctors. Because INN was supposedly separate, Amgen didn't have to include these discounts in its calculation of average wholesale or sales prices. "Once it started, INN had one real business—to get doctors to buy Aranesp through INN's distributor—and INN carried out that business in close consultation with Amgen," a trio of federal prosecutors wrote in a secret fifty-page memorandum detailing myriad scams related to EPO. One involved a claim that EPO was an effective medicine against AIDS, a dangerously false notion.

All the while, J & J publicly claimed that the money it was giving to American doctors had no effect on their prescribing habits. "We do not provide financial incentives for physicians to prescribe our products, including Procrit," a J & J spokeswoman said. "Consistent with industry practice, we do provide discounts that comply with federal government regulations."

The extent of the criminality uncovered in their investigation led to a debate among prosecutors about whether to charge individual executives.

"Rick Blumberg, the FDA's chief counsel for criminal enforcement, has all but begged us to charge individuals with misbranding in this case," a trio of federal prosecutors in charge of the EPO case wrote in a secret memo to a top prosecutor at the Department of Justice. "He argues that since 1999, there have been 27 civil and criminal off-label promotion cases and that, despite the more than $10 billion recovered in fines and penalties, the cases have had no deterrent effect. Instead, he believes the drug companies simply factor the price of a possible penalty into the cost of doing business and opt to engage in the conduct because of the profits involved."

But deterring crime is time-consuming. "The downside, of course, is that it guarantees the office a massive, complicated, and fiercely litigated trial without the prospect of any jail sentence or additional recovery for the work," the prosecutors wrote. Once again, taking on a huge conglomerate with scores of attorneys and a seemingly limitless budget for litigation seemed like a fool's errands, so the Justice Department did little but sigh.

No formal assessment has yet been undertaken, but EPO is a medicine used by millions that increases death rates by more than a third. One epidemiologist privately estimated that the death toll—which continues to mount to this day—is in the hundreds of thousands.

Indeed, the EPO disaster in many ways exceeds that of prescription opioids. The two have cost a similar number of lives, but opioid makers never ensnared as many doctors and revered medical institutions into greedily and knowingly participating in such blatant and systematized criminality. Opioids relieve pain in ways no other drugs can match, so patients can benefit from treatment. By contrast, since simple blood transfusions are far safer and more effective, EPO's only offering for nearly all patients is injury and death. And because EPO is so much more expensive than any opioid, the scale of the theft of tax, insurance, and patient dollars has been vastly greater.

CHAPTER 19

Miracle-Gro for Cancer

AGAIN AND AGAIN, JOHNSON & JOHNSON AND AMGEN DETERMINED
that they couldn't ethically give EPO to patients enrolled in clinical
trials because the drug was found to be killing patients. But all the
while, they continued to sell the drug to millions of patients outside
of closely monitored studies. It was a no-lose situation in terms of
profits, but very much a losing proposition for many cancer patients.

Having announced at the 2004 FDA advisory committee hearing
that they had launched a series of trials to finally assess EPO's risks,
neither Johnson & Johnson nor Amgen could bury their results—
although Amgen certainly tried.

Among the raft of studies in the next several years that confirmed
EPO's risks was the landmark Danish Head and Neck Cancer Study,
which found that among 513 patients, those receiving EPO were
about 38 percent more likely to see their tumors grow than those getting a placebo—a familiar number. The Danish study was supposed
to enroll 600 patients but was stopped on October 18, 2006, because
the independent safety-monitoring committee decided that it would
be unethical to continue giving patients a drug that was killing them.

Amgen kept the Danish results secret for months, refusing even
to divulge the outcome in its annual earnings call with analysts on

January 25, 2007, more than three months later. This was a clear violation of securities laws, since EPO was so crucial to the company's finances.

Paul Goldberg, the editor of *The Cancer Letter*, finally revealed the study's results in February 2007, and Amgen's chief executive (whom prosecutors would consider charging criminally) was forced to admit that the company should have said something earlier. Four days later, the *Journal of Clinical Oncology* published a Canadian study showing that EPO increased death rates in another group of cancer patients.

Goldberg wrote that "some implications of the new findings seem unthinkable: It could turn out that for nearly 15 years, oncologists have been giving cancer patients a biologic that was making their tumors grow."

The FDA called yet another meeting of its cancer experts. Such hearings are normally staid, collegial affairs. But this hearing in 2007 was different.

Dr. Otis Brawley, the longtime chief medical officer of the American Cancer Society, put the matter succinctly: "I'm concerned that this compound is a stimulant, a tumor fertilizer, for epidermal tumors." He then added a line that would come to define EPO: "What data do you have to assure me that this is not Miracle-Gro for cancer?"

FDA officials normally treat top officials from major pharmaceutical companies at such meetings with a deference bordering on obsequiousness. That was not the case this time. Dr. Vinni Juneja, an FDA medical officer, told the meeting that J & J had promised for years to conduct the right clinical trials but had not only failed to design its trials in a way that would uncover risks but had refused to share the information it had. "The primary data from five completed epoetin studies with no reported safety signals have not been submitted to FDA and these studies finished accrual as long as six years ago," she said.

J & J and Amgen officials said in the meeting that EPO was safe and that studies then underway would definitively prove that. Almost no one in the hearing room seemed to believe them, including

Roche's Hans Ulrich Burger, who was so puzzled by the slides presented by the two companies that he nudged a colleague during one presentation and asked how they could possibly be true. "Everybody in there could smell that something was fishy," Burger recalled.

By the end of 2007, eight large studies would convincingly demonstrate that EPO increased the risks of heart attacks, strokes, and tumor growth. The FDA put a black box warning, its strongest, on EPO drugs, saying doctors should use the lowest possible dose to help patients avoid blood transfusions. It added a note that Procrit should not be given to patients "when the anticipated outcome is cure."

It is difficult to explain the ongoing widespread use of EPO ever since. The only approved use of EPO in cancer is for patients who become anemic as a result of other chemotherapeutics. But cancer patients rarely take such toxic chemo unless they're seeking a cure, a situation for which they shouldn't be given EPO. The drug has not been proven to improve patients' quality of life and so is not appropriate for hospice patients either.

Doctors who continue to prescribe EPO say that it's helpful for their patients, many of whom are going to die anyway. But such prescriptions undermine almost everything oncologists say they stand for, since the drug can actually shorten life, and leave the victim's family impoverished financially as well as emotionally.

There was one more chance to push back on EPO and save lives accordingly. On July 30, 2007, the Centers for Medicare & Medicaid Services (CMS) released a National Coverage Determination that instructed doctors not to use EPO when patients' hemoglobin level rose above 10 g/dL. In an email dated September 20, 2007, the CMS division director who led the team that wrote the EPO coverage decision noted that an analysis of a small sample of EPO claims showed that 90 percent of the drug's use was in patients with hemoglobin levels above 10 g/dL. So agency officials knew that the new instructions would tank sales for J & J and Amgen. But officials also suspected the instructions would save thousands of lives.

The pharmaceutical industry is the largest donor to American political campaigns, and both J & J and Amgen called in their chits. Medical and patient groups, which are mostly supported by industry donations, flooded congressional offices with complaints. So, too, did oncologists.

The Senate soon passed by unanimous consent a "Sense of the Senate" resolution criticizing Medicare officials for responding to the FDA's alarm by asking doctors to use less Procrit. Every single Republican and Democrat in the chamber signed the measure—including Bernie Sanders, Barack Obama, and Joseph R. Biden, Jr. In the House, J & J got 224 signatures on a separate letter calling for fewer limits on Procrit.

Representative Edolphus Towns, a Democrat from Brooklyn who chaired the House Government Reform Committee, launched an investigation and sent CMS a blistering letter noting that the coverage decision "has been met with overwhelming opposition from oncologists and patients and representatives of numerous cancer and other health organizations."

The letter asked for documents relating to nineteen different issues. Nowhere, however, in Towns's letter, in the FDA advisory committee hearings, or in the stories about the controversy in the *Times* and other newspapers was there any mention of how many people might have died because J & J and Amgen had hidden the results of their studies for nearly two decades. No one thought to ask or wanted to know.

IN 2011, RESEARCHERS WORKING FOR THE CENTERS FOR MEDICARE & Medicaid Services released an eighty-four-page study declaring that among most kidney patients, the original market for EPO, no study had yet provided evidence that EPO made people feel better, improved their survival, or had any demonstrable clinical benefit besides a meaningless rise in a statistic related to red blood cell counts. Among cancer patients too, EPO has only downsides.

In short, the study suggests that EPO should be a niche drug, used only in the rarest of circumstances. Instead, it became the first big biotech franchise in history, made more than $100 billion in sales, and contributed to the deaths of perhaps hundreds of thousands of people.

That same year, Medicare changed the way it paid for EPO in kidney patients. Instead of paying doctors a separate markup for each EPO prescription, the federal government gave doctors a lump sum for the entirety of a patient's care. The change made EPO less profitable for doctors. Prescriptions plunged 20 percent in the policy's first year.

But the government never changed the way it paid for EPO use in cancer patients. Perhaps as a result, oncologists in the United States continued to use considerable quantities of EPO. In 2016, Johnson & Johnson's Procrit sales were $1.1 billion.

That same year, the study that Johnson & Johnson promised to conduct twenty-three years earlier was finally published in the *Journal of Clinical Oncology*. It showed that among 2,098 women with metastatic breast cancer, those who got EPO were twice as likely to suffer strokes, pulmonary embolisms, or acute coronary syndrome as those who did not. The EPO women were also likelier to die. The cancers in both sets of women behaved similarly until the twelfth month, when those who got EPO saw their tumors grow significantly bigger and faster than those who didn't. EPO was indeed Miracle-Gro for tumors.

The study definitively concluded that cancer patients who suffer serious anemia should be given blood transfusions to correct the problem, not EPO. In its wake, Procrit's sales have gradually declined. In 2021, they totaled $479 million.

Doctors who still prescribe EPO for many of their patients are invariably located in small towns and cities where care tends to be poorer. In 2018, the oncologist in the United States who used the most EPO was located in New Hartford, New York, a town of about 22,000 located halfway between Albany and Syracuse. The second biggest user was a nephrologist in Roseburg, Oregon. The third and fifth biggest users were oncologists in Little Rock, Arkansas, and the fourth was in Atlantis, Florida.

Not one of the five is affiliated with a major academic medical center where their EPO prescriptions would likely garner scrutiny. But for these oncologists in small towns, small markets, and small cities, prescribing EPO brings considerable extra income, helping them fight against many of the trends in medicine that might otherwise lead them to flee to bigger cities or cost them their ability to fund second homes.

CHAPTER 20

A Path to a Normal Life

RECURRENT PSYCHOSIS, WHICH IS MOST COMMONLY ASSOCIATED with schizophrenia but can also result from bipolar disease or severe depression, is one of the most troubling mental illnesses a human can suffer. It is defined as a break from reality in which people perceive things that others do not, and it is characterized by two different phenomena. One is hallucinations, which are commonly heard but sometimes seen as well. The second is delusions, in which someone perceives a narrative that doesn't square with consensus reality. Common delusions include paranoid thoughts of being followed or spied upon, or participating in a divine revelation or intervention.

A surprising number of people experience psychotic breaks once or twice in their lives. In children, they can manifest from a viral illness and high fever. In young adults, they sometimes result from heavy recreational drug use. No matter the cause, nothing has been shown to treat psychosis better than antipsychotics. The drugs' effects are immediate, and for those who can tolerate them, they offer a path to a normal life.

But for at least two-thirds of those who try them, antipsychotics have either minimal efficacy or intolerable side effects, which include rapid weight gain, intense sleepiness, diabetes, and strokes. Among the most dispiriting are something called "extrapyramidal side effects," which are tics and tremors that can continue even after a medicine is stopped. When these problems appear in people who are no one's idea of crazy—anxious grandmothers, children with ADHD, or just a guy going through a few bad months—they are horrifying. Those affected often become social pariahs—ostracized because many people find uncontrolled facial movements, like a thrusting tongue, unsettling. This is why prescribing antipsychotics to those with mild or brief mental illnesses can be problematic.

Children and the frail elderly are generally given the drugs when their behavior is deemed unacceptable by those with authority over them. In nursing homes, being too loud, too aggressive, or waking up in the middle of the night to complain can often lead nurses to insist patients be given an antipsychotic to shut them up. In the 1980s, the use of these medicines as chemical straitjackets had become so controversial that Congress passed a law in 1987 mandating restrictions and frequent reviews by independent pharmacists of antipsychotic prescriptions given to the institutionalized elderly. (Studies show that nursing homes still use antipsychotic pills to cut down on staffing costs.)

So, when Johnson & Johnson set out in the 1980s to discover a successor to Haldol—its popular and highly profitable antipsychotic, whose patent was expiring—the company knew what everyone wanted: an antipsychotic that worked better to quiet internal voices but didn't cause tics and tremors. And if the new medicine could be shown to actually help elderly patients with dementia rather than simply knocking them out, it would be a blockbuster.

That description is exactly what J & J's executives wanted the FDA to allow the company to say about Risperdal in 1993 when the company sought approval for the newly discovered drug. But the FDA wasn't buying it.

RISPERDAL WAS PART OF A WAVE OF DRUGS CALLED "ATYPICAL ANTIPSY-chotics," distinguishing them from older antipsychotics like Haldol, which are referred to as "typicals." Atypicals were sold as safer than typicals because they were supposed to cause fewer tics and tremors.

This benefit was enough to make the atypical class of medicines one of the most profitable in history. Since people with schizophrenia are often homeless or incapable of regular employment, state Medicaid programs, which provide healthcare for the poor, were the largest purchasers of such medicines. For about fifteen years, atypicals were Medicaid's single largest expense. But the prices of atypicals were so high that many state Medicaid programs ran out of money buying them and ended up having to kick thousands of poor people off their rolls as a result.

Perhaps this price would have been worth paying if Risperdal had been genuinely better or safer than Haldol, something psychiatrists were led to believe for years. Neither claim turned out to be true.

The best comparisons of the older and newer antipsychotics were done by government-funded researchers in the United States and Britain. In the CATIE trial (which stood for Clinical Antipsychotic Trials of Intervention Effectiveness), the first of these landmark studies, whose initial results were first published in September 2005, researchers randomly assigned 1,493 people with schizophrenia to receive one of five drugs and then followed them for eighteen months.

Three-quarters of those given Risperdal stopped taking the drug or switched to another, either because it was ineffective or because the side effects were too severe. Those taking an older Haldol-like drug tolerated the medicine a bit longer, which meant it was still the better drug despite costing a fraction as much.

Most remarkable was that the tics and tremors happened just as often in those taking Risperdal. The main selling point of atypicals, then—a reduction in extrapyramidal side effects—was false hype.

"Probably the biggest surprise of all was that the older medication produced about as good an effect as the newer medications, three of them anyway, and did not produce neurological side effects at greater rates than any of the other drugs," Dr. Jeffrey Lieberman of Columbia University, who led the study, said in an interview with Benedict

Carey, the mental health reporter for *The New York Times*. Further-more, a series of other independent studies conducted among teen-agers and elderly patients confirmed these findings and made clear that Risperdal and similar medicines are, for anyone who is not a confirmed schizophrenic, too toxic to be used beyond brief interven-tions.

Carey reasoned that a generous interpretation of the research comparing typicals and atypicals was that both classes of medicines were equally bad: the typicals probably caused somewhat more tics and tremors, while the atypicals had a worse effect on metabolism and weight. Teens gain about four pounds each month while on Ri-sperdal, studies show, and those on the drug for more than a few months often become seriously obese. The emotional impact of such weight gain could be devastating.

So the challenge Johnson & Johnson's executives faced was to take a medicine that was no better than its predecessor, slap a price on it that was forty times higher, and find ways to persuade psychiatrists, insurers, patients, patients' legal guardians, and everyone else in-volved in psychiatric care to prescribe and buy it.

The entire effort would have been much easier if the FDA from the start had allowed Johnson & Johnson to falsely claim that Risper-dal was a clear improvement over Haldol. This time, however, the FDA didn't roll over.

"The division has refused to accede to Janssen's demands because it believes that the side-by-side presentation of data obtained on Ri-sperdal and haloperidol assigned subjects invites a comparison that leads to the conclusion that Risperdal has been shown to be superior to haloperidol when, in fact, it has not," wrote Dr. Paul Leber, the FDA's director of neuropharmacologic drug products, to his boss in 1993.

Leber had told J & J many times that if the company wanted comparison data between Risperdal and Haldol to be listed on Ri-sperdal's official label, its scientists needed to conduct a head-to-head clinical trial in which they gave half the patients Risperdal and the other half Haldol, and then compared how the two sides fared.

Instead, J & J conducted a study in which every patient got Risperdal. The company then wanted to show how that trial's outcomes compared with an older study in which everybody got Haldol—an unfair comparison since outcomes invariably differ from one study to the next, even when using the same drug.

Did J & J's scientists and researchers know conclusively in those early years that Risperdal was no better, and probably a bit worse, than Haldol? There's no evidence in the drug's voluminous files that they did. But the company's refusal to follow the FDA's repeated prodding that it conduct a fair head-to-head comparison was a likely indication that its scientists suspected the truth.

In the end, the FDA held firm. On December 29, 1993, the FDA approved Risperdal, but did not allow the company to put on its label any comparison with Haldol.

BEYOND FIGURING OUT HOW TO SELL A MEDICINE THAT WAS NO BETter than an inexpensive predecessor, Johnson & Johnson had another problem: Those with schizophrenia comprise less than 1 percent of the U.S. adult population, and top company officials had set sales targets well above that relatively small market. "Aggressive expansion of Risperdal use in other indications," a 1994 sales plan draft explained, "is therefore necessary."

In order to do this, the company had to either persuade the FDA that Risperdal was an effective treatment for conditions other than schizophrenia or find creative ways to market the pill for other conditions without FDA endorsement.

In the end, J & J decided to do both. The company asked the FDA to approve other uses of Risperdal, and separately, it came up with an ingenuous scheme to work around the FDA and defy the law. To fool its own employees into going along with its illegal schemes, executives argued that since Risperdal was approved to treat schizophrenia, and since schizophrenics suffered almost every psychiatric illness and symptom imaginable, Risperdal could be sold as a treatment for everything.

Thus was born "Sell to the Symptoms."

CHAPTER 21

A Treatment for Everything and Everyone

THE "SELL THE SYMPTOMS" PLAN WAS AT THE HEART OF J & J'S EF-forts to break Risperdal out of the box the FDA had placed it in. In a summary of two years of secret grand jury testimony, prosecutors outlined what this meant: "In practice, a rep would sell to the symptoms by asking a doctor if that doctor had any patients who had certain symptoms such as anxiety, hostility, impulsiveness, agitation, etc. The rep would simultaneously show the doctor a sales aid which listed these symptoms on its cover. If the doctor said yes, he or she had patients with those symptoms, then the rep would tell the doctor that Risperdal was effective in treating those symptoms."

Janet Vergis, a top company executive, told the grand jury that she understood that the company "could promote Risperdal for treatment of any symptom in the PANSS scale," which is a measure commonly used to identify the severity of schizophrenia. PANSS stands for Positive and Negative Syndrome Scale, and its symptoms include anxiety, guilty feelings, depression, emotional withdrawal, tension, poor attention, pain, weakness, shortness of breath, poor impulse control, excitement, grandiosity, suspiciousness, hostility, lack of spontaneity, and on and on.

In short, the scale incorporates much of the human emotional palette, including states many people move through several times a day. Since sales reps couldn't possibly recite all of these symptoms in a brief sales call, the company shortened and tailored the list to those typically encountered by the doctors being pitched. For doctors who treated mostly elderly patients, there was one list. For pediatricians and child psychiatrists, another.

Anyone with even a minimal understanding of FDA's drug approval process would know that this was illegal. For comparison's sake, the symptoms of bacterial infections include headache, but antibiotics clearly cannot be promoted as a headache cure.

Johnson & Johnson's own regulatory experts told the grand jury that they knew a symptoms-based message was illegal. Among them was Edward Brann, director of Janssen's regulatory affairs group, who said that Risperdal wasn't approved to treat dementia and that if sales reps asked doctors to try Risperdal as a dementia treatment, "it would be improper." But he also said executives studiously avoided asking him and others in his group to vet Sell to the Symptoms.

Nonetheless, Sell to the Symptoms became the model across the industry, with Eli Lilly, AstraZeneca, Pfizer, and Bristol Myers Squibb all adopting some version of the concept.

THE JOHNSON & JOHNSON EXECUTIVE MOST RESPONSIBLE FOR TURN-ing Risperdal into a blockbuster was Alex Gorsky, and the adjective most commonly used to describe Gorsky is "determined." He ran marathons and competed in triathlons through middle age, until an arthritic hip forced him to get an implant.

Like J & J itself, Gorsky's origins are quintessentially American. The third of six children, he was born in Kansas City, Kansas. Three of his four grandparents were immigrants from Russia or Croatia. One grandfather was a grocer and the other worked in meatpacking. Gorsky's father was a Korean War veteran.

In Kansas City, Gorsky attended St. John the Baptist School, a Catholic institution. When he was eleven, the family moved to Fremont, Michigan, a small rural town where his father became a mid-level executive at Gerber Food Products and his mother volunteered as a special education teacher. Soon after moving, Gorsky learned that a family friend had been accepted to West Point. Looking at the man's yearbook, Gorsky became entranced with the idea of attending the academy and prepared by running four to six miles every day.

In high school, Gorsky played quarterback and linebacker, which his coach said was a testament to his mental and physical grit. He also swam and ran track. Well into his fifties, he told audiences that he had "an addiction of sorts to fitness."

Gorsky often told interviewers that he learned crucial lessons about leadership and himself in the military. Because of his actions at J & J, he's also told that to juries.

As a nineteen-year-old cadet, Gorsky attended U.S. Army Ranger School, a famously difficult physical and mental training course. Attendees are underfed, denied sleep, and forced on grueling marches near Stone Mountain, Georgia. Some become dangerously thin. Many fail to graduate.

Near the end of his session, Gorsky was leading a patrol when a branch snapped against his shin. The cut became infected. Gorsky got a fever and had to go to an emergency room for antibiotics. Against the doctor's advice, he returned to camp. The squad rallied and conducted its final patrol. Gorsky said he learned something about himself that final night: "No matter what obstacle you face, you are going to find a way to get over it, through it, around it, under it."

In 1988, after serving his six-year commitment to the army, much of it in Greece, Gorsky took a job in California as a sales rep for Janssen, J & J's main pharmaceutical subsidiary. After only eighteen months, he was promoted to sales manager in Pittsburgh. Two years after that, he was promoted again, to a marketing job at Janssen headquarters in New Jersey. In March 1995, he became a Janssen group director in the psychiatry, neurology, allergy, analgesia, and oncology franchises, with responsibility over Risperdal.

In 2001, he became president of Janssen, and eventually, company group chairman for J & J's pharmaceuticals business in Europe, the Middle East, and Africa. In 2004, he left Johnson & Johnson to head the North American division of Novartis.

He returned to J & J four years later as the leader of the company's device division and entered a two-person runoff for the top job against Sheri McCoy, another vice-chairman. A story in *Fortune* reported that the board picked Gorsky to lead the company because he was viewed as "tough," while McCoy was seen as more collaborative.

Gorsky told a class at the London School of Business in 2015 that the key to successfully climbing the corporate ladder was meeting sales goals.

"Performance is absolutely essential," he said. "You gotta be able to perform in good markets and bad markets."

When he took over the marketing of Risperdal, Gorsky was given sales goals that were unattainable without breaking the law. As he rose through the company's ranks, he would begin setting those impossible sales targets himself.

BECAUSE THEIR ILLNESS IS SO DISABLING, SCHIZOPHRENICS' HEALTHcare is generally provided by state Medicaid programs, and for years, the government bought about 85 percent of the Risperdal pills sold in the United States. A 2 mg tablet was priced at around $4.50, while the identical dose of generic Haldol cost ten cents—a forty-five-fold difference. If state Medicaid directors ever decided that Risperdal was not worth this vast difference in price, Johnson & Johnson would lose billions. So for Gorsky and J & J, convincing state Medicaid directors to keep spending taxpayer dollars for high-priced Risperdal pills was their top priority.

One way to do that was to put these directors on the company's payroll, even though doing so is generally illegal. The model for this strategy was Texas, which in 1995 created the Texas Medication Algorithm Project, or TMAP, to tell doctors in the state the best ways to treat schizophrenia.

Much of the money for TMAP initially came from the Robert Wood Johnson Foundation, which today is second only to the Bill and Melinda Gates Foundation as the nation's largest charity focused on healthcare issues. The foundation is supposed to operate independently of the company, though about half of the foundation's money at the time was invested in J & J stock, and several board members were former company executives.

The algorithm's lead author was Dr. Steven Shon, who was also the medical director of the Texas mental health department. Unveiled in 1996, the TMAP algorithm recommended that Risperdal be included along with older antipsychotics as first-line treatment, meaning doctors could use Risperdal or a host of other, cheaper pills.

It was a reasonable recommendation. Risperdal quickly became the most oft-used antipsychotic in Texas. By October 1997, the share of patients in Texas's state mental health facilities prescribed Risperdal was 68 percent.

Shon soon decided that TMAP needed an update.

This time, the process was almost entirely underwritten by Johnson & Johnson and other drug companies. And this time, only Risperdal and other similarly expensive atypicals made the recommended list. If doctors wanted to use the older, cheaper medicines, they had to justify doing so in writing—something busy physicians hate. The state also warned doctors and clinics that anyone who ignored TMAP could lose state funding. Use of the older medicines collapsed.

Johnson & Johnson then quietly lobbied the Texas legislature to pass a law mandating that doctors in Texas follow TMAP's guidance, all but making the use of the older and less expensive medicines illegal.

A cardinal rule in medicine is that patients whose illness has been stabilized by a particular medication should be allowed to continue on that drug, particularly when the illness has to do with mental health. TMAP made following that principle nearly impossible.

Having conquered Texas, Johnson & Johnson sought to export this success to other states.

The FDA had warned Johnson & Johnson against claiming that Risperdal was better than Haldol, something even company officials had agreed in discussions with the FDA that its studies failed to prove. But Shon and others from Texas used the company's money to make these false claims of superiority on the company's behalf. And as other state officials became company consultants, those states came up with their own versions of TMAP that put Risperdal on their preferred drug lists.

Shon was such a rock star for Johnson & Johnson's sales efforts that other drug companies began courting him.

"Note: Shon can and is influencing not only the $50 million atypical in Texas, but likewise in many other states," one internal J & J email dated March 20, 2001, stated. In another email in the same chain, an executive noted that Shon was "enjoying the vast attention and response he can command from industry. Laurie shared that Lilly is sending their corporate jet to pick up Steve and bring him to Lilly for a site visit. Obviously Steve has the right to be served by all industry. Let's hope he remains fair and balanced and remembers who placed him on the map." J & J executives also worried about efforts Pfizer was making to recruit their Texan superstar.

After *The New York Times* broke the story about TMAP on February 1, 2004, Shon sent the paper a long letter insisting he had never taken money from drugmakers. This was a lie, and one he continued to make for years—even under oath. He finally acknowledged as much in a devastating cross-examination during a court case in Texas in which the state sued the company for its illegal marketing efforts.

He insisted that he alone controlled the content of his speeches—until shown evidence that Johnson & Johnson required pre-clearance before he spoke. He said he never charged his state employer for time he spent giving marketing talks—until shown timecards proving that he had. He said he never illegally accepted money from J & J—until shown ledgers illustrating exactly that. Again and again, Shon recanted the lies he had just told.

"Dr. Shon, with respect to the thousands of dollars you received from Janssen in connection with these meetings and conferences, what did you do with the money?" a Texas state attorney finally asked him, after pointing out that accepting such funds was a felony offense.

"Deposited them in my personal account," Shon answered glumly.

Shon earned $25,000 from Johnson & Johnson while other state employees involved with TMAP got as much as $314,000. (The difference may help explain some of Shon's false statements. Did he see himself as fundamentally different from those making far more? This was not a question he was asked.)

Unfortunately for J & J, Shon's high profile encouraged Medicaid directors in other states (who probably thought he was making a fortune) to ask for similar funding. In Kentucky, for example, according to an internal J & J email, officials involved with adopting or rejecting TMAP "want a $200,000 grant from us."

An executive answered a colleague that one of the reasons the company dumped so much money in Texas was to create a model that other states would copy without much fuss. But Risperdal was just too important. J & J ended up paying officials in other states as well, despite its executives' awareness that doing so was illegal. (An official in Pennsylvania would eventually be convicted as a result.)

In the end, sixteen states as well as the District of Columbia adopted TMAP. For the rest, Johnson & Johnson had a backup plan.

THE STORIES OF PARENTS WHOSE TEENAGE CHILDREN SUFFER PSY-chotic breaks are among the most painful of medical narratives. They often follow a similar pattern: A shy but delightful child with a few intriguing oddities grows into a reclusive and worrying young teenager who suddenly has an awful and frightening disconnect with reality. Violent attacks and arrests by police often follow, along with a dawning realization by parents that they no longer know their child and, in some cases, fear them.

This is why the National Alliance on Mental Illness (NAMI), the nation's largest advocacy group for these parents, is such an effective advocacy organization. And it is why Johnson & Johnson made NAMI one of its most important partners.

In Texas, for instance, Johnson & Johnson gave the local NAMI affiliate $50,000 to support TMAP—and gave another $51,000 directly to Joe Lovelace, the affiliate's top executive, and flew him around the world to talk about the benefits of TMAP and Risperdal.

When Kentucky's Medicaid program went $230 million in the red in 2002, its formulary committee considered bumping the newer antipsychotics from its preferred list because they were the program's biggest expense. NAMI bused scores of protesters to a hearing in Frankfort, the state capital, placed full-page ads in Kentucky newspapers attacking the proposal, and sent angry faxes to state officials. These buses, ads, and faxes were all paid for by drug companies, though NAMI never disclosed this fact. In the end, Kentucky kept buying Risperdal but tightened rules for nursing home care, cutting off crucial support to thousands of ailing elderly patients.

NAMI also hosted popular barbecues for state legislators in almost every state capital, and its top members often contributed to the political campaigns of crucial legislators. Johnson & Johnson similarly contributed to these state campaigns. The combined attention from one of the nation's most sympathetic patient advocacy organizations and one of the world's biggest conglomerates was effective, and twenty-eight states passed laws specifically exempting drugs treating mental disorders from cost controls.

These battles were so intense not only because states were Risperdal's biggest customers but because J & J feared that if doctors returned to using older pills, they might discover they worked as well or better than Risperdal, and that might reduce sales across the board—something Gorsky and his fellow executives, to say nothing of J & J's shareholders, would not welcome.

For Johnson & Johnson, NAMI was a particularly effective lobbying force (all the more so because J & J could write its donations to the group off on its taxes, so federal and state governments were effectively funding the company's lobbying and sales efforts). There is nothing unusual about this. One study found that of 7,865 health advocacy groups in the United States, only a handful are completely independent of pharmaceutical industry money. A study published in March 2017 in *The New England Journal of Medicine* found that out of 104 organizations examined, "at least 83% received financial support from drug, device, and biotechnologies companies, and at least 39% have a current or former industry executive on the governing board." Full disclosure of these payments is rare, the study found.

In state after state, the alliance of NAMI and J & J successfully pressured state officials to leave Risperdal in place, even at the cost of cutting services because of the higher price point. Oregon's legislature dropped thousands of patients from its Medicaid program in 2003 rather than restrict purchases of Risperdal and similar medicines. Other states followed a similar pattern.

Serious Red Flags

BY THE END OF 1997, RISPERDAL'S SALES IN THE UNITED STATES totaled $589 million, a threefold jump from its first-year sales in 1994 of $172 million. TMAP and the company's partnership with NAMI had made Risperdal the dominant medicine among those with schizophrenia. And company analyses showed that sales were growing fastest among children and the elderly—both populations in which the potential for further growth was both limitless and, because marketing to them was illegal, perilous.

Beyond the legal issues, there were reasons to be worried about Risperdal's use in kids and seniors. From its earliest trials, Risperdal was shown to have a disturbing effect on patients' endocrine systems—the delicate and often mysterious set of glands that have profound effects on a whole series of bodily functions through their secretions of hormones.

This system is particularly delicate in children, in whom Risperdal led to elevated levels of prolactin, a hormone involved in the production of milk during pregnancy and one that is also vital to immune function. Even more problematic for J & J was the growing realization that no other antipsychotic, new or old, raised prolactin levels like Risperdal. And anecdotal reports were piling up that Risperdal caused severe weight gain in many patients and, in some unfortunate few children, death. Company sales representatives were increasingly hearing disturbing reports from psychiatrists.

The elderly were a different if equally disquieting story. The company's first trials had only eighty-five patients who were sixty-five years of age or older, but even in such a small subset, the drug raised blood pressure—a concern in older patients. But the potential sales that could result from the drug's use to treat dementia and Alzheimer's were so enticing that the company launched two early clinical trials. On January 20, 1998, J & J submitted the results to the FDA as part of an application seeking approval to sell Risperdal as a treatment for dementia.

A later publication would describe the results of these trials in glowing terms, but the FDA saw them differently. One of the studies failed to show any benefit in its primary outcome, and the second barely achieved statistical significance. Quite simply, the drug just didn't work well for elderly patients.

Even more worrisome: The patients given Risperdal died in greater numbers than those given a placebo. Johnson & Johnson ignored the difference, but agency reviewers were struck by it. In rejecting the company's application, the FDA wrote in a letter dated January 20, 1999, that the company had "failed to fully explore and explain what appeared to be an excess number of deaths."

These were serious red flags. None of them stopped Gorsky and his team from aggressively pushing Risperdal sales in children and the elderly.

In Risperdal's first three years, Johnson & Johnson used two different internal sales forces to pitch the drug to doctors: CNS and 500 Gold. CNS was a sales force that exclusively visited psychiatrists and psychiatric nurses. The 500 Gold force was the company's main sales division, and they visited primary care doctors.

In 1998, Gorsky decided that the elderly market was such a

spectacular opportunity that he created an eighty-three-member ElderCare sales force to sell exclusively to geriatricians, geriatric psychiatrists, and nursing home directors.

At the start, the ElderCare sales force sold four other drugs in addition to Risperdal. One was Propulsid, a problematic medicine for
treating dyspepsia. Another was Procrit, the deadly drug for cancer
patients. The other two were Duragesic and Ultram, both opioids.

Gorsky must have known that he was taking a considerable gamble. But if the FDA approved the company's application to sell Risperdal as a treatment for dementia, the timing of the ElderCare
launch wouldn't matter. Years of off-label and illegal sales can become
retroactively legal if a company eventually gets the agency's nod for
them. There is nothing in the law that justifies such a policy, but it is
one that the FDA still stands by. But if you market and sell a drug in
a way that remains beyond the bounds of the law, you are indisput-
ably acting illegally, with fingers crossed.

In a 2010 prosecution memorandum that is part of secret grand
jury files, prosecutors listed several reasons why Johnson & Johnson
knew that establishing a separate sales force to market Risperdal as a
treatment for elderly dementia was illegal.

For one, J & J had asked the FDA just weeks earlier to approve
selling Risperdal as a treatment for dementia. Why seek approval if
it's already legal? Executives also admitted in multiple presentations,
both internally and externally, that treating dementia was an unapproved use. Advisory boards, for instance, were told that dementia
was not an approved use. Such boards are made up of high-profile
doctors that the company wants to impress, and these doctors are
familiar with the FDA drug-approval process. Admitting the obvious
to them may have been inescapable.

Two years later, studies would prove that Risperdal's risks in children and the elderly were indeed severe. So, despite J & J's repeated
and increasingly desperate attempts to salvage its marketing efforts to
the elderly, the FDA would remain implacable.

. . .

BEYOND DOCTORS, MEDICAID DIRECTORS, AND PATIENT ADVOCACY organizations, Johnson & Johnson needed another major player in the system to ensure that sales to the elderly continued to increase: Omnicare.

Located in a bedroom community just across the Ohio River from Cincinnati, Omnicare was by far the nation's largest pharmacy benefit manager—PBM—for nursing homes, responsible for dispensing drugs to 1.4 million long-term care residents in forty-seven states. Two-thirds of these medicines were paid for by state Medicaid programs.

Omnicare was vital to J & J's drug sales for two reasons. First, while TMAP was helpful in mandating Risperdal's use in Medicaid patients, not all Medicaid patients and programs are directly administered by states. Instead, some states hire private insurers to oversee the programs. And while most nursing home patients get their care paid for by Medicaid—nursing homes represent the largest expense of the poverty program—a considerable share of residents are wealthy enough to have private insurance.

Managing the drug benefits for public and private payers is complicated. When a patient walks into a pharmacy with a prescription, that pharmacist must be able to find out instantly the patient's insurance status, copay, and other prescriptions that may conflict with the drug. With tens of thousands of pharmacies scattered across the country and hundreds of insurance programs with their own formularies and copayment plans, this is no easy task.

But once the data management issues are resolved, PBMs must content themselves with earning pennies on every transaction. The companies soon learned that drugmakers like Johnson & Johnson would pay them far more than pennies to nudge patients into getting more expensive medicines.

And when the patients are nursing home residents—many of

whom are in such frail mental and physical health that they are incapable of objecting or asking questions—the nudge becomes a shove. And since nursing home residents take an average of nine prescription drugs at a time, such shoves can be enormously profitable.

Omnicare had a powerful weapon when pushing Risperdal. A law passed in 1987 to discourage the use of antipsychotics as chemical restraints required that every antipsychotic prescription made to nursing home residents be checked monthly by an independent pharmacist. In 1997, Johnson & Johnson and Omnicare signed an agreement whereby J & J paid the Kentucky company kickbacks for every prescription of J & J's medicines they reimbursed, with Risperdal becoming Omnicare's "primary intervention."

So Omnicare used those required monthly checks as a unique opportunity to switch patients from older and cheaper antipsychotics to Risperdal. The very law designed to prevent overprescription of harmful medication thus ended up being co-opted by J & J and Omnicare to push overprescription of an even more expensive and harmful drug. And in addition to encouraging sales for Risperdal, Omnicare also pushed those for Procrit, Propulsid, Duragesic, and Ultram.

Omnicare executives were keenly aware that kickbacks from Johnson & Johnson were not only illegal but undermined almost everything for which the company claimed to stand. When on occasion Johnson & Johnson executives complained about various aspects of the deal, Omnicare executives responded with near incredulity that J & J would aggressively push what was such an obviously illegal and inappropriate scheme even further. And Johnson & Johnson did not want to bite the hand that was feeding it so well. (An executive described Omnicare's ability to switch market share from one drug to another as "scary.") For Johnson & Johnson, the deal with Omnicare was immensely profitable. One company executive calculated that every $1 million in kickbacks to Omnicare generated $3.4 million in sales—a nearly fourfold return on investment. Drugs like Risperdal have profit margins in excess of 90 percent.

And for Omnicare, kickbacks provided 60 percent of the company's profits, demonstrating just how remunerative it is for players in America's health insurance system to increase rather than control costs—even when the company's entire stated purpose is to push in the opposite direction.

But by 2001, when the two companies inked their second four-year contract, storm clouds were brewing.

AS A RESULT OF A MASSIVE (AND MASSIVELY MISLEADING) ADVERTISING campaign and frequent visits from ElderCare sales reps, and despite a growing list of competitors, Risperdal soon dominated the elderly market, with 89 percent of the drug's use in those over sixty-five being in patients without a diagnosis of schizophrenia. Indeed, half of Risperdal's elderly patients—a far larger share than with any other similar antipsychotic—were given the drug to treat dementia. Not only was Risperdal not approved for this use, trials had already clearly demonstrated using it in this manner was notably unhelpful.

On January 5, 1999, Lisa Stockbridge of the FDA's Division of Drug Marketing, Advertising, and Communications wrote Johnson & Johnson to say that its ads about Risperdal's benefits for the elderly were misleading, which meant they were illegal.

"Presentations that focus on this population are misleading in that they imply that the drug has been found to be specifically effective in the elderly population," Stockbridge wrote. "Risperdal is indicated for the management of manifestations of psychotic disorders," she continued. "However, Janssen is disseminating materials that imply, without adequate substantiation, that Risperdal is safe and effective specifically in treating hostility in the elderly."

Fifteen days later, the agency formally rejected the company's application to sell Risperdal as a treatment for dementia, a move that considerably increased the legal risks associated with the company's ongoing efforts to do just that.

Gorsky's decision to establish the ElderCare sales force in 1998 could no longer be explained away as a minor problem of timing. As prosecutors later pointed out, these sales reps were now pitching Risperdal for a use that the FDA had explicitly rejected.

Three months before the FDA's rejection, Gorsky had been promoted to become Janssen's vice president for sales and marketing. He now had full responsibility for selling Risperdal, Duragesic, Propulsid, Ultram, and other drugs. Sales to the elderly were growing faster than those to almost any other patient group and would soon comprise more than a quarter of Risperdal's prescriptions. If Gorsky closed down the ElderCare sales force, Risperdal's sales growth might stall and perhaps even decline.

So instead of shuttering ElderCare, in 1999 Gorsky expanded it to 136 people. The company's Risperdal business plan for the year 2000, which Gorsky approved in July 1999, envisioned the company's sales reps making 707,000 calls on doctors throughout the country and giving $51 million in grants—a pleasant-sounding term for what were often simple payoffs. The drug's two key growth areas, according to the plan, were dementia in the elderly and use among children, both illegal.

By the end of 1999, Risperdal's sales were $892 million annually—a fivefold increase from 1994.

CHAPTER 23

A Big Target

W HEN CHILDREN BECOME EXCEEDINGLY DEFIANT OR VIOLENT AT
school these days, a suspension is often followed by the intervention
of a mental health professional. If the child's behavior continues,
poor grades or school expulsion may follow. Some of the children are
variously diagnosed as having attention deficit hyperactivity disorder
(ADHD) or conduct disorder (CD).

The temptation in many such cases to prescribe antipsychotics
can be strong because, unlike antidepressants and some other psychiatric medicines, their effects are immediate and profound. These
drugs were originally called "major tranquilizers."

This was Johnson & Johnson's target, and it was a big one. The
company estimated that drug sales in 2000 for just this pediatric use
would reach $821 million annually in the United States alone. So the
company sponsored clinical trials to assess Risperdal's effect on conduct disorders.

More than half of children given Risperdal in clinical trials reported feeling tired and sleepy. Nearly a third experienced headaches,
one fifth vomited, and one sixth suffered stomachaches. Of course,
kids who are sleepy, headachy, or queasy tend to stop lashing out.
Since, in clinical trials, the benefits of the drugs are measured by a

reduction in behaviors such as "talks back to teacher, parents, or other adults," "stubborn, has to do things own way," and "disobedient," it wasn't hard to claim Risperdal was doing as promised.

But tranquilizing children over even modest periods of time can have serious consequences, like reduced life expectancy, obesity, diabetes, and permanent motor disorders. Children gain on average between four and six pounds every month while taking Risperdal. A few months of drug use leads many to become grossly obese, weight that many find impossible to lose. In rare occurrences, children suffer heart attacks, strokes, and sudden death—the very risks that make Risperdal so deadly in the elderly.

To their credit, FDA officials were deeply skeptical of J & J's plans to make Risperdal the drug of choice in defiant children, characterizing the range of behaviors that J & J targeted as "aggressive behaviors that annoy others." FDA officials were also so worried that Risperdal's hormonal effects would interfere with normal childhood development that they asked Johnson & Johnson to conduct animal studies first to assess how the drug might hinder maturation. The company refused.

AROUND THE TIME AUSTIN PLEDGER TURNED THREE, HIS MOTHER, Benita Pledger, took him on a visit to her sister in Illinois. The sister took Austin along with her one morning on her rounds as a school bus driver and returned home with a sobering observation: "I think Austin is autistic."

"I was shocked," Benita Pledger recalled. "I mean, what is that?"

Her sister noticed that Austin seemed disconnected from other children and hadn't responded appropriately to adults. Back home in Alabama, Austin was officially diagnosed as autistic by a pediatrician just before he began kindergarten—a label that got Austin special help from the local elementary school.

"He could recite the alphabet from a poster at school, sing songs in English or even Spanish that he had heard once," his mother said. "But he couldn't read 'cat.'"

Most worrisome were Austin's unpredictable rages, when he would suddenly erupt into fits of confusion or anger and bang his head against the floor, bite his hands or arms, or hit other students. "He couldn't handle any change," his mother said. "Even moving from one room to another might set him off."

Benita soon quit her job as a machinist at a paper mill. She wanted to be there in case something happened at school. Her husband worked at a car repair shop a brief walk from their home. They were not going to let Austin down.

"We had tried thirteen years to conceive Austin," Benita Pledger said. "He was a gift."

In April 2002, as Austin was nearing the end of first grade, Benita had a meeting at the school with the second-grade team scheduled to be working with Austin in the fall. A teacher's aide suggested she take Austin to see Dr. Jan Mathisen, a pediatric neurologist in Birmingham.

"I figured we'd drive into Birmingham [about fifty miles] to see this guy," Phillip Pledger said. "But if he prescribed some drugs right off the bat, that would be a negative. We weren't looking for drugs just to calm him down."

But Mathisen reassured them, and he spoke about Austin in a way that resonated.

"He explained that Austin cannot read any cues," Benita said. "That it's as if this wonderful, sweet boy who knows so much has landed in a foreign land and doesn't understand the language and the social cues. It mystifies him and then it frustrates him."

Mathisen did not prescribe medication but told them it was something to consider. "He told us he had started giving some patients something and it seemed to work, but he did not push it on us," Benita said. "He told us to think about it."

Within weeks, Austin's frequent outbursts had begun to really trouble the Pledgers, and they agreed that it was time to consider taking the next step. Benita brought Austin to Mathisen again on June 17, 2002, and this time she said she was ready to try medication.

A month earlier, a J & J salesman had made his first sales call on Mathisen and spoke about the benefits of using Risperdal for children with behavior disorders. The salesmen left behind 140 starter packages meant for children.

A few weeks later, a different J & J salesman visited Mathisen and left even more samples. Over the next two and a half years, this salesman visited Mathisen twenty more times and dropped off thousands of child-sized doses.

Mathisen explained to Benita Pledger that Risperdal would not cure Austin but would take the edge off his darker moments. But he warned that it would likely cause some weight gain.

"We were okay with that," Benita Pledger said. "Austin was pretty thin, and I'm big on healthy foods, so we thought we could handle that."

Still, the Pledgers remained worried. Before starting Austin on the drug, Benita and Phillip Pledger read through the drug's physician prescribing label, a complicated document. And they twice called a hotline number listed on the label to ask about the drug's side effects. They were told to talk to their doctor.

On June 20, 2002, the Pledgers put a 0.5 mg dose of Risperdal into a glass of water and asked Austin, seven, to drink it. By then, nearly two years had passed since Johnson & Johnson had received the interim results from a study about which Austin's parents needed to know. What would happen to Austin Pledger was horrifying—and once again, J & J had known it might happen.

AUSTIN'S PRESCRIPTION WAS PART OF AN EXPLOSION IN THE USE OF antipsychotics in children. From 1994 to 2003, the number of American children and adolescents treated for bipolar disorder increased fortyfold. In 2003, about eight hundred thousand children were treated for the disorder, or about 1 percent of the population under age twenty—a share that continued to increase.

Dr. Mark Olfson of the New York State Psychiatric Institute at Columbia University Medical Center told Benedict Carey of *The New York Times* that no other psychiatric diagnosis had ever increased that rapidly. "I have been studying trends in mental health services for some time, and this finding really stands out as one of the most striking increases in this short a time."

The increase made bipolar disorder more common among children than clinical depression. Psychiatrists made almost 90 percent of the diagnoses, and two-thirds of the young patients were boys. At that time, more than a third of the nation's psychiatrists were serving as part-time sales reps for makers of antipsychotic medicines, and most of the rest were taking significant gifts of food, travel, and other valuable items. The Pied Piper of this vast increase in bipolar diagnoses was a fiercely confident psychiatrist named Dr. Joseph Biederman of Harvard University.

Biederman was born in communist Czechoslovakia in 1949, and his parents took him to Argentina when he was six months old. He graduated from the Faculty of Medical Sciences in Buenos Aires and got an internship at Hadassah University Hospital in Jerusalem. He went to Harvard-affiliated Boston Children's Hospital for more training and rose through the ranks.

Like almost every other prominent psychiatrist of his age, Biederman's success depended largely on his close relationship with drugmakers, which funded much of his research and paid him to deliver talks about his findings. But he was also beloved by patients and their parents alike.

While many prominent psychiatrists pass off their most difficult patients to junior faculty, Biederman insisted on treating them himself. He often gave parents his home phone number in case of emergencies. His concern for them was heartwarming and real.

Charismatic and persuasive, he did more than any other person to convince the field of psychiatry that bipolar disorder—which, like schizophrenia, had long been thought to appear only in adulthood—afflicted children as young as one and two years old. And that the condition could be effectively treated with cocktails of powerful medicines that often included Risperdal and other antipsychotics.

While Biederman could be charming, he also could be demanding and tempestuous—especially when he didn't get paid the money J & J had promised him. "Dr. Biederman is not someone to jerk around," John Bruins, a company liaison to top academic figures in New England, wrote after Biederman said he'd been shorted $3,000. "He is a very powerful national figure in child psych and has a very short fuse."

Johnson & Johnson quickly paid Biederman the missing $3,000, and Biederman was soon pitching the company on a multimillion-dollar investment in his center that he promised would increase Risperdal's sales.

As an email from a top J & J executive explained, Biederman had "approached Janssen multiple times" to ask that the company fund a center named for it to study bipolar disorder in children. Biederman promised that if Johnson & Johnson invested in his research, the study results would increase the company's sales. When asked about this in a deposition, Biederman said: "We were talking to an interlocutor that was a commercial entity, so there has to be something for them."

The company gave the Harvard team $2 million for the center and spent beyond that to hire Biederman to give talks about his results. The investment paid huge dividends, as the Harvard group published findings from a string of drug trials from 2001 to 2006 that seemed tailor-made to make Risperdal appear as beneficial as possible.

The trials were as primitive as the office experiments from the Victorian era. Yet medical journals like *The Journal of the American Academy of Child and Adolescent Psychiatry* dutifully published them as "studies," claiming "significant reduction" in symptoms. Not surprisingly, the studies found that giving young children tranquilizers makes them seem more tranquil.

Despite his trials' obvious deficits, Biederman and his colleagues at Harvard succeeded in persuading many psychiatrists and the public that bipolar disorder, a serious condition typically diagnosed in adulthood or the late teens, was epidemic in young children.

Some child psychiatrists watched with alarm as huge numbers of children were given powerful tranquilizers. It wasn't just that Risperdal was largely untested in young children. It was the diagnosis itself. The most rigorous investigation of child mental health, the Great Smoky Mountain Study, found virtually no evidence of mania before the teen years. Nor has evidence since emerged that the children Biederman and his colleagues diagnosed as having bipolar illness carried the disease into adulthood. Biederman and his team were effectively treating a condition that didn't exist—and drawing the entire field into their dangerous game.

"Biederman was a crook," David Shaffer, former head of child psychiatry at Columbia Medical School and the author of a classic textbook on child development psychology, told Dr. Andrew Scull for Scull's book on psychiatry's recent history, *Desperate Remedies: Psychiatry's Turbulent Quest to Cure Mental Illness*. "He borrowed a disease and applied it in a chaotic fashion. He came up with ridiculous data that none of us believed. It brought child psychiatry into disrepute and was a terrible burden on the families of the children who got that label."

Johnson & Johnson—which paid a ghostwriting firm to draft write-ups for some of Biederman's studies—was the vital partner in making Biederman and his theories gain such broad acceptance.

A June 2002 email message to Biederman from Dr. Gahan Pandina, a top member of Johnson & Johnson's Risperdal clinical trial program, included a brief abstract of a study of Risperdal in children with disruptive behavior disorder, the target for which the company was hoping the FDA would approve the drug. The message said the study was intended to be presented at the 2002 annual meeting of the American Academy of Child and Adolescent Psychiatry. Pandina asked Biederman to sign a form listing himself as the author so the company could present the study to the conference, according to the message. Biederman responded that he would "be happy to sign the forms if you could kindly send them to me."

In another planned study presented to the company, Biederman proposed testing Risperdal in preschool children—those under six—and promised before the trial was conducted that its results "will support the safety and effectiveness of risperidone in this age group."

And then there were the continuing medical education classes—known as CMEs—which doctors are forced to take in hopes of keeping them sharp. A secret prosecution memorandum in the Risperdal case explained that most CMEs were typically supported by grants from pharmaceutical companies, which often exerted control over conference content. Most courses are offered either at annual medical conferences in sunny locales like San Diego or in the ballroom basements of nearby hotels. Funding from drugmakers means doctors don't have to pay for the lecture or the food that accompanies it.

Johnson & Johnson took great care in choosing speakers for CMEs. And of the hundreds and perhaps thousands of psychiatrists who participated in this sophisticated disinformation scheme, none offered a more effective or more dangerous sales pitch than Biederman. One of the great advantages he offered, Pandina explained, was that he was viewed as being unbiased. In fact, Biederman was so in J & J's pocket that in at least one presentation he took a direct shot at Eli Lilly's Risperdal competitor, Zyprexa.

Even though Biederman spent years as J & J's most highly paid and effective sales rep for Risperdal, he was eager to preserve his reputation for independence. In 2008 the office of Senator Charles Grassley, a Republican from Iowa, was exploring just how rich the consulting arrangements between drugmakers and academics could be, as well as how forthright academics were about these relationships. When Grassley's staff asked Biederman how much J & J was paying him, his response was less than straightforward.

At first, Biederman and two of his colleagues reported receiving about $150,000 from multiple drugmakers over many years, a seemingly modest amount. But Grassley's office had already heard directly from the companies that they had paid Biederman and two of his colleagues $1.6 million over several years—over ten times more than what Harvard reported. So Grassley's office told Harvard officials that Biederman and his colleagues needed to recheck their disclosures.

The corrected reports the university provided had numbers vastly higher than the earlier ones but still not close to the actual amounts. In just one example, Biederman originally reported no income from Johnson & Johnson for 2001. His corrected form showed that he had gotten $3,500. Johnson & Johnson reported paying him $58,169 that year. Similar discrepancies were discovered with other companies he'd taken money from.

At the time, the policy at Harvard (since changed) was that researchers were forbidden from conducting clinical trials if they received payments of over $10,000 from the maker of the drug being studied. Biederman had clearly broken that rule, and he had done so with children—a population for whom such protections are considered nearly sacred.

In an emailed statement, Biederman said, "My interests are solely in the advancement of medical treatment through rigorous and objective study," and he said that he took conflict-of-interest policies "very seriously." These revelations mattered little to Harvard or to the wider field of psychiatry. After a yearlong investigation into Biederman's faulty income disclosures, Harvard did little to punish him.

The Biederman case demonstrates not only how thoroughly drugmakers can fool an entire medical specialty but how persistent the resulting mythology can be. Despite a cascade of subsequent revelations that emerged during litigation demonstrating his terrible medical ethics, Biederman's studies remain among the most often cited and admired in child psychiatry. Despite helping to author one of the worst pediatric drug disasters in history, when he died in January 2023, he still had his Harvard affiliation and was among the most respected leaders in psychiatry.

Biederman was particularly helpful to J & J as competitors like Lilly's Zyprexa and AstraZeneca's Seroquel sought to dent Risperdal's dominant position. In their first years on the market, none of these drugs had approval to sell to children. All did anyway. With so many sales representatives visiting child psychiatrists and neurologists, the sniping among them got nasty. An important part of sales in such a competitive environment is "counter-detailing," a polite term for trashing the other guy's product. For Eli Lilly and AstraZeneca representatives, a big counter-detailing narrative was that Risperdal had that prolactin problem. Higher prolactin levels can lead boys to develop female breasts—a condition known as gynecomastia—and young girls and boys to start leaking milk.

For boys, the development of breasts is permanently disfiguring, since the tissue never goes away unless removed in a double mastectomy, a serious operation that can leave deep scars. Indeed, Risperdal's FDA-approved prescription label had a precaution that it caused excessive levels of prolactin, adding that "although disturbances such as . . . gynecomastia . . . have been reported with prolactin-elevating compounds, the clinical significance of elevated serum prolactin levels is unknown for most patients." Elsewhere, the label reassured that gynecomastia was a rare occurrence, meaning it happened in fewer than one patient in a thousand. This reassurance was wearing thin, though, and doctors were starting to complain. Given the odds, the more successful J & J was in its push for Risperdal's prescription, the more gynecomastia, and the more likelihood of boys getting double mastectomies.

In hopes of finally and fully dismissing this problem, the company sponsored a yearlong study in mentally disabled children in which researchers were asked to check for gynecomastia by physically inspecting patients' chests at the trial's beginning and then at the three-, six- and twelve-month marks. The study was named RIS-INT-41.

From the start, the ethics of this trial were problematic. Federal rules regarding human research mandate that unless researchers believe the purported benefits of a drug far outweigh any risks, a trial cannot be conducted on children. But helping these children was never the primary corporate purpose of the trial. Instead, the main goal was to see whether they would grow breasts.

Interim results arrived on November 2, 2000, and they were awful. Of the 319 patients enrolled at the time, eleven had gynecomastia, for a rate of 3.4 percent—more than thirty times the rate Risperdal's label warned about. By the time the study was completed, the number of cases of unexpected, permanent breast development climbed to twenty-five—a rate of 8.3 percent.

Despite these dismal results, the company continued the highly questionable study for another full year. Although most of the kids in the study dropped out, the rate of gynecomastia among those who remained jumped to 13 percent.

Ultimately, Johnson & Johnson's study showed that about one boy in ten suffered a permanently disfiguring side effect—one that few parents would knowingly risk, particularly not when Risperdal was the only drug in its class that had this effect and was no more effective than competing antipsychotics.

Risperdal's sales in 2000 totaled $1.08 billion, with Gorsky exceeding the company's goal of $1.05 billion. Much of that success came from selling for use in children—a market that would be jeopardized if the true results of RIS-INT-41 ever got out.

So the company set about burying those numbers, a years-long effort that involved statistical sleights of hand and, when that wasn't enough, complete fabrication. But it worked. Prescriptions for children continued to grow, and every year thousands of boys grew breasts.

In 2000, 1,176,000 Risperdal prescriptions for children were written in the United States, with patients spending an average of three months on the drug, according to company documents. If half were boys, and that is almost certainly an undercount, that meant more than twelve thousand boys were disfigured in that year alone.

FOUR MONTHS AFTER THE DISASTROUS RESULTS OF RIS-INT-41, GORSKY and his team received data in March 2001 from RIS-AUS-05, a trial in 345 elderly nursing home patients in Australia and New Zealand suffering dementia.

Dr. Ivo Caers, the head of the Risperdal clinical development program, told the study's investigators to shelve their plans for a quick announcement of the results. "I am very reluctant to have these data in the public domain that soon," he wrote in an email dated March 22, 2001. The reason was that the patients in the trial given Risperdal had suffered too many strokes and heart attacks—known as cardiovascular disease adverse events, or CVD AEs.

"You may have noticed in the topline results that there are substantially more CVD A.E.'s in the Risperdal group. These are of substantial concern to us and we are reviewing all the narratives of these cases as well as CVD A.E. in our other dementia studies," the email continued. "It is crucial we have a better understanding of these data before we make the data public. I propose to keep this discussion and concern in house, though, until we have better understanding."

The Australian study was the third Johnson & Johnson had conducted in hopes of persuading doctors as well as the FDA that Risperdal could be an effective treatment for Alzheimer's and dementia. These illnesses afflict about half of nursing home patients and 8 percent of the population over sixty-five—a huge market.

The first two of these studies were published in 1999, and company sales representatives had been using them in pitches ever since. But unmentioned in the study publications was the fact that the trials indicated an increase in deaths among those taking Risperdal. The FDA reviewers, however, had noticed, and they told Johnson & Johnson the deaths were worrying.

Now results from Australia made clear the reason for those excessive deaths: a sharp rise in heart risks. The problem became plain when researchers examined the three studies together—something Caers and his team did almost immediately. By May 2001, a company statistician confirmed that there was a statistically significant association between Risperdal use and strokes, heart attacks, and death.

Many seniors dread strokes more than any other affliction. Among their effects are paralysis, fatigue, muscle weakness, balance problems, mental deficits, and an inability to control bowel movements. Strokes can wipe out decades of memories and leave sufferers speechless, bewildered, and bedridden. They can change personalities, leaving those affected irritable and profoundly different. The loss of basic dignity is sometimes their worst toll.

As with the pediatric results received just five months earlier, Gorsky, Caers, and others on the Risperdal team faced a terrible dilemma. From a safety perspective, the company's three trials told them several things conclusively. First, that Risperdal offered little cognitive or behavioral benefit to elderly patients with dementia other than to make them more compliant to caregivers. Second, that it significantly increased their risks of heart attack and stroke. And third, that it was deadly.

The FDA had rejected two years earlier the company's application to sell Risperdal as a dementia treatment in part because of hints that the drug increased deaths. With that problem now proven conclusively, any hope of an FDA nod was almost certainly gone—and with it the belated legal blessing for the ElderCare sales force.

Just as the results from Australia arrived, the company's Risperdal marketing team created a new aid for the ElderCare sales force titled "Primer on Dementia." The new material stated that Risperdal offered an excellent combination of safety and efficacy in treating dementia.

The legal risks surrounding such aids were mounting. They were not only false, but now, in the wake of the Australian results, prosecutors might view them as recklessly and intentionally misleading. But Risperdal was by then the most popular pill for elderly patients suffering dementia. J & J estimated that it controlled more than half of the antipsychotic market among the elderly, and it had no intention of surrendering that dominance.

At a meeting on September 4, 2001, the company's top leaders met to discuss how to resolve the dilemma. Dr. Harlan Weisman, who would within weeks be appointed Johnson & Johnson's top scientist, told the gathering that he thought Risperdal was the most dangerous pill of its kind, according to notes of his remarks uncovered by prosecutors. Continuing to market Risperdal as a treatment for dementia would lead to a huge toll of injury and death, something that the FDA might soon figure out.

A slide set that accompanied the meeting was titled "Risperdal in BPSD"—an acronym for "behavioral and psychological symptoms of dementia." The agenda included four items: "Status of project," "How we can terminate the program," "Ethical, regulatory and commercial implications," and "Alternative proposal."

A big question was how J & J scientists, executives, and sales reps would explain to the medical and advocacy communities that the company had decided to stop asking the FDA for a formal approval to use Risperdal in elderly patients with dementia. For years, many of the company's sales representatives had explained away the company's illegal marketing efforts by saying that formal FDA approval of the drug's use in the elderly was in the offing. Admitting that such an approval was never going to happen might make doctors and even sales reps uneasy.

Then there was the "ethical/moral" slide. Instead of addressing the ethical and moral aspects of illegally selling a harmful drug, it noted that ending the company's marketing of Risperdal's use in the elderly population would "relinquish obligation to patients, caregivers & providers." That is, that J & J had a *moral obligation* to continue marketing Risperdal for the elderly because otherwise the company would be seen as abandoning a needy population.

Gorsky and his team decided to not only continue their sales efforts targeting the elderly but expand them. A new four-year kickback agreement with Omnicare was approved to push sales of Risperdal, Duragesic, and Procrit in nursing home patients. The company increased its investments in continuing medical education classes on using Risperdal to treat dementia patients. And in January 2002, Gorsky directed one of the company's largest primary care sales forces to make pitching Risperdal as a treatment for dementia in elderly patients a primary mission, adding 500 additional sales reps to ElderCare's 136. A month later, Gorsky got promoted to become president of Janssen.

In March 2002, the results of yet another Risperdal study on elderly dementia patients became available, and these were the worst so far. The drug not only proved to be no more effective than placebo in treating dementia, but those getting the drug suffered an even higher incidence of strokes than in earlier trials.

Publication of RIS-AUS-05 and the newest trial would be delayed for years. When the Australian study was finally published, the authors suggested that the fivefold difference in heart events (fifteen in the treatment group and three in the placebo arm) resulted from a problem with randomization—the part of the trial when patients are assigned by chance to receive either Risperdal or a placebo. "Patients suffering a cerebrovascular adverse event had significant predisposing medical risk factors," the study said. "This study, however, was not designed to stratify by risk factor across treatment and placebo groups."

But dementia is itself a significant predisposing medical risk factor for heart events, so every patient in the trial—not just those who suffered strokes and heart attacks, and not just those receiving Risperdal—were by definition at risk. The explanation given in the study for the huge increase in heart problems was disingenuous at best.

In all, Johnson & Johnson undertook seven studies to test the use of Risperdal in treating dementia, and in five of the seven, the drug failed to show any benefit for patients. J & J suppressed this information for years, and in most cases never allowed the studies to be published.

A scientist involved in the March 2002 study complained that "this trial is on its face nearly completely negative . . . Janssen has been sitting on the trial results for a long time. Yet it has a moral and ethical responsibility to publish quickly and in a way that can be understood." Instead, in 2007, the company published a pooled analysis of patients cherry-picked from four separate trials to suggest the drug actually worked.

After studying the issue for sixteen months, the FDA wrote to Johnson & Johnson in September 2002 that the company would have to add a warning to Risperdal's label about the increase in strokes and heart attacks. Through a series of meetings and proposals, the company managed to delay the change until April 2003—two years after RIS-AUS-05 had confirmed the problem.

A RECENT ANALYSIS BY RESEARCHERS AT MEMORIAL SLOAN KETTERING Cancer Center found that between 2000 and 2019, Risperdal and similar antipsychotic medicines caused as many as 1.2 million needless deaths among the elderly. Considering that Risperdal was approved for sale in 1993—seven years before the researchers began their assessment—the death count is a significant underestimate.

To this day, Risperdal and similar medicines kill between twenty thousand and sixty-five thousand patients every year, the Memorial researchers found. By comparison, overdoses involving prescription opioids caused about sixteen thousand deaths in 2020, according to the Centers for Disease Control and Prevention.

There is no document or interview in the grand jury files suggesting that J & J executives knew that their decision to continue marketing Risperdal to elderly patients would contribute to the deaths of more than a million Americans. But undoubtedly they knew the numbers would be substantial. Weisman had been entirely correct when he argued that Risperdal was the most dangerous pill of its kind.

IN THE ENSUING YEARS AFTER STARTING RISPERDAL, AUSTIN SEEMED to have fewer tantrums, though they didn't go away entirely. Some of his improvement was wondrous. Along with impressing his parents with his extraordinary memory—Austin could recite long passages from books by heart—he started being able to read.

But at the same time, he gained a significant amount of weight. Even more worrisome was that the weight was distributed almost entirely in his chest. "He started to get really self-conscious about it," Benita Pledger said, not even allowing his parents to see him without a shirt on.

The weight gain was so terrible that after four years of treatment, the Pledgers decided to switch to a different antipsychotic medicine. Austin stopped gaining weight as quickly, but he still carried a lot of fat on his chest.

"When I was wearing my nightgown at night he looked at me and you could tell he thought he looked like me up there," Benita Pledger said. "Not like the other boys he knew."

In 2011, Benita Pledger was watching TV with Austin when she realized that her son's fat might not be just fat.

"Suddenly a commercial comes on," she said, "you know one of those 1-800 things, and the announcer says something like 'Did your son take Risperdal and develop breasts?'" The announcer mentioned gynecomastia, though I didn't know what that meant at the time. And then there was the 800 number you could call to talk to a lawyer about suing the drug company."

Shaking, she grabbed a pen and quickly wrote down the number. She hustled Austin to bed and then dialed the 1-800 number. She reached a law firm in Texas, and a woman on the line asked her a few questions and then suggested she email a few photos of a shirtless Austin.

Benita Pledger went to her son's bedroom and asked if she could take a few pictures of his muscles.

"So he took off his shirt and flexed," Benita recalled. "He was so proud. Then I asked him to turn so I could take another picture from the side."

The law firm in Texas called back almost immediately.

At a trial that began on January 23, 2015, Benita Pledger was asked to describe Austin's awareness that his body was different from that of other boys.

"I mean, he can see me with my clothes on. He can see my husband without his shirt on. And he knows. . . . He just doesn't have the capacity to ask me why."

Her attorney asked her what she thought as Austin began growing breasts.

"I thought it was the weight gain, and I thought that as long as I kept trying to help him with his weight and exercise, that's all I could do. I would just have to fight the weight as much as possible. I did not know that his breasts were for any other reason than that," she said.

The attorney asked her if she knew at any time that there was a risk her son might develop gynecomastia.

"No. I knew nothing of that," she said. "I did not know boys could develop breasts or [if] it was a side effect from the medicine at all."

Would she ever have allowed her son to be on the drug if she had known of that risk?

"Absolutely not. I— I can— I can't fight breast growth. I felt like with the weight gain, we could exercise. . . . You can't fight something like that. I didn't even know that was a possibility." But J & J had.

CHAPTER 24

Ice Cream and Popcorn Parties

In AUGUST 2003, JOHNSON & JOHNSON LAUNCHED A "BACK-TO-School" marketing campaign for the new M-tab version of Risperdal, which quickly dissolves in a child's mouth.

Sales reps held ice cream and popcorn parties in child psychiatrists' offices and passed out lollipops and Risperdal-branded Lego toys and candy jars. One sales manager explained that "Risperdal popcorn" was intended to "butter up docs."

The intensity of the marketing efforts came about in part because while Risperdal remained the dominant antipsychotic in both the elderly and the pediatric markets, its rivals were growing stronger. In an email to district sales managers, one top executive noted that Abilify, an antipsychotic made by Pfizer, was gaining ground with child and adolescent psychiatrists, "and we need to make sure Risperdal is growing with this customer segment. Let's make it happen!"

In a later deposition on the company's marketing of Risperdal to children, Gorsky claimed there was a distinction between "marketing" and "selling" plans. This supposed distinction has since been cited repeatedly by the company's lawyers.

All of the annual business plans describing in explicit detail illegal efforts to sell to children were, J & J insisted, just aspirational "plan-

202 · NO MORE TEARS

ning exercises," dry runs in case the company won the FDA's approval to sell to children. They argued that these planning exercises had nothing to do with the many sales reps who were visiting thousands of child psychiatrists, dropping off drug samples in dosages intended for children and handing out lollipops and branded Lego blocks.

Some sales reps testified that they visited child psychiatrists and child neurologists because those doctors might on rare occasions treat adults. Jason Gilbreath, a J & J sales rep, pitched Risperdal to Austin Pledger's child neurologist twenty times over two years. He brought the doctor free drug samples in dosage sizes intended for children. But Gilbreath testified that he didn't know the doctor exclusively treated children.

The plaintiff's attorney asked, "You literally had to walk over toys and small people furniture to get in to see him, correct?"

"I don't recall seeing toys," Gilbreath testified. "It's possible they were there. I don't recall seeing them."

Meanwhile, the company was engaged in a high-stakes effort to publish the results of RIS-INT-41 in a way that wouldn't scare away child psychiatrists or alert the FDA that Risperdal's label needed a far stronger warning label about the risks of breast growth in boys.

The first thing executives did was to water down the study's numbers by combining them with results from two other studies. In neither of the other studies had investigators undertaken the kind of close chest examinations conducted in RIS-INT-41. Since children often become grossly obese on Risperdal, breasts can get lost in the folds, so chest inspections are crucial. Not looking for gynecomastia, the investigators in these other studies didn't find it.

Having cherry-picked its studies, Johnson & Johnson hired a statistical analysis firm to run the numbers on gynecomastia and other prolactin-related problems. Unfortunately, the analysis failed to make the problem disappear. The rate of gynecomastia dropped to 5.1 percent in boys—but that was still too high. Worse, an accompanying analysis made clear that there was a statistically significant relationship between the onset of gynecomastia and elevated prolactin levels for children after two months of therapy. That proved that instead of being a random event, the gynecomastia cases had been directly caused by Risperdal.

The first draft of the study gloomily conceded that this was an important result.

Ethical rules of science mandate that, before a meta-analysis is conducted, scientists must create an analytical plan and then publish the results no matter what. Rejiggering the analytical plan after the results have been seen—particularly when those results are disappointing—is unethical. So the company's first draft should have been its last.

But the company rejiggered the analytical plan anyway, though the second draft wasn't much better. Then someone got the idea of excluding all the children who were ten and older. The justification was that kids ten and older were approaching puberty, and breast growth in boys during that time could be a random occurrence. Most of the breast growth in the study had occurred in older boys. They rejiggered things again.

Company scientists presented this analysis to its pediatric advisory board at a November 15, 2002, meeting at the Palace Hotel in New York City. These advisors were prominent pediatricians, and since they were being paid by Johnson & Johnson, they could not be described as independent. But they said they could not agree to an analysis excluding all patients ten and older, and they told the company that a table including every patient had to be in the final publication. In an email dated November 18, 2002, a company executive said the advisors concluded that failing to include such a table "would be hiding data."

So a fourth draft of the paper was written. The main addition in this one was a statistical table—largely ignored in the study's text—that listed the number of prolactin-related adverse events such as gynecomastia in all trial participants. The table was printed alongside the study's now-primary analysis, which, despite the disagreement of the J & J–paid advisors, looked only at children under ten.

But both tables suffered from an almost juvenile sleight of hand in which the ratio of children suffering problems was divided by the wrong number. For the ratio of boys suffering prolactin-related problems, the top number was the number of boys suffering a problem, as it should have been. The bottom number should have been the total number of boys in the study. Instead, the researchers used the total number of all the children in the study, including the girls. This nearly halved the boys' ratio.

Dr. Denis Daneman, a professor of pediatrics at the University of Toronto and one of the study's two co-authors, who only worked part-time for J & J, would later say that he had been tricked.

"They never showed me that table," he said. "There can be no debate about what they did. They crossed the line. What they did in withholding data was unconscionable." (He said he had since donated the money that the company paid him.)

In courtroom testimony, Ivo Caers, the head of the Risperdal clinical development program, later acknowledged that the company not only suppressed the breast data from publication but refused even to tell the FDA about that data despite laws requiring the company to do so. "We decided that is not an analysis that makes sense to send to the FDA," he said.

The lawyer followed up: "You ultimately would want the FDA to see anything that they might interpret to be a red flag, correct? Would you agree with that?"

"No," Caers responded.

"You'd rather make that decision yourself?"

"Yes."

When it was finally published in *The Journal of Clinical Psychiatry*, nearly four years after the company got the results of RIS-INT-41, the meta-analysis study falsely concluded, "Although in some cases prolactin levels did remain above those seen prior to the initiation of risperidone therapy, there is no evidence that untoward effects related to prolactin are likely to be seen at those dosing levels." Once again, J & J had shamelessly buried the truth.

. . .

IN SEPTEMBER 2003, MORE THAN TWO YEARS AFTER J & J LEARNED conclusively that Risperdal was deadly to elderly patients and caused breasts to grow in boys, the FDA sent a letter to Johnson & Johnson ordering the company to place a warning on the drug's label that it and similar medicines could lead patients to become diabetic.

The agency acknowledged that while the science proving whether and how drugs like Risperdal cause blood sugar problems and diabetes wasn't certain, "increased attention to the signs and symptoms of diabetes mellitus may lead to earlier detection and appropriate treatment and thus reduce the risk for the most serious outcomes."

The connection between antipsychotic therapy and diabetes had been known for decades. In 1956, four years after the launch of the first antipsychotic drug, Thorazine, the *Journal of the American Medical Association* published a report about five patients receiving Thorazine who developed diabetes that went away after they stopped taking the drug.

Similar case reports peppered the medical literature in the 1950s and '60s, although they were overshadowed by growing alarm about the permanent and disquieting tics and spasms the drugs also caused. Finally, in 1968, a study went beyond case reports and noted that diabetes rates among patients in a mental hospital had quadrupled since the introduction of Thorazine.

With Risperdal and other atypicals, the association between antipsychotic therapy and diabetes grew stronger. Patients on the newer drugs gained weight faster and became diabetic sooner than they had on the older drugs. But there were clear differences in degree.

The worst of the new class was Lilly's Zyprexa, on which patients ballooned. With Lilly and J & J locked in a fierce battle for antipsychotic supremacy, J & J made the most of this difference by sponsoring multiple observational studies claiming that, while Zyprexa patients became diabetic, those on Risperdal didn't.

The enmity between the Zyprexa and Risperdal teams was intense. The FDA's files are filled with letters from Lilly and J & J complaining about the other's marketing practices. And since both companies regularly and deliberately broke the law, the complaints were usually accurate.

In early 2003, the FDA asked every antipsychotic maker to submit all studies that might shed light on weight gain. At the time, Johnson & Johnson was examining the results of a study showing that children given Risperdal became significantly overweight. The Risperdal team again decided against publishing the results or sending them to the FDA.

With the worst of its data hidden and Zyprexa's even more troubling problems widely acknowledged, J & J executives had some hope that the agency might slap a diabetes warning on the prescribing labels of Zyprexa and perhaps another competitor, AstraZeneca's Seroquel, but not on Risperdal's. Such differing treatment would have been a marketing boon.

In the end, however, FDA officials decided that all of the newer antipsychotics needed identical warnings, and in September 2003 the agency mandated that their makers send similar letters to every doctor in the country warning of yet another life-threatening danger.

The perceived inequities of the letter so outraged the Risperdal team that they undertook something that has never been done before or since: the exact opposite of what the FDA ordered the company. In a letter sent to all doctors, the company claimed that "a body of evidence from published peer-reviewed epidemiology research suggests that Risperdal is not associated with an increased risk of diabetes when compared to untreated patients or patients treated with conventional antipsychotics.

"Evidence also suggests that Risperdal is associated with a lower risk of diabetes than some other studied atypical antipsychotics," the letter continued.

Johnson & Johnson did not, as is customary, clear this letter with the FDA before sending it out. Federal officials were forwarded a copy and six months later—the kind of delay that is routine with the

FDA—sent the company a warning letter mandating that J & J issue a new letter to doctors alerting them of Risperdal's actual diabetes risks and stop promoting Risperdal as less likely to cause the illness than other antipsychotics. The FDA's letter had an air of upcoming legal action should J & J not do as told.

J & J finally sent the commanded letter in July 2004. The missive acknowledged that the company had minimized a potentially fatal safety risk and had made misleading claims in promotional materials. "The FDA did not think we had provided enough information, so that is why further notification was done," explained Carol Goodrich, a J & J spokeswoman.

But for ten months, J & J sales reps had continued to brag that Risperdal—alone among antipsychotics—in no way contributed to this devastating and deadly illness.

Even after sending the corrected letter, the company continued to falsely suggest in marketing messages that Risperdal was protective against diabetes. But it was these very same claims that would ultimately lead to an investigation that likely pushed Gorsky to leave the company, at least for a while, and cost Johnson & Johnson dearly.

CHAPTER 25

A Turning Point

VICKI STARR LEFT HER HOTEL ROOM JUST BEFORE 6 A.M. WITH HER heart in her throat. She had lied to her roommate, saying she was going to the business center to fax a document needed to refinance her mortgage. In fact, she headed to a different room for a secret meeting J & J would never have wanted her to have, and which they would regret forever after.

Starr had been a J & J sales rep for just two years, her huge Oregon territory stretching from Salem to Ashland. A pharmacist, she had spent six years as a sales rep for Eli Lilly, but when an opportunity to switch to Johnson & Johnson presented itself in 2001, she jumped. In her mind, J & J was the biggest, best, and most ethical company in the pharmaceutical industry. She was proud when she got the job.

She arrived just as the company's CNS sales team was fully transitioning to a "Sell to the Symptoms" strategy. Previously, that strategy had been wholly adopted by the company's ElderCare and 500 Gold teams because those sales forces so rarely saw doctors who actually treated patients with schizophrenia.

The CNS team, however, largely visited psychiatrists, who were perhaps more keenly aware than their peers in other specialties that antidepressants were approved to treat depression, anxiolytics to treat anxiety, and antipsychotics to treat psychosis. Telling psychiatrists that antipsychotics treated almost every emotional state was risky.

"We had a big national sales meeting with all the CNS reps across the country, and the new sales message went from talking about a patient with schizophrenia to talking about a patient with a broad spectrum of symptoms," Starr said.

The sales meeting even produced a new acronym: DART, which stood for depression, agitation, and racing thoughts. Speakers told the gathered throng that small doses of Risperdal had been found to hit different receptors in the brain than larger doses, and they showed huge and colorful PET scans of brains to illustrate the concept. These scans couldn't be used in their sales calls, the speakers said—the FDA wouldn't allow that—but the speakers wanted the sales reps to know the science themselves.

"I thought it was fascinating, really cool science," she said. "It was fascinating to see how the drugs could impact the brain on that level. Looking back, I realize that it was all speculative, and it wasn't right."

Once she got home, Starr's district manager offered to provide her an entire binder of studies about off-label uses of Risperdal. Many sales reps received these sorts of binders, which were filled with illegal, off-label sales messages. He told her that she shouldn't hand out any of the studies to her psychiatrists, since doing so would be frowned upon by the FDA. But, he said, she could discuss the findings with doctors if the doctors asked first.

The reps were financially incentivized to use those messages, though they were also later told in formal compliance meetings not to use illegal, off-label sales messages. Johnson & Johnson's lawyers always pointed to those compliance meetings as proof that if sales reps used the illegal messages that the company provided them, they did so in defiance of the company's instructions.

"They tell us to do the right thing, and you can't do this and you can't do that," one sales rep said. "But then they give us these sales goals and challenges that put you in a position where you're afraid if you don't do those things and don't meet your sales goals, you lose your job."

Starr appreciated having the binder. As a pharmacist, she felt that she could understand it. She didn't realize why she was being discouraged from sharing the materials as part of the symptoms-based sales message.

"I knew it was a little shady, but I didn't really connect the dots and think about it in terms of a very vulnerable patient group," she said. "Even just a couple of months before speaking to the lawyers, I knew that these were maybe inappropriate marketing tactics, but I didn't really consider that what they were doing was downright illegal."

She now marvels at her own naïveté. "I was an idealist. I lived in a fantasy," she said. "I thought these people were out there to do the right thing."

The company's pitching and payback schemes didn't bother Starr too much. Instead, the company's culture was the problem. For her, Lilly had been a comfortable fit. Half the sales reps there were pharmacists like her, as opposed to almost none at J & J. If a Lilly district manager suggested something that was obviously unethical, people there would speak up, because they were more knowledgeable, she said.

"But at J & J, I felt like the national sales meetings were somewhere between a football game and some weird religious conference. There was all this chanting. It was creepy," she said. "People were drinking the Kool-Aid."

The money was good, though. Her base salary was $120,000 annually, with quarterly bonuses that added another $40,000, and that was in 2003 and 2004 dollars. The best she could do if she returned to a pharmacy was $120,000 annually, and she'd probably have to work longer hours. But over two years, her discomfort became overwhelming. After she and her husband spent a lot of time talking about it, they eventually agreed they could get along without the extra money.

The final straw was the issue of gynecomastia. Her psychiatrists were telling her they were seeing too many boys with breasts. She relayed the doctors' concerns to her boss and other executives, hoping to get some explanation for the problem and offer her doctors a way to resolve or prevent it. "But they were like, 'No, this doesn't happen.'"

Starr was far from alone in what she was hearing from the psychiatrists she encountered. Internal documents show that J & J executives were acutely aware of how widely held these concerns were among psychiatrists. In 2000, J & J hired a market research company to interview child and general psychiatrists about Risperdal's effects in children. The survey simply confirmed what J & J already well knew about the damage caused by increased prolactin levels, weight gain, male breast development, and lactation. (Especially with the latter, noted one of those surveyed, "everyone panics and we have to stop Risperdal.")

For Starr, the blanket denial of these problems was not just false but immoral. Her nephew and her best friend's son were both taking Risperdal at the time, and she wanted to be certain that the drug was safe.

"That's why I decided to leave," she said. "They were like used car salesmen."

She told a former colleague from Lilly that she was going to quit. He told her they had to meet first. She agreed, and that's when she first heard about filing a whistleblower lawsuit, something her former colleague had already done against Lilly because Lilly had copied J & J's illegal symptoms-based marketing scheme for Zyprexa.

That a Lilly sales rep would be the inspiration for the first Risperdal whistleblower claim against J & J was oddly appropriate. Many of the warning letters that Johnson & Johnson received from the FDA over its Risperdal ads resulted from complaint letters from Lilly. Now it would be prosecutors who were alerted to the company's illegal activity by a Lilly connection.

Starr remained in her job at J & J for a few months to gather evidence. She met with prosecutors, who twice flew her out to Philadel-phia to meet with them. But, unable to stand J & J any longer, she left for a job helping nursing homes manage prescriptions. Soon after the switch, she signed up to attend a conference in Eugene, Oregon, on caring for nursing home patients and learned that a J & J sales team would be there pitching Risperdal as a treatment for dementia (with a free breakfast included for those who attended).

She called prosecutors, telling them that they had to monitor the conference. The Risperdal investigative team decided an agent should fly up to Eugene so Starr could wear a wire.

When she got to the rendezvous room, Special Agent Janet Lange told Starr to take off her blouse. Lange taped a recording device the size of a credit card onto Starr's skin at the small of her back, and then she taped microphones onto her skin around her front.

"She was so nice and professional," Starr said of Lange. "And while she's talking, I'm thinking, 'This is so crazy. I don't even know what I'm doing here.' "

When Starr first decided to participate in a whistleblower lawsuit, she assumed she'd provide some sales aids, emails, and a bit of context and then step away. Wearing a wire for a surveillance operation was nowhere in her plans.

But having returned to the pharmacy side of things, she spent much of her time reviewing the prescription records of nursing home residents being given antipsychotics, as required under the 1987 law. Many of her patients continued to be given Risperdal despite clear evidence that they were already suffering tics, spasms, and other per-manent movement disorders.

Many prescriptions were listed as PRN—an acronym for *pro re nata,* a Latin phrase that means "as needed." That meant the drug was not being used to treat schizophrenia or psychosis, approved uses that require daily and consistent medication. Instead, it was being used on occasion to knock out the loud, unruly, or annoying.

"So I'd write in there that this is an inappropriate use of the med-icine, since antipsychotics should not be used 'as needed,' " Starr said.

"You're using the side effect of the drug to incapacitate the patient. That's totally inappropriate."

Again and again, Starr wrote in patient records that there were more effective and less dangerous alternatives. But she was often ignored, and inappropriate use of Risperdal remained rampant, which made her increasingly angry.

So she went to the breakfast meeting, gulped down a coffee before the presentation began, and then sat quietly and recorded the entire event. She was going to get them.

VICKI STARR WAS THE FIRST OF AT LEAST FIVE WHISTLEBLOWERS WHO filed suit against Johnson & Johnson in 2004 and 2005 alleging that the company was illegally promoting Risperdal for off-label uses. Similar whistleblower claims were filed against Eli Lilly, AstraZeneca, Pfizer, and Bristol Myers Squibb—all for following J & J's lead in marketing their antipsychotics illegally. The equivalent of citizens' arrests, such suits are called "qui tam" cases and have their origins in a law passed during the Civil War that encouraged employees of firms that supplied rancid meat to the Union Army to blow the whistle on their bosses. Whistleblowers are required to show proof that they told their employers about the problems but were ignored or fired. If they prove their cases, qui tam "relators" are entitled to a share of monies recovered.

Although it possessed the power and tools to police the drug and device industries' conduct itself, the FDA stopped using these powers in the early 1990s—the same time that the agency began relying for much of its budget on industry fees. As a result, whistleblower cases became the primary tool to crack down.

Qui tam cases are filed under seal by private attorneys and are so secret that even their targets are supposed to be kept in the dark about the claims until federal prosecutors decide whether to join on the side of the whistleblower. But just as in academic and medical communities, J & J and its counterparts have extensive contacts in the nation's legal circles and almost invariably find out about whistle-blower claims long before they're officially informed.

Word of the growing threat of whistleblower cases involving antipsychotics began to leak out in the spring of 2004. At Lilly, Michael Bandick, the top executive most closely associated with the company's illegal Zyprexa sales effort, was pushed out. A month later, Alex Gorsky left J & J and took a job as the chief operating officer of the American subsidiary of Novartis, a Swiss drug giant, where he would remain for four years before returning to J & J at an even higher executive level.

In December 2004, after an internal assessment found that its gravest legal risks involved its marketing efforts to children, J & J decided that it needed to stop sending sales reps into child psychiatrists' offices and stop paying bonuses based upon prescriptions written to children. A December 13, 2004, internal communication cheerily stated that henceforth, sales reps should ask every doctor they normally visited a qualifying question: "Doctor, do you treat patients who are over the age of seventeen for schizophrenia or bipolar mania?" Anyone who answered in the negative—a group that should have included most of the nation's child psychiatrists and neurologists—would no longer be sold on Risperdal.

Soon enough, the company's lawyers would force a reckoning on its sales efforts to the elderly as well. And that would lead to a cascade of actions that would put Johnson & Johnson in real legal peril.

CHAPTER 26

One of the Most Alarming Warnings

O N APRIL II, 2005, THE FDA ANNOUNCED THAT RISPERDAL AND ITS sister medicines would have to carry one of the starkest and most alarming warnings the agency has ever placed on widely prescribed drugs:

WARNING: INCREASED MORTALITY IN ELDERLY
PATIENTS WITH DEMENTIA-RELATED PSYCHOSIS

See full prescribing information for complete boxed warning.

Elderly patients with dementia-related psychosis treated
with antipsychotic drugs are at an increased risk of death. Risperdal is not approved for use in patients with
dementia-related psychosis.

The warnings were hardly a surprise. Risperdal's drug label had since 2003 carried warnings about heart attacks, strokes, and diabetes—all of which can lead to death. Nonetheless, the announcement removed any wiggle room that executives, drug reps, and doctors may have had about the advisability of the drugs in elderly dementia patients. Not only does Risperdal kill, the warning announced, it also has no proven benefits for elderly patients with dementia-related psychosis.

While Gorsky had left J & J, his legacy in the form of the Elder-Care sales force lived on, with 132 reps spending their days telling doctors that Risperdal was a safe and effective treatment for dementia and Alzheimer's. They had done this for years, even though Risperdal never had FDA approval for this use. But now that the world had finally been told the truth about Risperdal and the elderly, could the company possibly continue to send sales reps into nursing homes to push the drug onto this exceptionally vulnerable demographic?

Of course it would. Johnson & Johnson not only kept the illegal efforts going but gave sales reps two new messages to transmit to the doctors they would continue to meet with. The first was to reassure them that they would never be sued for prescribing Risperdal to dementia patients who subsequently died, because no one would be able to distinguish between those the drug had killed and those who passed away naturally.

In 2010, J & J sales rep Tim Humphries testified to a grand jury that regional business director Roger Golden and district manager Greg Miller told him that the brand team had met with doctors and discussed their concerns about getting sued in connection with strokes related to Risperdal use.

Humphries testified that Golden and Miller said they told the doctors that "it's so rare that—you know, how are they going to prove that? How's an attorney going to prove that Risperdal itself caused that? Versus, you know, an eighty-five-year-old with the risk of stroke in the first place." The two men argued that detecting the cause "would be practically impossible."

The second message was to tell doctors that if they wanted to avoid scrutiny from federal regulators and state medical boards, they should diagnose their dementia patients with schizophrenia. In fact, though the condition is virtually nonexistent, diagnoses of late-onset schizophrenia soared from then on.

These two sales messages proved extraordinarily successful. Risperdal's sales grew 18 percent in 2005, to $3.6 billion, and rose another 17 percent in 2006, to $4.2 billion. To this day, some 21 percent of nursing home residents are given Risperdal and other antipsychotics—mostly to keep them quiet. And in more than half of these patients, doctors diagnose them with schizophrenia— mostly to try to hide what they're doing from the scrutiny of nursing home regulators.

Winston E. Smith, a manager in Lilly's long-term care division, which sold Zyprexa as a treatment for dementia, said that Lilly sales reps didn't even pretend that Zyprexa would help elderly patients. The point of the drug was to knock out the unruly or bothersome so staff could have quieter and easier shifts, he said. As he told prosecutors, "Zyprexa was in nursing homes more for the nursing home staff than for the patient."

In 2009, Lilly agreed to plead guilty and pay $1.4 billion for promoting Zyprexa as a treatment for dementia and Alzheimer's disease. Smith blamed J & J for Lilly's fall, telling prosecutors that he was "confident Lilly began marketing in nursing homes because Janssen was already in that marketplace with their schizophrenia drug, Risperdal."

Nursing homes in the United States use antipsychotics in elderly patients far more than nursing homes in other wealthy countries, mostly because American facilities have lower staffing levels. Some nursing homes, many of them owned by private equity firms, will not accept dementia patients unless they're being prescribed an antipsychotic.

The nursing home industry has been shrinking for years. Part of this is deliberate, as the government, since 2013, has shifted spending to in-home and community-based services, which many elderly people say they prefer. Covid accelerated nursing home closures, as families saw the facilities as death traps. The United States lost at least six hundred nursing homes between 2018 and 2023, and the industry's capacity has for many years lagged behind the growth in the ranks of older Americans.

For the sickest patients, however, these trends are problematic. With fewer beds generally, nursing homes can be picky about whom they choose to serve. This leads to an awful bind for doctors and families. Dementia patients often suffer a bewildering list of illnesses beyond their lost mental acuity, so comprehensive management of their symptoms is so complex that full-time attention is often necessary. But American families often need two incomes just to scrape by. Usually, no one can stay home to make sure grandma takes her pills and doesn't wander off, takes a fall, or sets the house on fire.

So, for some doctors and family members, getting full-time care outside of the home is worth the increased risks of death that antipsychotics bring. Indeed, when the Biden administration began a crackdown on antipsychotic use in dementia patients, some geriatricians complained that their patients were worse off.

In 2023, the Biden administration introduced another rule change to combat the use of antipsychotics to paper over staffing shortages, this one requiring facilities to maintain minimal staffing levels—something 75 percent of nursing homes failed to provide at the time.

To be sure, in some cases family members are quietly hoping their elderly relatives die sooner rather than later. In such circumstances, the effects of antipsychotic prescriptions may even be partially welcome. "This is euthanasia with plausible deniability," said a top FDA official, who insisted on anonymity. Such terrible choices are almost certainly rare exceptions, but for some, the choice is made terrible by economic circumstance. Rich dementia patients are less likely to get antipsychotics than poorer ones, and that's not because rich people love their mothers and fathers more. The poor simply don't have the money for more supportive care.

FOR SOME JOHNSON & JOHNSON SALES REPS, APRIL 2005 WAS A BREAKing point.

"My conscience and convictions are strong enough that I wouldn't do it, and I'm certainly not dumb enough to document it," said one former sales rep. "They told us that most of these people don't actually have dementia. That what they have is late-stage schizophrenia. That this schizophrenia was never diagnosed and now that they're eighty-five it's emerged," the former sales rep said. "It was horseshit, and I wouldn't do it."

By then, this sales rep had become convinced that the company's efforts to sell Risperdal as a dementia treatment were illegal and that he could be arrested if he continued doing so. When his district manager pestered him to adopt the new sales message, he asked her if she was going to take care of his legal defense. She told him they could talk about it later, but instead of an answer he just received further harassment to get with the program.

It's notable that over the past thirty years, it's been the sales reps—not the executives or even the scientists—who have filed almost every whistleblower case against the industry. Many have a moral foundation that their more educated and better-paid supervisors and scientific colleagues seem to lack.

Some said they had head-smacking moments when they finally saw the truth. Mark Hodge, a sales rep who visited nursing homes, testified to the grand jury on November 29, 2007, that he'd been talking to his boss—Michael Monaghan, a regional business director—about the company's routine compliance training, and Monaghan "made a comment that, you know, it's interesting that with all this compliance training, here we are in a division that is entirely off-label." The comment, Hodge said, "was like an epiphany."

Anecia Thedford, who worked as a sales representative in Missouri and Illinois for eleven years, told the grand jury on March 12, 2009, that her managers told her to summarize her sales calls in computerized descriptions as being about schizophrenia, even if "you weren't talking about a schizophrenic patient when you were in front of that doctor."

Comparing the J & J and Lilly grand jury files, J & J was clearly more successful in manipulating its own employees. Many of the documents in the case against Lilly suggest that its employees realized much earlier than J & J's that the company was breaking the law. J & J's employee indoctrination—with constant references to the credo and the 1982 Tylenol poisoning case—proved hard to break. But for some, break it did.

"I was a depressed and broken person from repeated moral injury, and knew I couldn't continue," recalled one rep who left J & J after fully realizing what he was doing by pushing a drug that caused so much terrible harm to children and the elderly. "It was a culture of ickiness."

After quitting, he stopped drinking, and to future bosses at other companies he passionately asserted that he would never do anything illegal—a preemptive insistence that was met with puzzled reassurances. From his drug-pushing experience, he had assumed that corporate America was rife with criminality. But in the two decades since his departure, nothing else has ever come close to the shady tactics of J & J, he said.

"I honestly thought that everything J & J did was what every other company did."

CHAPTER 27

They Knew They Were a Good Company

IN NOVEMBER 2005, SIX MONTHS AFTER RISPERDAL'S LABEL BEGAN carrying a death warning for patients with dementia, Johnson & Johnson finally disbanded its ElderCare sales force. Employees were asked to apply for jobs on other sales forces or in other parts of the company. Some failed to find new positions and were forced to leave the company.

Many of those pushed out said in interviews that they had no hard feelings about J & J, a company they said they still admired. But others suspected that they'd been blackballed specifically because they had protested illegal sales tactics. So they called lawyers and complained. A few of these lawyers got in touch with the Justice Department.

Johnson & Johnson had been the target of criminal investigations many times in the past, and its executives violated the law on a day-to-day basis. But the threatened penalties had always been a pittance, and, with one notable exception in which executives were charged with obstruction of justice after employees destroyed records related to illegal marketing of Retin-A, executives had never faced personal legal peril. This time would be different, prosecutors vowed.

Soon after, the company's rivals began admitting to illegal sales tactics, which they'd all copied from J & J. Bristol Myers Squibb was the first, striking a deal in September 2007 with the Justice Department to pay $515 million because, among other charges, it "knowingly promoted the sale and use of Abilify, an atypical antipsychotic drug, for pediatric use and to treat dementia-related psychosis."

Next came Eli Lilly, which pleaded guilty in January 2009 to criminal charges because it "sought to convince doctors to prescribe Zyprexa to treat patients with disorders such as dementia, Alzheimer's dementia, depression, anxiety, and sleep problems." They paid a whopping $1.4 billion.

Nine months later, Pfizer settled its criminal charges related to Geodon as well as other drugs for an astonishing sum of $2.3 billion.

In each case, lawyers and executives pointed to J & J as the pioneer they had copied. But while prosecutors and investigators saw J & J as the worst of the worst, the company's attorneys refused to concede, claiming that J & J's executives "thought they had a First Amendment right to sell products that they believed in, and they knew they were a good company."

The First Amendment argument was a bold one, but by 2009, breaking the law at Johnson & Johnson had become not the exception but the rule. So finding some sort of loophole for making false promises was more essential than ever. Marketing efforts for nearly all the company's biggest selling drugs and medical devices relied on illegal sales tactics, including physician bribery and false medical claims.

For example, by 2009, company executives knew that Johnson & Johnson's factories in Pennsylvania and Puerto Rico were churning out contaminated bottles of Tylenol, Motrin, Benadryl, and Zyrtec—some specifically for children. The law required the company to inform the FDA, announce a massive public recall of more than one hundred million bottles, and fix the plants. J & J did none of those things. Instead, the company sent secret shoppers to retail stores across the country to buy every tainted bottle they could find—an act federal officials would eventually term a "ghost recall." But the company's manufacturing operations were so dysfunctional that its plants continued to churn out contaminated products, so the total number of contaminated bottles on store shelves actually *increased,* despite the secret shopper plot. The FDA wouldn't learn of the problems until 2010.

The fact that three of J & J's rivals had already paid massive fines for marketing practices identical to the ones they themselves employed—which in fact these other companies had largely adopted from J & J—was immaterial to J & J executives, who saw themselves as untouchable.

On October 23, 2009, a team of Johnson & Johnson's lawyers arrived at the Department of Justice to try to persuade prosecutors that J & J shouldn't be charged. They displayed a 127-page deck of purple slides outlining why marketing Risperdal as a treatment for dementia was appropriate. (J & J's lawyers later sent the slides to prosecutors along with a note insisting that they be kept secret.)

The lawyers' first and most oft-made argument was that a marketing campaign based on symptoms instead of diagnoses was legal and appropriate, and that J & J had years earlier sent the FDA 175 symptoms-based promotional items, to which the agency never objected.

The lawyers further explained that "ElderCare carried multiple drugs, all of which were appropriate for use in the LTC [long-term care facilities] setting." And they argued vehemently that the "actions of a few field sales employees are not evidence of widespread pervasive wrongdoing at Janssen."

Negotiations continued for years because J & J wouldn't budge, and unlike with Renova decades before, the FDA didn't penalize the company while it was under investigation, because the agency was so dependent on the company's financial support. More so than any other drugmaker, the company's legal strategy has been to fight until the end and never back down.

And then on February 21, 2012, Johnson & Johnson announced that its board of directors had selected Alex Gorsky to become the company's next chief executive. Gorsky had returned to J & J from

Novartis four years earlier and was put in charge of the company's device division. His elevation to the company's top job must have startled federal prosecutors in Boston, who filed a brief as part of a discovery dispute over whether Gorsky should be required to appear for a deposition in a civil suit prosecutors had brought regarding J & J's marketing of Risperdal to Omnicare. The brief asserted that Gorsky was "actively involved" in fraudulent matters and that he "has firsthand knowledge of the alleged fraud."

Company executives explained to reporters that an important reason for Gorsky's selection was his role in purchasing Synthes, a large maker of surgical power tools and orthopedic implants that J & J was currently in the midst of buying for $20 billion. J & J bought Synthes because it had offerings in trauma care and child orthopedics that J & J didn't. At the time, this was the largest acquisition in J & J's history.

Synthes was already infamous for conducting among the grisliest recent cases of illegal human experimentation, killing at least five people on the operating table with a liquid cement that surgeons injected into spines. (This was after experiments in pigs had led the animals to die within seconds, and even though the FDA had pointedly told the company not to try anything similar in humans.) Four of the company's executives were sent to prison and the company paid a $23 million fine.

The April 2011 press release announcing the acquisition—issued at the same time the four executives were awaiting prison terms—stated that J & J and Synthes "have very similar company cultures."

At his first annual shareholders meeting as chief executive in April 2012, Gorsky spent more than thirty minutes reading sections of the company credo and telling brief anecdotes that demonstrated, as Gorsky told the audience, how "the credo is so relevant and so essential to who we are."

Three weeks later, Gorsky was forced to sit for the first of what would end up being many depositions as chief executive, this one regarding his central role in the Risperdal saga.

On November 4, 2013, Attorney General Eric Holder announced that Johnson & Johnson and its subsidiaries had agreed to pay $2.2 billion and plead guilty to a misdemeanor to settle its illegal marketing of Risperdal. The government complaint noted that J & J lied about the risks of Risperdal to elderly patients with dementia, lied about its tendency to cause diabetes, and illegally promoted its use in children despite knowing that the drug would cause many boys to grow breasts and both boys and girls to lactate.

Three days later, a phalanx of lawyers from the U.S. Attorney's office in Philadelphia and from Johnson & Johnson assembled at the federal court building in Philadelphia before U.S. District Judge Timothy J. Savage to formally enter J & J's guilty plea. There to admit to the company's crimes was Joseph Braunreuther, a deputy general counsel for the company and a former federal prosecutor.

Braunreuther said that the company "is responsible for the delivery of valuable therapy that changes people's lives around the world, has been and remains committed to improving human life going forward with its therapies—"

But Savage cut him off. "Does it do that from altruistic motive or a profit motive?" the judge asked.

"I think . . ." Braunreuther began.

"You can't make it sound like they are out there doing all of these good works and . . ." the judge began, before Braunreuther conceded that profit was a motive.

Savage continued with a blistering denunciation. "The defendant marketed a drug approved for schizophrenia to elderly patients with dementia and mentally disabled children, which were not approved uses," he said. "It did so despite its clear and unequivocal study showing the drug increased the risk of stroke and fatality among elderly patients suffering dementia. It did so in a calculated manner. It was not coincidental nor accidental. It was intended to maximize profit without regard to risk."

J & J's admission of guilt was a landmark event that led to front-page stories in leading newspapers, in light of the large fine. But the years of delay and prior pleas by competing drugmakers meant that in the mainstream media it was only a one-day story. And the agreement glossed over much of the underlying troubling behavior.

For one thing, though Johnson & Johnson pleaded guilty to bribing thousands of psychiatrists and doctors to prescribe Risperdal in unapproved ways, none of the doctors who actually accepted these bribes and then prescribed the drug, thereby endangering the lives of their patients (and in hundreds of thousands of cases these patients did end up dying), were ever charged. It was just too much work, with too little resources to carry it off. Investigators interviewed psychiatrists who in some cases admitted that they prescribed Risperdal because they were being paid by Johnson & Johnson. But before long, prosecutors gave up on the idea of charging doctors altogether.

No company executives were charged either, although in one secret memorandum, prosecutors listed four executives who could potentially be charged criminally. Gorsky—while mentioned elsewhere—was not among them. The problem, they wrote, was that they had no smoking-gun documents in which executives explicitly instructed subordinates to knowingly break the law. And having well-dressed and seemingly concerned executives at the defense table could blow up the entire case.

Federal prosecutors are famously reluctant to file any charges or undertake any case if there is any doubt that they will win. Company executives routinely consent to guilty pleas and large fines when doing so penalizes only shareholders. It's possible, though, that another, separate reason these prosecutors ultimately decided to stand down may have been their concern that such an aggressive strategy might jeopardize their careers. And it's here where the Johnson & Johnson difference is so profound.

Johnson & Johnson has long been one of the biggest individual patrons of corporate law firms in the world. Between 2010 and 2021, J & J spent $25 billion on litigation, a number that is likely higher than that of any other company in the Fortune 500. Any lawyer hoping to get hired by a big corporate law firm after aggressively targeting

Johnson & Johnson's executives would be confronted with a significant challenge. Almost every prospective employer would either be actively representing J & J or hoping to. These firms would face significant disincentives in hiring someone loathed by J & J.

Dave Hoffman, the first prosecutor assigned to the Risperdal case, left in the midst of the investigation. He went to work for Sidley Austin, a huge global law firm that lists Johnson & Johnson as a client. Then it was assigned to Christopher R. Hall, who left a year later and became a partner at Saul Ewing Arnstein & Lehr, where his specialty is defending drug companies. It was then briefly assigned to another assistant U.S. attorney before landing on the desk of Michael J. Bresnick, who went on to become a partner at the huge national law firm Venable LLP, which also lists Johnson & Johnson as a client.

There is no hint in the investigative files found so far that any investigator, prosecutor, or supervising attorney sought to interview epidemiologists or any other witnesses who could answer the most basic question about the case: How many boys grew breasts and how many elderly dementia patients died as a result of Risperdal use? It's a telling omission.

Had they discovered that the marketing efforts Johnson & Johnson pioneered caused tens of thousands of vulnerable boys to be permanently disfigured, or resulted in more deaths than the opioid crisis, prosecutors' decision to eschew charging doctors and executives might have been difficult to justify.

So instead, they simply didn't ask.

CHAPTER 28

An Epidemic Foretold

THE OPIOID EPIDEMIC (OPIOIDS ARE SEMISYNTHETIC DRUGS DE-
rived from opium) is often said to have started on December 28, 1995,
with the FDA's approval of OxyContin. Dr. Curtis Wright, director
of the agency's office for painkillers, allowed Purdue Pharma to assert
that OxyContin was safer than most other pain-relieving options.

"Delayed absorption, as provided by OxyContin tablets, is believed to reduce the abuse liability of the drug," the pill's approved
package insert stated, even though the small Connecticut drugmaker
provided no evidence to support this utterly false claim.

A year later, Wright took a job with Purdue making nearly
$400,000 a year, and OxyContin quickly became the most abused
opioid ever marketed.

But five years before OxyContin's approval, Wright oversaw the
approval of a fully synthetic opioid that would also feed the epidemic.
Johnson & Johnson's Duragesic is a patch that was supposed to provide a steady supply of fentanyl over seventy-two hours. But from the
start, Duragesic didn't work as intended—something Wright knew
very well.

Both OxyContin and Duragesic used simple timed-release tech-
nologies to make drugs that usually provided pain relief for at most

six hours last much longer. For OxyContin, the trick was a coating around the pill that slowed its absorption. For Duragesic, it was a well of medicine that gradually leached through a bandage placed on the skin.

But both of these slow-release mechanisms could be easily bypassed, allowing patients to receive immediate, intense, and possibly fatal doses. OxyContin could be crushed or dissolved. Duragesic could be chewed.

The FDA would later say it didn't know at the time of OxyContin's approval just how easily its timed-release mechanism could be defeated. But the agency never said the same about Duragesic because Wright foresaw almost everything that went wrong.

A year before Duragesic's approval, Wright asked J & J about "the potential for extraction of fentanyl from used or unused systems." He suggested ways the company could reduce the patch's potential for abuse, including by adding to the patch a bit of naloxone, a medicine that reverses an opioid overdose.

Wright told Johnson & Johnson that Duragesic would "need special precautions to keep this product on target for the cancer pain population." His worry, Wright said, was that "once the clinicians learn that the TTS [Transdermal Therapeutic System] fentanyl system can provide continuous opioid analgesia through the night, that the system will be used in a much broader clinical population than intended."

Wright also pointed out that Duragesic's patch technology was not very good at meting out appropriate doses and that even Johnson & Johnson's studies "indicate that all of the TTS patches deliver more fentanyl than expected . . . on the average, all of the subjects in the studies received 150% of the target dose in 24 hours."

Despite his worries, Wright approved Duragesic in August 1990.

Seventy-five times more powerful than morphine, fentanyl can lead patients to stop breathing and die, which is exactly what started happening even in patients who used it appropriately. On January 14, 1993, a seventeen-year-old Florida boy was prescribed Duragesic after oral surgery. He put on the patch just as his doctor instructed and died in his sleep.

Distraught, Donna Schilling, the boy's mother, started investigating how such a thing could have happened. This was in the pre-internet days, so she had to request from the FDA the file on Duragesic's adverse events. She discovered that between May 1991 and August 1993, fifty-two Duragesic patients had suffered deaths similar to her son's.

She wrote a letter to U.S. senator Connie Mack, a Florida Democrat, who forwarded it to FDA Commissioner David Kessler.

"I am convinced that this drug represents an enormous safety hazard and that its safety risks far outweigh the benefits received from this drug," Schilling wrote.

Kessler responded forcefully and met with Wright and others in the agency's painkiller division. "Dr. Kessler clearly expressed that it was the proper role of the agency to take prompt, firm, and aggressive action," a memorandum summarizing the meeting noted. "He was willing in this (and similar cases) to use the resources of the agency to try to prevent tragedies of this kind, even when the problem was not the safety of the drug as labeled, but the result of misuse."

The memo also suggested that future opioids be given greater scrutiny: "Dr. Kessler then asked that we ensure that we review our plans for other new opioid products subject to similar misuse (such as Fentanyl Oralet) to prevent, rather than remedy, such cases in the future." Had Kessler's advice been followed, the opioid epidemic might have been prevented.

Nonetheless, as a result of Donna Schilling's efforts, the agency slapped on Duragesic's label a black box warning stating that the fentanyl patch shouldn't be used for acute, postoperative, or mild, intermittent pain. And it required Johnson & Johnson to send a letter to every doctor in the country highlighting this warning.

In a press release announcing the change, the FDA quoted Kessler as saying that "there is evidence that this product is being misused in ways that put patients in danger.

"We are taking steps to protect future patients by making sure that the drug is prescribed safely," Kessler said.

About a year later, a new marketing executive took over the Duragesic franchise. His name was Alex Gorsky.

UNTIL OXYCONTIN, OPIOIDS WERE LARGELY MARKETED IN THE UNITED States as drugs for brief use or end-of-life care. Patients got them after major surgery or while dying of cancer. Their addictiveness was so widely understood and feared that few doctors were willing to prescribe them in anything but the most extreme circumstances.

For the first five years of Duragesic's sales, Johnson & Johnson mostly adhered to this tradition. A patch that provides seventy-two hours of fentanyl, Duragesic was given almost exclusively to cancer patients who had trouble swallowing. Sales were modest, and the company's sales reps rarely mentioned Duragesic.

And then, in the last days of 1995, Purdue Pharma launched Oxy-Contin. Coming right out of the gate with an aggressive marketing plan, the company's message was that too many patients suffered chronic pain needlessly, and that addiction fears about opioids were overblown. Along with these messages, the company showered money on doctors, academics, and medical education companies.

The problem for a company marketing its painkilling product to cancer patients is that they often die, limiting sales. But patients with lower back pain, arthritis, or a host of other kinds of chronic pain issues can live for decades. And once they're physically addicted— a common outcome when opioids are used for longer than three months—patients are highly motivated to serve as repeat customers.

"Purdue had a brilliant marketing plan," said Oklahoma attorney general Mike Hunter in his opening remarks during a 2019 trial in which he sued Johnson & Johnson for its role in causing the state's opioid crisis. "They believed there was a huge market that they could exploit, and they could, and ultimately did, make billions by doing it.

"Well, J & J had been in the field," Hunter continued. "They had sales reps here, too. They saw what Purdue was doing and it did not take long for Johnson & Johnson to see their own opportunity. And so sometime in 1997, Johnson & Johnson decided to relaunch or start a new promotion of Duragesic. What they started doing was using Duragesic as something that should be marketed broadly and widely for everyday chronic pain."

Hunter actually underplayed J & J's role in the crisis. An important reason Purdue was so successful so quickly is that J & J had been laying the groundwork for years. Johnson & Johnson's initial efforts to get doctors more comfortable prescribing opioids began in the 1980s, well before Purdue Pharma did so, when it started to shower money on a set of industry-friendly academics and patient-pain organizations. One of J & J's biggest-selling products in those days was Tylenol with codeine (an opioid), and the company's success at making doctors comfortable prescribing it in many ways laid the foundations for the epidemic to come.

The American Pain Society, which a 2018 Senate investigative report would list as a key facilitator of the opioid epidemic, was originally founded with a grant from J & J.

"The necessary conditions for this crisis may have arisen, in part, due to the financial relationships between opioid manufacturers and patient advocacy groups and medical professional societies—the precise terms of which parties to these transactions rarely disclose," the 2018 Senate report stated. "Patient advocacy organizations and professional societies play a significant role in shaping health policy debates, setting national guidelines for patient treatment, raising disease awareness and educating the public."

In late 1996, just as Johnson & Johnson's donations to these groups began soaring, the American Pain Society and the American Academy of Pain Medicine issued a statement titled "The Use of Opioids for the Treatment of Chronic Pain," which the groups claimed was a consensus statement citing the best science endorsing opioids as the most effective option for chronic pain and claiming that the risk of resulting addiction was low. The document sought to overturn decades of unease among doctors about using opioids outside of hospice.

Among the statement's co-authors were Robert T. Angarola, a J & J lawyer, and Dr. J. David Haddox, then a paid speaker for Purdue who would later become a Purdue vice president. Johnson & Johnson and Purdue printed hundreds of thousands of copies and passed them out to doctors around the country.

The consensus statement and Johnson & Johnson's subsequent marketing efforts were designed to get doctors to prescribe opioids to patients who would use them for years. In this, it was a massive success. "This document may be one of the single most damaging documents when we look back at the history of our opioid crisis," Dr. Andrew Kolodny, one of the nation's top experts in the opioid epidemic, testified in 2019.

"Our objective is to convince physicians that Duragesic is effective and safe to use in moderate to severe chronic pain such as back pain and degenerative joint disease like osteoarthritis," the company's 2002 Duragesic marketing plan stated. To do so, J & J promoted Duragesic as having a lower incidence of constipation, wooziness, and other functional impairments than oral opioids like OxyContin. All these claims were false.

In a March 1998 letter, the FDA told Johnson & Johnson that, far from being easier to take, Duragesic patients tended to report worse side effects and poorer pain relief than those taking pills.

The company "failed to disclose that the incidence of abdominal pain, dyspnea, and sweating were markedly higher with the use of fentanyl transdermal system and that more patients required rescue medication with the use of Duragesic than with the use of sustained-release oral morphine," the agency wrote.

The FDA further warned that the company's marketing tag line ("It stops the pain. Not the patient") was false and misleading because it implied that Duragesic was "not associated with impairment of mental or physical abilities," even though the patch's official prescribing information had a precaution that patients often suffered impairment of mental or physical abilities needed for potentially dangerous tasks like driving.

For motivation, J & J sent reports to its sales staff highlighting OxyContin's sales numbers and strategies. J & J was so enamored of OxyContin's success it created an initiative called "Project Pearl," exploring a partnership with Purdue to co-promote Duragesic and OxyContin. The idea was that the two drugs could be "positioning all brands in a relevant way to physicians" and proposed to "mirror Purdue and Janssen sales forces."

Then, in February 2001, Barry Meier of *The New York Times* wrote a landmark story detailing OxyContin's devastating impacts in Appalachia. Instead of seeing OxyContin's travails as a cautionary tale, though, Gorsky and his team saw an opportunity.

CHAPTER 29

Opium Blossoms in Tasmania

T ASMANIA IS AN ISOLATED AND ENORMOUS ISLAND OFF AUSTRALIA'S southeastern coast with spectacular natural beauty but an economy that has long struggled. One answer for its economic difficulties was a collaboration in the 1960s between Glaxo, a predecessor of Glaxo-SmithKline, and the Tasmanian Department of Agriculture to test whether the local climate—cool and wet—was suitable for the cultivation of opium poppies.

It was: Poppies grew like gangbusters. Cool springtime temperatures were ideal for the flowers' initial growth, while drier air in the summers meant there was little need for expensive post-harvest drying. Farmers on Tasmania's northwest coast soon learned that poppies were perfect for seasonal rotation with vegetable crops, while those in the island's midlands and south cycled them between wheat and other cereals.

Opium production is traditionally a labor-intensive process in which workers lance poppy pods and then return later to scrape off the latex gum—raw opium—that bleeds out of the cut. In Tasmania, Glaxo discovered that it could employ heavy machinery instead of manual labor at every step in the process by harvesting the entire flower and stem, not just the gum. Glaxo converted an abandoned milk powder factory into a processing facility and recruited hundreds of small farmers as growers.

Because of the obvious potential for abuse, legal cultivation of opium poppies is governed by international and national laws that strictly limit how much acreage can be devoted to the plant, and where. Glaxo was able to get legislation passed in Australia legalizing its Tasmanian operations in part because of the island's isolation.

In 1975, Abbott Laboratories and a Polish firm called Ciech Polfa took advantage of Glaxo's work to establish a second Tasmania-based opioid production company, Tasmanian Alkaloids. As sales of the combined Tylenol and codeine pill soared in the 1970s, Johnson & Johnson bought Tasmanian Alkaloids in 1982 and built a new codeine plant in Westbury, a local town.

With J & J's financial muscle behind it, Tasmanian Alkaloids blossomed and was soon making far more supply than the Tylenol franchise needed. J & J began supplying other companies with the active ingredient for their opioids, a market that exploded after the company successfully lobbied the American government to lift restrictions on opioid imports.

J & J soon became the largest supplier of the active ingredient in opioids in the United States, responsible for providing enough for about half of all opioid pills sold. Among its American customers was Purdue Pharma.

THE EARLY 1990S WERE POOR YEARS FOR JOHNSON & JOHNSON'S TAS-manian opioid cultivation business. Duragesic's fentanyl was a synthetic opioid made from chemicals, not poppies, and opioid prescriptions in the United States had barely budged for decades. Indeed, the amount of land devoted to opium poppy cultivation in Tasmania fell between 1991 and 1993.

But in 1994, the mood rapidly shifted. Executives at Purdue told their counterparts at Johnson & Johnson that Purdue was soon going to need a lot more supply—so much more that the land available in

Tasmania for opium production might not suffice. Purdue Pharma had just submitted its application to the FDA to sell OxyContin.

Realizing that demand for opioid production was likely to sky-rocket, Johnson & Johnson needed to find a way to harvest more opioids out of each acre of poppies. It decided the best way to do that was to start a years-long research effort to engineer a new poppy, one with far higher yields.

Johnson & Johnson was soon screening a thousand seedlings a week, only a tiny fraction of which made it to the second round of testing. Those that passed the second round were even more rare.

The production of oxycodone, the opioid present in OxyContin, requires an unusual mix of alkaloids, including one known as thebaine. So Johnson & Jonson's screening program focused on finding plants that produced high levels of thebaine. After more than a year of looking, the company settled on the 233rd plant that made it through two levels of screening. Called Norman, this poppy had a recessive gene that coded alkaloid production that didn't include morphine, a dominant constituent of most opium latex. Instead, the mutant produced almost nothing but thebaine.

In 1996, farmers in Tasmania planted about five hundred hectares of Norman poppies, a number that increased between 50 percent and 100 percent every year thereafter.

"The development of the Norman poppy coincided with the release of a slow release formulation of oxycodone in the USA," Anthony J. Fist, a J & J agricultural scientist who invented the Norman poppy, wrote in a 2002 paper. "The new formulation was very successful, and there was greatly increased demand for the thebaine raw material used for its manufacture." The paper further described the development of the Norman poppy as a "major turning point in alkaloid production" that would not have happened if not for the expertise that Johnson & Johnson brought to opioid production.

The result of this genetic work was that Australia and Johnson & Johnson came to dominate the production of the crucial ingredients needed to manufacture opioids. Australia's alkaloid yield per acre soon became eight times greater than Turkey's, twice Spain's, and 30 percent higher than France's.

Even with these efficiencies, Johnson & Johnson could barely keep up with the exploding demand from its partner, Purdue Pharma, and eventually from other companies producing opioids, such as Mallinckrodt. Tasmanian acreage planted with poppies almost tripled between 1993 and 2000.

To make sure that kind of production was kept up, J & J began offering incentive payments, such as all-expense-paid vacations and luxury cars, to its Tasmanian farmers. Fields of carrots and cauliflower were replaced with carpets of pink, white, and mauve poppies. Black Mercedes sedans began appearing in front of red barns. One company accountant joked that the economics of opium production was such that the company could give each farmer a 747 and, if it resulted in more poppy acreage, the incentive would still be worth it.

Eventually, seventy-four thousand acres of Tasmania's arable land were devoted to poppies. In the United States, Johnson & Johnson soon supplied 65 percent of the country's oxycodone, 54 percent of its hydrocodone, 60 percent of the codeine, and 60 percent of the morphine.

In a letter that Johnson & Johnson sent to Purdue, J & J promised that if Purdue signed a long-term supply agreement with Noramco—its American subsidiary that turned its Tasmanian supplies into opioids—then J & J would provide Purdue everything it needed to sell OxyContin around the world.

The intense back-and-forth between J & J and Purdue reflected Purdue's abiding worry that supply constraints would impede OxyContin's explosive growth. In one letter, Michael Friedman, Purdue's chief executive, wrote that "the principle barrier to a higher sales achievement before year-end is product supply."

J & J executives sought to put those fears to rest by promising to invest millions in facilities to provide all the opioids that Purdue would ever need. Two months later, the two companies signed a four-year agreement in which Johnson & Johnson agreed to supply not only all of Purdue's needs for thebaine but also that of Mallinckrodt.

David Kessler, the former FDA commissioner, said in a deposition that without J & J's extraordinary efforts in Tasmania, the United States would not have experienced the explosion in opioid prescriptions that it did.

CHAPTER 30

Less Prone to Abuse

Euphoria envelops your body in a warm, cozy hug. Problems dissolve. Limbs tingle. Life feels perfect.

These are the sensations that drug addict Christopher Coughlin says he felt using OxyContin, a highly addictive opiate that is sweeping Maine, from the streets of South Portland to the rural communities of Washington County.

"It's more addictive than any pill I know of," said Coughlin, a 32-year-old convicted drug dealer serving eight years in state prison. Coughlin was caught in May with a gym bag full of heroin and OxyContin.

"There's a lot of it on the street right now," he said. "It's the drug of choice . . ."

This was the beginning of a story published on July 30, 2000, in the *Portland Press Herald*, Maine, about the soaring abuse of Oxy-Contin. Two weeks later, a similar story appeared in *The Roanoke Times* about increasing rates of addiction in Virginia. More stories followed in newspapers in New Orleans, Charleston, Asheville, and Cincinnati until *The New York Times* did its version.

Thousands of stories and an entire shelf of books have since been written about the opioid epidemic, but it's remarkable how many of the crucial elements of this uniquely American disaster—payments to doctors, FDA failures, co-optive patient advocacy, and Sackler wealth—were captured in those first pieces.

That the epidemic nonetheless continued to build despite the press's strident warnings is one of the most astonishing governance and law enforcement failures in American history. And one of the principal reasons for this failure was the actions of Gorsky and his team at Johnson & Johnson.

Purdue first built OxyContin into a sales and addiction juggernaut in large measure because the company promised doctors that OxyContin was less addictive than other opioids. The press quickly proved that this promise was false, and this reality check had a profound impact on OxyContin's sales. Until February 2001, OxyContin's prescriptions were steadily rising every month. After the first wave of stories, they plateaued.

But in OxyContin's place, Duragesic's prescriptions soared. And a big reason was that Johnson & Johnson began making the very same false promise to doctors that had worked so well for OxyContin: Duragesic isn't addictive.

Today, almost everyone has heard of fentanyl, but back then, most Americans would not have been able to tell you what it was, or what it did. Duragesic's fentanyl is seventy-five times more powerful than morphine, and far more addictive and dangerous than the medicine in OxyContin. The reason J & J could somewhat believably claim that it wasn't addictive was a quirk of the Drug Abuse Warning Network, a hospital surveillance system widely known as DAWN. Overseen by the U.S. Substance Abuse and Mental Health Services Administration (SAMHSA), DAWN is a report that aggregates tests taken in hospital emergency rooms showing the presence of opioids in patients' urine.

As OxyContin abuse soared, so did the numbers in DAWN. But DAWN had a crucial weakness: the urine tests that hospitals generally conduct don't detect synthetic opioids like fentanyl, so DAWN can't be used to track illnesses or death from fentanyl abuse.

It's a weakness that SAMHSA often warned about. Internal emails show that J & J executives were aware of this. Johnson & Johnson's own Chronic Pain Scientific Advisory Board unanimously told the company in 2001 to stop citing DAWN as proof that abuse of Duragesic was low.

"Over-promising on the lack of abuseability is what got OxyContin in trouble. Duragesic should not repeat the same mistake," the board stated.

But with OxyContin the subject of so much press attention about addiction and abuse, selling Duragesic as a no- or low-abuse alternative became J & J's most successful strategy.

Every Duragesic business plan between 2001 and 2004 said that the product's strength and point of differentiation in the marketplace was that it was minimally addictive. Bad press for OxyContin was good for Duragesic, and abuse concerns for oral opioids were the primary driver of increased Duragesic sales.

A study by the management consulting firm ZS Associates found that worries about abuse were "the main reason for decreasing OxyContin" and that "lower abuse potential and fewer peaks and troughs are the most commonly cited reasons for increasing prescribing of Duragesic." Sales aids provided to reps in 2002 and 2003 cited DAWN data to falsely claim fentanyl accounted for less than 1 percent of emergency room visits, stating that "physicians should not let concerns of physical dependence deter them from using adequate amounts of opioids in the management of severe pain when such use is indicated." At trial in Oklahoma in 2019, prosecutors read through dozens of notes written by sales reps describing their interactions with doctors, and in call after call the sales reps referred doctors to DAWN data to prove that Duragesic had little risk of abuse or addiction.

In 2002, McKinsey & Company, perhaps the world's most famous management consulting firm, recommended that J & J do a better job selling Duragesic as an unapproved treatment for chronic back pain, a huge market. The firm added that Johnson & Johnson needed more patients under the age of forty, and singled out as the best business prospects those who were at high risk of abusing opioids. "Target high abuse-risk patients (e.g., males under 40)," the McKinsey report instructed. Another goal was to extend the average treatment period. Both strategies ensured soaring addiction and death rates.

In the middle years of Gorsky's career, his success in making Duragesic such a blockbuster was cited as among his greatest accomplishments. Later, Duragesic disappeared from his career highlights.

Under Gorsky's direction, J & J put together a sophisticated targeting system for doctors, with those writing the most OxyContin prescriptions receiving the most sales calls. One 2000 memo to the sales force said that Duragesic sales pitches should be focused on the eight thousand doctors in the country prescribing the most opioids "with an even greater emphasis being placed on the top 1,000 who account for 20% of all the dollars in the pain market."

Some of these doctors were running obvious pill mills, with parking lots filled with out-of-state license plates and mobs of desperate-looking addicts in clinic hallways. Sales reps knew exactly what these doctors were doing because Johnson & Johnson had precise reports summarizing doctors' prescriptions. A September 2002 presentation noted that, like OxyContin, much of Duragesic's sales came from a fairly small group of doctors. Four doctors wrote at least 1,442 prescriptions of the highly addictive patch each year. As a result, the reps knew where to go and who to target. In doing so, they were visiting the blazing heart of a raging epidemic of abuse and pouring gas on the flames.

Purdue Pharma executives could hide behind a fig-leaf explanation that initially they didn't know their aggressive marketing schemes for OxyContin would lead to so much death. And then once the money was pouring in, the company became too addicted to the profits to stop. Purdue was a one-trick pony. There was nothing else on which to fall back.

Gorsky and J & J had no such fig leaf or dependence. They copied Purdue's strategy after the resulting death toll was clear. And they did so for products that collectively represented a fraction of Johnson & Johnson's total revenues. J & J didn't need Duragesic, Noramco, or the rest of its opioids franchise to thrive.

A host of Hollywood and literary renderings have portrayed Purdue as the paragon of sociopathic corporate greed. Purdue was certainly bad, but it's far from being the worst offender in the pharmaceutical industry.

BRANDED DRUG COMPANIES ARE SO ADEPT AT DELAYING THE LAUNCH of cheap generic competitors that their actions rarely merit much media attention, even though these efforts cost consumers billions of dollars.

Purdue Pharma managed to do this with OxyContin by reformulating the pill just before its patent expired and then persuading the FDA to declare the old version of the pill—the one that both Purdue and the FDA had insisted for nearly two decades was perfectly fine—too unsafe to allow generic versions to copy.

Johnson & Johnson needed a similar strategy for Duragesic, which by the time of the product's original patent expiry in 2003 had become a $1.6 billion seller, with sales cresting at $2 billion in 2004. The low-abuse message and physician targeting had certainly worked. Of course, as the drug's sales surged, so, too, did the number of deaths and abuse reports linked to Duragesic. But that was of no real concern. Generics were.

To protect its turf, the company adopted a widely used industry playbook.

First, Johnson & Johnson sued Mylan Labs, which had filed to sell a generic version of the Duragesic patch. The litigation delayed the launch of Mylan's competing patch until 2005.

Delaying Mylan just a year was enormously lucrative, given the strength of the market; even a delay of a month meant tens of millions of profits that otherwise might have been lost. But stalling Mylan's launch was just a first step. Next, J & J developed a marketing plan to smear the Mylan version. This campaign highlighted the fact that Mylan's patch used "matrix" technology, wherein fentanyl is embedded in an adhesive layer, while J & J's patch used a "reservoir" method.

The company created ads that asked, "The Matrix Fentanyl Delivery System: Why Take the Chance of Abuse and Diversion?" and "The Matrix Fentanyl Delivery System: A Threat to Patient and Public Safety?" The ads suggested that doctors who allowed their patients to get Mylan's generic could face lawsuits from addicted patients. (Doctors can stipulate on prescription forms that only a branded drug be dispensed, although doing so usually raises costs and copays for patients.)

J & J put together a list of talking points for its sales reps that echoed the ads, warning that Mylan's version "falls far short of the high public safety standard of Duragesic." Not only could the matrix fentanyl "be easily extracted from the patch by chewing, soaking, or other means—thus creating the potential for a real public safety problem" but it could be cut into smaller pieces, making it a serious risk of widespread diversion—or so J & J claimed.

The sales rep script further stated that "Duragesic is not attractive to abusers" and that Duragesic had "an extremely low rate of abuse," both claims the company knew to be untrue. The script then warned of a possible looming epidemic of abuse from Mylan's product that was, of course, already happening:

"As we've seen with oxycodone, this is exactly what abusers are looking for—a delivery system that both contains a lot of drug and can be easily defeated to get a quick high. Each one of these little matrix systems contains all the potential for another epidemic— which means another crisis not only for the public, but for prescribers as well. Furthermore, it could negatively impact patients with chronic pain by limiting access to the effective pain therapy they legitimately need."

All these risks could be avoided if doctors just stuck with J & J's product, the script concluded.

On November 12, 2004, J & J filed a citizen petition with the FDA—something anyone can do—that made the same arguments. The petition asked the FDA to reverse its decision that Mylan's copy-cat drug was the equivalent of J & J's Duragesic. However, the FDA noticed that J & J's petition included interviews with patients who said they had negative experiences with matrix patches even though such patches weren't available at the time the interviews were conducted. The agency rejected the petition.

About the time that J & J was telling the FDA that Mylan's planned matrix patch was a public health menace, J & J launched in Europe a matrix patch identical to Mylan's. To prepare for the launch, J & J hired a consultant to assess whether a matrix patch would be more likely to be abused than a reservoir one, as it had been arguing to the FDA and American doctors. The consultant concluded that it was "highly unlikely" that a matrix system would "trigger more significant diversion" than the reservoir system.

In early 2008, the FDA forced J & J to issue a recall of its Duragesic reservoir patches in the United States because of manufacturing defects. The problems arose just as J & J was undertaking other ghost recalls of consumer medicines like Tylenol because of contamination.

As the FDA got wind of just how broadly J & J's quality control problems extended, the agency told the company that it would not take kindly to a new set of Duragesic recalls. So, pulling a 180, the company decided in 2009 to switch to exclusively selling its matrix patch in the United States as well.

CHAPTER 31

Evolve the Value Discussion

IN THE OPIOID DISASTER, THE FDA'S FAILURES HAVE BEEN WIDELY documented. But the agency's blind spot regarding Johnson & Johnson's role in the crisis may be the most remarkable.

When Purdue Pharma and three of its top executives pleaded guilty on May 10, 2007, to criminal charges that they misled regulators, doctors, and patients about OxyContin's risk of addiction and its potential to be abused, it confirmed what everyone in the pharmaceutical industry, academic medicine, and news media already knew: Purdue Pharma was the worst of the worst.

But while thousands of stories had been written about Purdue's aggressive and illegal marketing tactics and the epidemic of abuse and death that followed, the nation's opioid crisis continued to get worse. Why did doctors continue to believe these notions even after it had become crystal clear that Purdue had been lying the entire time?

Because it wasn't just Purdue they were dealing with. All of what they'd been hearing about the benefits of opioids was also being endorsed and propagated by the largest and what many believed to be the most ethical healthcare conglomerate in the world. The FDA repeatedly warned Johnson & Johnson to stop claiming that fentanyl was minimally addictive but then did nothing when it continued to make these dangerous and false assertions. And it would not have continued to make them if doctors weren't listening.

In 2008, Johnson & Johnson launched Nucynta, yet another opioid. To sell the pill, the company sent sales reps into doctors' offices around the country to once again tell doctors that opioids were rarely addictive and that patients were suffering from a vast undertreatment of pain.

The plan was to start selling an immediate release pill that gave four to six hours of relief and then a year later sell an extended-release version that doubled those hours. The one-two punch was intended to replace OxyContin, according to the company's business plans.

"Evolve the value discussion to displace the oxycodone molecule," one of the business plans stated.

At the core of the company's sales pitch was the same false promise that had made OxyContin and Duragesic such blockbusters: Nucynta was less prone to abuse.

The FDA made clear to the company that it believed that Nucynta, whose generic name is tapentadol, was just as risky as other opioids. In a November 4, 2008, memo, FDA reviewers said that studies of Nucynta suggested a "high abuse potential comparable to that of hydromorphone, a drug that is associated with high levels of abuse." The lowest dose of Nucynta, the FDA wrote, "produced comparable opioid effects."

These concerns grew with the long-acting version of the drug, called Nucynta ER. "The controlled release properties of the TRF [tamper-resistant] formation can be readily overcome by multiple simple physiochemical manipulations," agency reviewers wrote. Further, "withdrawal symptoms, including insomnia, depressed mood, depression, suicidal ideation, and disturbance in attention, occurred after extended-release formulation tapentadol was stopped."

The agency concluded: "Upon approval and marketing, the drug product should continue to be monitored for abuse, misuse, overdose and withdrawal."

In an August 3, 2011, summary review, the FDA medical reviewer noted that "extended-release tapentadol may have abuse potential and dependence/withdrawal characteristics similar to long acting opioids."

In other words, Nucynta ER was just like OxyContin.

Per usual, J & J's marketing campaign boasted that Nucynta was an improvement over oxycodone in ways that it was in reality no better, such as gastrointestinal side effects.

On August 26, 2011, the FDA sent J & J a letter telling the company to stop making these claims, which the agency said "misleadingly imply that Nucynta is clinically superior (i.e., safer) compared to oxycodone and tramadol for DPNP patients. Specifically, it implies that Nucynta has been shown to have less GI (gastrointestinal) adverse reactions (i.e., constipation, nausea, and vomiting) . . . when this is not the case."

Call notes from sales reps uncovered in litigation reveal that sales reps discussed Nucynta's "favorable GI profile" thousands of times. Yet Johnson & Johnson responded to the letter by stating it was "not aware of promotional activities or material for Nucynta that contains statements/claims such as those described."

After Purdue executives pleaded guilty to illegal marketing tactics, partly on the basis of records of sales rep pitches, J & J cannily changed its computer system to make it harder for authorities to track its opioid activities. Instead of sales reps writing down the actual sales messages they used with doctors, the new system offered a drop-down menu of approved messages. The record of how J & J sales reps pitched Nucynta in doctors' offices after 2008 is thus relatively limited. Sales reps still sent emails, however, and many of them were damning.

"Ronald Myers MD is a HUGE Nucynta target for me," one rep wrote in a September 2010 email. Myers was indicted in 2016 for operating an opioid pill mill. "He has two other doctors and a PA (physician's assistant) that practice pain management in his clinic," the rep added. "These practitioners are not targets for me, but it would be insane for me not to call on them while I am at the clinic."

Per its norm, beyond its massive sales effort for Nucynta, J & J underwrote an expensive and wide-ranging effort to support speakers, groups, medical education seminars, and bloggers that repeated the message that millions of Americans still suffered from untreated pain, a far more concerning epidemic than the one of opioid abuse and death. A slide routinely included in talks sponsored by J & J and copied in a brochure titled "Finding Relief" said this: "Myth: Opioid medications are always addicting. Fact: Many studies show that opioids are rarely addicting when used properly for the management of chronic pain."

By 2010, according to the CDC, there were enough prescription opioids being sold in the United States to medicate every American adult with a typical dose of 5 mg of hydrocodone every four hours for a month. No other industrialized country experienced anything close to such a tidal wave of opioid use, and no other country suffered the resulting death toll.

Fifteen years into one of the worst public health disasters in American history, and J & J was aggressively pushing a marketing plan for a new opioid with all of the same elements that had started and accelerated the epidemic in the first place. Company executives knew exactly how deadly their actions were, but they went on with them anyway because they also knew just how profitable they might be.

Documents show that J & J was able to pay off or influence in some other way almost every source of information doctors relied upon in treating their patients. The company's marketing teams put together sophisticated targeting plans for every organization, stakeholder group, and regulatory authority that had any impact on doctors' prescribing decisions.

One such plan was a flow chart titled "Number of Stakeholders That Influence Pain Prescribing Is Becoming More Complex." The flow chart had twenty-six separate boxes with arrows that eventually led to the central box on the page, which was labeled "Doctors, Nurse Pract., PAs, Nurses, Pharmacists." Among the surrounding boxes were those labeled, "Professional Groups Associations," "FDA," "DEA," "State Pharmacy Boards" and "Medicare, VA, DOD."

By 2007, Purdue's reputation was so diminished that it no longer had the credibility to maintain this kind of industry-wide influence. But J & J did, which is why its role in accelerating the opioid crisis long after the dynamics of the epidemic were clear was so crucial.

Purdue is often the primary or even the exclusive target in a library's worth of books on the addiction epidemic, for which Purdue's OxyContin launch was the starting gun. But Andrew Kolodny, the world's foremost expert on the opioid crisis, said that J & J was more at fault than Purdue. Of the corpses that appeared in morgues across the country during the height of the prescription epidemic, the vast majority had a J & J product in their systems, not a Purdue one.

"J & J was clearly the kingpin of the opioid epidemic, not Purdue Pharma," Kolodny said. "They were not only marketing their own branded opioids but were supplying almost every manufacturer with the crucial active pharmaceutical ingredient."

Stung by widespread criticism of its inaction during the opioid crisis, the FDA hired Dr. Mark McClellan of the Duke-Margolis Institute for Health Policy to hold a two-day meeting in October 2021 to discuss the role of prescriber education in mitigating the disaster. A former FDA commissioner, McClellan has served on J & J's board of directors since 2013. The agency had hired a top official from a company that may have done more to create the opioid crisis than any other to discuss how the agency could work better to resolve it.

If the agency had hired someone who worked for Purdue Pharma, the reaction would have been intensively negative. But J & J has such an extraordinary ability to avoid public accountability that no major publication even noted McClellan's problematic dual roles.

"When I'm at dinner parties, everyone wants to talk about Purdue and the Sacklers, and I'll often respond by talking about J & J," said Kolodny. "But people just aren't interested in hearing about J & J or look at me oddly when I mention it.

"They've branded their company brilliantly."

SECTION VII: ORTHO EVRA BIRTH CONTROL PATCH

CHAPTER 32

The Pill and the Patch

F OR MOST OF THE COMPANY'S HISTORY, JOHNSON & JOHNSON IN-
troduced new products onto the market with every expectation that
they would be safe and effective.

Sometimes, after the products were already approved or being
sold it learned about serious problems or dangers and it chose, irre-
sponsibly, to withhold that information from the FDA and the public. But sixty years passed between the introduction of Johnson's Baby
Powder and clear evidence that it contained asbestos. Nearly twenty
years separated Tylenol's introduction and the discovery that it was
the most dangerous over-the-counter medicine on the market. Even
with Procrit, a couple of years passed between the drug's introduction
and clear evidence that it was deadly. Likewise with Risperdal. With
Duragesic, the product's dangers were known before launch, but the
company took some years before it decided to lie so thoroughly about
them to doctors and patients.

In each case but Duragesic's, executives were in a bind. They decided not to disclose the dangers they'd subsequently discovered,
choosing to defend products and brands in which the company, consumers, and patients were already deeply invested. Revenue streams
had been established that would have been difficult to surrender. And

executives knew that disclosing those product risks could invite mass litigation, since the products were already in widespread use. Companies can be and often have been destroyed that way.

But once the FDA had been effectively neutered and become dependent on industry for funding, there was a shift. In some of their new products, Johnson & Johnson discovered dangers long before launch. Executives then chose to lie about those risks to the FDA and introduce products they had every reason to believe would harm or kill thousands. Instead of backing into disasters, executives made death and injury integral parts of their then-undisclosed plans. There was a clear shift in intentionality.

Even when Johnson & Johnson was caught, the consequences were minimal. In 1995, J & J paid a $7.5 million fine and pleaded guilty to obstructing a federal investigation into its marketing of Retin-A, an acne drug—a grain of sand on the beach for a product that had brought in half a billion dollars a year.

Three years later, dozens of federal agents raided the company's LifeScan unit after it failed to notify the FDA that its widely used glucose-monitoring device could return dangerously inaccurate readings. After two employees blew the whistle, the company pleaded guilty to criminal charges in 2000 and agreed to pay $60 million in fines. Again, it was nothing in comparison to the profits J & J had made by selling the device.

Both cases received minimal press coverage, and neither had any impact on the reputations of Johnson & Johnson or its CEO at the time, Ralph S. Larsen. Feeling emboldened by their state of impunity, the company let its internal guardrails gradually wither and then disappear altogether. Of their top-seven-selling drugs in 2003, J & J used illegal marketing tactics that included bribes, kickbacks, and lies to the FDA for six of them.

In the late 1970s, Larsen was part of a team that turned Tylenol from a reasonably profitable consumer medicine into a blockbuster drug with $500 million in sales. That success came from promoting the Extra Strength version of the medicine and accepting a level of danger that no other widely sold medicine came close to matching. His professional success arose from embracing but also publicly obscuring serious risks. Those risks had paid off: During his tenure, Johnson & Johnson's market value rose thirteenfold, from $14 billion to $182 billion. Near the end of his time as chief executive, the company's revenues from drugs grew faster than those of any other major pharmaceutical company in the world. He and the company's other top executives were lionized on Wall Street and in the media as proof that companies could do well and do good simultaneously. It was all heady stuff that made putting the brakes on this kind of behavior all but impossible.

THE BIRTH CONTROL PILL WAS ONE OF THE MOST IMPORTANT SCIEN-tific advances of the twentieth century. Much has been written about how it revolutionized sexual and social relationships, even the entire culture. Less well known is how much it transformed the FDA.

Many of the steps that underlie modern drug approvals—extensive clinical trials, routine referrals to outside experts, continual assessments of a medicine's safety, and direct communications between the FDA and patients—were pioneered to deal with evolving concerns about the Pill's safety.

The horrors of thalidomide led to the 1962 Kefauver-Harris drug amendments, which required drugmakers to prove in every application to the FDA that their medicines worked as intended. Even before that, though, the FDA demanded that the drug company Searle prove that Enovid, the first birth control pill, actually prevented pregnancy by tricking the body into believing it's already pregnant. In one of the first large clinical trials ever, Searle tested Enovid in 897 women, mostly from Puerto Rico and Haiti. On June 23, 1960, the FDA approved Enovid. Sales soared.

Then in November 1961, a British physician reported in *The Lancet* that a young woman had developed a blood clot and died while taking the Pill. Within months, two similar fatalities were reported in the United States, and by August 1962, the FDA had received twenty-six reports of users suffering blood clots.

Researchers soon realized that estrogen therapy was risky, and for the next two decades drugmakers gradually lowered hormonal doses. On April 15, 1988, Johnson & Johnson and two other manufacturers announced that they would stop making medium-dose estrogen birth control pills because of the risks of blood clots. The FDA said no such pills would be approved ever again.

Four years later, Johnson & Johnson introduced Ortho-Cyclen and Ortho Tri-Cyclen, joining a wave of popular low-dose birth control pills already on the market that reduced not only a woman's risk of stroke but also a host of other estrogen-related side effects like breast tenderness and bloating.

Even with these improvements, the Pill wasn't perfect. Pregnancies still occurred. The reason was primarily forgetfulness. Women would accidentally skip a day's pill and the drug would lose its efficacy.

Having already achieved financial success with the fentanyl patch, Duragesic, Johnson & Johnson decided to apply its patch technology to contraceptives as well. The new patch would be called Ortho Evra. Instead of a daily pill, women would only have to remember to replace the patch once a week. J & J suggested that since the body would not break down hormones delivered via the patch as readily as those from the Pill, lower doses of estrogen were needed, which would lower the risks of strokes and other side effects, like nausea, even more.

In 1996, the company told the FDA that it planned to develop the Ortho Evra patch. If Ortho Evra succeeded, it would likely result in an avalanche of sales. But patches are finicky—witness Duragesic's providing 50 percent more fentanyl on the first day than promised.

To see how Ortho Evra fared, the company gave the patch to a group of women, measured their blood estrogen levels, and compared those with estrogen levels from women taking three popular low-dose birth control pills. In March 1999, the company got the results of the study, which it called PHI-017.

They weren't good. Patch patients on average had blood estrogen levels three times *higher* than the women taking two of the pills and twice those of the third pill. In fact, because up to half of the estrogen in pills is lost in the digestive tract before it reaches the blood, the study suggested that the patch delivered an amount of estrogen that could be as high as a pill containing 76 mcg of estrogen—a level unseen on the market for decades, almost four times the amount in low-dose pills.

Another problem was that estrogen doses among patch users were totally inconsistent. Twelve percent of patients got less than 25 mcg of estrogen while more than a quarter got more than 75 mcg. The variability suggested that some patch users might get pregnant while too many others would suffer strokes and death. These dangers were readily apparent in the company's clinical trial program, in which two women suffered dangerous clots in their lungs.

J & J thus faced several unpalatable options. First, it could disclose the results to the FDA and possibly see its application rejected. Second, it might persuade the agency to approve the product, but with warnings that would ensure that its sales were always small. Third, it could go back to the drawing board and redesign the patch in hopes of achieving a lower estrogen dose. Or fourth, it could abandon the project altogether.

An email on July 11, 2000, from a top company executive asked the Ortho Evra team to estimate the costs to redo the clinical trials, suggesting there was some consideration given to starting over. But that was not the option J & J ultimately chose.

Instead, the company picked a fifth path: willfully deceiving the FDA about the patch's estrogen problem.

·   ·   ·

ON NOVEMBER 1, 2001, THE FDA APPROVED ORTHO EVRA WITH A LABEL stating that it released the same amount of estrogen as a low-dose birth control pill. J & J was fully aware that this claim was untrue.

A dozen years earlier, J & J had alerted the FDA before Duragesic's approval that its patch could leach excessive levels of fentanyl. But this time, it straight up lied to the agency. The company scientists in charge of Ortho Evra's application had applied a "correction factor" to the amount of estrogen that women absorbed from the patch, reducing the quantities found in clinical trials by 40 percent. The company mentioned this alteration only once in its 435-page FDA application, and only within a complex mathematical formula.

Dr. Larry Abrams, the lead scientist on the Ortho Evra team, later said in a deposition that he applied this correction factor to adjust for the different ways the body breaks down hormones from pills and patches. But this was contrary to the protocol that he promised to follow in a plan previously submitted to the FDA, and Abrams hadn't applied this correction to norelgestromin, the other hormone in the patch. And when J & J sent the results of its estrogen study to the agency, the study synopsis made no mention of a correction factor. Instead, J & J submitted all the tables and data in the synopsis showing only the altered or "corrected" results, without explaining that every estrogen number had been reduced by 40 percent. Similarly, in the application's clinical report, only the altered data were presented, with no mention of a correction.

And that was hardly the end of it. The company didn't provide the agency with the results of PHI-017, the study that compared estrogen levels between the patch and low-dose birth control pills, until October 2001—two years after the study's completion and just one month before the product's approval. Even then, it was buried under a mountain of other data, with no explanation in the cover letter to draw attention to this crucial bit of information.

J & J was successful: The FDA never noticed the correction factor. Similarly, J & J withheld PHI-017, its patch/pill comparison study, from European drug regulators until after the independent reviewer of the product's application had finished his analysis and submitted his recommendation in favor of approval. Only then, in June 2001, did Abrams and a colleague fly to London and disclose the results of PHI-017. Concerned, the reviewer told Abrams to disclose the results to both the European Medicines Agency and the FDA. The company did neither.

In 2004, worries about the number of deaths and strokes caused by Ortho Evra had grown. So regulators in New Zealand insisted on first seeing results of PHI-017. Once they saw the results, New Zealand regulators refused to approve Ortho Evra because "evidence from the clinical trials showing a higher rate of oestrongenic side effects than COCs (combined oral contraceptives) is now supported by additional AUC data from pharmacokinetic study PHI-017."

DRUG COMPANIES OFTEN HAVE TRUCKS FILLED WITH PRODUCT READY to roll the minute the FDA announces its approval, since every hour of lost sales is an hour that can never be regained. But Johnson & Johnson didn't start selling Ortho Evra until April 2002, a full six months after approval, because the company couldn't figure out how to scale up production of an exact replica of the patch used in its clinical trials, which the FDA requires. Eventually, more concerned with sales than safety, it simply started selling a version of the patch that released even more estrogen than the one used in testing, worsening an already dangerous problem. It wouldn't tell the FDA about the disparity until years later.

Johnson & Johnson launched Ortho Evra with a major advertising campaign featuring women who pulled down the sides of their panties to reveal what looked like a wishbone-shaped Band-Aid. Sales took off, with Ortho Evra quickly capturing 10 percent of the contraceptive market.

Soon, the FDA started receiving an alarming number of reports of young women having heart attacks, strokes, deep vein thrombosis, and lung clots. In a few cases, women were dying, including Zakiya Kennedy, an eighteen-year-old college freshman from New York, and Stephanie Rosfeld, a twenty-five-year-old assistant volleyball coach at the University of Cincinnati who was in the peak of health and had only been on the patch for a month.

At the same time, the agency started receiving reports about surprise pregnancies from women who claimed to have used the patch appropriately. J & J also started hearing from doctors that many patients didn't like the patch because of its excessive side effects. A study later conducted at ten academic medical centers revealed that patch users had longer and more painful menstrual periods and suffered more frequent nausea, mood swings, and skin rashes than those using other contraceptives. Patch users in the trial said they preferred a pill, and half said they had a patch fall off at least once. Trials conducted at Planned Parenthood clinics found that patch users were more likely to stop using birth control and get unintentionally pregnant than those on the pill, defeating the entire purpose of the patch in the first place.

An executive on J & J's Ortho Evra team quit and, in his resignation letter, said he was leaving "because young women were dying of massive pulmonary embolisms" and "there was not enough sense of urgency."

With injuries mounting, European drug regulators told J & J that they wanted to see a study that compared blood estrogen levels between women on the patch and those taking a popular low-dose pill. Unaware that J & J had already conducted just such a study and then hidden the results, the Europeans demanded a new one, and they demanded it quickly. Called NED-1, the study was supposed to measure estrogen levels at weeks one and three. NED-1 started in July 2002 and ended in July 2003. The comparison pill was Cilest, J & J's own low-dose pill. In the first week, patch users had estrogen levels 66 percent higher than those on the pill. In the third week, their levels were 60 percent higher.

In an internal email, Dr. Patrick Caubel, a member of the Ortho

Evra team, wrote: "I want to avoid that the take home message from this preliminary report is that EVRA is equivalent to a 43 mcg OC (and not to a 35 mcg OC as previously claimed)."

So the team got rid of that calculation. And since a product delivering 60 percent more estrogen than a 35 mcg pill would in fact be equivalent to a 56 mcg pill—higher than those long since banned—those numbers weren't included either.

Instead, the company submitted its bare-bones data to the Europeans on October 28, 2003, and waited to provide it to the FDA until January 19, 2004, when it was included as part of the product's annual report. These reports are phone book–sized compendiums of largely useless information. If something important is included, that information is supposed to be flagged at the front of a report. J & J, however, stated, "There is no significant new information to report."

While the FDA didn't catch the crucial data, as reports of women having strokes continued piling up, the agency demanded a meeting with the company. On May 19, 2004, J & J provided the agency a briefing package for that meeting, which contained the relevant data from NED-1.

The meeting was held on June 29, 2004, and among the twenty-four people in attendance—ten on the agency's side, fourteen on the company's—none was aware, according to later depositions, of the "correction factor" applied to the original estrogen data.

There is no evidence that company officials raised or discussed PHI-017, the earlier patch/pill study whose numbers were even worse than NED-1's. In fact, there is no evidence in the notes that FDA officials were aware of PHI-017 at the time, or even years later. In briefing books prepared by J & J for its meetings with the FDA in 2004 and 2005, the company never mentioned PHI-017 or its damning results. The study was never published.

So, unaware of all the other research that had been done, to the FDA, NED-1 was an outlier.

FDA officials Dr. Daniel Davis and Dr. Scott Monroe kept pressing the company about the excessive number of strokes. But J & J's

Caubel, among other company officials, said the numbers weren't that bad and argued that comparing exposures from patch and pill "presents inherent technical challenges."

FDA officials also said they were concerned by reports of a large number of unintended pregnancies, and that they were worried that the marketed patch might not be exactly the same as the one used in clinical trials. That was true, of course. But the meeting notes gave no indication that company officials admitted this problem. Instead, company officials promised to "continue to assess the appropriate specifications for this product."

The two sides promised to get together again in early 2005 to "discuss our path forward."

IN NOVEMBER 2005, THE FDA FINALLY SLAPPED A WARNING ON ORTHO Evra's label that it delivered at least 60 percent more estrogen than a pill with 35 mcg of estrogen. Sales plunged. There were 10 million prescriptions written for Ortho Evra in the United States in 2004, but by 2010, that number had dropped 87 percent to 1.3 million.

At the insistence of European regulators, the company had sponsored two epidemiological studies, one by the Boston Collaborative Drug Surveillance Project and another by the i3-Group. The Boston study used insurance billing records to check if women taking the patch had more heart attacks and strokes, while the i3-Group analyzed actual medical records.

Insurance billing records are a famously unreliable way to study health outcomes because the underlying entries are intended to elicit payments, not direct care. They often miss major events like death or out-of-network emergency room visits. As a result, the J & J official overseeing the two trials testified that he knew the i3 study would be the more reliable of the two.

It certainly was the more inconvenient. The Boston study initially found no difference in serious problems between patch and pill users, while the i3 study found a 100 percent increase in heart attacks, strokes, and other clot problems among those taking the Ortho Evra patch.

Johnson & Johnson immediately published the preliminary and reassuring numbers from Boston in the February 2006 edition of the journal *Contraception*. The company waited another year before publishing the far more worrisome i3 results.

Between these two publications, another top Ortho Evra executive—their name has never been revealed—submitted a blistering resignation letter denouncing the company for this strategy.

The FDA has repeatedly considered yanking Ortho Evra from the market but has decided against doing so because women need as many contraceptive options as possible. And for a small number of women, the patch's increased side effects do not seem to bother them.

At an FDA advisory committee meeting in 2011, Dr. Joanne Waldstreicher, J & J's chief medical officer, estimated that Ortho Evra increased the risks of a woman having a stroke or heart attack to about nine events per ten thousand woman-years of use. Independent estimates suggested the risks were even higher.

At the time of the hearing, Ortho Evra had more than 5.5 million years of product use in the United States. So, by her own calculations, 4,950 women had heart attacks and strokes as a result of using Ortho Evra. It was a calculation that Ortho Evra executives could have made even before the company launched the product. But neither the FDA nor the women who used it in those early years had any idea of such risks.

This was the kind of choice that would be made repeatedly by the new Johnson & Johnson.

Part III

Medical Devices

CHAPTER 33

The FDA Goes Looking for a Savior

JOHNSON & JOHNSON HAS LONG BEEN ONE OF THE WORLD'S LARG-
est manufacturers of medical devices. The company has nine major
device subsidiaries that manufacture a host of crucial products, including bandages, surgical sutures, staples and instruments, cardiac
stents, and implants for hips and knees.

For decades, medical devices didn't need government approval
before being sold. Tongue depressors, thermometers, and blood pressure cuffs are medical devices, but human trials would have been an
expensive nuisance.

As medical devices became more complex, deaths and injuries associated with their use mounted. Then came the Dalkon Shield, an
intrauterine contraceptive device whose faulty design led more than
three hundred thousand American women to sue claiming pelvic inflammatory disease, ectopic pregnancies, spontaneous septic abor-
tions, and perforated uteri.

The scandal led Congress to pass legislation in 1976 mandating
that complicated and high-risk devices—particularly those inserted
into the body—undergo testing in people before getting FDA approval for widespread sales.

While the FDA put together a list of the devices that would need to go through human trials, Congress allowed device makers in the interim to use a loophole called the 510(k) process to make small modifications to already approved complex devices without having to conduct entirely new and expensive clinical trials.

A year passed. Two years. Ten years. The FDA never got around to making its comprehensive list. Instead, it continued approving risky devices through what was originally intended to be only a brief 510(k) transition period. Losing patience, Congress passed a law in 1990 requiring the agency to establish a schedule to finally finish this transition. But to this day, the FDA hasn't produced its list.

Every year, the disjunction at the heart of the 510(k) process deepens. To win approval, manufacturers must tell the FDA that their devices come from before 1976, the era of rotary phones and Selectric typewriters. To win sales, however, companies must brag to doctors that their devices spring from cutting-edge advances in artificial intelligence and quantum computing.

Few doctors are aware that so many complex devices are approved without proof of safety or efficacy. In lawsuits involving unsafe devices, highly trained surgeons testify under oath again and again that they had no idea that the devices they implanted in thousands of patients had never undergone human testing.

One reason the FDA has allowed the 510(k) loophole to persist is a remarkably close relationship between regulator and medical device industry. Each part of the FDA negotiates separately with the industry it regulates for the money it needs. The agency's drug center negotiates directly with the branded pharmaceutical industry, its generics center negotiates with generics makers, and so on.

Dominated by many small and midsized companies, the medical device industry is fundamentally different from the pharmaceutical industry, and it has its own distinct relationship with the FDA. While huge drug companies see the FDA as a vital shield against lawsuits and as a guarantor of patient confidence, many small device makers view the agency as an expensive annoyance.

In 2011, a collection of these small companies took control of the agreement committee at the Advanced Medical Technology Association, the device industry trade association (known as AdvaMed). When they announced they'd had enough, the already budget-feeble FDA responded by significantly paring back its funding requests.

AdvaMed responded to the FDA's revised proposal of $681 million over five years with $447 million over five years, 39 percent less than the agency's bare funding minimum. Industry negotiators also insisted on an aggressive new set of "performance goals" regarding device review that the FDA's top staff said were unreasonable.

If a deal could not be okayed by Congress, come the end of September, hundreds of agency device reviewers would lose their jobs. Needing an industry partner that could get the smaller players at AdvaMed in line and then use its vast lobbying power to sell the resulting deal on Capitol Hill, top FDA staff suggested that Commissioner Margaret Hamburg reach out to Alex Gorsky, who at the time headed Johnson & Johnson's massive device division, as well as Steve MacMillan, chief executive and chairman of Stryker Corp., a large device manufacturer headquartered in Kalamazoo, Michigan. Both men sat on AdvaMed's board of directors.

Though a conservative Republican, Gorsky had attended the inaugural balls of the Obama administration and had contacts all over town in both political parties. No one in the device industry had more clout either inside or outside the industry.

Hamburg sent the agency's latest proposals to the two men, and Gorsky responded via email the next day.

"Dr. Hamburg . . . thank you very much for sending along the proposals outlined below," Gorsky wrote, adding: "Steve and I remain committed to working with our peers to reach an agreement that will address the issues noted below in a reasonable and timely manner."

For Gorsky and J & J, the timing couldn't have been better. FDA's funding-vulnerable device staff was currently reviewing a petition to ban and recall Johnson & Johnson's vaginal mesh. Almost simultaneously, *The Lancet* published a study finding that Johnson & Johnson's

Pinnacle metal-on-metal hip implants failed at much higher rates than other brands and said they should be banned, too.

The damage caused by both of these devices meant a potential tsunami of lawsuits from injured patients. An FDA ban or urgent recall for either or both devices would not only lead to even more lawsuits but vastly increase the amounts the company would have to pay each patient. Worse, J & J had lied to the agency about the devices' specifications and dangers and had even begun selling one of them without waiting for the agency's approval. Agency staff could easily have referred both cases to federal prosecutors.

There was also ongoing fallout from J & J's secret "ghost recall" of hundreds of millions of tainted pills, prosecutors were still in settlement talks about Johnson & Johnson's illegal marketing of Risperdal and other drugs, and then there was J & J's role in fueling the nation's skyrocketing opioid crisis.

Two of Hamburg's aides said they were deeply uneasy about the pact, but Johnson & Johnson executives were almost giddy about being thrust into the role of FDA savior. Hamburg and Gorsky hammered out the basics of an agreement. J & J browbeat AdvaMed into accepting the deal, and the company's lobbyists—among the most influential in Washington—pressed lawmakers on Capitol Hill to pass the measure expeditiously.

Now, having saved the agency, Gorsky had his assistant reach out to the agency on April 4, 2012, with an important request.

"As you may have read, Alex will become the CEO of J&J during our Annual Shareholders Meeting at the end of April," wrote Minnie Baylor-Henry, Gorsky's assistant, to one of Hamburg's top deputies. "He asked me today, if I could work with you to get a meeting with Commissioner Hamburg, Jeff Shuren, Stephen Spieldberg and Janet Woodcock, possibly during May."

The four were FDA's top officials, including those overseeing devices, drugs, and other medical products. They had enormous sway over the myriad regulatory and criminal investigations facing Gorsky and J & J. The email concluded that Gorsky "wants to continue to build a good relationship with FDA in his new role and to make a commitment to the agency regarding J&J. Can you help me with this task?"

Deb Autor, the chief of the FDA's inspections division, recommended against the meeting at J & J, but if Gorsky wanted to hop on the corporate jet and fly down, that would be fine, aides advised.

Gorsky got the meeting. The FDA's medical device staff—whose jobs had just been saved by Gorsky—decided against banning or recalling the unsafe devices. And the agency subsequently issued statements tailor-made and perfectly timed to help J & J as its legal troubles surrounding opioids, Risperdal, and Baby Powder worsened.

To be fair, the FDA is now so wholly captive to those it supposedly regulates that agency officials routinely refer to drug and device companies as their main customer and concern, not consumers or the American public. Even so, the agency's deference to J & J has been remarkable.

CHAPTER 34

Two Terrible Dilemmas

ONE FRIDAY, JUST ONE BUSINESS DAY BEFORE JOHNSON & JOHNSON planned to submit to federal regulators an application to sell a new hip implant it called Pinnacle, an engineer discovered that one of the five pairs being tested was falling apart in the simulator.

The problem on this Friday, November 10, 2000, was not with the simulator but with the implant itself, said Andrew Goldsmith, a J & J research engineer, in an email to Frank W. Chan, the company's senior research scientist, and to Leanne Turner, who was managing the program and putting the finishing touches on its application to the FDA.

Goldsmith speculated that the gap between Pinnacle's moving parts was too narrow. Doubling the gap might solve the problem, he wrote.

"This might lose us some wear performance, but not that much, and would avoid this frictional locking risk," he wrote.

At 7:13 P.M. that same Friday, Chan responded with alarm.

"Yikes!" he wrote. "Thanks for the update and I fully share your concern."

Chan endorsed Goldsmith's recommendation to double the gap

between the implant's moving parts and described in his email several engineering reasons why the smaller gap might be causing a problem.

"Leanne, what are the engineering and production implications for making a design change in 36 mm liner ID [as the product was known internally] at this time as Andrew suggested?" Chan asked, and perhaps even more importantly: "What about regulatory issues?"

For ten months, the company had set Monday, November 13, as its deadline for submitting its 510(k) application to the FDA. That was the very next business day. Reworking the application to account for the design change and then redoing the simulator testing would take months, forcing the company to miss its target.

Worse, any implant with such a wide gap was likely to spook FDA officials, since earlier hip implants using the same materials had similarly wide gaps and had all failed in spectacular fashion, crippling tens of thousands. Given that, the agency might insist that Johnson & Johnson test its new implant in real people, not just a simulator. Clinical testing would take years, cost millions, and surrender tens of millions in profits—potentially fatal blows to the entire Pinnacle program. Admitting the need for such a change was a huge risk.

The FDA application demanded a sworn affidavit from a company executive declaring that all the product descriptions included were accurate. So the company faced a terrible set of dilemmas.

On the one hand, if the FDA application disclosed the sudden design change, the entire Pinnacle program might fail. But if the change was not disclosed, the application would be based on false specifications that could later compromise the FDA's approval of the device. And there was an even wider dilemma: Would the company risk wounding, crippling, and in some cases killing tens of thousands—perhaps hundreds of thousands—of vulnerable people around the world by selling a device that its own executives and engineers now had ample reasons to suspect would fall apart soon after implantation because the device was now just like ones that had previously done just that?

· · ·

HIP AND KNEE REPLACEMENTS HAVE FOR DECADES BEEN THE MOST common elective surgeries in the United States, a multi-billion-dollar market. In 1998, Johnson & Johnson entered the business by spending $3.5 billion to purchase DePuy Orthopaedics, a company founded more than a century earlier in bucolic Warsaw, Indiana. The price would have been higher if DePuy's hip implants had been selling better. But for years, DePuy had been losing market share to rivals.

With J & J's financial muscle behind it, DePuy's new executive team hatched a bold plan to turn around the company's hips business. At the center of this scheme was a risky idea: reviving metal-on-metal hip implants.

When hip implants were first invented in the 1950s, the linings between the steel cups and balls were made of Teflon, a material intended to mimic the body's natural cartilage. But surgeons discovered that Teflon wore away too quickly, forcing recipients to undergo painful re-surgeries. Manufacturers started making linings out of heavier plastic in hopes they would survive longer.

Then, in the early 1960s, G. Kenneth McKee and J. Watson-Farrar, English surgeons, decided to get rid of the plastic altogether and design an implant using a stem and socket made from a super-hard alloy of cobalt and chrome. The idea was that while plastics invariably degrade, metal lasts a lifetime.

Bad idea. Friction between the cup and ball created hundreds of millions of tiny metal shavings that killed surrounding tissue, loosened the joints, and released toxic ions that poisoned patients' hearts, brains, and eyes. Some recipients died of heart attacks, others lost cognitive function, and some were blinded. Most were crippled with pain that was often worse than what they had suffered from their naturally degrading hips. Nearly all McKee-Farrar implants had to be yanked out and replaced with implants using plastic liners. But since the metal shavings often killed nearby tissue, new implant surgeries were often impossible or far more involved than the original ones. Many McKee-Farrar recipients died or were crippled for the rest of their lives.

Despite this disaster, some in orthopedics continued to believe that metal-on-metal was the way to go. By the mid-1990s, surgeons began speculating that McKee-Farrar had failed because the gap between cup and ball had been too wide. If modern metallurgical and machining techniques could narrow that gap, bodily fluids would work themselves into the divide and never allow the two sides to touch. With no touching, there'd be no friction, wearing, or toxic shavings. The implants would not only last forever but, because metal is so resilient, allow recipients to go back to skiing, running, and other active sports.

That was the theory. But there were plenty of reasons to doubt this notion. In a 1995 internal memo, Dr. Graham Isaac, an engineer who was DePuy's development manager for hips, wrote that plastic linings had improved so much that taking a risk on metal-on-metal implants made little sense. But incremental changes to existing plastic liners were not going to vault DePuy into becoming the leading maker of hip implants.

This was the conundrum that Johnson & Johnson inherited when it purchased DePuy. The company could play it safe by sticking with plastics and allowing an expanding market to lift all boats. Or it could take a long-shot risk on a new metal-on-metal hip implant and—an even longer shot—on selling it without testing it in a single patient.

By itself, DePuy might not have been able to pull off this longer shot. But it wasn't by itself anymore.

ON MONDAY, NOVEMBER 13, 2000, LEANNE TURNER WAS AMONG A handful of J & J executives who signed declarations in the company's FDA application that its descriptions and claims were accurate. The application included engineering specifications for a design the company had just abandoned. Turner later testified that the inaccurate technical descriptions were unintentional.

"And when I found out in 2005 that this mistake had been made in 2000, I was shocked and I was devastated," she said, choking up on the stand, adding: "So the suggestion over and over that I'm—that I'm a liar and that I did it on purpose, I take that very personally. All right?"

A year later, the company submitted a similar application to Canadian health authorities, but the J & J executive in charge of the submission realized that the product's actual engineering specifications were different from the descriptions that had been provided to the FDA. For two months she tried unsuccessfully to figure out why. Finally, she sent an email to a top American J & J executive, who forwarded it with urgency to Turner. Turner responded that the subsequent changes were "very minor."

On December 2, 2004, Johnson & Johnson submitted a 510(k) application for another metal-on-metal hip implant called ASR XL. This time, the company said that ASR had a wide clearance, just like the company's Pinnacle implants, and thus should be approved on the basis of that similarity—as well as the similarity with three previous metal-on-metal hip implants made prior to 1976, even though they had all failed. (Such is the strange world of the 501(k) process that a company can cite its similarity with a product that failed in spectacular fashion as support for clearance.)

On January 26, 2005, the FDA responded to J & J's application for the ASR XL, noting its concern about the implant's wide gap, since reviewers believed that was what caused the failure of the first generation of metal-on-metal devices. The agency also said the proposed clearance of the ASR XL was roughly twice that of the Pinnacle, which was then on the market, and that such a significant change would likely require testing in humans.

On May 23, 2005, Johnson & Johnson wrote back that the FDA's information on Pinnacle clearances was incorrect, and that Pinnacle's actual clearance was roughly double what the FDA believed—the same gap proposed for ASR XL.

On July 12, an FDA official called a company executive to say that the company's 2000 Pinnacle application listed a narrower clearance. After some delay, the executive phoned back to say that the company had made a mistake in its original submission.

The agency's device division held an internal meeting to decide what to do about such a popular implant being cleared for sale under false pretenses. Should the agency order J & J to stop selling it? The FDA's orthopedic division, known by its acronym ORDB, decided against taking such a tough step.

According to current practices, a doubling like this could not be approved without clinical data, the FDA said. "However, after searching the Medical Device Reporting Program for adverse events associated with the Pinnacle 36 metal-on-metal liners, only 5 adverse events were reported," the agency wrote J & J on August 5. Given such a safe track record, and the fact that implants made by other manufacturers had a similar number of problems, the FDA told Johnson & Johnson that it could continue selling Pinnacle without reapplying for an FDA approval.

What J & J didn't tell the FDA was that the company was sitting on dozens of additional revisions and complaint reports that it had never forwarded to the agency. (Federal law requires companies to forward such reports to the FDA in an expeditious manner.) So the FDA's reassurance that Pinnacle seemed to be performing well resulted because the company had illegally kept the agency in the dark.

A later FDA review of J & J / DePuy's complaints department found significant deficiencies, as did subsequent assessments done by J & J's own auditors, which declared that the department was inadequately resourced and overreliant on temps without medical expertise. These problems led to a huge backlog in complaints waiting to be assessed and forwarded to the FDA.

J & J had two options for resolving the complaint crisis. The first was to increase staffing in the complaints department to a level commensurate with the increasing number of problems being reported.

The second option was to "retrain sales force not to report every revision," which are re-surgeries to remove and replace defective implants. The benefits of this option, according to the internal review, was that it would "result in far fewer complaints," "free up sales reps time for selling" and there would be "far fewer MDRs"—problem reports sent to the FDA.

The J & J auditors didn't mention that such a tactic would be even more illegal than understaffing a complaints department to such an extent that it was unable to forward problems to the FDA in the timely manner required by law.

During an October 2016 trial against J & J claiming that the company was grossly negligent in selling Pinnacle, Mark Lanier, a plaintiff's attorney, confronted Dr. Pam Plouhar, J & J / DePuy's head of clinical studies, about these options.

"Ma'am, isn't it appalling that y'all would even put down as an option to retrain the sales force not to report every revision? Isn't that appalling?" Lanier asked.

"It's an option. I think that we were trying to identify what the options were," Plouhar replied.

"Ma'am, that's like, 'I'm going to have trouble paying my bills this month, all right, let me look at the options. One option is I can rob a bank.' I mean, who sits there and looks at those options? There's some things that should be off the table, right?" Lanier said.

"I would agree, but I don't think that— I think that they were just putting what the options were."

CHAPTER 35

God, Nazis, and Hip Implants

As was the case throughout the healthcare industry, when it came to getting doctors to implant something, there was usually a generous sales rep not far away. In September 2007, every major orthopedic device company entered into a deferred prosecution agreement with the Justice Department over allegations that they routinely bribed orthopedic surgeons to use their products. Thinly disguised as consulting contracts, the bribes were solely intended to influence which devices surgeons chose to use in their patients, prosecutors said.

J & J / DePuy paid an $84.7 million fine and agreed to be closely monitored for nearly two years.

Whether J & J and other device companies subsequently stopped bribing surgeons is disputed, but all agree that payoffs prior to 2007 were endemic. So, when J & J / DePuy was planning the launch of its new Pinnacle metal-on-metal hip implant in 2001, the company knew that it was going to have to create some serious payoff schemes. In addition to rich consulting agreements, the company put together a plan for a research study called PIN whose primary purpose was to funnel even more money to surgeons.

Given that the Pinnacle hip system was cleared for sale by the

FDA on December 13, 2000, without any clinical data, there was no regulatory reason for J & J / DePuy to conduct any studies of its safety and effectiveness. Postapproval studies, also known as "seeding trials," are a tried-and-true method of paying doctors to prescribe a drug or buy an implant. PIN was conceived by the company's marketing department, because payoffs were its primary purpose. In internal documents, company executives wrote that the PIN study would have a "new business focus" and an opportunity for "new business building" with a "focus on key accounts." Notably absent from these descriptions was any scientific rationale.

In an email dated June 5, 2000, a top company executive gave "an overview of the strategy for collecting survivorship data on Pinnacle while maximizing our impact in the market." The company planned to use forty surgeons, evenly distributed over five sales districts, each of whom would initially enroll twenty-five patients, for a total of one thousand patients.

When human trials are conducted for a genuine scientific purpose, participants almost invariably receive care for free and are sometimes paid to compensate for the risks they shoulder. When marketing is the goal, patients pay their own way. PIN patients paid, which made the study profitable for J & J / DePuy as well as the participating surgeons.

"Total study cost of $345,000 over 5 years," the email stated. "The sales revenue estimate for this study is $4.2 million"—a twelvefold return.

The study's expenses ballooned beyond this initial plan as J & J / DePuy decided to give more money to participating surgeons. Nine of them were designated as "designers" of the implant and earned millions in royalties even though not one of them was listed on the product's patent. The company paid others to give speeches and participate in other marketing activities.

Among the cardinal rules for ethical research is that before a trial begins, study plans known as "protocols" must be approved by ethics committees known as institutional review boards, or IRBs. Another is that before taking a drug or getting an implant, patients must sign consent forms acknowledging that they understand the risks they face.

J & J's policies mandate that every investigator employed by the company follow these rules, which one company document notes resulted from the 1947 Nuremberg trials of Nazi physicians charged with committing atrocities in the name of science. Another company document compares the rules to the Ten Commandments. So J & J referenced both Nazis and God to encourage compliance—and then worked mightily to do the opposite. Not one PIN patient signed a consent form until 2003, and not one investigator got IRB approval until 2004. Four study sites never got IRB approval, and 806 of the trial's 1,183 patients came from sites that had not yet or never would secure IRB approval.

In many cases, surgeons used standard medical release forms— the kind patients sign to allow their medical records to be shared— instead of informed-consent ones. At one study site, the company photocopied the top of the PIN study case report form onto thirty- one medical release records that patients had signed for a different study. Someone crossed out the name of the earlier study by hand and scribbled "Pinnacle" below.

The study's protocol about patient enrollment was fairly good, but these and other study rules were routinely violated in favor of cherry-picking. One investigator performed an average of 600 Pin- nacle implants a year but enrolled only 277 patients over the seven years he was involved in PIN. If he'd been enrolling patients prospec- tively and consecutively, as he was supposed to, he would have en- rolled 4,200 patients. At a different clinic, a quarter of the patients enrolled didn't get the appropriate implant.

Things changed in 2004. Investigators started asking IRBs for ap- proval. J & J / DePuy started becoming more insistent about receiv- ing copies of some kind of patient consent form, even those that were obviously retrospective, fraudulent, or jury-rigged.

There are three possible reasons for these changes. One is the arrival at the end of 2003 of Pam Plouhar as director of clinical research for J & J / DePuy. Plouhar, in sworn testimony, said she "was appalled that we were conducting a study without IRB approval."

Another is that J & J caught wind of the Justice Department's investigation into the near-universal use of kickbacks in orthopedic surgery. While subpoenas wouldn't arrive at company offices until early 2005, Johnson & Johnson's extraordinary intelligence network might have learned of the probe beforehand, so converting the PIN study from an obvious kickback scheme into something approximating research may have been part of the company's legal defense.

A third possible reason is that the company's marketers might have realized that data from the PIN study would only be useful if published in some kind of peer-reviewed journal or poster presentation. And to get that, the company would have to claim that the study had been conducted ethically, which meant getting patient consents and IRB approvals.

Whatever the cause, the newfound commitment to ethical appearances didn't go well. Three IRBs refused to approve the study's protocol. The Mayo Clinic's IRB voted 12 to 0 against it, and its comments were scathing.

"The Board was primarily concerned that there was not a sound scientific basis for conducting the study and that the sponsor's main aim might be to foster use of the implant in preference to other implants," the Mayo ethics committee stated in prescient remarks.

"Well, they're dropping like flies! Gavin Duffy [a Mayo surgeon involved in the J & J / DePuy effort] just called me and said he won't be able to participate in the PIN study due to a very nasty letter from the Mayo IRB (surprise, surprise!)," Amy Chan, the study coordinator at the time, wrote in a May 2002 internal email. She suggested switching Duffy's work over to another doctor.

The IRB at Baptist Medical Center in Jacksonville, Florida, said sanctions could be applied against Dr. Steven Lancaster, a local orthopedic surgeon who was a PIN investigator.

"At the Institutional Review Committee meeting today, you

stated the above-mentioned study has been conducted at your institution for three years," Dr. Michael Joyce, the Baptist IRC committee chairman, wrote to Lancaster on September 14, 2005. "Because IRC approval has never been granted, this is a direct violation of Baptist Medical Center, IRC and OHRP (Office for Human Research Protection) policy. Please be advised you are to cease all activities associated with this study, until such time as the IRC can make an informed decision about whether or not this study should be approved. This includes accepting new subjects and collecting data on the subjects you have already 'enrolled.'"

Lancaster told the Baptist IRB that his participation in the first phase of the study had been approved by a different IRB, an assertion that Joyce soon discovered was false. Seemingly chastened, Lancaster wrote back that "I no longer desire to pursue any participation in this study." He further promised to notify J & J / DePuy of his decision to withdraw from the project. But in an email he sent to J & J / DePuy's Marilyn Cassell soon after, he wrote that he would secretly keep going with the study but not tell his hospital's IRB committee.

"I will continue to send follow ups in the study from the first arm as it predated the fiasco with the IRB," Lancaster wrote. "I am not going to communicate that with Dr. Joyce since it does not involve Baptist Hospital, and he most surely will have a problem with that. I assume DePuy still feels comfortable with the legality and consents from the first arm of the study." Lancaster subsequently admitted nineteen new patients into the study in operations he performed at Baptist Medical Center, so the hospital's IRB should have been told. He continued to send J & J / DePuy follow-up data on other patients.

Having gathered the results of their Pinnacle surgeries from the company's consultants, J & J put together a PIN study poster presentation that was first displayed in February 2007 at the annual meeting of the American Academy of Orthopaedic Surgeons, held in San Diego.

The poster made five false claims. The most important was "At 5 years, acetabular cup survival was 99.9%." The implication was that only one of the 1,183 cups implanted during the study had to be replaced after five years. In fact, only 21 patients had passed the five-year mark by the time the study was concluded. And of these 21, five had their implants removed by the time of publication, meaning nearly a quarter had failed.

In 2006, an acceptable implant failure rate was widely deemed to be 1 percent per year, which translates to 5 percent at five years. With the launch in 1997 of the heaviest plastic liners, the acceptable failure rate soon fell to 0.5 percent annually and 2.5 percent at five years.

So, according to the actual results of J & J's own study, Pinnacle metal-on-metal hip implants were failing at a rate almost ten times higher than that of metal-on-plastic ones being sold at the time—and they were failing quickly. Among the total of 1,183 implants, 20 failed by January 2, 2007.

In sworn testimony, Plouhar said that J & J / DePuy knew about almost none of these failures. The first problem with Plouhar's claim is that in the same month the company publicized PIN's supposed 1-out-of-1,183 result, the company sent a letter to French regulatory authorities stating that 11 cups had failed (the actual number by that date was 16).

The second problem is that two of the unreported failures were in patients of surgeons listed as authors of the PIN study, including the lead author. Internal documents demonstrate the company ghost-wrote the study—unethical, when it comes to medical research papers—and the listed authors had almost nothing to do with its writing. So company executives were caught in a bind: they could either admit to ghostwriting, which would mean the surgeons' failure to provide appropriate data about their own cases in a timely fashion would be at least mildly explicable. Or they could claim the authors actually did the writing, and thereby throw them under the bus for deliberately misreporting the results of their own surgeries.

In trial testimony, Plouhar tried to navigate between these two unpalatable choices.

LANIER: You're saying that the doctor sat on it and didn't give the information to the company. Is that what you're saying?

PLOUHAR: We did not have the case report forms.

Q: I'm sorry, ma'am, is that what you're saying?

A: I'm saying that they were not reported to the company.

Q: You understand some of these doctors that y'all claim wrote this paper (indicating) are the same doctors that you're saying sat on the information and didn't give it to you.

A: I'm saying that we did not have all the case report forms.

LANIER: Objection, nonresponsive.

JUDGE: Sustained.

PLOUHAR: We had not received the case report forms from the sites.

LANIER: Ma'am, that still wasn't my question. I said you understand the doctors that you say wrote this paper are some of the very doctors that you're now saying they never told us about the data.

A: I'd have to look in detail at the case reports. I don't know which surgeons submitted the case report forms. I know—

Q: Dr. Barrett was one of them?

A: Yes. Dr. Barrett was one.

Q: So Dr. Barrett himself, if he truly wrote this paper, you sure would think he doesn't have the excuse of saying, well, I didn't know that I'd revised that hip?

A: I don't know. You would have to talk to Dr. Barrett.

Q: I mean, but you're sitting here telling—by the way, you won't agree this was ghostwritten, even though y'all ghostwrote it?

A: It was not ghostwritten.

Q: Yeah. You think Dr. Barrett actually wrote this paper?

A: He participated in it.

Q: He didn't write a word of this paper, did he?

A: He participated in it.

Q: By participated, you're telling us he hid his revisions from you?

A: No.

Q: Did y'all know about his revisions?

A: We knew that he had a case that had been revised for infection.

Q: Did y'all know about the other revisions, or did your investigators hide 'em from you?

A: I don't think that they were hiding them from us. Sometimes
it just takes time to get data.

CHAPTER 36

Never Stop Moving

MIKE KRZYZEWSKI IS AMONG THE GREATEST COLLEGE BASKETBALL coaches in history. A fixture at Duke University from 1980 until his retirement in 2022, he has thirteen Final Four appearances—more than any division one men's basketball coach in history.

Among his extraordinary accomplishments, he coached the men's Olympic team to three gold medals, the first in 2008. During those Olympics Krzyzewski, widely known as "Coach K," served as the chief pitchman for the largest orthopedic advertising campaign in history.

Titled "Never Stop Moving," the TV spots featured Coach K, the recipient of two J & J / DePuy plastic-on-metal hip implants, playing basketball—proof that his hips were working well.

"Thanks to his DePuy Hip replacements, Coach K is back in the game," the ads stated. "In fact, Pinnacle has a 99.9 percent survivorship at five years!"

J & J bought $40 million in TV advertising from NBC to run during the two weeks of the Olympics. The TV ads were complemented by printed ones in weekly newspaper supplements like *Parade* and magazines like *Better Homes and Gardens* and *Golf Digest*.

The campaign was expected to reach 90 percent of American

adults in the crucial thirty-five to sixty-four age category more than five times each. And when it ended, the company estimated that it got 317,000 responses, leading 139,000 people to take action and at least 18,000 to visit a "DePuy surgeon." No other orthopedic advertising campaign had ever come close to costing as much.

By then, Pinnacle had already surpassed $1 billion in sales, but a tidal wave of problems was building. In March 2008, a group of surgeons at Oxford University wrote a journal article highlighting four patients who had received metal-on-metal hip implants and subsequently developed what the surgeons described as pseudotumors—huge internal boils resulting from the body's inflammatory response to metallic debris.

In July, surgeons at Norfolk and Norwich University Hospital in England, which had a long and close association with J & J / DePuy, sent the company a report on the experiences of 545 patients who had received a total of 652 hip implants (some patients got both hips done) over a seven-year period.

"Up to 31st January 2008, 82 patients with 90 hips were revised," the report stated. "The failure rate has been 16% at 5 years." By comparison, the failure rate among patients receiving metal-on-plastic implants was between 1 percent and 2 percent, they reported.

The Norfolk and Norwich team added that "the metal ions released have killed the bone and soft tissue around the hip replacement resulting in:

a. Fluid collection often under high pressure causing pain.
b. Tendon rupture causing hip dislocation.
c. Bone death resulting in fractures around the implant."

J & J / DePuy responded by telling the English surgical team that the problems they were reporting had not been seen anywhere else in the world. This was a lie.

That same month, the Oxford team authored a piece in *The Journal of Bone & Joint Surgery*, the field's premier medical journal, expanding the number of patients whom they had treated suffering pseudotumors to seventeen, all of them women.

"There may be a toxic reaction to an excess of particulate metal wear debris or a hypersensitivity reaction to a normal amount of metal debris," they wrote. "We are concerned that with time the incidence of these pseudotumours may increase."

In September, the Hip Society—a specialty organization among orthopedic surgeons—held a meeting attended by Dr. Thomas Schmalzried, one of DePuy's top surgical consultants. Some of the surgeons shared pictures of patients whose metal-on-metal Pinnacle hips had to be removed.

"Visually, the MoM cases discussed looked alarming and concerning, unlike squeaking ceramic where there was no images associated with it. The images for MoM reaction looked bad," stated Michael Rhee, a top J & J / DePuy product director, in an email to Paul Berman, J & J / DePuy's director of hip marketing.

"There were no clear indicators from the data set or cases presented on direct cause of adverse metal reaction, but 80% of the attendees had seen this type of tissue reaction."

Berman reassured Rhee, "We will manage through this."

There was also an Australian orthopedic surgeon who had examined that country's registry of implants—something the United States doesn't have—and found that "larger diameter metal-metal had the highest early revisions rate." The largest of such implants was ASR XL followed by Pinnacle, both sold by J & J / DePuy.

Forwarding this email to Berman, Rhee wrote: "Another one." Berman responded, "Train wreck. It is going to be an uphill battle." Rhee wrote back: "It's all in or nothing. Who is planning to scream the loudest at this point. Best case might be a category issue, how do we protect pinnacle. Ult xl. Need to start looking at that strategy ASAP."

Yet, perversely, as the number of ASR XL and Pinnacle hips that had to be yanked out and replaced soared, so, too, did J & J / DePuy's sales. During such operations, surgeons often left untouched the cup and stem, the ends of the devices attached to bone, since after a few years bones tend to fuse with the implant. The surgeons generally replaced the metal ball, liner, or both, usually with plastic liners that functioned far better than the metal ones. But since they had to fit a J & J / DePuy cup and stem, the surgeons purchased new parts from J & J / DePuy as well.

Internally, this was cause for celebration. The company got to profit from its own disaster.

"Team, it's time to dial up the volume around DePuy's Hips Revisions portfolio. Clearly revisions are fueling our above market growth," Berman wrote in an April 1, 2009, email to his hips team. "This revision segment is on fire and we must dominate it in the same way we did primaries."

Another strategy the company used to deflect complaints about its metal-on-metal implants was to slightly tweak their design and then claim these changes resolved the problems. Of particular concern was the rapid failure of the company's ASR XL implants. Half of the company's hips revenues were coming from metal-on-metal implants, so finding a way to get ahead of the growing controversy was crucial. Between 2008 and 2009, the company designed and began selling the aSphere implant, which had a slightly modified shape.

"Team— We continue to hear questions about hypersensitivity and ions from surgeons and sales reps in the US," Berman wrote in an email on August 20, 2008. "While we don't have evidence of a real problem, particularly with DePuy MoM implants, the situation represents a significant opportunity to further differentiate Pinnacle MoM technology and protect our MoM franchise with aSphere heads. aSphere is now, more than ever, a critical project for the US hip business, and we must do everything we can to keep this project on schedule. We have reliable intelligence that there will be up to 10 papers at the AAOS on issues with MoM bearings. We cannot go into the AAOS meeting without approval of aSphere."

To an extraordinary degree, J & J / DePuy managed to keep complaints about its implants quiet, often telling surgeons who reported problems that they were alone in having issues. In mid-2009, a team from Johnson & Johnson's corporate parent arrived at the Indiana headquarters of J & J / DePuy to troubleshoot its hip problems. After the second meeting, the corporate team told J & J / DePuy they should employ a four-part defense. The first step was to blame surgeons for having poor technique and then offer to strengthen the company's training program. If that didn't work, the company should move to blaming patients and say that, as a result of anatomical differences, some patients may not be appropriate for the company's metal-on-metal implants. The third was to claim that the products' global results were good. If none of those three worked, the J & J corporate team said J & J / DePuy needed to develop some "soft landing strategies" associated with product phase-outs.

As J & J began rolling out the first of these strategies, more surgeons started complaining. Dr. Jack Irving, a Connecticut orthopedic surgeon, wrote the company extensive letters detailing his experience, including the fact that his re-surgical rate with the company's metal-on-metal hip implants was ten times higher than his rate with metal-on-plastic implants. Since he had been diligently sending all this information to J & J / DePuy, he said the company should know all about this growing disaster.

"I do not feel DePuy is doing enough to understand the extent of Pinnacle MOM hip disease. I believe it borders on unethical to continue to market the product until the issues are elucidated. These products are harming patients."

Another concerned doctor was Dr. Antoni Nargol, an orthopedic surgeon from Middlesbrough, England, who performed so many hip surgeries that DePuy hired him to train other surgeons, not only in Great Britain but in India and other parts of the world.

But beginning in 2007, Nargol started seeing serious problems in his metal-on-metal patients. In particular, blood tests he performed showed some of his patients suffering toxic levels of metal ions. The company was also seeing such problems all over the world but didn't tell Nargol. Rather, DePuy engineers and executives told Nargol he needed to change his surgical technique.

"They tried to suggest ideas to improve cup positioning," Nargol told a jury in October 2016. "And I went along with this, thinking that it was my fault that my patients had high metal ion levels, and I thought we needed to change the way we were putting the cups in."

In 2008, as more of his patients with J & J / DePuy hips needed their implants removed and replaced, Nargol decided to stop using the ASR XL. The next year, he stopped using Pinnacle. J & J / DePuy sales reps and executives in England sent alarmist emails back to headquarters about Nargol's decisions. Executives responded by sending teams to visit him.

"I was told they are coming to see me because they have never seen this before and I'm the only person with this problem," Nargol testified. "So this is totally— I was isolated, and I was thinking there's something wrong with what I am doing, how could I be the only surgeon with this problem. I blamed myself."

At the time, Nargol was overseeing a study measuring blood metal ion levels in patients receiving J & J / DePuy hip implants. A similar study was underway in Italy. In 2008, J & J / DePuy ended its funding for both studies. J & J / DePuy proposed to Nargol that the high ion levels he found in his patients may have been caused by contaminated local water supplies. Neither study was ever published or completed.

Finally, in April 2012, Nargol and three other surgeons from his hospitals attended a meeting in London with representatives from the British FDA, Britain's orthopedic association, and a team from DePuy.

Several weeks before the meeting, DePuy executives had run a report showing the failure rate of Pinnacle hips among twenty surgeons in the United States who, like Irving, were participating in a computerized reporting network called the DePuy Outcome Tracking System, or DOTS. The report showed a five-year failure rate of 14 percent for the company's metal-on-metal hip implants—six times the failure rate of metal-on-plastic implants. And these were the company's handpicked surgeons.

At the April meeting in Britain, J & J / DePuy mentioned nothing about these data or any of its American problems. Instead, executives told meeting attendees that Nargol's problems were unique to him, and that "because the Pinnacle was released in America a few years earlier [than in Britain], they said if we were going to see a problem, we'd see it in America first," Nargol testified. "And it was just total denial."

Several months later, the FDA held a meeting of its medical devices advisory committee, and a representative from J & J / DePuy made a similar presentation. He didn't mention the concerning data from the company's own registry.

Patients who had gotten J & J / DePuy's metal-on-metal hips told the panel the devices had ruined their lives. Among them was Alisa Moore, a fifty-seven-year-old wife, mother, and executive director of a community service agency employing 750 people. In April of 2008, she received an ASR XL, which soon failed and began poisoning her. In July 2011, she got it replaced. But the metal debris had so weakened her tissues that the new implant dislocated three months later, causing excruciating pain. Two more surgeries and a waist-to-thigh brace for six weeks were needed to reset it. She said she had never experienced a day since without intense pain, and the resulting strain on her other hip meant it would need to be replaced as well.

"When I think about the fact that DePuy was able to market the ASR hip without premarket clinical studies, I feel like a human guinea pig," she told the panel, adding: "When I read news articles indicating DePuy was aware of the problems with the ASR prior to the time I was implanted with it but remained heavily involved in promoting it and failed to warn doctors and patients until years later, my sense of outrage increases."

It wasn't just an issue of a corporation not warning doctors and patients but of doctor complicity. Nine prominent surgeons were collectively paid $184 million by DePuy. These surgeons were deployed for years by the company to persuade their colleagues to buy the product. They were even given a royalty on every Pinnacle sale other than those for their own patients.

In depositions, many of these surgeons said they stopped using Pinnacle metal-on-metal implants in their own patients in 2009 or 2010. They did not make these decisions public, and several continued to urge other surgeons to use the devices.

Australian health authorities, who have among the best device registries in the world, forced J & J / DePuy to stop selling the ASR metal-on-metal hip in December 2009. In the United States, the ASR was recalled in August 2010. J & J / DePuy stopped selling Pinnacle metal-on-metal hip implants in the United States in 2013 after the FDA strengthened hip implant regulations, but the company said declining sales and not the FDA rules were the reason.

Johnson & Johnson settled the many lawsuits involving problems with ASR XL implantations for $2.5 billion. Nearly ten thousand lawsuits from those who received Pinnacle would be filed in the coming years.

CHAPTER 37

A Cure for Sag

JILL MESIGIAN WAS A PETITE MOTHER OF TWO AND GRANDMOTHER of three who told a Philadelphia jury in 2019 that the surgical insertion of a Johnson & Johnson mesh had caused her immense harm.

"I feel like I'm being ripped apart when we have sex, last time," Mesigian, seventy-five at the time, said in her clipped British accent. "We haven't had it since."

She had five separate surgeries to fish jagged pieces of plastic out of her vaginal walls and said she would need many more. The wounds hadn't healed and never would. She had to wear pads to staunch a constant drip of blood and occasional gushes of urine. She couldn't swim with her grandchildren or dress in anything other than pants, something that filled her with regret and shame.

"I didn't expect my life to end this way," she added haltingly. "Didn't expect our marriage to end this way."

Millions of women have been treated with pelvic mesh implants to address urinary problems caused by sagging bladders pressing against the vagina. The implants often proved ineffective and caused serious injury, including bleeding and severe pain. Mass tort litigation brought against the manufacturers of these devices, including

Johnson & Johnson, has resulted in nearly $8 billion paid to resolve the claims of more than 100,000 women.

J & J's experience with vaginal mesh represented the final step in its moral descent. With Ortho Evra, company executives knew the patch delivered twice as much estrogen as low-dose birth control pills but chose to introduce the product anyway and lie about the risks to the FDA. With Pinnacle metal-on-metal hip implants, the company launched a product nearly identical to those that had failed a quarter of a century before, while also misrepresenting crucial product specifications to the FDA.

But in both cases the company never conducted an actual clinical trial before launch that demonstrated these dangers. So executives had some small amount of wiggle room to claim that they didn't conclusively know that the products were killers.

With J & J's vaginal mesh, however, that wiggle room disappeared. And rather than lie to the FDA about these proven dangers, the company simply didn't consult the agency at all.

HUMANS SAG BOTH INSIDE AND OUT AS THEY AGE. THE MIRACULOUS flexibility that allows women to carry babies to term while still having fully functional organs works against them in old age in this battle against internal subsidence.

As the muscles in the abdomen weaken, they often lose their grip on organs, which consequently bump into one another. Bladders often press against vaginas, causing urine leakage, chronic constipation, a feeling of pelvic pressure, vaginal bulge, lower back pain, and discomfort during sex. This is called pelvic organ prolapse, or POP.

A related problem is stress urinary incontinence, or SUI, when the muscles that control the release of urine weaken. Women with SUI often leak urine when laughing or lifting because the muscles around the urethra can no longer resist strong forces from the abdomen.

Cures for prolapse and urinary incontinence are myriad. Women are often given pelvic exercises intended to strengthen interior muscles. Another common but ancient treatment is a pessary, which in its modern form is a silicon pebble or sponge inserted into the vagina like a diaphragm or tampon. Many seek surgery. About half of women experience some symptoms of prolapse and somewhere between 7 and 19 percent in the United States get surgery—millions upon millions.

For years, surgeons used women's own tissue to strap organs down within their abdomens. But in many cases, this tissue disintegrated or stopped working, leading to re-surgeries. In the 1990s, surgeons began testing whether the plastic meshes they had been using for decades to repair abdominal hernias might work for POP and SUI. The first pelvic mesh was approved by the FDA in 1996, and it was essentially a plastic sling cinched around the bladder.

Among the many problems with these early procedures was that they were performed by cutting into the abdomen, making recoveries painful and lengthy. Looking for an easier and quicker way to insert mesh, surgeons soon settled on the vagina. But inserting mesh or anything else through and around the vagina presented an entirely different set of problems.

The first is that vaginas are teeming with bacteria that can never be entirely sterilized away. Plastic mesh brushed along vaginal walls and then inserted into the abdominal cavity creates an ideal environment for systemic bacterial contamination, which can be lethal. Another problem is mechanistic. Unlike the abdominal walls, vaginas are extraordinarily flexible organs, a characteristic crucial to childbirth and pleasurable sex. But hard plastic mesh isn't flexible. Wrapping a vagina in plastic limits its flexibility.

A third problem is that when women go through menopause, their vaginal walls thin. Mesh implanted behind vaginal walls can erode through these thinning walls to emerge on the other side. Penises that scrape along jagged plastic mesh often emerge injured.

Among the largest manufacturers of surgical supplies, J & J made a variety of plastic meshes—Gynemesh, UltraPro, and TVT were among them—that surgeons started using in prolapse abdominal surgeries. Initial results were mixed.

One surgeon wrote J & J in 2000 that he had used Gynemesh for prolapse surgery but after the surgery his patient "had a 2 cm erosion coming out of and into the right side wall at three months." He added, "Sex is like screwing a wire brush, according to her spouse. I have excised it. Any explanations?"

Problems became so common that a top surgeon approached J & J to suggest that the company publicize the best ways to *remove* problematic mesh. Unsurprisingly, a J & J executive warned in an email dated October 3, 2000, that the company should do nothing to promote such techniques.

But that particular surgeon was hardly alone in confronting problems with Johnson & Johnson's meshes. From 1994 through 2004, J & J hired Dr. Uwe Klinge, an abdominal surgeon at the University of Aachen in Germany, to study how the human body responded to mesh.

"When we started to use surgical meshes in the beginning of the '90s, we got aware that we have to face several complications that are related with these mesh materials, mainly at the occasion of some revision operations where we saw what happens to these meshes after getting incorporated. And we wanted to learn more about these meshes to avoid these complications," Klinge said in a sworn deposition.

With the support of Ethicon, a J & J surgical device subsidiary, Klinge soon proved that plastic meshes had a much more troubling impact on the human body than had been commonly believed. After examining hundreds of meshes taken out of patients, he concluded that the body invariably attacked them as invaders, a never-ending inflammatory response that can create considerable scarring.

"It doesn't stop after three weeks or four weeks, but it stays there as a chronic wound until the end of the life of the patient," he testified. "And this chronic wound leads to a permanent tissue irritation." That scarring leads the mesh to contract and shrink, he said, which can result in chronic pain. That pain can lead to dyspareunia, or painful sex, as well as "erosions and organ dysfunction," he said.

Klinge said he shared these findings with J & J researchers and executives in frequent meetings. He published many of his findings, including them in more than one hundred articles in peer-reviewed journals and about fifty books and book chapters. And, most importantly, he found a fix: The mesh's pore size is a critical element in the strength of the body's reaction to mesh. The smaller the pore size, the more intense the scarring. So he suggested that meshes have much larger pore sizes, a suggestion he published in a seminal paper in 2002.

J & J sold both Gynemesh, which had very small pore sizes, and UltraPro, with far larger pores. Citing Klinge's and others' work, Gene Kammerer, a J & J engineer, suggested in 2005 that the company consider telling surgeons to use UltraPro exclusively in prolapse surgeries and stop using Gynemesh, because UltraPro was far safer.

"Without going into too much detail here, this mesh could reduce the scar contraction and lower the density of the scar formation resulting in fewer cases of recurrence of prolapse and erosion," Kammerer wrote.

The request was rejected because it wouldn't be as profitable.

"I don't believe that UltraPro can be used due (to) commercial limitations," Dr. Dieter Engel, a top J & J executive, told Kammerer. "Gynemesh PS market price is much higher than that of UltraPro (I think at least twice as much if not more). This high price strategy has been very successful. Gynemesh PS is expected to sell about $15 million by year end which is only slightly less than Vypro and UltraPro together. Replacing Gynemesh by UltraPro would either reduce the market price, which is not good business, or the UltraPro price would have to be increased, which is not possible."

IN 2002, THE SAME YEAR KLINGE PUBLISHED HIS SEMINAL PAPER ON pore size, J & J had received approval from the FDA to market

Gynemesh for prolapse repair—the first preconfigured mesh ever granted such an approval by the agency. But at that point, Gynemesh was still largely being used by highly trained urogynecological surgeons who inserted the mesh in complex and invasive abdominal surgeries.

For the mesh to become a huge seller, J & J needed a simpler and less invasive surgery that could be performed by less trained but far more numerous OB-GYNs. So the company hired a French surgical team who developed a method of cutting the plastic sheets into a special shape with six tabs, or arms, that they used to sew the mesh into the tissue between the vagina and bladder. Seeing a huge potential market, J & J adopted the prototype, combined it with a few common surgical tools, and created an all-in-one kit that the company branded as Prolift.

In fact, almost two years before the company launched Prolift, the members of the French surgical team who invented the device were expressing deep unease about its safety. In an email dated July 19, 2003, Dr. Michel Cosson, one of the inventors, wrote that the mesh was protruding into the vaginal canal (one result is dyspareunia— painful sex) in far too many patients and that the company should consider going "back into the concept stage."

In an email dated May 10, 2004, Ophelie Berthier, a J & J executive, wrote that Dr. Bernard Jacquetin and Cosson, two of the inventors, were concerned with "the shrinkage of the mesh which may lead to pain, dyspareunia. . . . Indeed now that they have tremendously improved the technique and lowered the erosion rate what needs to be improved is the shrinkage of the mesh (in this case gynemesh soft)."

Again and again, J & J executives asked surgeons who were using an early version of the product how well it was working. In email after email, executives reported that the surgeons were worried.

In one email sent on January 18, 2005, two months before Prolift's launch, an executive reported that an Italian surgeon had infections in 8 percent of his cases and serious problems with painful sex and scar contraction.

"Contraction pulls against the side wall and causes pain," the email stated. "It causes a hard tissue which can be felt by patient and sexual partner."

That same month, an Italian surgical team published a study on the use of an early version of Prolift contending that it caused too many problems in women, including a sharp increase in painful sex.

"We believe that the use of prolene mesh should be abandoned," the study concluded.

J & J executives dismissed these concerns and, in March 2005, began selling Prolift anyway, without asking the FDA for approval: a highly unusual step that the agency later protested.

Just as Prolift was being introduced, the product's French inventors published a study detailing the preliminary results of their experiences. Thirty-four of the 277 women in the study, or 12 percent, experienced mesh protrusions (known as "exposures") into their vaginal canal, and 25 needed surgery within a month.

The study's final numbers would turn out to be even worse, but the preliminary ones were so bad that the authors advised that "caution be exercised when carrying out this new surgical procedure."

The French team suggested that Johnson & Johnson conduct "experimental studies and clinical trials . . . in order to reduce the level of exposure to less than 5 percent of cases." In subsequent interviews, Cosson said he and his coinventors told J & J executives that the company needed an entirely new mesh but they "just ignored us."

Meanwhile, Johnson & Johnson had to decide whether to warn surgeons about these risks in an instruction manual sent with its product, known in the device world as the IFU (instructions for use). One of the company executives working with the French team urgently requested that the company add a warning to its instructions: "Early clinical experience has shown that the use of mesh through a vaginal approach can occasionally/uncommonly lead to complications such as vaginal erosion and retraction which can result in an anatomical distortion of the vaginal cavity that can interfere with sexual intercourse."

Scott Ciarrocca, a top J & J executive, wrote back that the product instructions had already been printed, and that any new warnings would have to be included in future revisions—something that didn't happen for years.

Sean O'Bryan, who as Prolift's senior project manager for regulatory affairs was responsible for the IFU, said in a later deposition that the excuse about printing was unacceptable. O'Bryan left the company just as Prolift launched.

AS PROBLEMS WITH PROLIFT MOUNTED, J & J EXECUTIVES DISCUSSED whether to reveal the risks of the procedure in meetings with doctors. The first medical conference the Prolift team targeted took place soon after the product's launch. At the conference, J & J offered scientific information on its mesh product.

"I would like that we spin it more on the safety aspect rather than complications," wrote Laura Angelini, a J & J executive, in a March 24, 2005, email. "Can we include that in the title as well?" The response: "I have attached a draft for our internal review only. Vince (Lucente) felt it was unethical to exclude the dyspareunia data." Next response from Angelini: "I accept that we need to report the case of dyspareunia, because I agree that it would be unethical not to mention, since we know about it. However, the way it is presented in the abstract is going to kill us."

After several more back-and-forths, the team chose to eliminate the dyspareunia data entirely.

Johnson & Johnson supported Prolift's 2005 introduction with a two-year marketing budget of $7.7 million and a budget for clinical costs of just $600,000. The company didn't need much money for relevant clinical costs because it didn't intend to do any further clinical studies in women. Executives predicted a market with $400 million in sales.

Surgeons, many of whom were paid consultants to Johnson & Johnson, took to Prolift quickly and hundreds of thousands of women around the world were soon having plastic mesh stitched into their vaginal walls. Signs of serious problems were apparent from the start, with many doctors complaining that the surgery was more difficult and complicated than they expected.

As problems piled up, J & J's Prolift team met in September 2006 to discuss fixes. According to a PowerPoint presentation delivered at the meeting, the group agreed on some steps to address the customers' many unmet needs, including "Minimize shrinkage, pain," "Lower the rate of recurrence due to less tissue contraction," and "Minimize exposure."

Executives in the pharmaceutical and biotech industries frequently talk about "unmet medical needs" or "unmet customer needs," but they're usually referring to problems unresolved or unaddressed by current drugs or devices. The Prolift issues were caused by the treatment itself. A simple cure would have been to avoid using Prolift.

That was not a solution the executives offered. But they did point to another answer: UltraPro, which a separate slide promised would "cause less inflammation than traditional meshes. Induce less fibrosis compared to small porous meshes. Generate less foreign body reactions than heavyweight meshes. Get better integrated to host tissue. Lower patient complaints. Provoke less pain compared to traditional heavyweight meshes. Improve patients' quality of life."

And it would do this all, the slide promised, "without any negative side effects compared to traditional heavyweight meshes!" It was essentially the same solution Klinge had come up with in 2005. But, as before with Gynemesh, substituting UltraPro for Prolift would have reduced profits because UltraPro was cheaper, so J & J didn't make the substitution.

Six months later, the team met again with a list of "unmet clinical needs" similarly long and damning. So many women were suffering serious problems that the number of surgeons expressing alarm was growing at an increasingly worrisome rate. In February 2007, the American College of Obstetricians and Gynecologists (ACOG) published a practice bulletin emphasizing that, as a result of the risks and uncertain benefits of vaginal mesh, "the procedures should be considered experimental and patients should consent to surgery with that understanding."

Not only are experimental procedures rarely reimbursed by private insurers, but performing procedures that are deemed experimental can expose doctors to considerable liability. Within days of the bulletin, a top official of the Providence health system in Oregon sent a note to its OB-GYN department members warning of the potential malpractice risks of performing vaginal mesh surgeries.

For J & J, this was real trouble. If the ACOG bulletin stood, Prolift's soaring sales numbers might level off or decline.

J & J executives swung into action. Drug and device makers underwrite most medical-specialty societies, and their consultants often lead them. On August 26, 2007, Dr. Vincente Lucente, an ACOG official as well as a paid J & J consultant, wrote an email to Price St. Hilaire, an executive at Ethicon, the J & J subsidiary that manufactured the mesh, promising that ACOG would soon issue a new practice bulletin supporting vaginal mesh, which it did.

"I led the charge on this and never thought we would get a complete replacement of the earlier bulletin. This is a major victory," Lucente wrote.

St. Hilaire responded: "I AM DOING THE HAPPY DANCE!!!! I LOVE YOU MAN!!!! :)"

In April 2008, the company received a report from surgeons who were doing a brisk business in mesh removals. The report concluded that all meshes "without exception" induce a foreign-body response, and that pain, erosion, folding, and shrinkage were extremely common.

The next month, ACOG held its annual meeting in New Orleans, and one of the biggest topics of discussion were the dangers of vaginal mesh, which a J & J executive described in an email to headquarters.

"The lecture hall was standing room only, and the main topic for discussion, consternation was 'mesh,'" the email said. "As you walked into the room where the posters were located, the first row had six posters, the first four all related to mesh complications." The executive bemoaned the fact that any posters presenting positive findings on Prolift were located toward the back corner.

And those were just the posters. The first video presentation was, according to the executive, "from Dr. Park at the Cleveland Clinic titled 'Transvaginal Mesh Excision for Complications Following Transvaginal Mesh Placement.'"

The email described several more presentations from surgeons practicing at prestigious academic institutions who had been forced to perform delicate surgical procedures to remove vaginal mesh. It then continued: "After Dr. Ridgeway's presentation about handling mesh complications related to erosion, a doctor walked to the microphone and asked everyone in the audience to raise their hand if they have had to manage a mesh erosion surgically.

"Roughly 90 percent of the room raised their hand, at which point it was obvious the tenor of the meeting was starting to change."

The email concluded: "At one point, Peggy Norton, well known and vocal opponent of mesh use, approached the microphone and chastised the members of SGS for not taking a stance against mesh. And she implied that SGS should place a moratorium on the use of mesh in vaginal POP surgery. Peggy explained that the members of SGS were hurting patients and that mesh use has not been scientifically proven as a sound surgical option."

Chief of urogynecology and pelvic reconstructive surgery at the University of Utah, Norton's office had been flooded with women needing to have their mesh removed. At first, she blamed the surgeons and called J & J and other manufacturers and pleaded with them to either train doctors better or stop selling them mesh.

"These doctors would sign up for a weekend course," Norton said. "They'd fly him in, give him a nice dinner and show him how to do this. And they'd have the rep standing in the OR during his first few procedures."

When patients started experiencing problems, those surgeons largely refused to have anything more to do with those patients.

"These doctors said, 'You need to go to the university,'" Norton said. "'We put it in but they take it out.'"

One reason was that insurers paid doctors less to remove mesh than they did to implant it, Norton said. But delicate removal procedures were vastly more complicated, lengthy, and expensive. Norton's hospital lost money on every excision.

"My hospital said to me, 'You have to stop doing these surgeries,'" Norton recalled. "And we said, 'Who else is going to do this?'"

The same month as the ACOG meeting, J & J hired a firm to conduct phone interviews with the top twenty surgeons in the United States using Prolift. The interviews were scathing.

Several months after the ACOG meeting, the French team who invented Prolift published the final analysis of the 684 women they had implanted from October 2002 through December 2004. The results were far worse than their preliminary numbers. Fully a third of the women (33.6 percent) experienced serious side effects within six months of the procedure—most from vaginal erosions and mesh contracture.

Johnson & Johnson ramped up sales efforts anyway.

"Seize the moment and let's conquer!" a top company executive wrote in an email to sales representatives in June 2009. Revenues surged.

CHAPTER 38

"Usually Minor and Well Manageable"

T HE FDA RARELY ISSUES CORRECTIONS. BUT IN JULY 2011, THE
agency released a significant revision to its 2008 vaginal mesh alert,
which had said that serious complications from the devices were rare.

"The FDA determined that (1) serious adverse events are NOT
rare, contrary to what was stated in the 2008 PHN," the new alert
said, "and (2) transvaginally placed mesh in POP repair does NOT
conclusively improve clinical outcomes over traditional non-mesh
repair." The agency promised to hold an advisory hearing in September to discuss whether vaginal mesh products like Johnson & Johnson's should be yanked from the market.

The announcement came in the wake of a study that J & J
launched under pressure from the FDA and conducted with six surgeons at Stanford, Yale, and Washington Hospital Center. Such studies often serve to delay serious regulatory actions. In the study, women
with prolapse problems were randomly assigned to have prolapse surgery either with Prolift or without it. But unlike most studies, the
trial used a remarkable control to try to keep surgeons from influencing the outcome: The doctors who examined women after surgery
didn't know whether the patients had gotten mesh or not.

This may explain why Prolift failed so spectacularly. The trial was halted midstream by a safety committee after sixty-five women had been recruited (thirty-two got Prolift and thirty-three had surgery with their natural tissue) because 15 percent of the women who had gotten Prolift had seen the plastic erode through their vaginal walls. Almost as bad was the finding that women in the Prolift group were just as likely as those in the control group to have their prolapse symptoms return. Bad outcomes and no benefit. The investigators concluded that continuing to give Prolift to additional women would be unethical.

Outside of a clinical trial, however, J & J kept selling, and the number of women with injuries continued to pile up. In 2010, at least one hundred thousand American women had plastic mesh inserted around their vaginas.

In August 2011, Public Citizen, the rare public advocacy organization that does not take money from J & J, sent the FDA a formal citizen's petition asking the agency to ban vaginal mesh and force J & J and other makers to recall their remaining supplies of the products. If the agency had agreed, J & J's liability problems would have significantly worsened.

At the advisory committee hearing in September 2011, Dr. Piet Hinoul, a top J & J executive, told the experts that Prolift was working well. Hinoul pointed to a study published weeks before in *The New England Journal of Medicine* that offered support for the use of vaginal mesh in some patients. Two years later, the journal would issue an unusual correction of that study, stating that it had failed to note that J & J, in addition to paying the authors consulting fees, had reviewed the original study protocol and a presubmission draft of the manuscript—both breaches of the usual publication procedure. The revelations of J & J's influence on the study came only as a result of subsequent lawsuits.

In his remarks, Hinoul acknowledged that many women saw plastic mesh protrude through their vaginal walls but said this problem "is usually minor and well manageable."

A primary selling point for Prolift was the notion that using a plastic mesh instead of a woman's own tissue would ensure that women didn't have to go back under the knife as early or as often. FDA officials disagreed, saying that more than half of women who experienced mesh erosions into their vaginal walls needed surgical corrections.

Examining claims from the federal Medicare program to see how quickly women who got vaginal mesh had to have another surgery compared to women who had prolapse surgery without mesh, "we found that women who were initially treated with mesh underwent re-surgery 2.26 times more often than women who did not have mesh placed," Dr. Colin Anderson-Smits, an FDA epidemiologist, told the committee.

In January 2012, the FDA ordered J & J and other mesh implant makers to conduct formal studies to determine whether the products' benefits outweighed their risks. In June 2012, J & J announced that it would stop selling Prolift and three other vaginal mesh devices. It had made millions by hiding what it had known for years. It had also ruined countless lives along the way.

In 2019, the FDA banned all vaginal meshes for prolapse repair after independent research proved that the products offered no benefits while exposing many recipients to devastating and irreversible injuries. Had the agency agreed with Public Citizen's petition in 2011 seeking this very result, hundreds of thousands more women might have been spared life-altering injuries.

As thousands of women began complaining, bills in Congress began circulating to change the FDA's device approval process, proposals that agency officials endorsed in part because of vaginal mesh. Partly thanks to the power and campaign generosity of J & J and its competitors, the bills never passed.

Johnson & Johnson was soon facing nearly fifty thousand lawsuits from injured women. Among the first plaintiffs was Linda Gross, a forty-seven-year-old nurse from Watertown, South Dakota, who won $11.1 million in damages in a trial in February 2013.

Gross told the jury that Prolift had made her unable to work, have sex with her husband, or sit comfortably for more than twenty minutes at a time. She had eighteen revision surgeries but still suffered constant pain.

The documents showing that J & J had known about Prolift's many problems before introducing the device caused such consternation that state attorneys general began suing Johnson & Johnson as well. Many won multi-million-dollar settlements.

In Australia, the company became the target of the country's largest products liability class-action lawsuit ever, with more than eleven thousand claimants. Australian media were filled with stories about the vaginal mesh disaster. In 2018, the Australian Senate released the results of its own inquiry.

"We believe this is a catastrophic failure of the health system to protect women and ensure they have access to safe health care," the report concluded. "We feel that women have been let down by their doctors, by the manufacturer of mesh and by the TGA [Therapeutic Goods Administration] as the regulator."

Greg Hunt, Australia's minister for health, offered a public apology to women injured by vaginal mesh and promised significant changes to address their concerns.

In the United States, J & J settled tens of thousands of lawsuits, but thousands more remain unresolved. Johnson & Johnson's lawyers continued to argue in court that Prolift was safe, and that the women had only themselves and their doctors to blame for devastating injuries. But the company had trouble finding respected surgeons to go along with these claims and instead had to hire obscure, sometimes unemployed doctors as defense witnesses.

In 2007, J & J had entered into a deferred prosecution agreement with the Department of Justice in which it agreed to pay an $84.7 million fine for using consulting agreements with surgeons as bribes to get them to use the company's devices. The company promised to stop the bribes.

But in vaginal mesh cases, plaintiffs' attorneys showed juries that these inducements continued long after 2007, and that they were an important reason that surgeons continued using vaginal mesh after Prolift's dangers had become plainly clear. It was all just business as usual.

PART IV

Vaccination

CHAPTER 39

A Rare Shot at Redemption

O N MARCH 10, 2021, FLANKED BY PRESIDENT BIDEN TO HIS RIGHT and Merck chief executive and chairman Ken Frazier to his left, Alex Gorsky strode to the White House podium in the South Court Auditorium of the Eisenhower Executive Office Building, a more camera-friendly space than the usual press briefing room. To Gorsky's right, a ten-foot-high poster titled "Expanding Vaccine Substance Production" featured a giant picture of machinery that represented two centuries of extraordinary progress in the science of human immunology. To his left was another giant poster titled "Accelerating Vaccine Fill Finish," which depicted a machine involved in vaccine packaging that demonstrated more than seventy years of stringent efforts to ensure that whatever substance emerged from vaccine plants was safe. It was a picture that J & J and its partner had for months failed to live up to.

But for Biden, having the chief executives of two of the most storied pharmaceutical manufacturers in the world by his side just six weeks after taking office in the midst of the worst global pandemic in a century offered invaluable PR benefits. Gorsky in particular was a catch. Gorsky had been among the last to leave President Trump's manufacturing council following what were widely perceived as racist remarks by the president. And he led one of the most admired and trusted corporations in the world, one that cast a halo on all associated with it. J & J just might save the world, and Biden wanted to be sure he was close by Gorsky's side when it did.

Meanwhile, for Gorsky, the opportunity to introduce POTUS at a White House event represented an extraordinary moment in his own life and career. A former army officer, Gorsky was now sharing the stage with the commander in chief. His staff in Washington believed that Gorsky had long toyed with the idea of running for Congress himself.

Six months earlier, he'd helped lead an effort by nearly two hundred chief executives, including the leaders of Apple, Pepsi, and Walmart, to redefine the role of business in society. He co-authored a statement from the Business Roundtable on "the purpose of a corporation," stating that companies needed to look beyond narrow shareholder interests and invest in their employees, protect the environment, and deal fairly and ethically with their suppliers. The effort was a transparent attempt by Gorsky to whitewash his past.

"There were times when I felt like Thomas Jefferson," Gorsky told a reporter from *The New York Times*.

Now he was at the White House and was introducing the president himself.

"Good afternoon, everyone," Gorsky said. "I really couldn't be more honored to be here celebrating this landmark collaboration today between Johnson & Johnson, Merck, and the Biden administration to further accelerate production of our one-shot Janssen–Johnson & Johnson Covid 19 vaccine."

The press conference was originally scheduled to be held at the Baltimore manufacturing facility of Emergent BioSolutions, the contract manufacturing company that J & J had hired to make its Covid vaccine. But a *Times* investigation published four days earlier lambasting Emergent for a history of shady contracting practices led aides to switch the venue to the White House. No one from Emergent was invited onto the stage.

Emergent's problems were one in a series of woes that had quite suddenly started piling up against the massive conglomerate. On August 26, 2019, a judge in Oklahoma ruled that Johnson & Johnson had intentionally played down the dangers and oversold the benefits of opioids, in a disaster that cost thousands of lives in the state. He ordered the company to pay $572 million in what promised to be the first of possibly dozens of government-led opioid trials that would collectively cost the conglomerate billions and leave a lasting stain on its reputation.

Two months later, the FDA announced that it had found asbestos in Johnson's Baby Powder. Unlike the Tylenol poisoning case thirty-seven years before, executives couldn't blame a faceless madman for the contamination.

Executives had known for decades that if Americans ever found out that the company deliberately violated the emotional bond created between Johnson's Baby Powder and the public, the consequences to the company's brand could be catastrophic.

Hell hath no fury like a consumer scorned.

By the end of 2019, the company was facing lawsuits from nearly 18,000 women claiming that Baby Powder had given them cancer, with tens of thousands more to follow. At the same time, J & J was being sued by 11,000 claiming injuries from the company's hip implants, nearly 21,000 over its pelvic meshes, 11,900 over Risperdal, 29,000 because of blood thinner Xarelto, and 400 from its diabetes drug Invokana.

The world was finally catching on to J & J's penchant for bad behavior. The company's ranking on *Fortune*'s listing of the most admired companies in the world dropped to twenty-sixth place from eleventh place in 2015. A crude measure, the listing had long been a deep source of pride by top J & J executives and a focus of envy from counterparts at other drug companies.

And then, a few weeks into 2020, J & J executives learned that a virus emanating from Wuhan, China, might threaten humanity. Suddenly, the rarest of opportunities presented itself to the planet's largest healthcare conglomerate—a chance to redeem itself by saving the world.

The press conference was intended to reward Gorsky for agreeing to accept help from a rival. These sorts of photo ops—the North Portico, Air Force One, the Oval Office—are powerful tools the White House can deploy to cajole reluctant business executives into doing its bidding. The images are PR gold and often end up framed and hung in the offices and homes of some of the nation's most powerful CEOs.

There was deep irony, however, in Gorsky and Johnson & Johnson being hailed as Covid saviors. Aside from the ensuing failure of J & J's vaccine, part of Gorsky's legacy was his oversight of illegal marketing tactics for Risperdal, which played a significant role in the overprescription of antipsychotics in American nursing homes. One way that Risperdal kills is by making patients more susceptible to respiratory infections, and Covid, of course, is a respiratory infection. Of the more than one million Americans whose deaths were linked to Covid, 40 percent were nursing home residents. How many were taking an antipsychotic like Risperdal? It's not a question that researchers ever answered.

Beyond that, Gorsky played leading roles in twin J & J device disasters that led tens of thousands to be crippled by poisonous metal hip implants and hundreds of thousands of women to suffer dreadful vaginal wounds. He insisted that J & J continue selling Johnson's Baby Powder despite clear evidence that the product was contaminated with asbestos.

He was also a prime contributor to the nation's opioid crisis, which had already cost more than five hundred thousand American lives. And yet while the Sackler family name was widely reviled by then, Gorsky's name had largely been spared controversy and opprobrium. Indeed, Gorsky was even given the Humanitarian of the Year Award at the Community Anti-Drug Coalitions of America's sixteenth annual Drug-Free Kids Campaign awards dinner in Washington, D.C., on October 8, 2014, for his "commitment to preventing youth drug use."

Gorsky was no stranger, then, to bitter irony when he received his praise from President Biden in March 2021.

"I want to thank the scientists and researchers at Johnson & Johnson for the literal heroic effort that began when Covid-19 first spread and led to the safe and effective vaccines that are now being co-produced," the president gushed.

That same day, the House of Representatives passed a $1.9 trillion stimulus measure dubbed the American Rescue Plan that had already passed the Senate. The bill was among the greatest legislative achievements of any president in decades. And now the world's largest healthcare conglomerate was joining the fight.

"So there is real reason for hope, folks, there's real reason for hope, I promise you," Biden said.

Nothing better encapsulates the more-than-140-year history of Johnson & Johnson than having its leader be rewarded and publicly celebrated for actions that in reality helped to foster or worsen the country's worst public health crises. Few companies in American history have had a wider gap between their public reputation and their actual conduct than J & J—a gulf it bridged with enormous advertising budgets, ingenious public relations campaigns, and massive piles of money.

Of the company's seven top-selling drugs in 2003, legal proceedings would eventually show that the company used illegal marketing tactics—including bribes, kickbacks, and lies to the FDA—for six of them.

Procrit, Risperdal, and Duragesic alone helped cause three distinct and enduring drug crises that have contributed to the deaths of as many as two million people and counting. In addition to those deaths, J & J's decision to aggressively and illegally market Risperdal to children likely caused at least sixty thousand of the country's most vulnerable boys to grow permanent breasts, and young girls and boys to briefly express milk.

Beyond those infamous products, Johnson & Johnson sold at least a half-dozen others from 2003 onward with undisclosed dangers. Among them was the company's power morcellator, a tiny blender that surgeons used to grind up and extract uteruses during hysterectomies. The procedures splattered women's abdominal cavities with endometrial cells that in far too many cases turned out to be cancerous. One in three hundred women who underwent the procedures developed metastatic cancer, according to the FDA.

Another huge seller in 2003 was the company's Cordis franchise of Cypher stents, with sales of $2.7 billion each year. Later research demonstrated that such stents are, for most patients, nothing more than an exceedingly expensive and risky waste.

Not long after 2003, the company became one of the largest manufacturers of breast implants. For decades, thousands of women complained they suffered from brain fog, fatigue, and other health issues collectively known as "breast-implant illness," while the breast implant manufacturers continued to claim their products were perfectly safe. J & J failed to conduct promised clinical trials and adequate registries that might have confirmed these problems. Finally, in October 2021, the FDA concluded that some breast implants are associated with a rare and deadly cancer. The agency thereafter mandated that women who are considering implants must be given a checklist of potential problems such as pain, scarring, asymmetry, and infection.

Yet another problematic drug was J & J's blockbuster diabetes medicine, Invokana. In March 2014, Invokana's medical safety team strongly advised the company to warn the FDA and drug regulators in Europe that, in rare cases, Invokana could cause a potentially deadly increase in blood acid levels known as diabetic ketoacidosis.

Ketoacidosis and related reactions accounted for four thousand of the roughly twenty-three thousand potentially drug-related problems in Invokana patients reported to the FDA from 2013 to 2020. More than 450 deaths were linked to Invokana during the period.

But managers decided against the warning and soon pushed out the medical safety team leader who'd advocated for it. The next year, the FDA mandated just such a warning that, along with others, tanked sales.

Again and again and again, Johnson & Johnson sold dangerous products and hid the risks from patients and regulators, all while being widely praised for a high standard of ethics. That praise most often emanated from a professional class—doctors, lawyers, and academics—that J & J sponsored with huge payments that compromised their ethics.

On top of all that, Johnson & Johnson's colossal influence operation in Washington—one begun in the nineteenth century—successfully neutered nearly all federal efforts at taming it. A small but significant measure of this achievement is that Johnson & Johnson remains the only corporation in the world that can freely use the symbol of the Red Cross, because of special legislation passed by Congress. No other company in the world owns such license. The Red Cross symbol is the most cherished in healthcare—one that engenders feelings of trust, respect, and admiration. J & J's ability to link its own brand with a universally recognized emblem of care and reassurance is priceless.

That cross is just one of the iconic brands fueling the most effective smokescreen in capitalism. But the company couldn't have created such an enduring mythology about itself were it not for a complementary myth about an agency widely regarded as the best and most impactful regulatory body in the world.

And as for saving the world—well, it hadn't worked out exactly as hoped.

DR. DAN BAROUCH WAS ALWAYS THE SMARTEST GUY IN THE ROOM. HE went to Harvard and majored in biochemistry, widely considered one of the toughest majors at one of the toughest schools anywhere. In 1993, he graduated summa cum laude.

He landed a prestigious scholarship to attend Oxford, where he earned a PhD in immunology in just two years. He returned to Harvard to attend medical school, where he once again graduated summa cum laude, even though he spent much of his time working on HIV research in his own laboratory.

He never left Harvard, soon becoming a full professor of immunology at its medical school. In 2012, he was named the founding director of the Center for Virology and Vaccine Research at Beth Israel Deaconess Medical Center, a Harvard-affiliated hospital in Boston.

For decades, some of the smartest people in virology have attempted to make a vaccine against HIV/AIDS. They've all failed. Barouch nonetheless set himself this nearly impossible task. He soon came up with a vaccine candidate with enough promise that Johnson & Johnson, the National Institutes of Health, and the Bill & Melinda Gates Foundation all decided it was worth spending the enormous resources needed to test the vaccine candidate in people.

On January 10, 2020, Barouch was hosting his lab's annual retreat on the top floor of Boston's Museum of Science when the conversation turned to news of a mysterious cluster of forty-one pneumonia cases in Wuhan, China.

"Forty-one cases seemed like a lot at that point," he said.

For years, China had been the source of a series of deeply worrisome virological illnesses like SARS and bird flu that many feared would become global pandemics. The most recent cases sounded like SARS, a disease caused by a coronavirus—a weird family of spiky respiratory viruses that usually cause mild colds. In 2002, SARS had spread to twenty-nine countries, struck more than eight thousand people, and led authorities to briefly shutter Hong Kong. Nearly eight hundred people died before the outbreak finally and almost miraculously petered out.

Barouch's team chatted about whether they should set out to try to make a vaccine against the new threat. But without a sample or sequence, which is a precise genetic code, they couldn't even start work. Everyone went home.

That night, Dr. Kathryn Stephenson, the director of the center's clinical trial unit, sent Barouch a brief email from her iPhone that contained a link she'd seen on Twitter. The link led to an open-access virology site on which Chinese scientists had posted a file containing the full genetic sequence—about thirty thousand genetic letters. Barouch forwarded the link to several scientists on his team.

"Can one of you extract the new coronavirus sequence from this file?" he asked.

This back-and-forth took place on a Friday night. All four scientists were back in the lab early the next morning and then again on Sunday. By Monday, they were starting to think they might have something.

Vaccines prime the immune system to fight viral invaders by exposing it to a harmless virus or virus-like particle that is similar enough to the disease-causing one that the body knocks out both. The first vaccine was for smallpox. Edward Jenner, an English physician, inoculated an eight-year-old boy with the pus he scraped from blisters on the hands of a local milkmaid, who had become infected with cowpox—a virus that wasn't as deadly or virulent in humans as smallpox but was similar enough that it gave immunity for the worse illness. Cows soon became production factories for vaccines (the word derives from the Latin word for cow).

But not all viruses have such innocuous and prevalent cousins, and an ongoing challenge is finding a vehicle that will spread a weakened virus around the body enough to train the body for attack. Barouch's insight was to use a cold virus called an adenovirus in which he nestled the genetic code for the disease he was fighting. The altered virus then infects cells, which adopt the genetic instructions inserted into it and begin manufacturing the disease-like virus themselves. He initially began working with Crucell, a Dutch company that was purchased by Johnson & Johnson in 2011.

His first approved vaccine using an adenovirus came against Ebola. When Zika became a threat in 2016, his team created a vaccine against it, though they eventually shelved the project after Zika receded. They knew that the best way to attack a coronavirus was to train the immune system to recognize its distinctive surface spike proteins.

As his team sculpted a workable adenovirus, the outbreak in Wuhan worsened. In late January, he emailed Johan Van Hoof, the head of vaccines at J & J.

"I am writing today because the coronavirus outbreak in China is looking bad," Barouch wrote. "Are you interested in making a rapid Ad based vaccine like we did for Zika in 2016-2017?"

Two minutes later, Van Hoof replied: "Would a call work now?"

Four days later, they signed a collaboration agreement.

The dozens of scientists, medical doctors, grad students, and assistants in Barouch's lab all dropped their work on other projects to focus on Covid. The most important initial task was to isolate the genetic instructions for the production of Covid's spike proteins and insert them into an adenovirus. They came up with ten initial candidates, each slightly different from the others. Another vital chore was to build a test for spike antibodies in the blood of animals that would be infected with the candidates. By late February, the team had both. They began infecting animals. Just as the world was shutting down in March, the team injected their spike-protein candidates into monkeys and then exposed them to the coronavirus.

One morning in early March, just as the streets of Boston were turning desolate, the team got back the results: One of the adenoviruses had clearly protected the monkeys. Their plan was going to work.

At the same time, a separate team of Johnson & Johnson researchers in the Netherlands was feverishly working to create vats of specially engineered cells to serve as the production factory. Manufacturing vaccines is a tricky business. Some viruses that work great in the lab flop once the engineers at production plants try to grow them, because the cells that serve as the modern version of Jenner's cows don't like them. So teams sometimes have to make difficult choices between candidates that generate great immunity in the lab and candidates that respond well to the cells that produce them in great quantities. Even a small difference in reproduction rates could leave Johnson & Johnson with a terrible shortfall in vaccine doses, which the team knew would be needed by billions of people.

"It can mean you have three hundred million vaccines or thirty million," said Paul Stoffels, J & J's chief scientific officer.

But the track record of adenoviruses gave J & J confidence. First, the vaccines are fairly stable, which means they don't require super cold storage, as the vaccines from Pfizer and Moderna would. And since doses of adenoviruses cannot be given within two months of each other, J & J decided early in its development to focus on providing a single-dose vaccine—in contrast with those from Pfizer and Moderna, which J & J knew would require two doses.

J & J's vaccine would eventually prove to be only 65 percent effective in preventing illness from Covid, compared to 95 percent for Pfizer's and Moderna's shots. But the added convenience of only having to get a single shot made the option from J & J preferable for many people.

J & J was so confident that it negotiated a $1 billion contract with the Trump administration to deliver enough doses for eighty-seven million Americans by the end of May 2021. The company pledged to provide the vaccines at cost, a huge concession for a conglomerate that for decades refused to provide low-cost versions of its HIV/AIDS medicines in Africa or to license their patents to the United Nations, as every other major HIV medicine manufacturer does.

But storm clouds were brewing.

J & J's EXECUTIVES KNEW THEY FACED TWO SERIOUS HURDLES. THE most concerning was that adenoviruses—which had become a popular vehicle for vaccines and gene therapies—were known to cause problems with platelets and coagulation, essential elements of wound-healing and clots. Clots can cause strokes and heart attacks, but an inability to clot can also lead to excessive bleeding and strokes.

Bizarrely, adenoviruses seemed to cause both problems, and the scientific literature was filled with speculation as to why. In a vaccine given to billions, even a tiny increase in clotting can be deeply problematic.

The other problem was manufacturing. J & J wasn't a presence in the international vaccines market, so it didn't have the staff or facilities needed to quickly ramp up production on a global scale. J & J could have struck a manufacturing deal with a fellow giant such as Merck in the United States or GlaxoSmithKline and Sanofi in Europe, each of which has vast vaccine manufacturing, filling, and distribution capabilities.

But that might have meant surrendering some credit for the project to a rival with a public-relations infrastructure nearly as sophisticated as J & J's. Pfizer's Covid vaccine, for instance, was discovered and developed by BioNTech, a German company. Pfizer came into the project late, to supervise the vaccine's human testing and production. But Pfizer's brand is the one widely remembered because its massive press apparatus overwhelmed BioNTech's.

So, in April 2020, J & J struck a manufacturing deal with Emergent BioSolutions, a tiny company with a facility in Baltimore known as Bayview, which the federal government had been supporting for years to serve precisely this function: to make a pandemic vaccine.

The federal government had a half-billion-dollar contract to reserve manufacturing space at Emergent's facilities. Emergent didn't have to do much to get that money besides train staff and presumably be ready when they were needed. Rather than make stuff, the plant simply had to persuade the government that it *could* make stuff. So top company officials encouraged employees to disregard federal standards they were required to maintain.

Virus manufacturing is the most difficult production challenge undertaken by drugmakers. Contamination risks are legion, and several steps in the process are extremely delicate. Nearly all such plants are single-product facilities because switching from one viral seed to another involves massive cleaning challenges to protect against cross-contamination. But Emergent signed deals to manufacture not only J & J's vaccine but one being developed by AstraZeneca that also used an adenovirus. An audit conducted by AstraZeneca just as J & J was signing its deal highlighted the risks of cross-contamination between the two. The warning went unheeded.

Now Emergent had a huge amount of work to do and very little time to do it. Meanwhile, one of its few nongovernmental clients was suing the company for providing a vaccine that Emergent failed to properly test before releasing. Emergent's own top executive for manufacturing later said he had warned the company's senior executives "for a few years" about the company's deficient quality systems, saying that "room to improve is a huge understatement."

Audits and investigations conducted throughout 2020 by Johnson & Johnson, AstraZeneca, two federal agencies, and Emergent's own quality evaluators—all of whom were focused on helping Emergent get ready to make Covid vaccines—found that Emergent was not following basic industry standards. They listed repeated problems in efforts to disinfect and prevent contamination. Emergent's auditors noted that errors "are not investigated to determine root cause, or are not investigated adequately" and that "investigations are terminated without sufficient cause."

In one case, Emergent's auditors said mold had been repeatedly found in a room where cell cultures were grown. But Emergent's workers conducted "essentially no investigation" beyond checking the wheels of one cart for mold and incorrectly classifying the incident as minor.

Johnson & Johnson's auditors identified several major concerns that they feared might hamper the plant's ability to deliver a sufficient quantity of safe vaccines. Among them: "The site virus contamination control strategy is deficient"; "The disinfectant program used in the facility is deficient"; there were "mold issues," "inadequate gowning/wipe down procedures," and "no process" for the handover of cell banks and viral seed banks from the warehouse to manufacturing. AstraZeneca noted that Emergent repeatedly relaxed monitoring standards in hopes of passing its own tests but then failed them anyway.

Inspectors from the government's Biomedical Advanced Research and Development Authority classified the plant's risks of microbiological contamination as "critical." In June, a top federal pandemic official warned in an internal assessment that solving Emergent's many problems "will require significant effort" and that the company "will have to be monitored closely."

As production began to ramp up in the fall, Emergent's inspection problems metastasized into real manufacturing ones. Between October 2020 and January 2021, contamination issues forced Emergent to throw out five lots of the AstraZeneca vaccine—each of which contained roughly two to three million doses.

In November 2020, an outside consultant for Emergent wrote a blistering email warning that Emergent was continuing to violate current good manufacturing practices, or CGMP. Such violations are illegal and dangerous.

Johnson & Johnson had a small production facility in the Netherlands, but it was counting on Emergent's Bayview site to provide the vast majority of its doses. Tracking Emergent's missed milestones, the White House became so concerned that Jeffrey D. Zients, President Biden's coronavirus response coordinator, and David Kessler, who managed vaccine distribution for the White House, reached out to Alex Gorsky, the company's chief executive, with a blunt message: "This is unacceptable."

Gorsky was at the time the point person for one of Johnson & Johnson's biggest and most sophisticated PR campaigns ever, publicizing how the world's largest healthcare conglomerate was about to save humanity from Covid-19. Among other efforts, the company produced a multi-million-dollar weekly TV series hosted by CNN journalist Lisa Ling that would eventually include twenty episodes featuring top executives, movie stars like Sean Penn, and other luminaries.

Putting himself at the center of this effort, Gorsky spent weeks visiting many of the nation's most-watched and friendliest TV news programs, including NBC's *Today* show, CNBC's *Squawk Box,* and Bloomberg TV.

White House officials said later that they couldn't get Gorsky and others at J & J to understand just how far offtrack the company's partnership with Emergent had gotten. Simultaneously, officials reached out to Ken Frazier, Merck's chief executive, in hopes of persuading the giant to put its considerable vaccine-manufacturing expertise and facilities at J & J's disposal. The government agreed to pay Merck $269 million for the effort.

As the talks were underway, FDA inspectors again visited Emergent's plant in February. By then, Emergent suspected that J & J's vaccine batches might have serious contamination problems. Employees placed yellow tags on containers holding at least one batch of J & J's vaccine to flag it for further testing. Just before FDA inspectors arrived, however, employees removed the tags, only replacing them after the inspectors left.

Still, the FDA identified a host of issues, though it allowed the company some leeway to correct them. By this point, though, it was all too little, too late.

JOHNSON & JOHNSON DISTRIBUTED ITS FIRST BATCH OF VACCINES ON March 2, 2021. They'd all been manufactured in the Netherlands. The company had promised to deliver thirty-seven million doses by the end of March, but delays at the Baltimore facility led executives to cut that number to twenty million.

Another FDA inspector arrived at Bayview, this time sampling some crucial inputs. The results were concerning enough that the FDA asked Johnson & Johnson to thoroughly test its vaccines.

On March 25, Emergent and J & J reported the results to the administration: J & J's vaccines had been contaminated with AstraZeneca's—exactly what AstraZeneca had warned about a year before. More than fifteen million doses of J & J's vaccine had to be discarded, though this was only a small fraction of the nearly four hundred million doses that Emergent would eventually toss.

With some vaccine distribution sites providing only J & J's shot, the supply shortfall had immediate effects around the country. Some states had created special vaccination programs focused on college students and those living in remote areas that exclusively distributed the J & J vaccine, since it required less specialized handling and only one shot.

California officials announced that they would receive four hundred thousand fewer doses the following week than the previous week, a drop of 15 percent. In Virginia, the state's vaccine coordinator described the J & J shortfall as having a "huge" effect on plans to broaden vaccine availability to the entire adult population. Other states said the shortfall would significantly slow their vaccination efforts, too.

Two weeks later, J & J suffered an even greater setback. On April 13, the FDA announced a mandatory pause in the administration of J & J's vaccines while the agency investigated six cases of a rare and severe type of blood clot called cerebral venous sinus thrombosis.

AstraZeneca's vaccine, not yet approved in the United States, seemed to cause similar problems, reports of which had led to pauses in vaccinations within Europe. Following the FDA's announcement, these countries also paused administration of the J & J vaccine. It was a risk that J & J and its scientists had known about from the start. So much had changed in the world, but J & J was still J & J.

By the time of the pause, seven million people in the United States had already received J & J's shot, representing about 5 percent of overall vaccinations.

The day after the FDA's announcement, a vaccine advisory panel sponsored by the Centers for Disease Control and Prevention debated how to handle the newly emerging risk. An FDA official recommended that the vaccine go back into use while researchers studied the problem. Others argued that too many patients might be harmed if vaccinations resumed without a better understanding of the clotting issues.

Among the concerns was that seven women who had suffered injury not only had severe clots in their brains but also low platelet levels, an odd combination. An important consideration for the experts was that the usual treatment for clots, the blood thinner heparin, was actually harmful given these circumstances.

The safety bar for vaccines is always extraordinarily high because they are given to healthy people. Even rare risks are considered unacceptable. For instance, the United States chose to withdraw the live polio vaccine because it caused illness in one person in a million—a risk deemed too high when a dead virus vaccine has no such problems.

Despite U.S. vaccines' incredibly high safety record, this pause in J & J's Covid vaccine led to a huge rise in antivax postings on Facebook, Twitter, and other social media. J & J's carelessness and mistakes accelerated antivaccination sentiment that would bedevil the United States' overall anti-Covid efforts and result in countless more unnecessary deaths.

Federal officials eventually lifted the pause on J & J's vaccine, but the damage was already done. Confidence in the shot cratered even further in July when the FDA warned of increased risks of Guillain-Barré syndrome, a rare and debilitating neurological condition. By the time of the warning, federal officials were reviewing more than one hundred suspected cases of Guillain-Barré among J & J recipients. Ninety-five percent of the cases were considered serious and required hospitalization.

The new warning and the shots' relatively poor efficacy left the roughly 13 million Americans who'd already gotten the J & J shot with a dilemma. Officials soon recommended boosters for all Americans, but—considering its many problems—should recipients of the first shot double up on J & J?

The National Institutes of Health tried to answer that question by testing antibodies in J & J recipients receiving three kinds of boosters—shots from J & J, Pfizer, or Moderna. Those who received a Moderna booster saw their antibody levels rise seventy-six-fold within fifteen days, compared to a four-fold rise among those who got another J & J shot. The Pfizer booster raised antibody levels thirty-five-fold.

By December 2021, fifty-four cases and at least nine deaths from the clotting disorder had been linked to J & J's vaccine. The risk was greatest among women thirty to forty-nine, with one in one hundred thousand suffering severe side effects—far too high for a vaccine.

The Centers for Disease Control and Prevention recommended that Americans stop being given J & J's shot altogether. Just 8 percent of Americans were vaccinated with J & J's vaccine, and that fell to less than 2 percent when counting boosters. Additional studies confirmed without any doubt that the effectiveness of J & J's vaccine was far lower than that offered by Pfizer's and Moderna's shots. This efficacy plunged even further when the Omicron variant suddenly started sweeping the world. Against Omicron, studies indicated that the J & J shot was close to useless.

As regulators around the world restricted access to J & J's vaccine, the company pushed back.

"Our vaccine is different," Penny Heaton, the company's top vaccine executive, said in public remarks. "It is long-lasting, it offers high levels of protection, and it provides breadth of protection. Our vaccine has flexible dosing, is easy to store and transport. In many low- and middle-income countries, our vaccine is the most important and sometimes only option."

In June 2023, the FDA quietly revoked its authorization for the J & J vaccine entirely. It had already, by that point, been unavailable in the United States for months. The company's effort to save humanity from Covid had failed.

In the end, Gorsky's decision to link both Johnson & Johnson's brand and his own personal brand with their Covid vaccine turned out to be a fatal mistake. Over time, J & J's vaccine became nothing more than a punch line.

"I don't want you to worry about me. I'm vaccinated. I got the Johnson & Johnson vaccine," comedian Dave Chappelle joked during his 2021 Netflix special. "I walk into the doc and I'm like, 'Give me the third best option. I'll have what the homeless people are having.'"

The crowd roared.

ON AUGUST 19, 2021, GORSKY ANNOUNCED THAT HE WAS STEPPING down as chief executive at the end of the year, handing the reins of the company to his longtime deputy, Joaquin Duato. Gorsky remained the company's chairman for a year but then left that job, too.

His departure marked the end of an era for J & J and the entire pharmaceutical industry. Both Gorsky and his predecessor, William Weldon, had gotten their starts as American sales representatives—part of a wave of sales personnel who rocketed to the top because they brought in more money than any other company functionary.

Gorsky told *The Wall Street Journal* that he was leaving in part because of health issues in his family. The paper lauded him for overseeing tremendous growth at the company.

"He navigated manufacturing issues that had plagued its signature consumer-health business, as well as thorny opioid and talcum-powder lawsuits," the story stated, without mentioning the fact that Gorsky had been responsible for many of the management decisions that led to those very lawsuits.

But the praise for Gorsky was not universal. Other reporters pointed out that under his leadership, J & J grew more slowly than its peer companies, and some even mentioned his checkered history.

Had the company's vaccine succeeded in saving the world from a once-in-a-century pandemic, Gorsky might have floated away on a chorus of hosannahs. Such acclaim might not have changed a subsequent decision by a federal appeals court regarding Baby Powder that cost the company dearly, but its absence certainly didn't help. The mountain of Baby Powder lawsuits eventually grew so high, and the potential liability so great, that J & J simply couldn't make it through as it always had since its earliest days in the 1800s: with a stable of iconic consumer products.

On November 12, 2021, Gorsky—in his final days as chief executive—announced that the company would soon expel its entire consumer products portfolio from J & J's corporate embrace. Iconic products like Johnson's Baby Shampoo, Tylenol, Listerine, Neutrogena, Aveeno, Band-Aids, and Motrin would now be put into a separate corporation to be called Kenvue Inc.

The company had already tried to shield itself from the Baby Powder disaster by placing those liabilities into a separate company that then declared bankruptcy. But that was just a delaying tactic. A complete consumer spin-off was a far more drastic measure, one that would sever Johnson & Johnson's link with its iconic past entirely and end the company as it had always been known.

Wall Street analysts largely cheered the consumer spin-off, with many saying they hoped it would protect the company from more large Baby Powder verdicts. But this turned out to be wrong. A federal appeals court later determined that J & J must still shoulder this financial burden—a ruling the company is appealing. Nonetheless, litigation payouts are likely to be modest.

While more than sixty-thousand women have sued and perhaps as many as twenty thousand more may do so annually for decades, nearly all of these cases are individual claims that must be fought separately because no judge has approved a class-action lawsuit and none is likely to. A series of business-friendly Supreme Court rulings in recent years have made such gargantuan cases exceptionally rare. The days of class-action lawsuits threatening the viability of major corporations are mostly gone.

Some ten thousand individual claims have been consolidated in federal court in New Jersey, in what's termed "multidistrict litigation," but the process for adjudicating these is likely to take many years. Federal courts are famous for being particularly kind to large corporate defendants like Johnson & Johnson. As a result, many plaintiffs' lawyers bring claims in state courts, but state judicial systems rarely have the capacity to deal with hundreds—never mind thousands—of individual cases.

Another factor working in Johnson & Johnson's favor is the stubborn insistence by some top plaintiffs' attorneys to focus on the dangers of talc rather than its hidden contamination with asbestos, a poison that is not even mentioned in many trials. These firms assembled their litigation strategies, files, and witnesses prior to the discovery of hundreds of documents proving asbestos contamination. The lawyers memorized their opening and closing arguments before Lanier won his landmark $2.5 billion verdict, and, puzzlingly, they refuse to pivot. Absent the fear-inducing word "asbestos," talc doesn't seem quite so much of a danger to many judges or juries. So these lawyers lose and keep on losing.

Johnson & Johnson, then, will undoubtedly continue to pay an ongoing financial penalty for its decades of deadly deceit regarding Johnson's Baby Powder, but the cost isn't anything it can't withstand. And the reputational injury it has to recover from may end up subsiding far sooner than expected with Johnson's Baby Powder now in another company.

On May 4, 2023, Kenvue went public and raised $3.8 billion in the largest initial public offering in eighteen months. J & J finished its share exchange with Kenvue in August, completing the deal. Even after the spin-off, J & J remains the largest and most diversified healthcare conglomerate in the world and is among the most profitable companies of any kind. Its name is still one of the most admired and valuable brands in history.

Even though J & J no longer sells Tylenol, the company will very likely continue successfully recruiting top candidates at the nation's best business schools because every student is still taught that Johnson & Johnson's response to the 1982 poisoning case was exemplary.

And by maintaining its medical products businesses, the company remains among the largest funders in the world of the FDA, academic medical centers, and white-shoe corporate law firms—ensuring ongoing regulatory servility, professorial obsequiousness, and prosecutorial pusillanimity.

In truth, the iconic American company that for decades sold prescription medicines, medical devices, and such beloved brands as Johnson's Baby Shampoo, Tylenol, and Aveeno died in 2023. But the power, privilege, and mythology that have long protected its executives and shareholders from ever paying truly significant penalties for their myriad misdeeds over the years? Those continue to endure.

An important reason for this endurance is a complementary myth about an agency widely regarded as the best and most impactful regulatory body in the world.

ITS BUDGET LARGELY UNDERWRITTEN BY INDUSTRY FEES, THE FDA HAS long been captive to the medical and food companies that it regulates. But most Americans are still under the mistaken impression that the FDA is a tough cop, one of the most strict and powerful regulatory agencies in the country. J & J and the rest of the pharmaceutical industry work hard to preserve this myth, in large measure because it is a vital defense in their many ongoing product liability cases.

"You know, if you listen to Mr. Upshaw [the plaintiff's attorney] talk, you would think that the FDA is some ghost agency up there that is being run over by pharmaceutical companies all over the country, that they don't have any police in effect, that they let you do whatever you want to do," Robert L. Johnson III, J & J's defense attorney, said in his opening remarks at a 2001 Mississippi trial involving Propulsid. "The evidence will prove otherwise."

Propulsid was a prescription heartburn medicine that was no more effective than Tums, the chewable tablets of calcium carbonate found in most convenience stores. But Propulsid could cause arrhythmias, particularly when taken alongside other common medications or even grapefruit juice. The drug was especially dangerous to infants, in whom it offered no benefits. J & J nonetheless quietly underwrote a marketing campaign that succeeded in getting one in five premature infants in the country to be given this dangerous and useless medicine.

As one baby after another died, the FDA slapped warning after warning on the medicine, none of which had much effect. J & J finally withdrew Propulsid from general sales in 2000 and was hit by a wave of lawsuits. For J & J, the most troubling document in the Propulsid cases was a slide that a top FDA official used in a March 1998 meeting that asked, "Is it acceptable for your nighttime heartburn medicine (i.e., something for which you could take Tums) to have the potential to kill you?"

It was a rhetorical question that reflected the agency's discomfort with the drug's poor balance between risks and benefits. That the FDA would allow sales of a prescription medicine that, while no more effective than over-the-counter Tums, could kill is a telling indication of its captivity to industry. But J & J's lawyer used the mythology around the FDA to dismiss this document altogether.

"If the answer to that question was, 'Well, yeah, you can take Tums for it,' would the FDA have approved a prescription medication when you had a Tums, an Alka-Seltzer, and all of that out there? No."

In reality, the FDA does often enough approve prescription medicines that are less effective, more dangerous, and more expensive than over-the-counter remedies. Agency standards simply require that a drug be proven effective. No comparisons with already-approved medicines—either from efficacy or safety standpoints—are generally required.

In many states, FDA approval offers blanket protection against negligence claims. In other states, it prevents juries from assessing punitive damages. The justification for these laws is the same as Johnson's argument: that the FDA is a tough and independent regulator filled with hard-working public servants solely concerned with the public's health. Only they have the expertise and independence necessary to balance the risks and benefits of drugs and devices. And their educated and fair decisions should not be second-guessed by juries comprising average citizens.

This false mythology surrounding the FDA has also been a crucial tool for Johnson & Johnson to corral the sales reps, doctors, academics, and others involved in sales schemes that sometimes cross ethical and legal boundaries.

Dawn Raybon, a J & J sales rep for Propulsid, was asked under oath during the 2001 Mississippi Propulsid trial why she had used in her sales presentations a brochure, CD, and video that all included blatantly false claims about the drug.

"I'm assuming that the only way we would have gotten it is if the FDA had approved them for generation among representatives," Raybon said.

Raybon's impression is common. In dozens of interviews, sales reps said that their obviously illegal sales aids must have been legal because the FDA must have approved them or at least would have forced J & J to stop using them. In many cases, sales reps said their bosses brushed aside their concerns by saying that the FDA wouldn't allow any illegal sales pitches in the marketplace, so why worry?

These reassurances rang true because the mythology of the FDA as a tough cop is so widely held that few believed J & J could have gotten away with ignoring the agency's repeated warnings that its sales materials were false. The FDA's presumed diligent oversight has been crucial in winning the willing participation of thousands of co-conspirators in so many criminal schemes. What they were doing couldn't be illegal, they reassured themselves, because the FDA—which everyone knows is super tough—would stop them if it were.

FDA regulations do require drug companies to submit to the agency all marketing materials, but there is no penalty for failing to do so, and companies often skip this required step. Nonetheless, the agency routinely receives more than thirty thousand promotional items a year from companies—a mountain of material that completely overwhelms the tiny office charged with reviewing them. In the summer of 2005, according to the General Accounting Office, that office had a single person with oversight over thousands of ads directed at consumers. Even when the office spots an obviously illegal promotion, the agency's process for issuing warning letters takes months and often more than a year—by which time the illegal promotion has long since had its effect.

The FDA's feeble efforts to police industry marketing are so hopeless that those assigned to the office serially quit or transfer out. So the office is always understaffed, making its efforts even more hopeless, leading to a vicious cycle of failure and despair.

But for doctors, the myth of an ever-vigilant FDA lulls many into a false sense of security. They routinely prescribe medical products that have serious side effects without hesitation or concern.

Dr. Kevin K. Howe, a board-certified orthopedic surgeon who practices in Santa Rosa, told a jury on November 2, 2016, that he had no idea that Johnson & Johnson's metal-on-metal knee implants had never been tested in people, and he expressed astonishment that the FDA would let that happen.

"In hindsight, the FDA let us down, because I didn't realize, you know, how they would release a product," Howe testified, adding: "We trusted the FDA like you guys trust the FDA. When the FDA says, 'Hey, this is safe,' you consider it to be safe."

Beyond sales reps and doctors, the unfounded confidence in the FDA may be an important reason Americans are so quick to try new medical products. Prescriptions of newly introduced medicines increase at a faster clip in the United States than in Europe, Japan, or any other industrialized country. Simply put, Americans like new drugs. And since patent terms are limited, this, along with sky-high prices, makes the United States a bonanza for drugmakers. That early bump in sales is irreplaceable.

Despite surveys that consistently show Americans generally distrust the pharmaceutical industry, a uniquely American belief in progress and invention seems to lead to a rapid, never-ending climb in new drug sales. The circle gets squared because Americans trust that the FDA is policing the drug industry.

Oddly enough, one of the most important reasons for Americans' confidence in the FDA results from a campaign by the agency's most influential critic.

FOR DECADES, *THE WALL STREET JOURNAL'S* EDITORIAL PAGE HAS harshly criticized FDA officials, arguing that excessive regulatory zeal has cost countless lives that might have been spared if not for the agency's meddling interference. But strangely, many of the complaints the editorials have made about the agency being overly risk averse, anti-industry, and antiprogress are actually about concessions the agency made at the very behest of industry.

"FDA Loves Kids So Much, It'll Make You Sick" was the headline of one of these pieces, which explained: "President Clinton announced that drug companies will be required to test whether the medicines they sell for adults are safe and effective for children, and to put the pediatric dosages on the label. The new requirement will increase the already astronomical cost of drug development by more than $200 million annually."

In fact, the administration proposed giving manufacturers an extra six months of exclusive sales rights for their medicines if they agreed to test how the medicines work in children. The tests are voluntary, but drugmakers almost invariably conduct them because doing so is immensely profitable.

While a pediatric trial might cost as much as $20 million, the extra months of exclusive sales often amount to hundreds of millions and sometimes billions of dollars. The law is an enormous giveaway to industry, which is why drugmakers pushed so hard for its passage. But the *Journal* opinion writer managed to portray it as anti-industry government overreach.

This kind of denunciation of government largesse or concessions to industry as somehow against the industry's interests—and by extension those of the general public—is routine for *Journal* editorial writers. For decades, they have served to hide the FDA's slow but unmistakable slide from enforcer of public interests to defender of industry priorities.

"The FDA Is Out of Control and a Danger to the Public" was the headline of another piece. "In recent years, the agency's long-standing risk-aversion and intrusion into the practice of medicine have soared. Nowhere is the phenomenon more evident than in the FDA's imposition of Risk Evaluation and Mitigation Strategies (REMS), which the agency can impose at will on drugs."

The piece explained that REMS programs were unnecessarily restrictive and imposed huge burdens on doctors and patients.

"The FDA is an agency out of control—a killer of jobs, of innovation and of Americans," it concluded.

Actually, the FDA adopted REMS at the insistence of the pharmaceutical industry so that unsafe medicines can avoid being withdrawn from the market entirely, which juries view as proof that a drug should never have been offered for sale in the first place. When a drug is withdrawn—an admission that it is unsafe—plaintiffs' attorneys win big verdicts. This was demonstrated during the opioid crisis when J & J and Purdue pleaded with the FDA to create a REMS program for opioid medicines, in hopes of fending off tougher measures with real effect and increasing the companies' protections against a growing tide of litigation. So the FDA created an opioid REMS, which did nothing to slow the epidemic.

The *Journal*'s editorial page is generally considered the second most influential in the country behind only that of *The New York Times*. In business circles, it is the most widely read by far. The pages' decades-long focus on the FDA—among its most consistent and far-reaching themes—has had a profound effect on the public's image of the agency. In 2011, a *Journal* editorial writer won a Pulitzer Prize for a series that included pieces slamming the FDA.

Again and again, *Journal* editorialists have denounced agency actions done at the behest of industry as anti-industry excesses. The writers of these pieces are some of the brightest minds in media. The consistency of their errors cannot be accidental.

But editorials are far from the only place in which the American media perpetuates FDA mythology to the benefit of J & J and other huge drugmakers. Many of the articles in even the best newspapers describe a tough FDA as a device to make stories seem more urgent or compelling.

An example was published in *The New York Times* on September 14, 2010. Under the headline "Meat Farmers Brace for Limits on Antibiotics," the story focused on a pig farmer who used a lot of antibiotics but was girding for the imminent imposition of strict limits.

"Now, after decades of debate, the Food and Drug Administration appears poised to issue its strongest guidelines on animal antibiotics yet, intended to reduce what it calls a clear risk to human health."

The new guidelines didn't go into effect until 2017—more than six years later. The *Times* reporter knew the restrictions were likely years away, but his editor told him that the story wouldn't get on the front page unless it suggested a more immediate crackdown. So he complied.

FDA reporters face this dilemma almost daily, and many recount examples of similar stories that—after editors' prodding—falsely aggrandized agency enforcement efforts, powers, or timelines. Making the agency appear tough gets stories attention. Revealing it to be a slow-moving, compromised bureaucracy generally consigns articles to the bottom of news feeds. "But the FDA is unlikely to take meaningful action for years" is a line that all but ensures a slashing edit and zero prominence. Reporters' most important constituencies—editors, readers, agency officials, politicians, and industry executives—are all invested in a false image of the agency, and reporters defy them at their peril.

Even brave reporters routinely find themselves outfoxed by an agency more adept than any other in the federal government at announcing tough-sounding initiatives that are camouflage for inaction. In the early 2010s, for instance, concerns grew that most drugs were tested almost exclusively on white males, leaving women and minorities uncertain of how common remedies worked for them. As the era of precision and genetic medicine progressed, these concerns intensified—leading some experts to call the problem the most critical in all of life sciences.

Advocates called for reforms. Members of Congress proposed legislation. Already facing rising costs for clinical trials, the industry quietly opposed these efforts but couldn't voice that opposition publicly. So in 2014, the FDA announced an "action plan" of "concrete steps" to boost diversity in clinical trials. The drug industry underwrote a public service messaging campaign titled "I'm In" to encourage minority participation in clinical trials and reassure advocates that real steps were being taken.

Eight years later, in 2022, researchers reported that these steps had had no impact whatsoever on the racial makeup of clinical trial participants. None. So the FDA announced a new initiative that is unlikely to have any effect either, hoping to buy the industry yet more time.

The FDA could require disclaimers on drug labels that the medicines were never adequately tested in women or minorities. Such acknowledgments—well within the agency's power—might affect sales enough to encourage the industry to solve its diversity problem. But drugmakers oppose such disclaimers, so the agency hasn't implemented them.

Another example came in 2021 when, after years of controversy about lead, arsenic, and other neurotoxins being found in baby food, the FDA finally announced a cleverly titled campaign called "Closer to Zero" to reduce these contaminants. A few months later, the agency quietly eliminated from its website all the timelines for action. Most baby food remains just as contaminated, and the FDA has no plans to change that.

Similar initiatives to tackle rising drug prices, nicotine levels in cigarettes, contaminated produce, dietary sodium, and other health concerns have been announced by agency leaders, often to great acclaim. In some cases, agency staff tasked with the promised work first heard about the initiatives when they read about them in the newspaper. In every case, no health impact has resulted.

To ensure positive coverage, agency press officers offer exclusive access to the most important or compliant reporters. Such exclusives are vital professional plums, and reporters who get them are incentivized to write stories in the most aggrandizing way possible to improve odds that they get more.

But it's not just the press that gets manipulated. Advertisements for schlock medical products often bolster the mythology of vigilance in hopes of inspiring consumer confidence. In ads for supplements, foot massagers, crystal healers, and similar products, announcers often boast that the product has been "registered with the FDA."

This claim often means nothing more than that the company spent ten dollars sending a certified letter to the agency declaring that the product is being sold. With neither the legal mandate nor the staff to police these products, the agency usually files these fatuous declarations in its outgoing trash.

In truth, no major government agency has failed as fully, frequently, or consistently as the FDA. From 1991 through 2015, pharmaceuticals manufacturers entered into 373 settlement agreements and paid $35.7 billion in criminal and civil fines. Similarly riddled with criminality, the device industry was forced into its own set of guilty pleas and fines.

While no one has estimated the resulting death toll from these myriad crimes, the number is certainly in the millions—more than the combined American toll from every war since the birth of the United States. And not only did the FDA fail to prevent this historic cascade of deadly malfeasance, it played almost no role in policing it after the fact, either. Nearly every legal case sprang from the bravery of whistleblowers rather than any agency enforcement.

Examples of other government agencies that underwent significant reforms in the wake of disaster are almost too numerous to count. Following the deadly attacks on 9/11, the federal government restructured the nation's intelligence and law enforcement agencies. After the terrible events of Hurricane Katrina, Congress reorganized the Federal Emergency Management Agency. And the 2008 financial crisis led to a wholesale reshaping of the nation's financial regulatory system.

But despite its widely acknowledged role in furthering the opioid crisis, which alone cost one hundred times more lives than all of those events combined, the FDA has never even faced a major government commission or a wide-ranging Congressional investigation. Like Johnson & Johnson, the agency is nearly untouchable because powerful interests protect it from scrutiny.

IN THE IMMEDIATE AFTERMATH OF THE 1986 EXPLOSION OF THE Challenger space shuttle, journalists blamed some high-octane NASA managers for overriding basic safety concerns. They painted a picture of gross incompetence bordering on criminal negligence on the part of a few bad actors.

But later, in a masterful reconstruction, Diane Vaughan, a Columbia University sociologist, made it clear that the disaster was in fact the result of a years-long, organization-wide drift from the very principles that NASA and its top managers claimed to hold so dear.

Launching rockets, after all, is an inherently risky endeavor. Even though NASA claimed to make the safety of its astronauts its paramount concern, some risks had to be accepted. Over time, however, the organization began accepting risks that—to an outside observer—would have seemed insane. To those inside, though, the many incremental steps that led to that crazy place were completely rational and normal, because they'd lost all perspective.

"Social normalization of deviance means that people within the organization become so much accustomed to a deviant behavior that they don't consider it as deviant, despite the fact that they far exceed their own rules for elementary safety," Vaughan said in an interview. "But it is a complex process with some kind of organizational acceptance. The people outside see the situation as deviant whereas the people inside get accustomed to it and do not. The more they do it, the more they get accustomed."

It's an apt description of the tragic decline of Johnson & Johnson, which for most of the twentieth century was among the most ethical major companies anywhere. But the dawning internal realization about the risks of Johnson's Baby Powder became a ladder down which the entire organization would eventually descend.

In the 1960s, the idea that tiny amounts of asbestos could represent a genuine safety risk must have seemed ludicrous. At the time, pure asbestos was everywhere—in homes, cars, airplanes, and ships. As concerns built, the company took clear and responsible steps to reduce exposures. Executives sold a talc mine in Johnson, Vermont, that was hopelessly contaminated. Documents suggest that they made sure that miners in their remaining facilities were more careful about spotting and avoiding the ribbons of asbestos that routinely snake through talc deposits.

In the early 1970s, the back-and-forth with the FDA must have seemed to many executives like a public-relations exercise. To placate the FDA and a newly energized consumer movement, J & J executives led the talc industry to adopt a testing standard that declared talc to be pure even when it contained up to 3 percent chrysotile asbestos and smaller quantities of other types of asbestos. But again, such small amounts probably seemed perfectly fine to them.

The United States didn't ban asbestos pipe insulation until 1975 or asbestos embers for home fireplaces until 1977. The EPA didn't propose a general ban on products containing asbestos until 1989. Pure asbestos remained fairly common into the 1980s. Why worry, then, about small amounts of contamination in talc powders?

Once the industry adopted the J4-1 asbestos testing standard, the problem seemed to go away. Many J & J executives likely never knew or may have forgotten that the protocol was deliberately created so that manufacturers wouldn't find small amounts of asbestos even when they were present.

Sometime in the 1980s, things took a darker turn. The company's lawyers started hiding documents. Executives began lying under oath. Studies linking chronic talc usage with elevated cancer rates made clear that Johnson's Baby Powder had to change, but executives instead worked to discredit the researchers.

Meanwhile, the 1982 Tylenol poisoning case confirmed to the entire world that Johnson & Johnson was the most ethical and upstanding major corporation in the world. Case studies at Harvard Business School began piling up declaring J & J as a capitalist's nirvana. Inside J & J, a belief solidified that the company was a uniquely beneficial force for good in the world.

The company's stable of baby products also gave J & J a level of emotional trust from consumers that was all but impossible to degrade. No matter what executives did or to what charges they pleaded guilty, consumers, doctors, business professors, and legislators continued to shower them with admiration and affection. They could do almost anything, it seemed, and still be admired. And bad behavior without consequence can be deeply corrupting.

So instead of just the unknowing slide into problematic behavior that had characterized the previous thirty years, Johnson & Johnson's executives then began taking what they must have known were much more ethically problematic steps to hide serious problems. And those steps got bigger and bigger.

By the mid-1990s, executives knew that Procrit's risks were much worse than the FDA or oncologists knew. But the drug had grown into the conglomerate's biggest and most profitable ever, representing 10 percent of overall sales and a far larger share of profits. Protecting that franchise became an almost existential priority.

Similar decisions seem to have been made regarding Risperdal and Duragesic, and in both cases, the mental gymnastics needed to maintain any notion that the company was acting ethically became Olympian. J & J copied Purdue's opioid playbook while Purdue was being widely derided as among the worst corporate criminals in history. Under the instructions of executives, its reps claimed that fentanyl was non-addicting—a more outrageous and dangerous sales pitch than any of Purdue's. Its Risperdal sales reps told doctors that they could escape legal culpability for prescribing a drug that offered no benefits for dementia patients and could potentially kill them.

Meanwhile, the company's executives created something of a cult around the credo. Every major meeting had a credo component. The company conducted annual surveys to ask employees how closely they and their colleagues adhered to credo principles. I never learned of any major corporate decision or strategy that was actually changed as a result of these credo discussions and analyses, but constant references to the credo supported the notion internally that J & J was truly special and good.

This was corporate gaslighting on an epic scale.

"Every drug has risks." That phrase was repeated countless times in my interviews with those involved in J & J's myriad drug disasters. This is an undeniable fact, known by everyone who works in healthcare. The real danger, though, comes when profit is the corresponding benefit. Whether or not anyone at Johnson & Johnson would have openly admitted this, their actions, from the highest levels down, indicate that they believed that since they were creating new products with the intent to help the sick, all their efforts must always be good, regardless of whether the tests of those new products actually bore those beliefs out. "Every drug has risks" became an excuse to tolerate any risk whatsoever for the sake of not risking the chance of making as much money as possible.

Long before the launch of Ortho Evra, Pinnacle metal-on-metal hip implants, and Prolift vaginal mesh, executives knew those products would disable and kill. The FDA applications for Ortho Evra and Pinnacle contained blatant falsehoods. With Prolift, executives didn't even bother lying to federal regulators—they just started selling without the agency's approval.

The clinical trial for Pinnacle violated almost every sacred rule regarding the ethical conduct of human clinical trials. Emails reveal that executives knew exactly what they were doing and joked among themselves about how fully their actions contradicted the central tenets of the company's credo.

The goal, of course, was not to kill. Theirs was the ruthless, sociopathic indifference of bank robbers eliminating anyone between them and a vault of gold. Executives' divergence from cardinal rules of polite society was sometimes revealed in court when simple questions about honesty and integrity seemed to flummox them.

"You agree that drug companies like Janssen and J & J need to be honest with the public, right?" a plaintiff's attorney asked on September 23, 2019, during a cross-examination of Dr. Gahan Pandina, the senior scientist leading J & J's Risperdal development program, in one of the many small moments that laid bare the company's deviation from basic decency.

"It's a very general statement, but they should abide by the regulations and rules," Pandina responded.

Surprised, the plaintiff's attorney tried again: "Sir, this is a simple— I promise you, it's not a trick question. Drug companies should be honest with the public, right?"

Pandina persisted: "Again, honesty is a very broad term. I would say they should abide by the regulations and rules."

Handed a gift, the plaintiff's attorney made sure the jury took note: "Okay. That's— In fact, I am going to write that one down so I remember it. 'Honesty is a broad term.'"

In depositions and court testimony in case after case after case, Johnson & Johnson's employees almost invariably come across as shifty and dishonest. When confronted with any piece of the mountain of damning documents uncovered in litigation, executives nearly always claim failing memories.

As one of its sales reps said, the company has "a culture of ickiness." This is the virus that Johnson & Johnson has never tried to find a shot for. And, if history proves anything, it has no plans to seek inoculation.

. . .

IN THE 1946 FRANK CAPRA MOVIE *IT'S A WONDERFUL LIFE,* JIMMY Stewart's character is given the chance to see what the lives of those he loves would have been like if he'd never been born. He soon learns that he contributed mightily to their happiness, transformed the face of his hometown, and even saved lives.

Would the world be a better place if Johnson & Johnson had never existed?

The company manufactures the sutures used in most surgeries around the world. It has brought to market a host of drugs and devices that save and improve lives. In 2022, the company introduced the first combination treatment drug to offer long-term HIV suppression to adolescents, a remarkable accomplishment. In 2018, it introduced Erleada, a first-of-its-kind treatment for prostate cancer.

In 2012, J & J won approval for bedaquiline, the first new drug for tuberculosis in over forty years. The pill has revolutionized treatment for drug-resistant infections. The company's biggest-selling drug by far is Stelara, a monoclonal antibody that suppresses the immune system. For those with ulcerative colitis or Crohn's disease, Stelara can offer a normal life. The company also revolutionized vision care when it introduced the first disposable contact lenses. Its early commitment to sterilization when the theory was still being debated saved countless lives, particularly those of wounded soldiers. Meanwhile, the company's financial success has made hundreds of thousands of shareholders and employees richer and happier.

At the same time, J & J has knowingly contributed to the deaths and grievous injuries of millions. And for much of the early twenty-first century, almost every one of J & J's top-selling drugs benefited from criminal marketing schemes. Many of its devices gained wide acceptance because of bribery.

Prisons are filled with people who lived good, productive lives but experienced one moment of bad judgment. A bank teller who faithfully served her employer for forty years and then, in a fit of greed, stole just one hundred dollars is forever branded as a thief. Likewise, J & J's executives, scientists, and salespeople cannot be excused for their bad behavior because of the good and helpful products they brought to market. That was their job, and what they were expected to do. But they also distinguished themselves by their deliberate, persistent, and frank criminality—year after year, decade after decade.

For all intents and purposes, Johnson & Johnson was a criminal enterprise. Indeed, mafia families get a large share of their income from strictly legal activities. But no mafia outfit ever consistently targeted the kind of vulnerable people that J & J exploited. And if one of the most admired corporations in the world is in reality a criminal enterprise and a killing machine, what else are we missing? How many other killers are out there?

So, what should be done?

In this reporter's opinion, first, doctors should be barred from taking money or gifts from drug and device companies while simultaneously treating patients. If physicians want to work for industry, they must leave clinical medicine. They can't do both because too many patients have died as a result.

The Centers for Medicare & Medicaid Services could accomplish this by—after a phase-in period—barring doctors from participating in the program if they have taken money from drug or device companies in the previous three years. Private insurers might soon follow suit.

A growing share of doctors are employed by hospitals and health systems, and many of these companies forbid their employees from taking money or items of significant value from drug and device makers. Such prohibitions should be universal.

Some doctors are paid by drug and device companies to participate in clinical studies. Much of this so-called research is simply marketing by a different name, and the payments are disguised bribes. Ending them would protect patients.

Instead, if doctors want to continue to participate in research, they can do so under the auspices of a university health system or the

National Institutes of Health. Drug and device makers could funnel their payments through these institutions, which in turn could hire doctors as they see fit. Such a system is already in place for pediatric cancer trials, and it functions well.

Second, states should stop certifying continuing medical education courses that are funded by drug and device companies. Too many of these classes are advertorials that make doctors worse at their jobs, not better.

Third, the FDA needs to be funded by taxpayers, not industry. But even that won't be enough to reform a culture that has become so entirely captive to the companies it is supposed to oversee. One model to consider is the one used in aviation. The Federal Aviation Administration approves new airplanes, while the National Transportation Safety Board—an entirely independent agency—investigates crashes.

The reason for the separate functions is that the FAA cannot investigate unsafe airplane designs that it was involved in approving. The same logic should apply to drugs, medical devices, and other products overseen by the FDA. An agency independent of the FDA needs to be charged with tracking the safety of medical products once they reach the market, as well as the marketing efforts involved in their sale.

Such an agency might have prevented the opioid crisis and countless others, saving millions of lives in the process. The FDA has never fulfilled this vital function effectively, and, unless things change radically, it never will.

Fourth, companies and their executives must be punished for lying under oath to the FDA and federal courts. It is astonishing how common this problem remains. In just one example, Novartis, a Swiss drug giant, submitted to the FDA in 2019 an application containing fraudulent data for Zolgensma, a gene therapy medicine for spinal muscular atrophy in infants.

Top company officials later admitted that they had known about the fraudulent data for months while the FDA considered the appli-

cation, but they decided to keep mum until after the agency announced its approval and even after the company disclosed the
treatment's controversial price: $2.1 million. When the price contro-
versy subsided, executives admitted the lie.

When this deception became public, the FDA issued a scorching
statement saying that the company could face criminal charges. But
Dr. Peter Bach, a researcher at Memorial Sloan Kettering Cancer
Center, tweeted his skepticism: "This whole thing has the 'wrongs
were committed but there were no wrongdoers' feel," Bach wrote. Dr.
Scott Gottlieb, who left the agency as its commissioner just five
months earlier, tweeted a response: "Based on the tone and substance
of the FDA statement today, Peter, I suspect there will be wrongdoers
here. And consequences."

Seven months later, Novartis quietly disclosed its punishment in
a little-noticed filing: a commitment to notify the agency within five
business days of any "credible allegation" in which manipulated data
may affect a pending marketing application.

In other words, Novartis's punishment for breaking the law and
lying to the FDA was a promise to tell the agency much sooner the
next time it decides to break the law and lie about a pending application. Lies about other matters are presumably not even covered by
the new guarantee. If the FDA had simply asked Novartis to surrender the revenue from Zolgensma's first one hundred sales, that would
have amounted to a $210 million fine. But no fine at all was levied.

Fifth, states should repeal laws that forbid personal injury suits or
punitive damages against makers of FDA-approved products. The
underlying premise of these laws—that the FDA's decisions are the
result of expert analysis and not industry lobbying—is fundamentally untrue.

The FDA is a creature of industry, and its decisions and judg-
ments should be seen as such. No legal protection should be afforded
to drug- and device makers just because the FDA agrees with them.

Sixth, American media organizations need to do some deep soul-
searching to figure out how they so thoroughly missed exposing the

monster in their midst. Johnson & Johnson's size and complexity made tracking and linking its myriad misdeeds challenging, to be sure, but still, they should have been uncovered years ago. As one of the leading reporters in the space, this failure was partly mine.

Was the company's massive advertising budget the key reason this story was missed? If so, newspapers and TV news programs ought now to take a close look across their advertisers to see who else might be hiding a dark history.

Finally, the story of Johnson & Johnson must lead to a wholesale reassessment of the very system in which the conglomerate was allowed to thrive. In a country that is now actively reassessing its past and searching for a better way forward, Johnson & Johnson's history must also be examined.

After all, Johnson & Johnson is "a quintessentially American company," as the CNBC anchor said. Its decades-long transformation from ethical to evil mirrors the slow-motion metamorphosis of American healthcare from best to worst, protected by smokescreens of disinformation and mythologizing.

No other healthcare system is as expensive or inefficient. None in the developed world loses a greater share of its participants to preventable deaths. Middle-class Americans have long accepted the system's downsides, under the mistaken belief that the poor are the only ones disadvantaged, and with the worry that a more equitable system might prove less innovative or convenient. J & J's deadly and cynical campaigns for such a wide array of products powerfully demonstrates just how wrong these assumptions really are. Almost every American family has suffered profoundly from J & J's misdeeds. That Johnson & Johnson has gotten away with so much is a devastating indictment of the country's for-profit healthcare model at large.

Maybe it's time it, too, underwent a fundamental change. Perhaps there is a way in which we can band together and create this greater immunity.

Acknowledgments

THE STORY TOLD IN THESE PAGES HAS BEEN HIDING IN PLAIN SIGHT for a very long time. Over the course of nearly five years, scores of people gave me important parts of this tale even though doing so was often spectacularly unwise for them.

J & J is one of the largest funders of academic medical centers in the world. Its lawyers are widely perceived as unusually aggressive. Its advertising budget is massive. Its associated charity, the Robert Wood Johnson Foundation, is one of the biggest grant-makers in healthcare. For many professionals—doctors, lawyers, academics, regulators, prosecutors, investigators, and even journalists—getting crossways with Johnson & Johnson is a ticket to career oblivion. For executives and former employees of the conglomerate, talking to me was even more fraught.

Nevertheless, scores of brave people did help—none more so than Dr. Peter Bach, formerly of Memorial Sloan Kettering Cancer Center. Bach is one of the world's foremost experts on drug pricing and a practiced epidemiologist. When no one else would agree to stake their reputation to a public estimate of the antipsychotic death toll, he and his terrific team at Memorial did.

The grand jury and investigative materials featured in this book were provided by people who left themselves at risk of criminal prosecution. Readers may yawn at such a description because of the highly classified national security documents that seem to appear regularly in the nation's top newspapers, Florida bathrooms, and Delaware garages.

But grand juries are the last truly secret institutions in American life. Their inner workings almost never become public. I'm incredibly grateful for the courage and passion of the people who not only broke laws but a host of near-sacrosanct legal covenants to provide them.

The initial draft of this book was nearly twice as long as the final. Samuel Nicholson did terrific work as my first editor in identifying extraneous material and ensuring the book carried a consistent tone. Geoffrey Shandler pared things down even more. I'm thankful for the careful and painstaking work of both fine editors.

Gail Ross, my agent, was the first person to tell me that a book about Johnson & Johnson would have an audience. She kept me on track when I wandered too far afield, and she whipped me into shape during days of grueling pitches to publishers.

A big shout-out to Andy Ward, Ben Greenberg, and Mark Warren of Random House, who collectively took a chance on my ability to fulfill an unusual set of promises. Tough investigations are increasingly rare in journalism as the legal risks surrounding this work have mounted, but Random House never wavered. Matthew Martin, Random House's in-house counsel, always looked for ways to include rather than exclude material—unusual in legal reviews. I would also like to thank the skilled copyediting team, Mimi Lipson and Dennis Ambrose.

Benedict Carey, a close friend who covered mental health for the *Los Angeles Times* and then *The New York Times,* provided invaluable encouragement and advice, particularly in the Risperdal section. Glenn Fine, Steven Shapiro, and Neil King were great sounding boards, and Conor Salcetti performed a needed final copyedit. James Gutman helped a lot in the Tylenol section. The Rockefeller Foundation's decision to hire me as a consultant during the Covid-19 pandemic saved my family's finances.

Like many reporters who turn to books, I left the endnotes to the last and then had to scramble to organize hundreds of crucial documents. Tran Hao Triet was invaluable in that process, and I relied heavily upon him not only to put together the vital listing at the end of the book but to create a website where those documents could be aggregated and permanently reside. I'm hoping it's a place where professors of medical, legal, and business ethics might find useful material for their work and classes.

My sons, Aden and Bram, are the center of my life. I couldn't have undertaken or finished this book without their love and support. I am so lucky to have them.

Finally, while I am critical in these pages of some of the nation's most important auditors of corporate conduct, including *The Wall Street Journal, The New York Times,* and the Food and Drug Administration, I want to acknowledge that all of these institutions have dedicated and remarkable professionals who work tirelessly to make American life better. Many of the failings I highlight in this book are almost beyond their capacities to correct. The kind of money that J & J spreads around American society is a nearly irresistible force.

I'm particularly grateful then that FDA staffers helped me, even when they knew I was bound to kick their beloved employer in the teeth. That kind of selfless dedication is a vital part of public service.

Notes

INTRODUCTION: A QUINTESSENTIALLY AMERICAN COMPANY

xiv **Eighteen years later:** Johnson & Johnson. "Johnson & Johnson Named a 2023 *Fortune* World's Most Admired Company and Ranked #1 on the Pharmaceutical Industry List." JnJ.com, February 1, 2023. Available at: https://no-more-tears.org/JJ-2023.pdf.

xiv **"If there is a more American":** Tirrell, Meg. "CNBC's Meg Tirrell Interviews Johnson & Johnson Chairman and CEO Alex Gorsky from CNBC's Healthy Returns Conference Today." CNBC, May 21, 2019. Available at: https://no-more-tears.org/Tirrell-2019.pdf.

xiv **Seven in ten patients:** Henderson, Jessica. "8 Johnson & Johnson Inventions We're Grateful For." JnJ.com, November 21, 2019. Available at: https://no-more-tears.org/Henderson-2019.pdf.

xv **First written in 1943, its credo:** Foster, Lawrence G. *A Company That Cares: A One Hundred Year History of Johnson & Johnson,* 1986. Available at: https://no-more-tears.org/JJ-1986.pdf.

xv **When a maniac tested the credo:** Rehak, Judith. "Tylenol Made a Hero of Johnson & Johnson: The Recall That Started Them All." *The New York Times,* March 23, 2002. Available at: https://no-more-tears.org/Rehak-2002.pdf.

xv **A Harvard Business School case study:** Greyser, Stephen. "Johnson & Johnson: The Tylenol Tragedy." Harvard Business School Case 583-043, October 1982.

xv **Johnson & Johnson is the largest:** Maurer, Mark. "Johnson & Johnson Prepares to Untangle Finances Ahead of Planned Split." *The Wall Street Journal,* December 6, 2021. Available at: https://no-more-tears.org/Maurer-2021.pdf.

xvi **I found that J & J was the *only:*** Jack, Andrew. "J & J Opts Out of HIV Rights Sharing Pool." *Financial Times,* December 24, 2011. Available at: https://no-more-tears.org/Jack-2011.pdf.

xvii **The first section details:** Johnson & Johnson. "Our Baby History." JnJ.com, 2008. Available at: https://no-more-tears.org/JJ-2008.pdf.

xvii **A crucial actor:** Kolodny, Andrew. "How FDA Failures Contributed to the Opioid Crisis." *AMA Journal of Ethics* 22, no. 8, August 2020: 743–50. Available at: https://no-more-tears.org/Kolodny-2020.pdf.

xvii **Like Johnson & Johnson, the FDA:** "The FDA's Poor Oversight of Post-marketing Studies." Editorial in *The Lancet* 374, November 7, 2009: 1568. Available at: https://no-more-tears.org/Lancet-2009.pdf.

CHAPTER 1: AN EMOTIONAL BOND

3 **Company surveys found:** Hsu, Tiffany. "Johnson & Johnson to End Talc-Based Baby Powder Sales in North America." *The New York Times,* May 19, 2021. Available at: https://no-more-tears.org/Hsu-2021.pdf.

3 **Talc products were:** Steinberg, W. H. Letter to Dr. Hildick-Smith, subject: "Johnson's Baby Powder Talc Aspiration." June 17, 1966. JNJNL61_000009898. Available at: https://no-more-tears.org/Steinberg-1966.pdf.

4 **"The association of":** Johnson & Johnson. "Our Baby History." JnJ.com, 2008. Available at: https://no-more-tears.org/JJ-2008.pdf.

4 **"Many companies have rational trust":** Cirillo, Marco. "Johnson & Johnson Equity Presentation." Corporate slide deck, 1996. Available at: https://no-more-tears.org/Cirillo-1996.pdf.

4 **"Olfactory learning occurs":** "Role of Fragrances in Johnson's Baby Products." 2009. Available at: https://no-more-tears.org/JJ-Fragrance.pdf.

CHAPTER 2: THREE BROTHERS GO TO NEW BRUNSWICK, 1860–1968

6 **To protect Robert, his parents:** Mates, Rich. "Carbondale Area Native Founded Johnson & Johnson." *The Times Tribune,* November 12, 2000. Available at: https://no-more-tears.org/TimesTribune-2000.pdf.

6 **In 1873, the two men:** Johnson & Johnson. "Seabury & Johnson Is Founded, 1873." Our Story. JnJ.com. Available at: https://no-more-tears.org/JJ-Seabury.pdf.

7 **In 1876, the two:** Johnson & Johnson. Our Story. JnJ.com. Available at: https://web.archive.org/web/20230408124554/https://ourstory.jnj.com/.

7 **An 1879 Seabury & Johnson catalog:** Shook, Robert. *Miracle Medicines: Seven Lifesaving Drugs and the People Who Created Them.* Portfolio, 2007.

8 **On July 18, 1885:** Gurowitz, Margaret. "Seabury & Johnson." Our Story. JnJ.com, October 2, 2009. Available at: https://no-more-tears.org/Gurowitz-2009b.pdf.

8 **On October 28, 1887:** Gurowitz, Margaret. "The Year Was 1886: The Story of How Johnson & Johnson Was Born." Our Story. JnJ.com, September 2, 2015. Available at: https://no-more-tears.org/Gurowitz-2015.pdf.

8 **Over the course of the next months:** Gurowitz, Margaret. "100 Years Ago: A

Modern Advertising Campaign." Our Story. JnJ.com, January 15, 2010. Available at: https://no-more-tears.org/Gurowitz-2010.pdf.

9 **Johnson & Johnson soon began:** Johnson & Johnson. "The First Band-Aid Brand Adhesive Bandage." Our Story. JnJ.com, March 9, 2017. Available at: https://no-more-tears.org/JJ-BandAid.pdf.

9 **Some of the ingredients:** Johnson & Johnson. "The Johnson's Promise." JnJ.com. Available at: https://no-more-tears.org/JJ-Promise.pdf.

10 **In 1901, Kilmer authored a book:** Johnson & Johnson. "The Birth of the First Aid Kit." JnJ.com, June 27, 2017. Available at: https://no-more-tears.org/JJ-2017.pdf.

11 **Robert Wood Johnson II was:** Cozby, Paul. "Robert Wood Johnson II Was a Drug Titan Ahead of His Time." *Investor's Business Daily,* March 14, 2016. Available at: https://no-more-tears.org/Cozby-2016.pdf.

11 **That summer:** Gurowitz, Margaret. "Young Robert Wood Johnson Joins the Company." JnJ.com, September 21, 2007. Available at: https://no-more-tears.org/Gurowitz-2007.pdf.

12 **For the 1918 flu pandemic:** Johnson & Johnson. "National Clean Up Weeks: A History of Spring Cleaning to Improve Public Health." JnJ.com, April 18, 2022. Available at: https://no-more-tears.org/JJ-2022B.pdf.

13 **In 1918, Johnson & Johnson launched:** Johnson & Johnson. "The First Band-Aid Brand Adhesive Bandage." Our Story. JnJ.com, March 9, 2017. Available at: https://no-more-tears.org/JJ-BandAid.pdf.

13 **Hugely successful:** Foster, Lawrence G. *Robert Wood Johnson: The Gentleman Rebel.* Lillian Books, 1999.

13 **J & J began to:** Berfield, Susan, Jef Feeley, and Margaret Cronin Fisk. "Johnson & Johnson Has a Baby Powder Problem." *Bloomberg Businessweek,* April 4–10, 2016.

14 **In 1926, as the beginning:** Gurowitz, Margaret. "Factories Can Be Beautiful." JnJ.com, December 4, 2008. Available at: https://no-more-tears.org/Gurowitz-2008.pdf.

15 **In 1959, the team landed:** Gurowitz, Margaret. "1959: McNeil Laboratories Joins the Family." 2009. Available at: https://no-more-tears.org/Gurowitz-2009.pdf.

15 **Just months after the McNeil:** Johnson & Johnson. "Johnson & Johnson Acquires Janssen Pharmaceutica, 1961." Our Story. JnJ.com. Available at: https://no-more-tears.org/JJ-Janssen.pdf.

15 **And months before closing the deal:** "Case AT.39685—Fentanyl." Summary of Commission Decision. *Official Journal of the European Union,* October 12, 2013. Available at: https://no-more-tears.org/OJEU-2013.pdf.

15 **Janssen eventually birthed seventy compounds:** "A Lasting, Far Reaching Legacy." Paul Janssen Award website, 2003. Available at: https://no-more-tears.org/JJ-2003.pdf.

16 **The bond between father and son:** Foster, Lawrence G. *Robert Wood Johnson: The Gentleman Rebel.* Lillian Books, 1999.

17 **In a bitter letter dated:** Foster, Lawrence G. *Robert Wood Johnson: The Gentleman Rebel.* Lillian Books, 1999.

17 **No family member would ever:** Oppenheimer, Jerry. *Crazy Rich: Power, Scandal and Tragedy Inside the Johnson & Johnson Dynasty.* St. Martin's Press, 2013.

CHAPTER 3: MINERAL TWINS

18 **In places like India:** Cheng, Ahn Dao, et al. "Skin-Lightening Products: Consumer Preferences and Costs." *Cureus: Journal of Medical Science,* August 17, 2021. Available at: https://no-more-tears.org/Cheng-2021.pdf.

19 **The first reports documenting dangers:** Johnson & Johnson. "Powder Presentation," 1999. JNJNL61_000106363. Available at: https://no-more-tears.org/JJ-Powder.pdf.

19 **In 1969 and again in 1981:** Mofenson, Howard C., et al. "A Warning: An Epidemic of Baby Powder Aspiration." *Pediatrics* 67, no. 1, January 1981: A68. Available at: https://no-more-tears.org/Mofenson-1981.pdf.

20 **In one terrible example:** Crandall, William "Rick," and Richard E. Crandall. "Revisiting the Hawks Nest Tunnel Incident: Lessons Learned from an American Tragedy." *Journal of Appalachian Studies* 8, no. 2, Fall 2002: 261–83.

20 **Studies published in 1942 and 1955:** Schepers, G. W., and T. M. Durkin. "The Effects of Inhaled Talc-Mining Dust on the Human Lung." *AMA Archives of Industrial Health* 12, no. 2, August 1955: 182–97.

20 **There were hints:** Cralley, L. J., et al. "Fibrous and Mineral Content of Cosmetic Talcum Products." *American Industrial Hygiene Association Journal* 29, no. 4, winter 1968: 350–54.

20 **In 1956, 1963, and 1968:** "Talc (Fibrous)." *American Conference of Governmental Industrial Hygienists (ACGIH),* 1963. Available at: https://no-more-tears.org/ACGIH-1963.pdf.

21 **As a bonus:** Rolle, Robert. "Proposed Specs for Analyzing Talc for Asbestos." Report sent to F. R. Rolle, May 16, 1973. JNJ000232679. Available at: https://no-more-tears.org/Pooley-1973.pdf.

21 **Between 1890 and 1968:** Roselli, Maria. *The Asbestos Lie: The Past and Present of an Industrial Catastrophe.* European Trade Union Institute, 2014. Available at: https://no-more-tears.org/Roselli-2014.pdf.

21 **But over the course:** International Agency for Research on Cancer (IARC). *Arsenic, Metals, Fibres and Dusts.* IARC Monographs on the Evaluation of Carcinogenic Risks to Humans, Volume 100C. IARC, 2012.

22 **Hints of asbestos's:** Roselli, Maria. *The Asbestos Lie: The Past and Present of an Industrial Catastrophe.* European Trade Union Institute, 2014. Available at: https://no-more-tears.org/Roselli-2014.pdf.

22 **More evidence emerged:** U.S. Food and Drug Administration. "Food Talc: What It Is and How It Is Used in Cosmetics." FDA.gov. Available at: https://no-more-tears.org/FDA-Talc.pdf.

22 **In a *British Medical Journal* paper:** Cooke, W. E. "Pulmonary Asbestosis." *The British Medical Journal* 2, no. 2491, December 3, 1927: 1024–25.

22 **Following up, between 1928 and 1929:** Merewether, E.R.A., and C. W. Price. *Report on Effects of Asbestos Dust on the Lungs and Dust Suppression in the Asbestos Industry.* H.M.S.O., 1930.

23 **In 1960, South African researchers:** Wagner, J. C., C. A. Sleggs, and P. Marchand. "Diffuse Pleural Mesothelioma and Asbestos Exposure in the North Western Cape Province." *British Journal of Industrial Medicine* 17, no. 4, October 1960: 260–71.

23 **Another team of South African:** Thomson, J. G., et al. "Asbestos as a Modern Urban Hazard." *South African Medical Journal* 37, no.3, January 1963: 77–81.

23 **Subsequent autopsy studies:** Selikoff, Irving J., and E. Cuyler Hammond. "Community Effects of Nonoccupational Environmental Asbestos Exposure." *American Journal of Public Health* 58, September 1968: 1658–66.

23 **Around the same time:** Lambert, Bruce. "Irving J. Selikoff Is Dead at 77; TB Researcher Fought Asbestos." *The New York Times,* May 22, 1992. Available at: https://no-more-tears.org/Lambert-1992.pdf.

23 **In 1965, a study:** Newhouse, Muriel L., and Hilda Thompson. "Mesothelioma of Pleura and Peritoneum Following Exposure to Asbestos in the London Area." *British Journal of Industrial Medicine* 22, no. 3, October 1965: 261–69.

24 **In 1964, his study:** Selikoff, Irving J., Jacob Churg, and E. Cuyler Hammond. "Asbestos Exposure and Neoplasia." *JAMA* 188, no. 1, April 1964: 22–26.

24 **In a study published in 1960:** Keal, E. E. "Asbestosis and Abdominal Neoplasms." *The Lancet* 276, December 3, 1960: 1211–16.

24 **In 1968, *The New Yorker:*** Brodeur, Paul. "The Magic Mineral." *The New Yorker,* October 12, 1968. Available at: https://no-more-tears.org/Brodeur-1968.pdf.

25 **Selikoff had recruited Langer:** Langer, A. M., Irving J. Selikoff, and Antonio Sastre. "Chrysotile Asbestos in the Lungs of Persons in New York City." *Archives of Environmental Health* 22, no. 3, March 1971: 348–61.

25 **He found that all:** "Meeting with Dr. Langer on July 9 Concerning Analytical Analysis of Talc." July 9, 1971. JNJ000265335. Available at: https://no-more-tears.org/JNJ000265335.pdf.

25 **In April 1968:** Cralley et al., "Fibrous and Mineral Content of Cosmetic Talcum Products."

25 **A year later:** Wright, G. W. "Asbestos and Health in 1969." *American Review of Respiratory Disease* 100, no. 4, October 1969: 467–79.

26 **Those impurities, Battelle noted:** Smith, W. L. *Progress Report on Further Studies on the Measurement and Correlation of the Physical Properties of Talc to Johnson and Johnson.* Battelle Memorial Institute, May 9, 1958. Available at: https://no-more-tears.org/Smith-1958.pdf.

26 **In 1964, Johnson & Johnson:** Miller, Roger. Letter to J. E. Burke, subject: "Review of the Italian Talc Source Societa Talco e Grafite Val Chisone." July 15, 1966. Available at: https://no-more-tears.org/Miller-1966.pdf.

26 **As Italy remained:** Miller, Roger. "Notes on Board of Directors meeting of 4/19/72 at New Brunswick." 1972. Available at: https://no-more-tears.org/Miller-1972.pdf.

26 **That colocation:** Petterson, D. R. Memo to D. D. Johnston, subject: "Windsor Minerals and Talc." April 26, 1973. JNJ000294872. Available at: https://no-more-tears.org/Petterson-1973.pdf.

26 **Once intermingled:** Nashed, W. Letter to Hearing Clerk, Department of Health, Education, and Welfare. October 11, 1972. JNJ000245230. Available at: https://no-more-tears.org/Nashed-1972.pdf.

26 **Predictably, Johnson & Johnson's tests:** Ashton, W. H. *Alternate Talc Sources Project #101.* 1967. Available at: https://no-more-tears.org/Ashton-1967.pdf.

27 **About a year and a half later:** Ashton, W. H. Memo to G. Hildick-Smith, subject: "Alternate Domestic Talc Sources File No. 101." April 9, 1969. JNJ000087989. Available at: https://no-more-tears.org/Ashton-1969.pdf.

27 **"Since the usage of these products":** Thompson, T. M. Letter to W. H. Ashton, subject: "Alternate Domestic Talc Sources." April 15, 1969. Available at: https://no-more-tears.org/Thompson-1969.pdf.

27 **In 1971, the Tenovus:** Henderson, W. J., et al. "Talc and Carcinoma of the Ovary and Cervix." *Journal of Obstetrics and Gynaecology of the British Commonwealth* 78, March 1971: 266–72.

28 **instead, the Tenovus team:** Meeting at Tenovus Institute of Cancer, Cardiff (transcript). April 7, 1971. JNJTALC000287135. Available at: https://no-more -tears.org/JNJTALC000287135.pdf.

28 **One aspect of that plan:** "Deposition of Tissues Obtained from Tenovus Institute." 1971. JNJTALC000287287. Available at: https://no-more-tears.org /JNJTALC000287287.pdf.

28 **The Johnson & Johnson employee:** Johnson & Johnson memo. "Meeting with Dr. Langer on July 9 Concerning Analytical Analysis of Talc." 1971. JNJ000265335. Available at: https://no-more-tears.org/JNJ000265335.pdf.

28 **"We also got a few surprises":** Langer, A. M. Letter to G. Hildick-Smith, November 10, 1971. JNJ000288077. Available at: https://no-more-tears.org /Langer-1971.pdf.

28 **"We also observed trace amounts":** Langer, A. M. Letter to Dr. Gavin Hildick-Smith. November 10, 1971. JNJ000288077. Available at: https://no -more-tears.org/Langer-1971B.pdf.

29 **The company had no interest:** Deposition of Susan Nicholson, March 6, 2019. Available at: https://no-more-tears.org/Nicholson-2019.pdf.

29 **So instead of publishing:** Kretchmer, Jerome. Letter to Elliott H. Richardson (Department of Health, Education and Welfare), June 28, 1971. JNJ000277594. Available at: https://no-more-tears.org/Kretchmer-1971.pdf.

29 **Johnson & Johnson promptly:** Johnson & Johnson. Statement issued to the *New York Daily News* and the *New York Post,* June 29, 1971. JNJ 000277629. Available at: https://no-more-tears.org/JJ-1971.pdf.

29 **The private meeting:** Wenninger, John. Memorandum of meeting, subject: "Asbestos Particles in Talc." July 8, 1971. Available at: https://no-more-tears .org/Wenninger-1971.pdf.

30 **Years later, a company:** *Barden v. Brenntag North America et al.* Trial testimony by John Hopkins. July 23, 2019. Available at: https://no-more-tears.org /Hopkins-2019.pdf.

   Q: This is the President of Windsor Mineral in a lawsuit saying, no evidence of the presence of asbestos in Windsor Minerals' product. And he included— I asked you, he included everything they'd ever sold, cosmetic and industrial, has ever revealed or been revealed by this testing.
   Here's the question. Was that true or was that false?
   A: On the face of it, it does not appear to be true.
   Q: So that makes it what?

A: Unless we've got other evidence. On the face of it, it would not be true. Unless—

Q: Which would make it?

A: It would make it false, unless there is other evidence that we don't have here. . . .

Q: And he was under oath, wasn't he?

A: I believe so, yes.

Q: And that is— You understand that is perjury, do you not?

A: I do.

CHAPTER 4: THE FDA CONDUCTS A SURVEY

31 **In August 1971:** Norwood, Robert E., and Harold D. Stanley. Memorandum, subject: "Asbestos in Talc 'Analytical Methodology Conference at FDA, Washington, D.C., 3 August 1971.'" PFI_KA_00000001. Available at: https://no-more-tears.org/Norwood-1971.pdf.

32 **In September 1972:** Lewin, Seymour. Letter to Dr. Alfred Weissler; "Tabulation of X-Ray Diffraction Analyses of Commercial Products Containing Talc" (table), August 3, 1972. Available at: https://no-more-tears.org/Lewin-1972.pdf.

32 **Kligman was a problematic:** Hornblum, Allen M. *Acres of Skin: Human Experiments at Holmesburg Prison.* Routledge, 1998.

32 **Kligman wrote a letter:** Kligman, Albert M. Letter to G. Hildick-Smith, December 10, 1971. JNJ000254366. Available at: https://no-more-tears.org/Kligman-1971.pdf.

33 **When J & J forwarded:** Stewart, Ian M. "Examination of Johnson and Johnson's Baby Powder." Altered report, October 27, 1972. HHS00000056. Available at: https://no-more-tears.org/Stewart-1972b.pdf.

33 **"DO NOT USE THIS REPORT":** Stewart, Ian M. "Examination of Johnson and Johnson's Baby Powder." Altered report, October 27, 1972. HHS00000056. Available at: https://no-more-tears.org/Stewart-1972b.pdf.

33 **"Two brands of talcum powder":** Lichtenstein, Grace. "High Levels of Asbestos Found in 3 Paints and 2 Talcums Here." *The New York Times,* June 16, 1972. Available at: https://no-more-tears.org/Lichtenstein-1972.pdf.

34 **The next day:** Lichtenstein, Grace. "Talc Warning Is Labeled False." *The New York Times,* June 17, 1972. Available at: https://no-more-tears.org/Lichtenstein-1972b.pdf.

35 **The analysis found:** Lightfoot, J., G. A. Kingston, and F. D. Pooley. "An Examination of Italian Mine Samples and Relevant Powders." *Department of Mineral Exploitation,* University College, Cardiff, September 8, 1972. Available at: https://no-more-tears.org/Pooley-1972.pdf.

35 **A few months later:** Shelley, T. H. Letter to Mr. Ian Sloan, February 20, 1973. JNJ000330927. Available at: https://no-more-tears.org/Shelley-1973.pdf.

35 **A month later, Shelley:** Shelley, T. H. Letter to Mr. H. L. Warner, subject: "Talc/Asbestos Patents." March 30, 1973. JNJ000302740. Available at: https://no-more-tears.org/Shelley-1973b.pdf.

35 **In an April 26, 1973:** Petterson, D. R. Memo to D. D. Johnston, subject:

"Windsor Minerals and Talc." April 26, 1973. JNJ000294872. Available at: https://no-more-tears.org/Petterson-1973.pdf.

36 **Villa created a pamphlet:** *Practical Guide to the Recognition of Impurities in Talc.* Società Talco e Grafite Val Chisone, 1974. JNJMX68_000009502. Available at: https://no-more-tears.org/SVC-1974.pdf.

36 **Ashton wrote that:** Ashton, W. H. Letter to Mr. G. Lee, subject: "Italian Talc Source Societa Talco e Grafite Val Chisone Talc Publication Matters Project No. 0503.00." October 31, 1974. JNJ000270495. Available at: https://no-more-tears.org/Ashton-1974.pdf.

36 **The J & J team emphatically:** Ashton, W. H. Confidential memo to Mr. G. Lee, Dr. D. R. Petterson, and Dr. B. Semple, 1974. JNJAZ55_000001101. Available at: https://no-more-tears.org/Ashton-1974b.pdf.

CHAPTER 5: BIRTH OF THE MODERN FDA

37 **The Food and Drug Administration:** Law, Marc E. "History of Food and Drug Regulation in the United States." Website of the Economic History Association, October 11, 2004.

38 **Tulsa medical authorities soon:** Ballentine, Carol. "Sulfanilamide Disaster." *FDA Consumer,* June 1981. Available at: https://no-more-tears.org/FDA-1981.pdf.

38 **But the requests were spotty:** Miller, Dennis. "10 shocking Things I've Learned as a Pharmacist." *Drug Topics,* June 21, 2016. Available at: https://no-more-tears.org/Miller-2016.pdf.

38 **In September 1960:** Seidman, Lisa A., and Noreen Warren. "Frances Kelsey & Thalidomide in the US: A Case Study Relating to Pharmaceutical Regulations." *The American Biology Teacher* 64, no. 7, September 2002: 495–500.

39 **In the wake of the story:** Wileman, H., and Arun Mishra. "Drug Lag and Key Regulatory Barriers in the Emerging Markets." *Perspectives in Clinical Research* 1, no. 2, April 2010: 51–56.

40 **Blush, hair tonics:** Bird, Tess, et al. "A Review of the Talc Industry's Influence on Federal Regulation and Scientific Standards for Asbestos in Talc." *New Solutions* 31, no. 2, August 2021: 152–69.

40 **After much back-and-forth:** U.S. Food and Drug Administration. "Proposed Rules: Asbestos Particles in Food and Drugs." Code of Federal Regulations, Title 21, parts 121, 128, 1331973. *Federal Register,* 38, no. 188, September 28, 1973: 27076. Available at: https://no-more-tears.org/FDA-1973.pdf.

40 **Unsurprisingly, the Cosmetic:** Nashed, W. Letter to Dr. Robert M. Schaffne, September 6, 1974. JNJNL61_000013575. Available at: https://no-more-tears.org/Nashed-1974.pdf.

41 **But that wasn't the end:** Lee, George. Memo to Talc Advisory Group, subject: "CTFA Cosmetic Talc Specification." August 26, 1975. JNJ000299776. Available at: https://no-more-tears.org/Lee-1975c.pdf.

41 **Prodded by their drug counterparts:** Spivak, Jonathan. "FDA Plans to Impose Limits on Asbestos in Certain Cosmetics." *The Wall Street Journal,* February 26, 1973. Available at: https://no-more-tears.org/Spivak-1973.pdf.

41 **One proposal involved:** Ashton, W. H. Letter to George Lee, November 24, 1976. JNJ000242147. Available at: https://no-more-tears.org/Ashton-1976.pdf.

41 **What the industry needed:** Sloan, I. W. *Letter to R. Rolle*, February 18, 1975. JNJ000326922. Available at: https://no-more-tears.org/Sloan-1975.pdf; Sandland, George W. "Minutes: CTFA Subcomittee of SAC on Asbestos in Talc." October 11, 1973. Available at: https://no-more-tears.org/Sandland-1973.pdf.

41 **And it needed one:** Steinberg, Wallace. H. Letter to Dr. Norman Estrin and John Menkart, subject: "Talc." December 17, 1974. JNJMX68_000009139. Available at: https://no-more-tears.org/Steinberg-1974.pdf.

41 **So the industry created:** Tran, Triet H., et al. "Talc, Asbestos, and Epidemiology: Corporate Influence and Scientific Incognizance." *Epidemiology* 30, no. 6, November 2019: 783–88. Available at: https://no-more-tears.org/Tran-2019.pdf.

41 **One of the most common:** Sandland, George. "Talc." CTFA Cosmetic Journal 8, no. 1, January/March 1976: 21–22. QE-CPC00001182. Available at: https://no-more-tears.org/Sandland-1976.pdf.

42 **But the failure:** Westman, Mort. "Minutes: CTFA Task Force on Round Robin Testing of Consumer Talcum Products for Asbestiform Amphibole Minerals." June 13, 1977. JNJNL61_000020521. Available at: https://no-more-tears.org/Westman-1977.pdf.

42 **J & J didn't notify:** Gettings, Stephen D. *"Meeting Minutes: Scientific Advisory Executive Committee."* April 12, 1995. PCPC001342. Available at: https://no-more-tears.org/Gettings-1995.pdf.

42 **Dr. Susan Nicholson:** Deposition of Susan Nicholson, March 6, 2019. Available at: https://no-more-tears.org/Nicholson-2019.pdf.

CHAPTER 6: THE POWER OF PRESSURE

43 **On November 29:** Hildick-Smith, Gavin. Letter to D. D. Johnston, subject: "Antagonistic Personalities in the Talc Story in the U.S.A." November 28, 1972. JNJAZ55_000005015. Available at: https://no-more-tears.org/Hildick-Smith-1972.pdf.

44 **Langer's last stand:** Langer, Arthur M. Letter to Dean Thomas C. Chalmers, subject: "The Ongoing Talc Study in the Environmental Sciences Laboratory." March 17, 1976. Available at: https://no-more-tears.org/Langer-1976.pdf.

44 **As soon as Pooley:** Lee, George. Memo to W. H. Ashton, et al., subject: "A. M. Langer Analysis of Talcum Powder Products—Edinburgh Meeting." September 9, 1975. JNJ000253056. Available at: https://no-more-tears.org/Lee-1975.pdf.

45 **Although Pooley had told:** Lee, George. Memo to Talc Advisory Group, subject: "Review of Talc Events at Brighton and Edinburgh Conference September 14–26, 1975." October 3, 1975. JNJ000329832. Available at: https://no-more-tears.org/Lee-1975b.pdf.

45 **In a memo, Langer:** Langer, letter to Dean Thomas C. Chalmers, March 17, 1976.

46 **All told Burros:** Johnson & Johnson Memo, subject: "The Mt. Sinai Samples Are OLD." March 18, 1976. JNJMX68_000009854. Available at: https://no-more-tears.org/JJ-1976.pdf.

46 **Johnson & Johnson's top executives:** Hildick-Smith, Gavin. Memo, subject:

"Meeting with Johnson & Johnson Personnel and the Mt. Sinai School of Medicine." March 31, 1976. JNJ000304421. Available at: https://no-more-tears.org /Hildick-Smith-1976.pdf.

47 **An initial draft:** Chalmers, Thomas C. Letter to Dr. Irving Selikoff, March 22, 1976. Available at: https://no-more-tears.org/Chalmers-1976.pdf.

47 **In the final statement:** Chalmers, Thomas C. Mount Sinai Retraction, March 23, 1976. Available at: https://no-more-tears.org/Chalmers-1976b.pdf.

47 **Langer was, unsurprisingly:** Yates, Ronald. Memorandum, subject: "Analytical Methodology for the Detection and Determination of Asbestos Minerals in Talc." March 22, 1976. HHS00000018. Available at: https://no-more-tears.org /Yates-1976.pdf.

48 **An instant fall classic:** Burros, Marian. "Eating Well." *The New York Times,* November 15, 1989. Available at: https://no-more-tears.org/Burros-1991.pdf.

48 **"But there is":** Burros, Marian. "Report on Talc Research 'Corrected.'" *The Washington Post,* March 25, 1976. JNJ000222906. Available at: https://no -more-tears.org/Burros-1976.pdf.

49 **The same day Burros's:** Burros, Marian. "Asbestos Fibers Found in Baby Powder." *The Washington Post,* March 8, 1976. Available at: https://no-more-tears .org/Burros-1976b.pdf.

49 **D. D. Johnston sent:** Johnston, D. D. Letter to Dr. Thomas C. Chalmers, March 26, 1976. JNJ000304381. Available at: https://no-more-tears.org/Johnston -1976.pdf.

50 **Langer's data:** Rohl, A. N., et al. "Consumer Talcums and Powders: Mineral and Chemical Characterization." *Journal of Toxicology and Environmental Health* 2, no. 2, 1976: 255–84.

50 **And with the Mount Sinai team:** Lee, George. Letter to D. D. Johnston, subject: "Status Report—Defense of Talc Safety." August 29, 1977. JNJMX68_000013482. Available at: https://no-more-tears.org/Lee-1977.pdf.

51 **For James E. Burke:** Tye, Joe. *All Hands On Deck: 8 Essential Lessons for Building a Culture of Ownership.* Wiley, 2010.

51 **"I had helped develop a new product":** Foster, Lawrence G. *Robert Wood Johnson: The Gentleman Rebel.* Lillian Books, 1999.

52 **He supported the aggressive:** Bartz, Scott. *The Tylenol Mafia: Marketing, Murder, and Johnson & Johnson.* New Light Publishing, 2012.

52 **Near the end of:** Rundle, Rhonda L. "Amgen and J & J Battle It out over a Very Hot Anemia Drug." *The Wall Street Journal,* September 30, 1998. Available at: https://no-more-tears.org/Rundle-1998.pdf.

CHAPTER 7: A MEETING AT A HARVARD HOSPITAL

54 **Three weeks earlier:** Cramer, D. W., et al. "Ovarian Cancer and Talc: A Case-Control Study." *Cancer* 50, no. 2, July 15, 1982: 372–76.

54 **Cramer in turn:** Cramer, D. W. "Opinion on the Relationship Between Ovarian Cancer and Cosmetic Talc Powder Use: Causality and Relevance to the Case of Jacqueline Fox." July 31, 2015. Available at: https://no-more-tears.org /Cramer-2015.pdf.

54 **Still, as an internal:** Phillips, Steven. Letter to George Lee, subject: "Talc and Ovarian Cancer Site Visit with Dr. Cramer." August 12, 1982. JNJ000029640. Available at: https://no-more-tears.org/Phillips-1982.pdf.

55 **Nonetheless, when in the:** International Agency for Research on Cancer (IARC). *Arsenic, Metals, Fibres and Dusts.* IARC Monographs on the Evaluation of Carcinogenic Risks to Humans Volume 100C. IARC, 2012.

56 **The result was:** Jones, D. F. Letter to J. Hopkins et al., subject: "J & J Worldwide Talc Steering Committee." September 22, 1993. JNJ000298949. Available at: https://no-more-tears.org/Jones-1993.pdf.

56 **Engelhard was a major:** Collins, David. Memo to H. E. Bailey et al., subject: "Eastern Magnesia Talc Co., Inc." September 22, 1965. IMERYS162826. Available at: https://no-more-tears.org/ https://no-more-tears.org/Collins-1965.pdf.

56 **For many, talc was:** "Versatile EMTAL TALCS—Do the job!" 1952. Available at: https://no-more-tears.org/Emtal-1952.pdf.

56 **"When we bought the mine":** Deposition of Glenn Hemstock, May 29, 2012. Available at: https://no-more-tears.org/Hemstock-2012.pdf.

56 **About two hundred National:** Deposition of Glenn Hemstock, May 9, 2012.

57 **Beginning in late January:** Nadkarni, R. A. Report to Dennis L. Caputo, subject: "Asbestos in Talc Samples." October 27, 1978. BASF02510. Available at: https://no-more-tears.org/Nadkarni-1978.pdf.

57 **Initial results were worrisome:** Deposition of Ellen Poole, March 29, 2012. Available at: https://no-more-tears.org/Poole-2012.pdf.

57 **Every single one:** Triglia, E. J. Memo to G. A. Hemstock, subject: "Talc Investigation." May 22, 1979. BASF _LOPEZ000000091. Available at: https://no-more-tears.org/Triglia-1979.pdf.

57 **Engelhard was in a bind:** Deposition of Glenn Hemstock, March 16, 1983. Available at: https://no-more-tears.org/Hemstock-1983.pdf.

57 **But much of the reason:** Placitella, Christopher M. Letter to Judge Dixon, subject: "Plaintiffs' Response to BASF Application for Findings Relating to Existing Documents." February 16, 2017. Available at: https://no-more-tears.org/Placitella-2017.pdf.

58 **And continuing to:** Fetzer, Howard. Letter to Lucy B. McCrone, August 29, 1977. BASF02499. Available at: https://no-more-tears.org/Fetzer-1977.pdf.

58 **But that warning sign:** *Westfall v. Whittaker, Clark & Daniels et al.* Third amended complaint. 1982. Available at: https://no-more-tears.org/Cannon-1982.pdf.

58 **Westfall's lawyer hired:** Placitella, Christopher M. Letter to Judge Dixon, subject: "Plaintiffs' Response to BASF Application for Findings Relating to Existing Documents." February 16, 2017. Available at: https://no-more-tears.org/Placitella-2017.pdf.

CHAPTER 8: SECRECY IS A TOP PRIORITY

59 **Hemstock grudgingly:** Deposition of Glenn Hemstock, March 16, 1983. Available at: https://no-more-tears.org/Hemstock-1983.pdf.

59 **A year earlier:** Lewin, Tamar. "Manville's Robust Bankruptcy." *The New York*

Times, December 10, 1982. Available at: https://no-more-tears.org/Lewin-1982.pdf.

60 **The attorneys demanded confidentiality:** *Kimberlee Williams v. BASF.* Decision on appeal. September 3, 2014. Available at: https://no-more-tears.org/Fuentes-2014.pdf.

60 **"It is the policy of ":** *Kimberlee Williams v. BASF.* Decision on appeal. September 3, 2014. Available at: https://no-more-tears.org/Fuentes-2014.pdf.

60 **Johnson & Johnson then helped:** Deposition of William H. Ashton, May 8, 1989. JNJ000059401. Available at: https://no-more-tears.org/Ashton-1989.pdf.

61 **Among those who signed:** Deposition of William H. Ashton, May 8, 1989. JNJ000059401. Available at: https://no-more-tears.org/Ashton-1989.pdf.

61 **Following this, Engelhard's:** Kluznik, Jack. Letter to Peter J. Brodhead, subject: "Engelhard/Eastern Magnesia Talc Co.—Tireworkers Litigation." October 2, 1989. BASF FC 0007755. Available at: https://no-more-tears.org/Kluznik-1989.pdf.

61 **John Beidler, J & J's:** Beidler, John N. Letter to Ronald B. Grayzel, subject: "Edley v. Windsor Minerals Inc." August 27, 1986. Available at: https://no-more-tears.org/Beidler-1986.pdf.

61 **Many years later:** *Barden v. Brenntag North America et al.* Trial testimony by John Hopkins. July 23, 2019. Available at: https://no-more-tears.org/Hopkins-2019.pdf.

61 **In 2004, Imerys:** "Material Data Safety Sheet—Talc." Rio Tinto Minerals, July 1, 2006. IMERYS 042245. Available at: https://no-more-tears.org/Rio-Tinto-2006.pdf.

62 **A top company executive responded:** Predale, Robert A. Letter to Dana Mickel, subject: *"MSDS Carcinogenic Rating."* January 23, 2005. JNJ000390337. Available at: https://no-more-tears.org/Predale-2005.pdf.

62 **In 2008, J & J's Global:** Johnson & Johnson. "Johnson's Intro to Project Jetpack." Global Design Strategy Team presentation, March 1, 2007. JNJTALC000351738. Available at: https://no-more-tears.org/JJ-2007.pdf.

62 **Sales analyses showed:** True, Todd. Email to Paul J. Serbiak, subject: "FW: Johnson's Baby Powder Naming Study Report." April 17, 2009. JNJ 000422800. Available at: https://no-more-tears.org/Koberna-2009.pdf.

62 **In an April 18, 2008:** True, Todd. Email to Frederick Tewell, subject: "Baby Powder—Not for babies." April 18, 2008. Available at: https://no-more-tears.org/True-2008b.pdf.

63 **In another email:** True, Todd. Email to Christopher Hacker, subject: "Johnson's Baby Powder—Unsafe for Babies?!" April 18, 2008. JNJ 000457189. Available at: https://no-more-tears.org/True-2008.pdf.

64 **The coalition simultaneously:** Cashen, Jill A., and Samuel E. Epstein for the Cancer Prevention Coalition. "Citizen Petition Seeking Carcinogenic Labeling on All Cosmetic Talc Products." November 17, 1994. FDA00000222. Available at: https://no-more-tears.org/Cashen-1994.pdf.

64 **The coalition noted that:** Douillet, Philippe. "Petition for Labeling of Warning of the Hazardous Effects Produced by Asbestos in Cosmetic Talc," received December 2, 1983. FDA00003595. Available at: https://no-more-tears.org/Douillet-1983.pdf.

64 **Relying on false reassurances:** Swanson, H.J.W. Letter to Phillippe Douillet,

subject: "Docket No. 83P 0404." 1986. Available at: https://no-more-tears.org/Swanson-1986.pdf.

64 **Relying on false reassurances:** Kennedy, Donald. Letter to Sidney M. Wolfe and Benjamin Gordon, January 11, 1979. HHS00000067. Available at: https://no-more-tears.org/Kennedy-1979.pdf.

64 **In response to the third:** Carr, C. Jelleff. "Talc: Consumer Uses and Health Perspectives." *Regulatory Toxicology and Pharmacology* 21, 1995: 211–15. JNJ 000024701. Available at: https://no-more-tears.org/Carr-1995.pdf.

64 **The CTFA sent the ISRTP:** Gettings, Stephen. Fax to Talc Interested Party Task Force, January 26, 1994. IMERYS 095258. Available at: https://no-more-tears.org/Gettings-1994.pdf.

64 **Most came from industry:** Bailey, John. Email to SST, subject: "Notes from Meeting with FDA on Talc." May 11, 2009. PCPC0005505. Available at: https://no-more-tears.org/Bailey-2009.pdf.

64 **In the end:** Bailey, John. Letter to Jill Cashen, subject: "Docket No. 94P-0420." July 11, 1995. FDA00000285. Available at: https://no-more-tears.org/Bailey-1995.pdf.

64 **But the entire process:** Wehner, Alfred P. Letter to Michael Chudkowski, September 17, 1997. JNJ000040596. Available at: https://no-more-tears.org/Wehner-1997.pdf.

65 **In 2008, the Cancer Prevention Coalition:** Epstein, Samuel. "Petition Seeking a Cancer Warning on Cosmetic Talc Products." May 13, 2008. FDA00001326. Available at: https://no-more-tears.org/Epstein-2008.pdf.

65 **After a lot of back-and-forth:** Bernard, Craig. Email to Mark Zamek, subject: "Meeting w/ J & J." November 3, 2008. IMERYS 250192. Available at: https://no-more-tears.org/Bernard-2008.pdf.

65 **Six months after:** Musser, Steven. Letter to Samuel Epstein, subject: "Docket Number 94P-0420 and FDA-2008-P-0309-0001/CP." April 1, 2014. Available at: https://no-more-tears.org/Musser-2014.pdf.

CHAPTER 9: A SACRED COW

67 **In 2009, Donna Paduano:** Deposition of David Swanson, June 15, 2009. Available at: https://no-more-tears.org/Swanson-2009.pdf.

67 **Engelhard (now owned by):** BASF. "BASF Makes All-Cash Proposal to Acquire Engelhard." Press release, January 3, 2006. Available at: https://no-more-tears.org/BASF-2006.pdf.

67 **Her father had worked:** Deposition of David Swanson, June 15, 2009. Available at: https://no-more-tears.org/Swanson-2009.pdf.

67 **The eighty-six-year-old:** Deposition of Glenn Hemstock, May 9, 2012. Available at: https://no-more-tears.org/Hemstock-2012c.pdf.

HEMSTOCK: However, they have a so-called expert on talc here who took an affidavit to the effect that it was true.

PLACITELLA: And if that expert was never supplied with any of the testing that you actually did or you had people do for you, what would you think about that?

A: Well, I would be pretty skeptical of it for sure at the very least, yes.

Q: This expert Ashton, he never called you to ask you about anything, did he?

A: Nor do I know who he is.

Q: Right, and if he called you and said was there asbestos in the Emtal talc, you would have told him what?

A: I would have told him, as I always said, there are traces to be sure of asbestiform minerals in our talc.

Q: So as it's stated here by the lawyers for Engelhard, asking for people to dismiss their lawsuits, that Engelhard's talc did not contain asbestos, is that a true or a false statement?

A: On the face it, it's a false statement.

68 **More legal wrangling ensued:** *Kimberlee Williams v. BASF*. Decision on appeal. September 3, 2014. Available at: https://no-more-tears.org/Fuentes-2014.pdf.

68 **With this blistering ruling:** *Kimberlee Williams v. BASF*. Decision on appeal.

68 **One top New York law firm:** Feeley, Jef. "BASF, Cahill Law Firm to Pay $72.5 Million in Talc-Scam Deal." Bloomberg News, July 23, 2020.

68 **"This case boils down to":** *Ingham et al. v. Johnson & Johnson.* Trial transcript. June 06, 2018. Available at: https://no-more-tears.org/Ingham-20180606.pdf.

69 **The company knew:** Johnson & Johnson. "Draft 1—Copy for Safetyand CareCommitment Website." 2013. JNJTALC000067661. Available at: https://no-more-tears.org/JJ-2013.pdf; Petterson, D. R. Memo to D. D. Johnston, subject: "Windsor Minerals and Talc." April 26, 1973. JNJ000294872. Available at: https://no-more-tears.org/Petterson-1973.pdf.

69 **Bicks began by thanking the jury:** *Ingham et al. v. Johnson & Johnson.* Trial transcript. June 06, 2018. Available at: https://no-more-tears.org/Ingham-20180606.pdf.

71 **Others were purchased:** Longo, William E., and Mark W. Rigler. Supplemental Expert Report & Analysis of Johnson & Johnson Baby Powder and Valeant Shower to Shower Talc Products for Amphibole Asbestos. March 11, 2018. Available at: https://no-more-tears.org/Longo-2018.pdf.

71 **And then Lanier:** *Ingham et al. v. Johnson & Johnson.* Trial transcript. June 18, 2018.

73 **Lanier showed Dr. Joanne Waldstreicher** *Ingham et al. v. Johnson & Johnson.* Trial transcript. June 18, 2018.

74 **The only asbestos expert:** McCarthy, Ed. Email to Julie Pier, May 13, 2011. IMERYS 308446. Available at: https://no-more-tears.org/McCarthy-2011.pdf.

74 **However, the RJ Lee expert:** *Ingham et al. v. Johnson & Johnson.* Trial transcript. June 28, 2018. Available at: https://no-more-tears.org/Ingham-20180628.pdf.

74 **J & J's lawyer then called:** *Ingham et al. v. Johnson & Johnson.* Trial transcript. June 29, 2018. Available at: https://no-more-tears.org/Ingham-20180629.pdf.

75 **The company had even:** Dunleavy, Kevin. "Pfizer, Roche, AstraZeneca and J & J Face Newly Revived Lawsuit Claiming They Funded Terrorism in Iraq." *Fierce Pharma,* January 6, 2022. Available at: https://no-more-tears.org/Dunleavy-2022.pdf.

76 **But the doctors' profound:** *Ingham et al. v. Johnson & Johnson.* Trial transcript. July 5, 2018. Available at: https://no-more-tears.org/Ingham-20180705.pdf.

76 **One of the company's experts:** *Ingham et al. v. Johnson & Johnson.* Trial transcript. July 9, 2018. Available at: https://no-more-tears.org/Ingham-20180709.pdf.

MARK LANIER: We'll look at them together. You got selected— and this just wasn't your area of research before you got hired to do this, was it?

KEVIN HOLCOMB: No.

Q: Okay. And these things— you haven't even seen this IARC Special Report until I just showed it to you, had you?

A: There's no new information on that IARC Special Report.

Q: That wasn't my question, sir.

A: No, I had not seen it, nor would it add to my knowledge.

76 **Lanier went first:** Johnson & Johnson. "Our Baby History." JnJ.com, 2008. Available at: https://no-more-tears.org/JJ-2008.pdf; *Ingham et al. v. Johnson & Johnson.* Trial transcript. July 11, 2018. Available at: https://no-more-tears.org /Ingham-20180711.pdf.

78 **At ten the next morning:** *Ingham et al. v. Johnson & Johnson.* Trial transcript. July 12, 2018. Available at: https://no-more-tears.org/Ingham-20180712.pdf.

80 **It cut the award:** *Ingham et al. v. Johnson & Johnson.* Decision by Judge Philip Hess. June 23, 2020. Available at: https://no-more-tears.org/Ingham -2020.pdf.

80 **Johnson & Johnson appealed:** Hurley, Lawrence. "U.S. Supreme Court Rebuffs J & J Appeal Over $2 Billion Baby Powder Judgment." Reuters, June 2, 2021. Available at: https://no-more-tears.org/Hurley-2021.pdf.

80 **In 2003, a TV station:** Bowker, Michael. "Quantitative Analysis Report: Asbestos in Bulk Material; Job ID: KCRA Television/Dave Walker." January 5, 2004. Available at: https://no-more-tears.org/Floyd-2004.pdf.

81 **Five months after the trial:** Girion, Lisa. "Johnson & Johnson Knew for Decades That Asbestos Lurked in Its Baby Powder." Reuters, December 14, 2018. Available at: https://no-more-tears.org/Girion-2018.pdf.

82 **getting her husband:** Harris, Gardiner. "F.D.A. Regulator, Widowed by Cancer, Helps Speed Drug Approval." *The New York Times,* January 2, 2016. Available at: https://no-more-tears.org/Harris-2016c.pdf.

82 **The Ingham documents:** *Ingham et al. v. Johnson & Johnson.* Trial transcript. June 6, 2018. Available at: https://no-more-tears.org/Ingham-20180606.pdf.

82 **At J & J, executives cloistered:** Montandon, Carol. Handwritten notes on talc. October 17, 2019. JNJTALC001321958. Available at: https://no-more -tears.org/Montandon-2019.pdf.

PLAINTIFFS' ATTORNEY: Okay. And then there's a line that says PR from the leaders. And then below that it says can we shut down the program; not adequately monitored and controlled; is it legal; coercion, threats, blackmail, question mark. Do you see that?

MONTANDON: Yes, I do.

Q: What was the reference to shutting down the program referring to?

A: I do not recall.

Q: And do you recall what your note about coercion, threats and blackmail is referring to?

DEFENSE ATTORNEY: Object to form.

A: No, I do not.

Q: What about your note that, is it legal, question mark, what does that note refer to?

A: I don't recall the context of this note.

Q: Was J&J considering trying to use coercion, threats or blackmail to shut down the FDA program?

DEFENSE ATTORNEY: Object to form.

A: Absolutely not.

Q: Then why on earth would you write coercion, threats and blackmail in your personal notes?

DEFENSE ATTORNEY: Objection, argumentative, form.

A: I don't recall the context of this exact section of these notes, but I know, having been at J&J for 27 years, in no instance has anyone ever talked about or mentioned coercion, threats or blackmail as an action the company would ever take.

Q: So was J&J thinking that they were the victim of coercion, threats or blackmail from the FDA?

DEFENSE ATTORNEY: Objection, asked and answered. The witness has testified extensively about this set of notes.

A: I do not recall the—the context of this note.

Q: Was it common for you to take notes about coercion, threats and blackmail in your work at J&J?

DEFENSE ATTORNEY: Object to form, argumentative.

A: No, it is not common.

Q: But you don't recall the situation here with these notes saying coercion, threats and blackmail, right?

DEFENSE ATTORNEY: Object to form, answer—asked and answered many times.

A: I do not recall.

83   **Four days later:** U.S. Food and Drug Administration. "Baby Powder Manufacturer Voluntarily Recalls Products for Asbestos." Constituent update, October 18, 2019. Available at: https://no-more-tears.org/FDA-2019b.pdf.

83   **Seven months later:** Johnson & Johnson. "Johnson & Johnson Consumer Health Announces Discontinuation of Talc-based Johnson's Baby Powder in U.S. and Canada." J&J.com, May 19, 2020. Available at: https://no-more-tears.org/JJ-2020.pdf.

83   **declared LTL bankrupt:** *LTL Management LLC v. Debtors.* Transcript. November 10, 2021. Available at: https://no-more-tears.org/LTL-2021.pdf.

83   **Known as "the Texas two-step":** Douglis, Sylvie. "J & J Tries the 'Texas Two-Step.'" NPR, January 5, 2022. Available at: https://no-more-tears.org/NPR-2022.pdf.

83   **Sometimes its retribution:** Strickler, Andrew. "J & J Says Plaintiff Firms Can't Hide From Talc Media Subpoena." Law360, September 13, 2021. Available at: https://no-more-tears.org/Strickler-2021.pdf.

84   **Hundreds of thousands:** Loftus, Peter. "Johnson & Johnson's Legal Challenges Mount." *The Wall Street Journal,* October 14, 2019. Available at: https://no-more-tears.org/Loftus-2019.pdf.

84   **In January 2023:** *LTL Management LLC v. Debtors.* Appeal before the Third Circuit. Opinion of the Court. September 19, 2023. Available at: https://no-more-tears.org/LTL-2023.pdf.

CHAPTER 10: AN INFAMOUS CRIME, THE BIRTH OF A MYTH

85 **Winter arrives early:** "Revisiting Chicago's Tylenol Murders." *Chicago,* September 21, 2012. Available at: https://no-more-tears.org/ChicagoMag-2012.pdf.

86 **Just as the Kellermans:** Bartz, Scott. *The Tylenol Mafia: Marketing, Murder, and Johnson & Johnson.* New Light Publishing, 2012.

86 **Paramedics returned her:** *"Revisiting Chicago's Tylenol Murders."*

88 **Dr. Edmund Donoghue:** Bartz, Scott. *The Tylenol Mafia: Marketing, Murder, and Johnson & Johnson.* New Light Publishing, 2012.

88 **Almost every newspaper:** Caesar-Gordon, Andrew. "The Perfect Crisis Response?" *PRWeek,* October 28, 2021.

88 **The first anyone at FDA:** Bartz, Scott. *The Tylenol Mafia: Marketing, Murder, and Johnson & Johnson.* New Light Publishing, 2012.

89 **Inspectors showed up late:** "FDA Uncovers More Problems at J & J Fort Washington Plant." Reuters, December 16, 2010. Available at: https://no-more-tears.org/Reuters-2010.pdf.

89 **That Friday evening:** Baumann, Ed, and John O'Brien. "Getting Away with Murder." *Chicago Tribune,* April 21, 1991. Available at: https://no-more-tears.org/Baumann-1991.pdf.

89 **Hours later, Chicago mayor:** Bartz, Scott. *The Tylenol Mafia: Marketing, Murder, and Johnson & Johnson.* New Light Publishing, 2012.

89 **Sales in 1982:** Pace, Eric. "Lingering Damage to Sales of Tylenol Is Expected." *The New York Times,* October 2, 1982. Available at: https://no-more-tears.org/Pace-1982.pdf.

89 **FDA officials faced:** Gerth, Jeff, and T. Christian Miller. "Tylenol Can Kill You." *Insider,* September 21, 2013. Available at: https://no-more-tears.org/Gerth-2013.pdf.

89 **The agency's core mission:** Lee, William M. "Public Health: Acetaminophen (APAP) Hepatotoxicity—Isn't It Time for APAP to Go Away?" *Journal of Hepatology* 67, no. 6, December 2017: 1324–31. Available at: https://no-more-tears.org/Lee-2017.pdf.

CHAPTER 11: PROBLEMS WITH THE NARRATIVE

91 **In the previous three years:** Bartz, Scott. *The Tylenol Mafia: Marketing, Murder, and Johnson & Johnson.* New Light Publishing, 2012.

92 **Almost twenty-nine hours before:** Malcolm, Andrew H. "Cyanide Case Focuses on Find in Parking Lot at All-Night Restaurant." *The New York Times,* October 5, 1982. Available at: https://no-more-tears.org/Malcolm-1982.pdf.

93 **In press conferences and interviews:** Bartz, Scott. *The Tylenol Mafia: Marketing, Murder, and Johnson & Johnson.* New Light Publishing, 2012.

94 **Roger Arnold struck fear:** Gutowski, Christy, and Stacy St. Clair. "The Tylenol Murders, Part 3: Chicago Police Zero In on a Suspect, and the Case Claims an 8th Victim." *Chicago Tribune,* September 29, 2022. Available at: https://no-more-tears.org/Gutowski-2022.pdf.

95 **A forty-eight-year-old dead-ender:** Marx, Gary, and Steve Mills. "Tylenol

Case Revisited." *Chicago Tribune,* February 8, 2009. Available at: https://no
-more-tears.org/Marx-2009.pdf.

95 **A week after the Tylenol murders:** Gutowski, Christy, and Stacy St. Clair.
"The Tylenol Murders, Part 3: Chicago Police Zero In on a Suspect, and the
Case Claims an 8th Victim." *Chicago Tribune,* September 29, 2022. Available
at: https://no-more-tears.org/Gutowski-2022.pdf.

97 **Instead, the FBI:** Levenson, Michael. "James W. Lewis, Suspect in the 1982
Tylenol Murders, Dies at 76." *The New York Times,* July 10, 2023. Available at:
https://no-more-tears.org/Levenson-2023.pdf.

98 **"All the pieces, all the tips":** Gutowski, Christy, and Stacy St. Clair. "The
Tylenol Murders, Part 3: Chicago Police Zero In on a Suspect, and the Case
Claims an 8th Victim. *Chicago Tribune,* September 29, 2022. Available at:
https://no-more-tears.org/Gutowski-2022.pdf.

99 **But a quick poll:** "Johnson & Johnson's Tylenol Scare—The Classic Example
of Responsible Crisis Management." In Robert F. Hartley, *Business Ethics: Mistakes and Lessons.* Wiley, 2004: 303–14. Available at: https://no-more-tears.org
/JJ-TylenolScare.pdf; Greyser, Stephen. "Johnson & Johnson: The Tylenol
Tragedy." Harvard Business School Case 583-043, October 1982.

99 **"It was a bitter irony:** Foster, Lawrence G. *Robert Wood Johnson: The Gentleman Rebel.* Lillian Books, 1999.

CHAPTER 12: NEVER AN ADVERSARIAL RELATIONSHIP

101 **Records that have only recently:** Gutowski, Christy, and Stacy St. Clair. "The
Tylenol Murders: Read the *Tribune* Investigation." *Chicago Tribune,* 2022.

101 **Partially, this was due to:** Torres, Christian. "Outsourcing Challenges FDA to
Strengthen Oversight Abroad." *Nature Medicine* 16, no. 2, February 2010: 139.

102 **(one reason its inspections):** Bartz, Scott. *The Tylenol Mafia: Marketing, Murder, and Johnson & Johnson.* New Light Publishing, 2012.

102 **In Congressional testimony:** Tamper-Resistant Packaging for Over-the-
Counter Drugs. Hearing before the Subcommittee on Health and the Environment. Testimony of David Collins. October 15, 1982.

102 **But only Dr. Arthur Hayes, Jr.:** Bartz, Scott. *The Tylenol Mafia: Marketing,
Murder, and Johnson & Johnson.* New Light Publishing, 2012.

103 **In public statements:** In the Matter of: Adulteration of Over-the-Counter
Drugs: The Tylenol Poisonings. Joint Public Hearing, California Senate Committee on Health and Welfare and Assembly Committee on Health, October
12, 1982. Available at: https://no-more-tears.org/Ketcham-1982.pdf.

104 **"The pattern of contamination":** Swit, David. *Product Survival: Lessons of the
Tylenol Terrorism.* Washington Business Information Inc., 1982. Available at:
https://no-more-tears.org/Swit-1982.pdf.

104 **Whether Hayes was aware:** Tamper-Resistant Packaging for Over-the-
Counter Drugs. Hearing before the Subcommittee on Health and the Environment. Testimony of David Collins. October 15, 1982.

104 **He also ludicrously defended:** U.S. Food and Drug Administration. "Over-

view of Drug Safety—The Adverse Event." World of Drug Safety Module. Available at: https://no-more-tears.org/FDA-AE.pdf.

104 **After the health department's:** Kurtz, Howard. "Hayes Planning to Resign as Head of FDA." *The Washington Post,* July 29, 1983. Available at: https://no-more-tears.org/Kurtz-1983.pdf.

CHAPTER 13: THE COST OF DOING BUSINESS

107 **Around Thanksgiving of 1982:** Hollie, Pamela G. "Making Products Tamper-Resistant." *The New York Times,* September 17, 1983. Available at: https://no-more-tears.org/Hollie-1983.pdf.

107 **For Anthony Benedi:** Bates, Steve. "A Bitter Pill for Winner in Tylenol-Damage Suit." *The Washington Post,* January 17, 1996. Available at: https://no-more-tears.org/Bates-1996.pdf.

108 **Aspirin, Motrin, and similar:** Ivey, K. J., and B. Settree. "Effect of Paracetamol (Acetaminophen) on Gastric Ionic Fluxes and Potential Difference in Man." *Gut* 17, 1976: 916–19. Available at: https://no-more-tears.org/Ivey-1976.pdf.

108 **(This problematic balance):** Prakash, Snigdha, and Vikki Valentine. "The Rise and Fall of Vioxx." NPR, November 10, 2007. Available at: https://no-more-tears.org/Prakash-2007.pdf.

108 **More than a century:** Toussaint, K., et al. "What Do We (Not) Know About How Paracetamol (Acetaminophen) Works?" *Journal of Clinical and Pharmacy Therapeutics* 35, 2010: 617–38. Available at: https://no-more-tears.org/Toussaint-2010.pdf.

108 **The ubiquity of ulcers:** Jordan, Jennifer, and Robert J. Sternberg. "Wisdom in Organizations: A Balance Theory Analysis." In *Handbook of Organizational and Managerial Wisdom,* edited by Eric H. Kessler and James R. Bailey, 3–19. Sage Publications, 2007. Available at: https://no-more-tears.org/Jordan-2007.pdf.

109 **Nonetheless, the FDA:** Gerth, Jeff, and T. Christian Miller. "Use Only as Directed." *ProPublica,* September 20, 2013. Available at: https://no-more-tears.org/Gerth-2013b.pdf.

109 **In September 1977:** Ameer, Barbara, and David J. Greenblatt. "Acetaminophen." *Annals of Internal Medicine* 87, no. 2, August 1977: 202–9.

110 **Liberated, J & J heavily advertised:** Jones, John Philip. *The Advertising Business: Operations, Creativity, Media Planning, Integrated Communications.* Sage Publications, 1999.

110 **Tylenol was so dominant:** McFadden, Robert D. "Maker of Tylenol Discontinuing All Over-Counter Drug Capsules." *The New York Times,* February 18, 1986. Available at: https://no-more-tears.org/McFadden-1986.pdf.

110 **By the next year:** McFadden, Robert D. "Poison Deaths Bring U.S. Warning on Tylenol Use." *The New York Times,* October 2, 1982. Available at: https://no-more-tears.org/McFadden-1982.pdf.

110 **Johnson & Johnson's surveys:** Tedlow, Richard S., and Wendy K. Smith. "James Burke: A Career in American Business (A)." Harvard Business School, 1989. Available at: https://no-more-tears.org/Tedlow-2005.pdf.

110 **The most important:** Altman, Lawrence K. "When the Doctors Are Their Own Best Guinea Pigs." *The New York Times,* October 9, 2005. Available at: https://no-more-tears.org/Altman-2005.pdf.

111 **At least 150 Americans die:** Cho, Minhee, and Christie Thompson. "Five Consumer Resources from Our Acetaminophen Investigation." *ProPublica,* September 26, 2013. Available at: https://no-more-tears.org/Cho-2013.pdf.

111 **Acetaminophen has for decades:** Canbay, Ali, et al. "Acute Liver Failure: A Life-Threatening Disease." *Deutsches Ärzteblatt International* 108, no. 42, October 2011: 714–20. Available at: https://no-more-tears.org/Canbay-2011.pdf.

112 **The brand's most iconic:** Gerth and Miller, *"Use Only as Directed."*

112 **A survey of forty-six patients:** Gerth, Jeff, and T. Christian Miller. "Tylenol Can Kill You." *Insider,* September 21, 2013. Available at: https://no-more-tears .org/Gerth-2013.pdf.

112 **A survey of forty-six patients:** Gerth and Miller, *"Use Only as Directed."*

113 **In 1993, the FDA asked:** Gerth and Miller, *"Use Only as Directed."*

114 **In an email uncovered in litigation:** Gerth, Jeff, and T. Christian Miller. "Use Only as Directed." *ProPublica,* September 20, 2013. Available at: https://no -more-tears.org/Gerth-2013b.pdf.

114 **In 2011, the agency limited:** Mays, James A. *Prescription Medication/Drug Misuse Andabuse: A Clear & Present Danger.* XLIBRIS, 2013.

114 **McNeil introduced Tylenol:** ProPublica, "Dose of Confusion." *ProPublica,* September 20, 2013. Available at: https://no-more-tears.org/ProPublica-2013b.pdf.

115 **But many safety experts:** Irwin, Richard S., et al. "Diagnosis and Management of Cough Executive Summary." *Chest* 129, January 2006: 1–23. Available at: https://no-more-tears.org/Irwin-2006.pdf.

115 **There was a commercial rationale:** Harris, Gardiner. "U.S. Reviewing Safety of Children's Cough Drugs." *The New York Times,* March 2, 2007. Available at: https://no-more-tears.org/Harris-2007d.pdf.

115 **But many safety experts:** Emry, Chris, and Stephanie Desmon. "Off the Shelves." *The Baltimore Sun,* October 12, 2007. Available at: https://no-more -tears.org/Desmon-2007.pdf.

115 **The FDA and J & J tussled:** Gardiner. *"U.S. Reviewing Safety of Children's Cough Drugs."*

115 **After their five-month-old:** ProPublica, *"Dose of Confusion."*

116 **Two weeks before the:** Harris, Gardiner. "Makers Pull Infant Cold Medicines." *The New York Times,* October 11, 2007. Available at: https://no-more -tears.org/Harris-2007e.pdf.

116 **With Tylenol, the agency:** Gerth, Jeff, and T. Christian Miller. "New Court Docs: Maker of Tylenol Had a Plan to Block Tougher Regulation." *ProPublica,* September 21, 2015. Available at: https://no-more-tears.org/Gerth-2015.pdf.

CHAPTER 14: A VALLEY OF DEATH IN DRUG DISCOVERY

119 **antidepressants like Prozac and Zoloft:** Lehrer, Jonah. "Head fake." *The Boston Globe,* July 6, 2008. Available at: https://no-more-tears.org/Lehrer-2008.pdf.

120 **Claritin and Allegra, for instance:** Fein, Michael, et al. "CSACI Position

Statement: Newer Generation H1-Antihistamines Are Safer Than First-Generation H1-Antihistamines and Should Be the First-Line Antihistamines for the Treatment of Allergic Rhinitis and Urticaria." *Allergy, Asthma & Clinical Immunology* 15, October 2019.

120 **Across the industry:** Harris, Gardiner. "Where Are All the New Drugs?" *The New York Times,* October 5, 2003. Available at: https://no-more-tears.org /Harris-2003b.pdf.

120 **In the midst of this crash:** National Institutes of Health. "International Consortium Completes Human Genome Project." April 14, 2003. Available at: https://no-more-tears.org/NIH-2003.pdf.

121 **The first was the creation:** Congressional Research Service. The Hatch-Waxman Act: Over a Quarter Century Later. Report for Congress, December 5, 2012. Available at: https://no-more-tears.org/Hatch-Waxman.pdf.

122 **The reason was:** Angell, Marcia. *The Truth About the Drug Companies: How They Deceive Us and What to Do About It.* Random House, 2004.

122 **One way they achieved:** Donohue, Julie. "A History of Drug Advertising: The Evolving Roles of Consumers and Consumer Protection." *The Milbank Quarterly* 84, no. 4, 2006: 659–99. Available at: https://no-more-tears.org/Donohue -2006.pdf.

CHAPTER 15: THE FIRST GREAT BIOTECH FRANCHISE IS BORN

123 **Speculation about the cause:** Cleveland Clinic. "Erythropoietin." My .clevelandclinic.org, reviewed on November 10, 2022. Available at: https://no -more-tears.org/ClevelandClinic.pdf.

124 **FDA's approval for EPO's:** Burns, Lawton Roberts, ed. *The Business of Healthcare Innovation.* Cambridge University Press, 2020.

124 **It was a compelling notion:** Tonelli, Marcello, et al. "Benefits and Harms of Erythropoiesis-Stimulating Agents for Anemia Related to Cancer: A Meta-Analysis." *CMAJ* 180, no. 11, May 26, 2009: E62–E71. Available at: https://no -more-tears.org/Tonelli-2009.pdf.

125 **A researcher named Athanasius Anagnostou:** Pollack, Andrew. "Risks of Anemia Drugs for Patients with Cancer to Get More Scrutiny." *The New York Times,* March 12, 2008. Available at: https://no-more-tears.org/Pollack-2008.pdf.

125 **Just as EPO was:** Chase, Marilyn. "How Genentech Wins at Blockbuster Drugs." *The Wall Street Journal,* June 5, 2007. Available at: https://no-more -tears.org/Chase-2007.pdf.

126 ***The Wall Street Journal:*** "Human Sacrifice." Editorial. *The Wall Street Journal,* June 2, 1987.

126 ***The Washington Post* published:** Kazman, Sam. "TPA Foot-Dragging Costs 30 Lives a Day." *The Washington Post,* November 3, 1987. Available at: https:// no-more-tears.org/Kazman-1987.pdf.

127 **So when, only a:** U.S. Food and Drug Administration. "Summary for Basis of Approval. Epoetin Alfa (Amgen)." Bethesda: FDA, 1993.

127 **Instead, the agency forced:** Ortho Biotech Inc. Procrit label. 1997. Available at: https://no-more-tears.org/Procrit-Label.pdf.

128 **About the time J & J:** Scandinavian Simvastatin Survival Study Group. "Randomised Trial of Cholesterol Lowering in 4,444 Patients with CHD: The Scandinavian Simvastatin Survival Study (4S)." *The Lancet* 344, November 19, 1994: 1383–89. Available at: https://no-more-tears.org/Pedersen-1994.pdf.

128 *Fortune* **named EPO:** Kim, Rachel. *Economics and Management in the Biopharmaceutical Industry in the USA: Evolution and Strategic Change.* Routledge, 2018.

128 **The sudden death:** López, Bernat. "The Invention of a 'Drug of Mass Destruction': Deconstructing the EPO Myth." *Sport in History* 32, no. 1, March 2011: 84–109. Available at: https://no-more-tears.org/Lopez-2011.pdf.

128 **A few months later:** Fisher, Lawrence M. "Stamina-Building Drug Linked to Athletes' Deaths." *The New York Times,* May 19, 1991. Available at: https://no-more-tears.org/Fisher-1991.pdf.

128 **Lance Armstrong famously won:** Cutler, Teddy. "Cycling in the EPO Era: 65 Per Cent 'Juiced' . . . And Probably More." Sporting Intelligence. Sports Journalists' Association, December 31, 2014. Available at: https://no-more-tears.org/Cutler-2014.pdf.

128 **In 1993, J & J announced:** Beasley, Deena. "FDA Panel on Anemia Drugs Has Investors Wary." Reuters, March 11, 2008. Available at: https://no-more-tears.org/Beasley-2008.pdf.

CHAPTER 16: HOW GIVING CASH TO DOCTORS BECAME
GOOD BUSINESS

130 **In the 1980s, drug:** Elliott, Carl. "Relationships Between Physicians and Pharma." *Neurology: Clinical Practice,* April 2014: 164–67. Available at: https://no-more-tears.org/Elliott-2014.pdf.

131 **No other corporate investment:** Staff. "Allergan CEO Sees Big Demand for Bladder Drug." Reuters, September 19, 2007. Available at: https://no-more-tears.org/Reuters-2007.pdf.

131 **So companies rebuilt themselves:** Saul, Stephanie. "Gimme an Rx! Cheerleaders Pep Up Drug Sales." *The New York Times,* November 28, 2005. Available at: https://no-more-tears.org/Saul-2005.pdf.

131 **On the other hand:** Jacob, Nilan T. "Drug Promotion Practices: A Review." *British Journal of Clinical Pharmacology* 84, 2018: 1659–67. Available at: https://no-more-tears.org/Jacob-2018.pdf.

131 **With payments as the goal:** Ornstein, Charles, Tracy Webber, and Ryann Grochowski Jones. "We Found over 700 Doctors Who Were Paid More Than a Million Dollars by Drug and Medical Device Companies." *ProPublica,* October 17, 2019. Available at: https://no-more-tears.org/Ornstein-2019.pdf.

132 **Many doctors' offices:** Fugh-Berman, Adriane, and Shahram Ahari. "Following the Script: How Drug Reps Make Friends and Influence Doctors." *PLoS Medicine* 4, no. 4, 2007: e150. Available at: https://no-more-tears.org/Fugh-Berman-2007.pdf.

132 **But many of the doctors:** Mitchell, Aaron, and Deborah Korenstein. "Drug Companies' Payments and Gifts Affect Physicians' Prescribing. It's Time to

Turn Off the Spigot." *STAT,* December 4, 2020. Available at: https://no-more-tears.org/Mitchell-2020.pdf.

132 **Even after rules were adopted:** "Pharmaceutical Companies Must Find New Ways to Market Products." Relias Media. Medical Ethics Advisor, November 1, 2002. Available at: https://no-more-tears.org/Relias-Media.pdf.

132 **A survey of medical residents:** Steinman, Michael A., Michael G. Shilpack, and Stephen J. McPhee. "Of Principles and Pens: Attitudes and Practices of Medicine Housestaff Toward Pharmaceutical Industry Promotions." *The American Journal of Medicine* 10, no. 7, May 2001: 551–57.

134 **Companies paid doctors:** Llamas, Michelle. "Big Pharma's Role in Clinical Trials." *Drugwatch,* April 24, 2015. Available at: https://no-more-tears.org/Llamas-2015.pdf.

134 **(In October 2001):** Petersen, Melody. "2 Drugmakers to Pay $875 Million to Settle Fraud Case." *The New York Times,* October 4, 2001. Available at: https://no-more-tears.org/Petersen-2001.pdf.

134 **Overwhelmed by the explosion:** Young, Frank. "1988 Product Approvals: An FDA Annual Report." *FDA Consumer* 23, no. 3, April 1989: 6–7. Available at: https://no-more-tears.org/Young-1989.pdf.

135 **Indeed, with Congress showing:** Woodcock, Janet, and Suzanne Junod. "PDUFA Lays the Foundation: Launching into the Era of User Fee Acts." U.S. Food and Drug Administration, 2012. Available at: https://no-more-tears.org/Woodcock-PDUFA.pdf.

135 **But each subsequent five-year:** Llamas, Michelle. "Misplaced Trust: Why FDA Approval Doesn't Guarantee Drug Safety." *Drugwatch,* May 16, 2017. Available at: https://no-more-tears.org/Llamas-2017.pdf.

135 **It was in a 1997:** Kulynych, Jennifer. "Will FDA Relinquish the 'Gold Standard' for New Drug Approval? Redefining 'Substantial Evidence' in the FDA Modernization Act of 1997." *Food and Drug Law Journal* 54, no. 1, 1999. 127–49.

135 **The person who taught:** Kligman, Albert M. Letter to Dr. T. M. Thompson, May 23, 1967. JNJTALC000088495. Available at: https://no-more-tears.org/Kligman-1967.pdf.

135 **The person who taught:** Hornblum, Allen M. *Acres of Skin: Human Experiments at Holmesburg Prison.* Routledge, 1998.

135 **In 1971, the FDA:** Gellene, Denise. "Dr. Albert M. Kligman, Dermatologist, Dies at 93." *The New York Times,* February 22, 2010. Available at: https://no-more-tears.org/Gellene-2010.pdf.

137 **Such marketing campaigns:** Associated Press. "Ortho Fined $7.5 Million in Retin-A Case." *The New York Times,* April 11, 1995. Available at: https://no-more-tears.org/AP-1995.pdf.

137 **Outraged by the purge:** Hornblum, *Acres of Skin.*

137 **Financially dependent on:** Manjoo, Farhad. "America Desperately Needs a Much Better F.D.A." *The New York Times,* September 2, 2021. Available at: https://no-more-tears.org/Manjoo-2021.pdf.

138 **The rise of managed care:** Rohman, Grant. "The Rise of Managed Care: A Study of Its Current Trends and Future Effects." 2001. Senior Thesis Projects, 1993–2022. TRACE: Tennessee Research and Creative Exchange Available at: https://no-more-tears.org/Rohman-2001.pdf.

139 **Medical societies and insurers:** Knaapen, Loes. "Evidence-Based Medicine or Cookbook Medicine? Addressing Concerns over the Standardization of Care." *Sociology Compass* 8/6, 2014: 823–36. Available at: https://no-more-tears.org/Knaapen-2014.pdf.

139 **Amidst all of these changes:** Fresques, Hannah. "Doctors Prescribe More of a Drug If They Receive Money from a Pharma Company Tied to It." *ProPublica,* December 20, 2019. Available at: https://no-more-tears.org/Fresques-2019.pdf.

139 **By the 1990s:** Thomas Katie. "Pills Tracked from Doctor to Patient to Aid Drug Marketing." *The New York Times,* May 16, 2013. Available at: https://no-more-tears.org/Thomas-2013.pdf.

CHAPTER 17: J & J'S BIGGEST-SELLING DRUG

141 **By 1998, Procrit had become:** Johnson & Johnson. "Annual Report Pursuant to Section 13 of the Securities Exchange Act of 1934 for the Fiscal Year 2001." Available at: https://no-more-tears.org/JJ-2001.pdf.

142 **Dr. Allen Nissenson:** "Discontinues Study of Higher Hematocrits in Dialysis Patients with Cardiac Disease." Business Wire Inc., 1996.

142 **Called the Normal Hematocrit Trial:** Coyne, Daniel W. "The Health-Related Quality of Life Was Not Improved by Targeting Higher Hemoglobin in the Normal Hematocrit Trial." *Kidney International* 82, 2012: 235–41. Available at: https://no-more-tears.org/Coyne-2012.pdf.

142 **When the study was published:** Whoriskey, Peter. "Anemia Drug Made Billions, but at What Cost?" *The Washington Post,* July 19, 2012. Available at: https://no-more-tears.org/Whoriskey-July 2012.pdf.

143 **In 1998, just as:** Brawley, Otis. *How We Do Harm: A Doctor Breaks Ranks About Being Sick in America.* St. Martin's Griffin, 2012.

143 **In one letter to the company:** Sharp, Kathleen. *Blood Medicine: Blowing the Whistle on One of the Deadliest Prescription Drugs Ever.* Plume, 2012.

143 **Drugmakers soon learned:** Goldberg, Paul. "FDA Examines Its Own Role in Allowing Misleading Ads." *The Cancer Letter* 33, no. 19, May 18, 2007: 4–6. Available at: https://no-more-tears.org/Goldberg-2007b.pdf.

143 **In 2001, the administration of President George W. Bush:** Dickinson, James G. "FDA Law Chief Troy Resigns." Medical Device and Diagnostic Industry. January 1, 2005. Available at: https://no-more-tears.org/Dickinson-2005.pdf.

144 **When Troy left the FDA:** Direct-to-Consumer Advertising: Marketing, Education, or Deception? Hearing before the Subcommittee on Oversight and Investigations of the Committee on Energy and Commerce, House of Representatives, May 8, 2008, Available at: https://no-more-tears.org/USGovernment-2008.pdf.

STUPAK: Anywhere in your advertising, did you say that use of Procrit for cancer patients who had tumors that Procrit would likely enlarge those tumors and endanger the lives of those patients?

TAYLOR: No, that was not a specific warning in the ads.

Q: But the FDA told you about that, and you didn't put it in there. Don't you think people should know that before they take your drug, that, in fact, it could worsen their condition, not make it better, by making tumors swell more and shorten their lifespan?

A: That is a theoretical concern that has been raised.

Q: Well, it has been documented, right? That tumors would swell with your stuff, the greater the Procrit they got, the quicker the tumors swell.

A: I don't believe that that is accurate, but what we did do with the ads is we included all of the side effects that were significantly different from placebo.

Q: That would be significantly different, wouldn't it, if you were a cancer patient and the tumors you had in your body swell when you took Procrit? Wouldn't that be significant, especially when it shortens your life?

A: These are significant results as measured in clinical studies, so the side effects that were there, such as diarrhea and edema, were those that were significantly different from placebo.

Q: Can you point to any of the documents you submitted, anywhere, where the FDA approved Procrit for off-label use for fatigue or weakness in patients? Can you point to any one document you submitted to our committee?

A: Procrit has been approved for chemotherapy-induced anemia. Our advertisements were specifically looking at using language that would be recognizable by a consumer such as—

Q: So I take it your answer is no because you cannot point to an exhibit, as FDA wrote to you . . . telling you not to be using your ads for tiredness, for weakness. There isn't a letter from FDA that said you can advertise for that.

A: In fact, all the way through, there have been discussions with the FDA about—

Q: I didn't ask about discussion. I asked about approval for the way you marketed Procrit for seven years for an off-label use that was not approved for Procrit. Do you have any document that can show me that?

A: We have consistently, throughout, had reassurances that the way we were communicating the symptoms of anemia, such as fatigue and weakness, was appropriate to the patient group we were reaching with the DTC.

144 **In 2001, the company had started:** Luksenburg, Harvey, Andrea Weir, and Ruth Wager. "Safety Concerns Associated with Aranesp (darbepoetin alfa) Amgen, Inc. and Procrit (Epoetin Alfa) Ortho Biotech, L.P., for the Treatment of Anemia Associated with Cancer Chemotherapy." Briefing for the FDA's Oncologic Drugs Advisory Committee, May 4, 2004. Available at: https://no-more-tears.org/FDA-2004.pdf.

144 **After enrolling 109 patients:** Cabanillas, Maria E., et al. "Epoetin Alfa Decreases the Number of Red Blood Cell Transfusions in Patients with Acute Lymphoblastic Leukemia, Lymphoblastic Lymphoma, and Burkitt's Leukemia/Lymphoma—Results of a Randomized Clinical Trial." *Cancer* 118, no. 3, February 2012: 848–55. Available at: https://no-more-tears.org/Cabanillas-2012.pdf.

CHAPTER 18: A BRAVE RESEARCHER BREAKS THE SILENCE

145 **In October 2003:** Grady, Denise. "Anemia Drug May Impair Some Cancer Treatments." *The New York Times,* October 17, 2003. Available at: https://no-more-tears.org/Grady-2003.pdf.

146 **Days later, Paul Goldberg:** Goldberg, Paul. "FDA's ODAC to Review EPO Agents in May; SEC Probes Amgen Delay in Study Disclosure." *The Cancer Letter,* 33, no. 8, March 2, 2007. Available at: https://no-more-tears.org/Goldberg-2007.pdf.

146 **Goldberg uncovered an obscure:** Goldberg, Paul. "Study Tests a 'Truth' in Radiation Oncology, Raises Questions About Anemia Treatment." *The Cancer Letter* 29, no. 39, October 24, 2003. Available at: https://no-more-tears.org/Goldberg-2003.pdf.

146 **By the time of Henke's:** Pollack, Andrew. "F.D.A. Warning Is Issued on Anemia Drugs' Overuse." *The New York Times,* March 10, 2007. Available at: https://no-more-tears.org/Pollack-2007.pdf.

146 **The reaction to Henke's:** Grady, *"Anemia Drug May Impair Some Cancer Treatments."*

146 **Michael Henke was born:** Sharp, Kathleen. *Blood Medicine: Blowing the Whistle on One of the Deadliest Prescription Drugs Ever.* Plume, 2012.

149 **EPO use resulted in more deaths:** Grady, *"Anemia Drug May Impair Some Cancer Treatments."*

150 **After learning of Henke's study:** "Erythropoiesis-Stimulating Agents: Continued Challenges." *Journal of Oncology Practice* 3, no. 5, September 2007: 248–53. Available at: https://no-more-tears.org/JOP-2007.pdf.

150 **Both the opioid and:** Ehley, Brianna. "Federal Scientists Warned of Coming Opioid Crisis in 2006." *Politico,* August 21, 2019. Available at: https://no-more-tears.org/Ehley-2019.pdf.

150 **While partners in making:** Pollack, Andrew. "Johnson & Johnson to Pay $150 Million in Amgen Suit." *The New York Times,* October 19, 2002. Available at: https://no-more-tears.org/Pollack-2002.pdf.

151 **But companies routinely lied:** Leap, Terry L. *Phantom Billing, Fake Prescriptions, and the High Cost of Medicine: Health Care Fraud and What to Do About It.* Cornell University Press, 2011.

151 **In 2005, to crack down:** Mullen, Patrick. "The Arrival of Average Sale Price." *Biotechnology Healthcare,* June 2007, 48–53. Available at: https://no-more-tears.org/Mullen-2007.pdf.

152 **In addition to drug markups:** Tesoriero, Heather, and Avery Johnson. "Suit Details How J & J Pushed Sales of Procrit." *The Wall Street Journal,* May 10, 2007. Available at: https://no-more-tears.org/Tesoriero-2007.pdf.

152 **J & J sales reps have:** Sharp, Kathleen. *Blood Feud: The Man Who Blew the Whistle on One of the Deadliest Prescription Drugs Ever.* Tantor and Blackstone Publishing, 2011.

152 **Such widespread fraud:** Grand jury files.

153 **A practice manager:** Sharp, *Blood Feud.*

153 **Looking at a different:** Tesoriero and Johnson, *"Suit Details How J&J Pushed Sales of Procrit."*

153 **"Once it started":** Grand jury files.

153 **"We do not provide:** Perrone, Matthew. "Lawmakers Ask J&J and Amgen to Hold Off Promoting Top-Selling Drugs During Safety Review." Associated Press, March 22, 2007.

153 **"Rick Blumberg, the FDA's":** Grand jury files.

CHAPTER 19: MIRACLE-GRO FOR CANCER

155 **But all the while:** Pollack, Andrew. "Trouble with Anemia Drug Is Reduced, but Issues Remain." *The New York Times,* September 30, 2004. Available at: https://no-more-tears.org/Pollack-2004.pdf.

155 **Among the raft of studies:** Overgaard, Jens, et al. "DAHANCA 10—Effect of Darbepoetin Alfa and Radiotherapy in the Treatment of Squamous Cell Carcinoma of the Head and Neck. A Multicenter, Open-Label, Randomized, Phase 3 Trial by The Danish Head and Neck Cancer Group." *Radiotherapy and Oncology* 27, no. 1, April 2018: 12–19.

155 **Amgen kept the Danish results:** Pierson, Ransdell. "Amgen Delays Earnings Report to Include Trial Data." Reuters, April 11, 2007. Available at: https://no-more-tears.org/Pierson-2007.pdf.

156 **Goldberg wrote that:** Goldberg, Paul. "A Streak of Bad News for EPO Products Brings FDA Scrutiny, Payment Curbs." *The Cancer Letter* 33, no. 7, February 23, 2007. Available at: https://no-more-tears.org/Goldberg-2007c.pdf.

156 **But this hearing in 2007:** Sharp, Kathleen. *Blood Feud: The Man Who Blew the Whistle on One of the Deadliest Prescription Drugs Ever.* Tantor and Blackstone Publishing, 2011.

156 **Dr. Otis Brawley:** Brawley, Otis. *How We Do Harm: A Doctor Breaks Ranks About Being Sick in America.* St. Martin's Griffin, 2012.

156 **He then added a line:** Pollack, Andrew. "F.D.A. Panel Seeks Limits on Cancer Patient Drugs." *The New York Times,* May 11, 2007. Available at: https://no-more-tears.org/Pollack-2007b.pdf.

157 **The FDA put a:** Janssen Pharmaceuticals. Procrit label. 2018. Available at: https://no-more-tears.org/Procrit-BlackBox.pdf.

157 **On July 30, 2007:** "Erythropoiesis- Stimulating Agents: Continued Challenges." *Journal of Oncology Practice* 3, no. 5, September 2007: 248–53. Available at: https://no-more-tears.org/CMS-2007.pdf.

157 **So agency officials knew:** "US Oncology, Inc. Reports Second Quarter 2007 Results." PRNewswire, August 14, 2007. Available at: https://no-more-tears.org/US Oncology, Inc.pdf.

157 **In an email dated:** CMS internal documents.

158 **The pharmaceutical industry:** Wouters, Olivier J. "Lobbying Expenditures and Campaign Contributions by the Pharmaceutical and Health Product Industry in the United States, 1999–2018." *JAMA Internal Medicine* 180, no. 5, May 1, 2020: 688–97. Available at: https://no-more-tears.org/Wouters-2020.pdf.

158 **In the House:** Goldberg, Paul. "Congress Urges CMS to Soften Proposal for Coverage of ESAs in Oncology." *The Cancer Letter* 33, no. 28, July 20, 2007. Available at: https://no-more-tears.org/Goldberg-2007d.pdf.

158 **Representative Edolphus Towns:** Johnson & Johnson's Recall of Children's Tylenol and Other Children's Medicines. Hearing before the Committee on Oversight and Government Reform, House of Representatives, May 27, 2010. Available at: https://no-more-tears.org/JJ-ChildrenTylenol.pdf.

159 **Instead, it became:** Berenson, Alex. "Treatment of Anemia Questioned." *The New York Times,* November 30, 2006. Available at: https://no-more-tears.org/Berenson-2006.pdf.

159 **That same year, Medicare:** Leyland-Jones Brian, et al. "A Randomized, Open-Label, Multicenter, Phase III Study of Epoetin Alfa Versus Best Standard of Care in Anemic Patients with Metastatic Breast Cancer Receiving Standard Chemotherapy." *Journal of Clinical Oncology* 34, no. 11, April 2016: 1197–207.

160 **But for these oncologists:** Whoriskey, Peter. "Anemia Drug Made Billions, but at What Cost?" *The Washington Post,* July 19, 2012. Available at: https://no-more-tears.org/Whoriskey-2012.pdf.

CHAPTER 20: A PATH TO A NORMAL LIFE

161 **But for at least two-thirds:** de Araújo, Arão Nogueira, et al. "Antipsychotic Agents: Efficacy and Safety in Schizophrenia." *Drug, Healthcare and Patient Safety* 2012, no. 4, November 2012: 173–80. Available at: https://no-more-tears.org/Araújo-2012.pdf.

162 **In the 1980s:** Gurvich, Tatyana. "Appropriate Use of Psychotropic Drugs in Nursing Homes." *American Family Physician* 61, no. 5, 2000: 1437–46. Available at: https://no-more-tears.org/Gurvich-2000.pdf.

162 **(Studies show that nursing homes):** Mattingly II, T. Joseph. "A Review Exploring the Relationship Between Nursing Home Staffing and Antipsychotic Medication Use." *Neurology and Therapy* 4, no. 2, December 2015: 169–75. Available at: https://no-more-tears.org/Mattingly-2015.pdf.

162 **Risperdal was part of:** Üçok, Alp, and Wolfgang Gaebel. "Side Effects of Atypical Antipsychotics: A Brief Overview." *World Psychiatry* 7, no. 1, February 2008: 58–62. Available at: https://no-more-tears.org/Ucok-2008.pdf.

163 **Since people with schizophrenia:** Frank, Richard G., Rena M. Conti, and Howard H. Goldman. "Mental Health Policy and Psychotropic Drugs." *The Milbank Quarterly* 83, no. 2, June 2005: 271–98. Available at: https://no-more-tears.org/Milbank-2005.pdf.

163 **The best comparisons:** Swartz, Marvin S., et al. "What CATIE Found: Results from the Schizophrenia Trial." *Psychiatric Services* 59, no. 5, May 2008: 500–506. Available at: https://no-more-tears.org/Swartz-2008.pdf.

163 **In the CATIE trial:** Lieberman, Jeffrey A., et al. "Effectiveness of Antipsychotic Drugs in Patients with Chronic Schizophrenia." *The New England Journal of Medicine* 353, no. 12, September 2005: 1209–23. Available at: https://no-more-tears.org/Lieberman-2005.pdf.

163 **"Probably the biggest surprise":** Carey, Benedict. "Little Difference Found in Schizophrenia Drugs." *The New York Times,* September 20, 2005. Available at: https://no-more-tears.org/Carey-2005.pdf.

164 **Teens gain about four pounds:** Wilson, Duff. "Weight Gain Associated with Antipsychotic Drugs." *The New York Times,* October 27, 2009. Available at: https://no-more-tears.org/Wilson-2009.pdf.

164 **"The division has refused":** *Jones v. Janssen Pharmaceutica, Inc.* Trial transcript. January 13, 2012. Available at: https://no-more-tears.org/Jones-20120113.pdf.

165 **Instead, J & J conducted:** Rattehalli, Ranganath D., et al. "Risperidone Versus Placebo for Schizophrenia." *Cochrane Database of Systematic Reviews* 12, 2016. CD006918. Available at: https://no-more-tears.org/Rattehalli-2016.pdf.

165 **There's no evidence:** Leber, Paul. Memo to Robert Temple, *subject:* "Approvable and/or Approval Action Memorandum NDA 20-272: Risperdal, Janssen Brand of Risperidone." December 21, 1993. J-TX 3322312. Available at: https://no-more-tears.org/Leber-1993.pdf.

165 **"Aggressive expansion of Risperdal":** Caers, Ivo. "Risperdal's Future in the New Competitive Environment." October 1994. J-TX6049306. Available at: https://no-more-tears.org/Caers-1994.pdf.

166 **Thus was born:** Brill, Steven. *America's Most Admired Lawbreaker.* Chapter 4: "Massaging the Data, Spreading the Word." *The Huffington Post,* Fall 2015.

CHAPTER 21: A TREATMENT FOR EVERYTHING AND EVERYONE

167 **The "Sell the Symptoms":** Janssen Pharmaceuticals. *Risperdal Sales Training.* 2000. JJRIS 00431761 Available at: https://no-more-tears.org/Janssen-2000.pdf.

Here is plaintiff's attorney Tom Kline discussing the strategy with Carmen Deloria, one of Johnson & Johnson's top marketing executives.

KLINE: And another thing that we know for sure, like, for sure, is that you can't sell on symptoms, correct?

DELORIA: You have to also give what the indication is so you can go within in the context of what's in the label.

Q: You can't sell on symptoms alone, can we agree?

A: Correct. . . .

Q: Do you see the key strategies?

A: Yes.

Q: The key strategies is, "Sell on symptoms, not diagnosis."

A: Correct.

Q: That's wrong before the autism label, correct? It's just wrong. You can't do it. Can we agree?

A: You have to provide the indication.

Q: I didn't ask for that. I asked you is it wrong what it says right here, to sell on symptoms, not diagnosis. That's wrong before the autism label change. Correct? Yes or no? Yes or no?

A: I would say no.

Q: Want another chance at it? And it's wrong after the autism label by the very thing you just told us, correct? Yes or no?

A: It says diagnosis, not indication.

J & J LAWYER: Objection, your Honor.

KLINE: Sir, I'll withdraw it and I'll apologize for saying it. Is it correct, yes or no? Let's start again. It's wrong, improper to sell on symptoms, not diagnosis at any time relating to Risperdal in children and adolescents, can you agree? Let's agree because it's so fundamental. Can you agree?

DELORIA: I would agree provided that . . .

Q: There's no provided, sir. That's what this document says. Does this document have any provided in it, yes or no?

A: No.

Q: The sales force was told to sell on symptoms, not diagnosis. In fact, not only— There's no wiggle room, is there? There's just no wiggle room because it says this is what you can't do and this is you can't do. It's two can'ts. You can't sell on symptoms unless there's a diagnosis. Can we agree? When you're stuck, you got to agree.

A: I'm not stuck, but when we say sell, we're talking about . . .

Q: No, sir. There's no question pending. No question pending at this point in the litigation. There's redirect examination. My job— I'm going to ask you one more time and then maybe we can be done. Can you agree if you were given a statement, "Sell on symptoms, not diagnosis," as to Risperdal in children and adolescents that that would be wrong. Will you agree with us at 4 P.M. today, sir? Yes or no?

A: No.

167 **Janet Vergis, a top:** *Commonwealth of Massachusetts v. Ortho-McNeil-Janssen Pharmaceuticals, Inc.* Complaint. May 6, 2011. Available at: https://no-more-tears.org/Coakley-2011.pdf.

167 **PANSS stands for:** Leucht, Stefan, et al. "What Does the PANSS Mean?" *Schizophrenia Research* 79, nos. 2–3, November 2005: 231–38.

168 **Since sales reps couldn't:** Szalavitz, Maia. "Prozac May Reduce Symptoms of Autism in Adults." *Time,* December 5, 2011. Available at: https://no-more-tears.org/Szalavitz-2011.pdf.

168 **Nonetheless, Sell to the Symptoms:** Shorter, Edward. *The Rise and Fall of the Age of Psychopharmacology.* Oxford University Press, 2021.

Q: Did you ever have any concern about selling Risperdal for the treatment of behavioral symptoms of dementia when Risperdal did not actually have that indication?

A: I felt uncomfortable, yes.

Q: Could you tell the grand jury about that?

A: I felt that it was something that is not my character. I couldn't really approach my district manager or my regional business director because out of fear I would lose my job.

Q: You were very concerned about this?

A: Yeah. I have a wife who has a disability. And I have a young daughter. And I needed to keep my job

168 **The Johnson & Johnson executive:** "Alex Gorsky Is the All-American CEO." *The Healthcare Technology Report,* April 9, 2019. Available at: https://no-more-tears.org/Gorsky-2019.pdf.

169 **Because of his actions:** *Barden v. Brenntag North America et al.* Trial testimony by Alex Gorsky. January 27, 2020. Available at: https://no-more-tears.org/Gorsky-2020.pdf.

ALEX GORSKY: Well, I learned about the importance of staying connected to your people as much as possible as you can. There is no leadership without fellowship. That making sure that people feel as though they can approach you and have access to you and not feel intimidated is always important, and those were lessons I learned. One thing I learned in the Army, and it was very important, was the difference between unintelligent and uneducated. I served with a lot of people who just hadn't had a chance to go to a college like I did, but they were incredibly bright people.

169 **As a nineteen-year-old cadet:** Norton, Leslie P. "Embracing the J & J Credo." *Barron's,* December 14, 2013.

169 **Gorsky said he learned:** Norton, *"Embracing the J&J Credo."*

169 **In 1988, after serving:** Johnson & Johnson. "Our Leadership Team: Alex Gorsky—Executive Chairman." JnJ.com. Available at: https://no-more-tears .org/JJ-Gorsky.pdf.

170 **Because their illness:** Shorter, Edward. *The Rise and Fall of the Age of Psychopharmacology.* Oxford University Press, 2021.

170 **The model for this strategy:** Miller, Alexander L., et al. "The Texas Medication Algorithm Project Antipsychotic Algorithm for Schizophrenia: 2003 Update." *The Journal of Clinical Psychiatry* 65, no. 4, April 2004: 500–508.

171 **Much of the money:** Root, Elizabeth E. *Kids Caught in the Psychiatric Maelstrom: How Pathological Labels and "Therapeutic" Drugs Hurt Children and Families.* Praeger, 2009.

171 **The algorithm's lead author:** Petersen, Melody. "Making Drugs, Shaping the Rules." *The New York Times,* February 1, 2004. Available at: https://no-more-tears.org/Petersen-2004.pdf.

171 **By October 1997:** *Jones v. Janssen Pharmaceutica, Inc.* Trial transcript. January 13, 2012. Available at: https://no-more-tears.org/Jones-20120113.pdf.

171 **Johnson & Johnson then quietly:** Applbaum, Kalman. "The Banality of Corporate Corruption: Janssen's Reimbursement Department Takes the Stand. (Risperdal On Trial, Cont'd.)." *Somatosphere,* January 15, 2012. Available at: https://no-more-tears.org/Applbaum-2012.pdf.

172 **But Shon and others:** *Jones v. Janssen Pharmaceutica, Inc.* Trial transcript. January 12, 2012. Available at: https://no-more-tears.org/Jones-20120112.pdf.

172 **"Note: Shon can and is":** Caplan, Paula. "Diagnosisgate: Conflict of Interest at the Top of the Psychiatric Apparatus." *Aporia* 7, no. 1, Fall 2015: 30–41. Available at: https://no-more-tears.org/Caplan-2015.pdf.

172 **He finally acknowledged:** *Jones v. Janssen Pharmaceutica, Inc.* Trial transcript. January 11, 2012. Available at: https://no-more-tears.org/Jones-20120111.pdf.

JACKS: When you spoke on TMAP, Dr. Shon, or at a continuing medical education conference that Janssen sponsored or funded in some way, isn't it true that—that Janssen required you to submit your PowerPoint presentation to them for their review and comment?

SHON: No.

Q: That's not true?

A: That's not true.

Q: Let me show you Exhibit 310, Dr. Shon. And you recognize this as an email from a woman named Ann Swink to you and others dated February 18th, 2002, subject matter slides for the Janssen symposia on treating schizophrenia. Do you see that?

A: Yes.

Q: This was a symposia that you participated in—

A: Yes.

Q: —in 2002?

A: Yes.

Q: Well, what it says is Ms. Swink asks you— she says in the third paragraph, "Please have your personal set of slides back to me by March 6th. We will return any feedback CNS might have on your slides to you by March 13th." Do you see that?

A: Yes, I do.

Q: Let's read the next sentence—sentence after that. "After Janssen has had an opportunity to review and comment on the slide, we will send you those comments to you by March 25th with final revisions due back to me from you by March 28th." Isn't that right?

A: Yes, that's what it says.

Q: So, sir, doesn't this email describe Janssen asking to review and comment on your slides before the Janssen symposia on treating schizophrenia?

A: Yes, it does.

. . .

Q: Dr. Shon, do you recall attending an outcome research advisory board for Janssen in Scottsdale, Arizona, from February 27th to March 1st, 2000?

A: I attended a couple of things in Scottsdale. It sounds familiar, but I can't remember the exact name of it.

Q: And Exhibit 317 is a couple of pages from your calendar, plus a check for $3,000 to you at the Texas Department of Mental Health, as well as some receipts and a draft agenda. Do you see that?

A: Yes.

Q: So you personally accepted a $3,000 honorarium for this event?

A: Yes. This includes the honorarium travel.

Q: Why did you think it was proper for you to accept honorarium for this event?

A: Because it— and this is one of the ones that I talked to Cathy Campbell about and she— she said, is this— does this involve anything with your job? Is your— in terms of any projects you're working on or anything that would influence your particular roles and functions, and I said no, this is primarily an educational program and a program where they get input.

Q: Okay, Well, if you look at your calendar on the first page, it looks like you left on Sunday, correct, on the very first page of that exhibit?

A: Oh, yes.

Q: And then when you have Janssen CNS Summit, it goes through February 28th, 29th and March 1st, and that's a Monday, Tuesday and Wednesday; is that correct?

A: That's correct.

Q: But it's your testimony to the jury that this was not job related?

A: That's correct.

Q: Did you— how did you record your time?

A: I think I took comp time or something along that line.

Q: If you could look at the times entered for those days that you were at the CNS Summit, could you tell the jury how you recorded your time, please? On the 28th and 29th, how do you record hours worked? Is it eight hours on Monday and eight hours on Tuesday under regular hours worked?

A: Yes, it is.

Q: Okay. On the last page, March 2000, how did you record your time for Wednesday, March 1st? It's at the top of that.

A: Oh, yes. Eight.

Q: Okay.

A: Eight hours.

Q: So for this trip to Scottsdale, Arizona, in which you accepted a $3,000 honorarium from Janssen from February 27th through March 1st, you not only accepted a $3,000 honorarium from Janssen, but you recorded your time with the State as eight hours of regular time worked, is that correct?

A: That's what it appears.

. . .

Q: You talked with Mr. McDonald about this Exhibit 667, which was a document that you created after the *New York Times* article came out.

A: Yes.

Q: A couple of the staff actually did it at your direction?

A: Yes.

Q: But you gave them the facts?

A: Or they gathered the facts and we all went over the facts together.

Q: Well, I want to look at page 4, sir, the last full bullet point on page 4. You said that "Dr. Shon did not accept compensation for his time in such cases because Texas state employees are prohibited from accepting compensation for presentations." Do you see that?

A: Yes.

Q: Now, that's not true, is it, sir?

A: Well, it was true as far as I— as I recall.

Q: Well, Dr. Shon, you did accept money from Janssen in the form of honorarium. We're going to go over some of them, but—

A: Yes. That was for— but not in relation to this project.

Q: Well, sir, you say here— Doctor, it's stated here on Exhibit 667— I take it you reviewed this—

A: Yes.

Q: —before it was finalized—

A: Yes.

Q: —to make sure it was right?

A: Yes.

Q: Okay. Correct?

A: Yes.

Q: It says, "Dr. Shon did not accept compensation for his time in such cases because Texas state employees are prohibited from accepting compensation for presentations, consultation and other work related to their employment with the state."

A: Yes.

Q: Did I read that right?

A: Yes.

Q: Okay. You know it's a felony to do that, isn't it, sir, to accept money as described in— on page 4?

A: Well, I don't know what level of— it is, but yes, I know that that is not—

Q: Well, it's against the law.

A: —appropriate, yes.

Q: All right. And, in fact, you did accept time and again money from Janssen for going out and speaking as a result of work related to your employment with the State of Texas?

A: No, I don't see it that way. This was not— the— the things that I went to related to my experience as an administrator across the board.

Q: Are you saying that you believe Janssen flew you all around the country and paid you thousands of dollars in honorarium because of your work in the state of California?

A: My work as an administrator for over 20 years, yes.

Q: Let me hand you what we'll mark as Exhibit 671 to see if I can refresh your recollection about this. Do you see a check dated 1/24/2003 made out to you—

A: Yes.

Q: —in the amount—

A: Yes.

Q: —of $3,000?

A: Yes.

Q: And you received that check—

A: Yes.

Q: —didn't you, sir? No doubt in your mind about that, right?

A: Yes. Yes.

Q: I'm going to hand you what we've marked as Exhibit 672. Now, Dr. Shon, you were participating, according to this document, in the strategic sales planning process. Do you see that?

A: Yes, I see that.

Q: And do you see that you're— you're listed on there as the medical director, State of Texas, Office of Mental Health and Mental Retardation?

A: Yes.

Q: All right. No— no mention there of your previous titles, is there, sir?

A: No.

Q: No mention of any work you've done for the State of California?

A: No.

Q: You're there because you're the medical director for the State of Texas, isn't that right, sir?

A: I don't know that that's the sole reason, but that was my title and that's what was listed, yes.

Q: Well, certainly a reason that you're there, you would agree with me on that?

A: Probably, yeah. Probably.

Q: I want to go back to your statement earlier on Exhibit— Exhibit 667 where you— we talked about on page 4 where you said that— or the exhibit was that you did not accept compensation because Texas state employees are prohibited from accepting compensation. But, in fact, sir, you accepted $3,000 in September of 2003.

A: Okay. That's what it appears.

Q: Well, sir, here's the thing. I mean, you answered all these questions from Janssen's lawyer about how various statements in Exhibit 667 were right and accurate and you were trying to correct the record, but when it came down to the money, Exhibit 667 is just flat wrong about that because you did take money from Janssen while you were and on— and on account of your position as a state employee. Isn't that right, sir?

A: Yes, actually I did. And I did that with other consultations, which we've talked about.

Q: But you— you agree that part of it, part of the reason you were being asked— even under your testimony, part of the reason you were being asked was because of your position as medical director of the State of Texas, isn't that correct?

A: That I was an administrator in the State of Texas as part of my career and that's part of what I was asked— why I was asked, I'm sure.

Q: Exhibit 674 is some information related to the very summit we were just discussing for which you received $3,000, right?

A: Yes.

Q: It's the meeting in Amelia Island, Florida, correct?

A: Yes.

Q: Now, one of the things that was discussed at this summit was Risperdal CONSTA, right?

A: I believe so.

Q: Isn't it true that as a matter of chronology, Dr. Shon, that after you attended the Amelia Island presentation and received $3,000 from the folks at Janssen, a presentation at which CONSTA was discussed, that subsequent to that, the folks from Janssen came to you and talked to you about the idea of putting Risperdal CONSTA on the TMAP algorithm? Is that true or not true?

A: The chronology is correct.

Q: Let me ask you this, Doctor. How many times did Janssen pay for you to go anywhere in the world before TMAP was implemented?

A: I don't think they did.

Q: How much— how many— how much cash money did Janssen pay you in the form of honoraria or otherwise at any time prior to the implementation of TMAP in Texas?

A: Probably nothing. I don't recall any.

Q: From last time and from this time, I count six different CNS conferences that you attend for which you received $3,000. Let me run them over with you.

A: Yes.

Q: So three in Arizona that you recall at 3,000 a pop, one in Florida that's 3,000. That's— that's four. We've established there's one in Princeton, New Jersey where you got 3,000. That's—

A: Yes.

Q: That's five.

A: Yes.

Q: Dr. Shon, with respect to the thousands of dollars you received from

Janssen in connection with these meetings and conferences, what did you do with the money?

A: Deposited them in my personal account.

Q: You didn't take those honoraria checks and give them to TDMHMR, correct?

A: Correct.

Q: Kept that money for your own personal use, correct?

A: Correct.

173 **Unfortunately for J & J:** *Jones v. Janssen Pharmaceutica, Inc.* Trial transcript. January 12, 2012. Available at: https://no-more-tears.org/Jones-20120112.pdf.

173 **In the end, sixteen:** Rosack, Jim. "Company Accused of Improprieties in Marketing Risperdal." *Psychiatric News.* American Psychiatric Association website. February 2, 2007. Available at: https://no-more-tears.org/Rosack-2007.pdf.

174 **This is why:** Brill, Steven. *America's Most Admired Lawbreaker.* Chapter 2: "Blowing Past the Label." *The Huffington Post,* Fall 2015.

174 **In Texas, for instance:** Applbaum, Kalman. "Marketing Clientelism vs. Corruption Pharmaceutical Off-label Promotion on Trial." In *Economy, Crime and Corruption in the Neoliberal Era,* edited by James G. Carrier. Berghahn Books, 2008. Available at: https://no-more-tears.org/Applbaum-2008.pdf.

174 **When Kentucky's Medicaid program:** Harris, Gardiner. "States Try to Limit Drugs in Medicaid, But Makers Resist." *The New York Times,* December 18, 2003. Available at: https://no-more-tears.org/Harris-2003.pdf.

175 **One study found that:** Committee on Homeland Security and Governmental Affairs, U.S. Senate. "Fueling an Epidemic." Minority staff report, February 13, 2018. Available at: https://no-more-tears.org/HSGAC-2018.pdf.

CHAPTER 22: SERIOUS RED FLAGS

176 **By the end of 1997:** Brill, Steven. *America's Most Admired Lawbreaker.* Chapter 1: "The Credo Company." *The Huffington Post,* Fall 2015.

176 **And company analyses showed:** Shorter, Edward. *The Rise and Fall of the Age of Psychopharmacology.* Oxford University Press, 2021.

177 **Even more worrisome:** *Commonwealth of Massachusetts v. Ortho-McNeil-Janssen Pharmaceuticals, Inc.* Complaint. May 6, 2011. Available at: https://no-more-tears.org/Coakley-2011.pdf.

177 **In rejecting the company's application:** Brill, Steven. *America's Most Admired Lawbreaker.* Chapter 3: "Sales over Science." *The Huffington Post,* Fall 2015.

177 **In Risperdal's first three years:** *Commonwealth of Massachusetts v. Ortho-McNeil-Janssen Pharmaceuticals, Inc.* Complaint. May 6, 2011. Available at: https://no-more-tears.org/Coakley-2011.pdf.

178 **But if the FDA approved:** *United States of America v. Janssen Pharmaceuticals, Inc.* Charges in the U.S. District Court, Eastern District of Pennsylvania. November 4, 2013. Available at: https://no-more-tears.org/Memeger-2013.pdf.

180 **And since nursing home residents:** Lau, Denys T., et al. "Potentially Inappropriate Medication Prescriptions Among Elderly Nursing Home Residents: Their Scope and Associated Resident and Facility Characteristics." *Health Ser-*

vices Research 39, no. 4, October 2004: 1257–76. Available at: https://no-more
-tears.org/Lau-2004.pdf.

180 **Omnicare had a powerful weapon:** *Lisitza v. Johnson & Johnson et al.* Complaint of the United States. January 15, 2010. Available at: https://no-more
-tears.org/Ortiz-2010.pdf.

180 **In 1997, Johnson & Johnson and Omnicare:** Janssen Pharmaceuticals. "LTC Group Monthly Report. January, 2002. JNJ 291257. Available at: https://no
-more-tears.org/Janssen-2002b.pdf; "Supply Agreement between Omnicare Inc. and Johnson & Johnson Health Care Systems Inc." March 31, 1997. Available at: https://no-more-tears.org/Janssen-1997.pdf.

180 **The very law designed:** Singer, Natasha. "Johnson & Johnson Accused of Drug Kickbacks." *The New York Times,* January 15, 2010. Available at: https://
no-more-tears.org/Singer-2010c.pdf.

180 **Omnicare executives were keenly:** U.S. Attorney's Office, District of Massachusetts. "Nation's Largest Nursing Home Pharmacy and Pharmaceutical Manufacturer Pay $112 Million to Settle False Claims Act Cases." FBI.gov, November 3, 2009. Available at: https://no-more-tears.org/FBI-2009.pdf.

180 **When on occasion Johnson & Johnson:** Bien, Timothy E. Letter to Bruce Cummins, February 14, 2001. OMNI-MA 040770. Available at: https://no
-more-tears.org/Bien-2001.pdf.

180 **(An executive described):** Russell, Dale. Email to Tim Forsthoefel, subject: "Omnicare Levaquin Initiative." 2002. Available at: https://no-more-tears.org
/Russell-2002.pdf.

181 **As a result:** Stockbridge, Lisa. Fax to Todd McIntyre, subject: "NDA #20-272, 20-588; Risperdal (Risperidone) Tablets; Risperdal (Risperidone) Oral Solution; MACMIS #6908." January 5, 1999. JJRP 00379434. Available at: https://
no-more-tears.org/Stockbridge-1999.pdf.

181 **As a result:** Janssen Pharmaceuticals. "Risperdal 1997 U.S. Strategic Offense Plan." February 1997. Available at: https://no-more-tears.org/Janssen-1997b
.pdf.

181 **On January 5, 1999:** Stockbridge, Lisa. Fax to Todd McIntyre, January 5, 1999.

182 **So instead of shuttering:** Brill, Steven. *America's Most Admired Lawbreaker.* Chapter 3: "Sales over Science." *The Huffington Post,* Fall 2015.

182 **The drug's two key growth areas:** Janssen Pharmaceuticals. "Risperdal 2000 Business Plan Summary." Available at: https://no-more-tears.org/Risperdal
-2000.pdf.

CHAPTER 23: A BIG TARGET

183 **These drugs were originally:** Braslow, Joel T., and Stephen R. Marder. "History of Psychopharmacology." *Annual Review of Clinical Psychology* 15, 2019: 25–50. Available at: https://no-more-tears.org/Braslow-2019.pdf.

183 **More than half of children:** Janssen Pharmaceuticals. Record of FDA Contact, subject: "Minutes of March 3rd Meeting to Discuss Risperdal Pediatric Exclusivity and Development Program for Conduct Disorder." March 3, 2000. Available at: https://no-more-tears.org/Janssen-2000c.pdf.

184 **But tranquilizing children:** Mano-Sousa, Bryan Jonas, et al. "Effects of Risperidone in Autistic Children and Young Adults: A Systematic Review and Meta-Analysis." *Current Neuropharmacology* 19, 2021: 538–52. Available at: https://no-more-tears.org/Mano-Sousa-2021.pdf.

184 **To their credit:** Leber, Paul. Letter to Janssen Research Foundation, September 17, 1997. RISPEDPA 004228639. Available at: https://no-more-tears.org /Leber-1997.pdf; Janssen Pharmaceuticals, Record of FDA Contact, March 3, 2000. Available at: https://no-more-tears.org/FDA-2000.pdf.

184 **FDA officials were also:** Katz, Russell. Memo, subject: "Action Memo for NDA 20-272/S-036 Risperdal (Risperidone) NDA 20-588/S-024 Risperdal Solution, & NDA 21-444/S-008, Risperdal Orally Disintegrating Tablets, in the Treatment of Irritability in Patients with Autism." May 9, 2005. Available at: https://no-more-tears.org/Katz-2005.pdf.

186 **Mathisen explained:** Brill, Steven. *America's Most Admired Lawbreaker.* Chapter 7: "A Multi-Front War" *The Huffington Post,* Fall 2015.

186 **By then, nearly two years:** Rothman, David J. "Expert Witness Report." October 15, 2010. Available at: https://no-more-tears.org/Rothman-2010.pdf.

186 **In 2003, about:** Kessler, Ronald C., et al. "The Prevalence and Correlates of Nonaffective Psychosis in the National Comorbidity Survey Replication (NCS-R)." *Biological Psychiatry* 58, no. 8, October 2005: 668–76.

187 **born in communist Czechoslovakia:** Biederman, Joseph. "Curriculum Vitae." May 7, 2008. Available at: https://no-more-tears.org/Biederman-2008.pdf.

187 **Like almost every other:** Harris, Gardiner, and Benedict Carey. "Researchers Fail to Reveal Full Drug Pay." *The New York Times,* June 8, 2008. Available at: https://no-more-tears.org/Harris-2008.pdf.

188 **While Biederman could be:** Harris, Gardiner. "Research Center Tied to Drug Company." *The New York Times,* November 24, 2008. Available at: https://no -more-tears.org/Harris-2008b.pdf.

188 **"Dr. Biederman is not":** Bruins, John. Email to Sohei Sachak, subject: "Dr. Joseph Biederman Payment." November 17, 1999. JJRE 02510305. Available at: https://no-more-tears.org/Bruins-1999.pdf.

188 **As an email from:** Gharabawi, Georges. Email to Janet Vergis and Christine Cote, subject: "Janssen-MGH Child and Adolescent Bipolar Center—Dr Joe Biederman." February 5, 2002. Available at: https://no-more-tears.org/Gharabawi -2002.pdf.

188 **Biederman promised:** Parry, Peter I., and Edmund C. Levin. "Pediatric Bipolar Disorder in an Era of 'Mindless Psychiatry.'" *Journal of Trauma & Dissociation* 13, 2012: 51–68. Available at: https://no-more-tears.org/Parry-2012.pdf.

189 **A June 2002 email message:** Harris, Gardiner. "Research Center Tied to Drug Company." *The New York Times,* November 24, 2008. Available at: https://no -more-tears.org/Harris-2008b.pdf; Shorter, Edward. *The Rise and Fall of the Age of Psychopharmacology.* Oxford University Press, 2021.

190 **And then there were:** "Industry Sponsored CME: Controversies Surrounding Pharma Funding." CMEList, June 14, 2019. Available at: https://no-more -tears.org/CMEList.pdf.

190 **A secret prosecution memorandum:** Grand jury files.

190 **Funding from drugmakers:** Rodwin, Marc A. *Conflicts of Interest and the Future of Medicine: The United States, France, and Japan.* Oxford University Press, 2013.

190 **One of the great advantages:** Brill, Steven. *America's Most Admired Lawbreaker.* Chapter 4: "Massaging the Data, Spreading the Word." *The Huffington Post,* Fall 2015.

191 **But Grassley's office:** Harris, Gardiner, and Benedict Carey. *"Researchers Fail to Reveal Full Drug Pay."*

192 **For Eli Lilly and AstraZeneca:** Deposition of Alex Gorsky, May 18, 2012. Available at: https://no-more-tears.org/Gorsky-2012.pdf.

McCORMICK: Turn to the top of the next page, please, page 261. See where it says, "Risperdal use in the child/adolescent population is exploding?" Is that correct?

GORSKY: That's what it says, yes.

Q: Then down below, it says, "Key Base Business Goals— Well, strike that. I'm sorry. "Risperdal use in the child/adolescent population is exploding," but in this time frame, 2001/2002, Risperdal is not indicated by the FDA for any pediatric use, is it?

A: Again, we did not have the specific indication, as we discussed earlier, until 2006. I don't remember exactly what the labeling said regarding use in children, but as I discussed earlier, there was a significant— there appeared to be a significant increase in the recognition of this condition in children and adolescents during this time, which was substantiated by data and its occurrence. And physicians have an opportunity to use a treatment that they perceive to be appropriate and effective in a particular patient population, and that's clearly what we were seeing happening in this area.

Q: Look down at the head that says, "Key Base Business Goals and Objectives." Do you see that?

A: Yes.

Q: And the fifth of the Key Base Business Goals says, "Grow and protect share in child/adolescents." Is that right?

A: Yes, that's correct.

Q: My question is, how can Johnson & Johnson grow a share in a child and adolescent market when the drug isn't even indicated for use in the child and adolescent market?

A: Well, my interpretation of that is, this is in fact a marketing plan, not a selling plan. As a marketing plan, its intent is to cover a wide range of activities regarding the development as well as the promotion of Risperdal. That being said, all of our actual promotion to the physicians would follow what was outlined in our package insert and all of our materials went through a significant review process, and that's the way our representatives were trained. And in an area such as this, this is a marketer versus a sales representative, their language. And when in fact physicians took it upon themselves and their patients to prescribe the product, their statement would in fact be correct: To ensure that when a physician made that choice, that it was in fact Risperdal.

Q: You were the vice-president of sales and marketing at this time frame, 2000/2001, correct?

A: It depends when this was actually previewed. I don't know if there's a date on here or not, but I think that's the case, yes.

Q: You became vice-president of sales and marketing in December of 1999, correct?

A: My statement related to— I believe I became president of Janssen in late 2001.

Q: Okay. Even if a doctor can prescribe Risperdal for an off-label use and create a market share, you still cannot or Janssen still cannot market the drug to that doctor, a pediatric doctor, for use, can you?

A: To the best of my knowledge, we did not promote the use of Risperdal in that patient vis-a-vis direct promotional programs.

Q: Okay. Even though it says grow the share in child and adolescents on this bullet point as a key base business goal, right?

A: Yes— again, this was a marketing document, not a sales-direction guideline.

Q: Well, it's a marketing document, but it's still an internal Janssen document. You don't think the people in marketing knew that Janssen didn't have— or Risperdal didn't have an indication for pediatric use?

A: I'm certain they realized that. And they realize, also, that all of the promotional materials would go through a review process to ensure that they were consistent with our labeling.

192 **Indeed, Risperdal's FDA-approved:** *Starr et al. v. Johnson & Johnson et al.* United States' Complaint in Intervention. November 4, 2013. Available at: https://no-more-tears.org/Delery-2013.pdf.

193 **Interim results arrived on:** Kessler, David A. Expert Report (Risperdal), September 17, 2012. Available at: https://no-more-tears.org/Kessler-2012.pdf.

193 **Risperdal's sales in 2000:** Brill, Steven. *America's Most Admired Lawbreaker.* Chapter 3: "Sales over Science." *The Huffington Post,* Fall 2015.

194 **Dr. Ivo Caers, the:** Caers, Ivo. Email to [redacted], subject: "RE: RIS-AUS-5 Presentation/Publication Plan." March 22, 2001. Available at: https://no-more-tears.org/Caers-2001.pdf.

195 **By May 2001:** *Starr et al. v. Johnson & Johnson et al.,* Complaint.

195 **Just as the results:** *McGowan and Doetterl v. Janssen Pharmaceutica, Inc. et al.* Complaint. December 21, 2004. Available at: https://no-more-tears.org/Oliverio-2004.pdf.

196 **At a meeting on September 4:** Janssen Pharmaceuticals. "Risperdal in BPSD." 2001. Available at: https://no-more-tears.org/Risperdal-2001.pdf.

196 **A slide set that:** Janssen Pharmaceuticals. "Risperdal in BPSD." 2001. RISP-EDPA003576591. Available at: https://no-more-tears.org/Janssen-2001c.pdf.

197 **Gorsky and his team:** *Lisitza v. Johnson & Johnson et al.* Complaint of the United States. January 15, 2010. Available at: https://no-more-tears.org/Ortiz-2010.pdf.

197 **The company increased its investments:** *McGowan v. Janssen. Complaint.* December 21, 2004. Available at: https://no-more-tears.org/Oliverio-2004.pdf.

197 **Publication of RIS-AUS-05:** [Redacted]. Email to [redacted], subject: "RIS-232." August 31, 2003. RISP-EDPA003488757. Available at: https://no-more-tears.org/RISP-EDPA003488757.pdf.

198   **After studying the issue:** Starr v. Johnson & Johnson, Complaint.
198   **A recent analysis:** Atypical antipsychotics: Decades of use, unfathomable harms. Drug Pricing Lab. May 31, 2022. Available at: https://no-more-tears .org/Bach-2022.pdf.

CHAPTER 24: ICE CREAM AND POPCORN PARTIES

201   **Sales reps held:** Brill, Steven. *Tailspin: The People and Forces Behind America's Fifty-Year Fall—and Those Fighting to Reverse It.* Vintage, 2018.
201   **In a later deposition:** Deposition of Alex Gorsky, May 18, 2012. Available at: https://no-more-tears.org/Gorsky-2012.pdf.
202   **Jason Gilbreath, a J & J:** *Pledger v. Janssen Pharmaceuticals, Inc.* Trial transcript. February 3, 2015. Available at: https://no-more-tears.org/Pledger-Janssen.pdf.

Q: And did you ever at any time have any discussion or any thought in your head that my boy is developing actual breast tissue?

PLEDGER: No. I thought it was the weight gain, and I thought that as long as I kept trying to help him with his weight and exercise, that's all I could do. I would just have to fight the weight as much as possible. I did not know that his breasts were for any other reason than that.

Q: Okay. And did you at any time know that there was any increased risk, of any kind, of your son developing what we in this courtroom have been calling gynecomastia?

PLEDGER: No. I knew nothing of that— I did not know boys could develop breasts or [if] it was a side effect from the medicine at all.

Q: If you knew that, would you have allowed your son to be on this drug?

PLEDGER: No.

Q: Can you tell that to us absolutely and categorically?

PLEDGER: Absolutely not. I— I can— I can't fight breast growth. I felt like with the weight gain, we could exercise— You can't fight something like that. I didn't even know that was a possibility.

202   **Meanwhile, the company:** De Smedt, C., et al. "Clinical Research Report." Janssen Research Foundation, November 2, 2000. JJRIS 02562360. Available at: https://no-more-tears.org/RIS-INT-41.pdf.
203   **In an email dated:** *Jones v. Janssen Pharmaceutica, Inc.* Trial transcript. January 10, 2012. Available at: https://no-more-tears.org/Jones-20120110.pdf.
203   **The main addition:** *Pledger v. Janssen Pharmaceuticals, Inc.* Trial transcript. January 28, 2015. Available at: https://no-more-tears.org/Pledger-Janssen-Kessler .pdf.
204   **"They never showed me":** Brill, Steven. *America's Most Admired Lawbreaker.* Chapter 12: "Showdown, Almost" *The Huffington Post,* Fall 2015.
204   **In courtroom testimony:** Brill, Steven. *America's Most Admired Lawbreaker.* Chapter 14: "The Good Soldier, the Good Mother, the Faded Star." *The Huffington Post,* Fall 2015.

Q: The truth is, there were how many people in the study?
A: 592.

Q: And how many had a prolactin-related adverse event, of those 592?

A: 2.2 percent.

Q: Sir, the jury is looking squarely at Table 2, okay. They see that there were 30 who had a— a SHAP, correct? That means . . .

A: SHAP A.

Q: Sir, let's put aside SHAP A and SHAP B—

A: No, that's crucial.

Q: —because you invented SHAP A—

A: That doesn't matter we invent. It's crucial.

Q: How many patients. How many patients— You know where this is going. You know that I'm going to show you the abstract, and the abstract only shows 2.2 percent.

A: Obviously.

Q: And you also know that that's misleading?

A: No, I don't agree.

Q: There's 592 patients, correct?

A: Yes.

Q: 30 of them had a prolactin-related averse event, correct?

A: Under the— under the definition of SHAP A.

Q: Yes. Under the definition of all the patients, if you took all the patients—

A: No, no. Under the definition of SHAP A.

Q: The definition of SHAP A is all the children in the study.

A: No.

Q: All the children with side effects in the study—

A: No, no, no, no.

. . .

Q: Sir, there are 592 patients, correct?

A: Yes.

Q: And there are 30 adverse events, correct?

A: In SHAP A.

Q: And that is 5.1 percent, correct?

A: Yes.

Q: What you do here in the abstract is you take the total number of patients, correct?

A: Yes.

Q: That would be SHAP A?

A: No, no, no.

Q: No, that would be—

A: Total number of patients.

Q: Total number of patients. Yeah.

A: Exactly.

204 **When it was finally:** Findling, Robert L., et al. "Prolactin Levels during Long-Term Risperidone Treatment in Children and Adolescents." *The Journal of Clinical Psychiatry* 64, no. 11, November 2003: 1362–69.

205 **In September 2003:** Rosack, Jim. "FDA to Require Diabetes Warning on Antipsychotics." *Psychiatric News.* American Psychiatric Association website, October 17, 2003. Available at: https://no-more-tears.org/Rosack-2003.pdf.

205 **In 1956, four years:** Hiles, Bettie W. "Hyperglycemia and Glycosuria Following Chlorpromazine Therapy." *JAMA* 168, no. 18, December 1956: 1651.

206 **And since both companies:** Prescription Medicines Code of Practice Authority. "Updated Code of Practice Agreed by ABPI Members." *Code of Practice Review* 40, May 2003: 1–67. Available at: https://no-more-tears.org/Code-of-Practice-Review.pdf.

206 **In the end, however:** Rosack, Jim. "FDA to Require Diabetes Warning on Antipsychotics." *Psychiatric News.* American Psychiatric Association website, October 17, 2003. Available at: https://no-more-tears.org/Rosack-2003.pdf.

206 **letter sent to all doctors:** *State of West Virginia v. Johnson & Johnson.* Decision on appeal. November 18, 2010. Available at: https://no-more-tears.org/Gaughan-2010.pdf.

207 **The missive acknowledged that:** U.S. Attorney's Office, Eastern District of Pennsylvania. "Johnson & Johnson to Pay More Than $2.2 Billion to Resolve Fraud and Misbranding Allegations." Justice.gov, November 4, 2013. Available at: https://no-more-tears.org/DOJ-2013.pdf.

CHAPTER 25: A TURNING POINT

208 **Starr had been:** Brill, Steven. *America's Most Admired Lawbreaker.* Chapter 6: "Trouble." *The Huffington Post,* Fall 2015.

209 **Johnson & Johnson's lawyers always:** Rothman, David J. *Expert Witness Report.* October 15, 2010. Available at: https://no-more-tears.org/Rothman-2010.pdf.

211 **The survey simply confirmed:** Liu, Jianjun, et al. "Randomized Controlled Trial Comparing Changes in Serum Prolactin and Weight among Female Patients with First-Episode Schizophrenia over 12 Months of Treatment with Risperidone or Quetiapine." *Shanghai Archives of Psychiatry* 26, no. 2, April 2014: 88–94. Available at: https://no-more-tears.org/Liu-2014.pdf; Janssen Pharmaceuticals. "Risperdal Pediatric Market Opportunity." August 2000. JJRE 01502238. Available at: https://no-more-tears.org/Janssen-2000e.pdf.

211 **(Especially with the latter):** Kessler, David A. Expert Report (Risperdal), September 17, 2012. Available at: https://no-more-tears.org/Kessler-2012.pdf.

211 **She agreed, and that's:** Brill, Steven. *America's Most Admired Lawbreaker.* Chapter 6: "Trouble." *The Huffington Post,* Fall 2015.

213 **Similar whistleblower claims:** Wilson, Duff. "Side Effects May Include Lawsuits." *The New York Times,* October 2, 2010. Available at: https://no-more-tears.org/Wilson-2010.pdf.

214 **At Lilly, Michael Bandick:** Grand jury files.

CHAPTER 26: ONE OF THE MOST ALARMING WARNINGS

215 **On April 11, 2005:** Janssen Pharmaceuticals. Prescribing Information for Risperdal. 2007. Available at: https://no-more-tears.org/Janssen-2007.pdf.

215 **Nonetheless, the announcement:** Harris, Gardiner. "Popular Drugs for De-

mentia Tied to Deaths." *The New York Times,* April 12, 2005. Available at: https://no-more-tears.org/Harris-2005b.pdf.

216 **They had done this:** *United States of America v. Janssen Pharmaceuticals, Inc.* Charges in the U.S. District Court, Eastern District of Pennsylvania. November 4, 2013. Available at: https://no-more-tears.org/Memeger-2013.pdf.

216 **sales rep Tim Humphries:** Grand jury files.

216 **Risperdal's sales grew 18:** Johnson & Johnson. "Management's Discussion and Analysis." Annual Report to the Shareholders. 2004. Available at: https://no-more-tears.org/JJ-2004b.pdf.

217 **To this day, some:** Thomas, Katie, Robert Gebeloff, and Jessica Silver-Greenberg. "Phony Diagnoses Hide High Rates of Drugging at Nursing Homes." *The New York Times,* September 11, 2021. Available at: https://no-more-tears.org/Thomas-2021.pdf.

217 **And in more than half:** Centers for Medicare & Medicaid Services. "CMS Announces Partnership to Improve Dementia Care in Nursing Homes." Press release, May 30, 2012. Available at: https://no-more-tears.org/CMS-2012.pdf.

218 **In 2023, the Biden:** Kamp, Jon, Melanie Evans, and Gretchen Lenth. *"The Upheaval at America's Disappearing Nursing Homes, in Charts." The Wall Street Journal,* August 23, 2023. Available at: https://no-more-tears.org/Kamp-2023.pdf; Centers for Medicare & Medicaid Services. *"Medicare and Medicaid Programs: Minimum Staffing Standards for Long-Term Care Facilities and Medicaid Institutional Payment Transparency Reporting (CMS 3442-P)."* Fact sheet, September 1, 2023. Available at: https://no-more-tears.org/CMS-2023.pdf.

CHAPTER 27: THEY KNEW THEY WERE A GOOD COMPANY

221 **Soon after, the company's:** Wilson, Duff. "Side Effects May Include Lawsuits." *The New York Times,* October 2, 2010. Available at: https://no-more-tears.org/Wilson-2010.pdf.

222 **Next came Eli Lilly:** Conn, Lawrence, and Lawrence Vernaglia. "Shining the Light on Physician–Pharmaceutical and Medical Device Industry Financial Relationships." *Journal of Vascular Surgery* 54, no. 185, September, 2011. 22S–25S. Available at: https://no-more-tears.org/Conn-2021.pdf.

222 **Marketing efforts for nearly:** Compton, Kristin. "Big Pharma and Medical Device Manufacturers." *Drugwatch,* 2021. Available at: https://no-more-tears.org/Compton-2021B.pdf.

222 **For example, by 2009:** Kavilanz, Parija. "Tylenol Recall: FDA Slams Company." CNN, October 19, 2010. Available at: https://no-more-tears.org/Kavilanz-2010.pdf.

222 **J & J did none:** Singer, Natasha. "More Disputes over Handling of Drug Recall." *The New York Times,* June 11, 2010. Available at: https://no-more-tears.org/Singer-2010.pdf.

222 **Instead, the company sent:** Johnson & Johnson's Recall of Children's Tylenol and Other Children's Medicines. Hearing before the Committee on Oversight and Government Reform, House of Representatives, May 27, 2010. Available at: https://no-more-tears.org/JJ-ChildrenTylenol.pdf; Krauskopf, Lewis.

"Documents Show J & J Bought Motrin Before Recall." Reuters, June 12, 2010. Available at: https://no-more-tears.org/Krauskopf-2010.pdf.

223 **on February 21, 2012:** Johnson & Johnson. "Alex Gorsky to Succeed Bill Weldon as CEO of Johnson & Johnson." JnJ.com, February 21, 2012. Available at: https://no-more-tears.org/JJ-2012.pdf.

224 **Company executives explained:** Armstrong, Drew, and Robert Langreth. "J & J Names Alex Gorsky CEO to Replace William Weldon." Bloomberg News, February 22, 2012.

224 **Synthes was already infamous:** Meier, Barry. "Synthes, Medical Device Maker, Accused of Improper Marketing." *The New York Times,* June 16, 2009.

224 **April 2011 press release:** Johnson & Johnson. "Johnson & Johnson and Synthes Announce Definitive Merger Agreement to Create World's Most Innovative and Comprehensive Orthopaedics Business." JnJ.com, April 27, 2011. Available at: https://no-more-tears.org/JJ-2011.pdf.

224 **At his first annual:** Todd, Susan. "Johnson & Johnson's New CEO Emphasizes Company Credo at Shareholder's Meeting." *The Star-Ledger,* April 26, 2012. Available at: https://no-more-tears.org/Todd-2012.pdf.

225 **On November 4, 2013:** U.S. Attorney's Office, Eastern District of Pennsylvania. "Johnson & Johnson to Pay More Than $2.2 Billion to Resolve Fraud and Misbranding Allegations." Justice.gov, November 4, 2013. Available at: https://no-more-tears.org/DOJ-2013.pdf.

226 **No company executives were charged:** Brill, Steven. *America's Most Admired Lawbreaker.* Chapter 10: "Chess, at $1,000 an Hour." *The Huffington Post,* Fall 2015.

CHAPTER 28: AN EPIDEMIC FORETOLD

228 **The opioid epidemic:** Egilman, David, et al. "The Marketing of OxyContin: A Cautionary Tale." *Indian Journal of Medical Ethics* 4, no. 3, July–September 2019: 183–93. Available at: https://no-more-tears.org/Egilman-2019.pdf.

228 **"Delayed absorption, as provided":** Zettler, Patricia J., Margaret Foster Riley, and Aaron S. Kesselheim. "Implementing a Public Health Perspective in FDA Drug Regulation." *Food and Drug Law Journal* 73, no. 2, 2018: 221–56.

228 **A year later:** Keefe, Patrick Radden. *Empire of Pain: The Secret History of the Sackler Dynasty.* Doubleday, 2021.

228 **Johnson & Johnson's Duragesic:** State of Texas v. Janssen. Plaintiff's original petition. September 3, 2019. Available at: https://no-more-tears.org/Texas-Opioid.pdf.

229 **OxyContin could be crushed:** United States General Accounting Office. *Prescription Drugs—Oxycontin Abuse and Diversion and Efforts to Address the Problem.* Report to congressional requesters, December 2003. Available at: https://no-more-tears.org/GAO-2003.pdf.

229 **Duragesic could be chewed:** Neergaard, Lauran. "FDA Says Some Doctors Dangerously Misusing Potent Painkiller." Associated Press, 1994.

229 **A year before:** Wissel, J., and M. Southam. "Regulatory Agency Contact Report." Record of meeting with Curtis Wright, August 29, 1989. JAN-MS-02908031. Available at: https://no-more-tears.org/Wissel-1989.pdf.

229 **Wright told Johnson & Johnson:** "FDA-DEA-NIDA Meeting." Minutes, February 21, 1990. JAN-MS-02909945. Available at: https://no-more-tears.org /Wissel-1990.pdf.

229 **His worry, Wright said:** Wright, Curtis. *"Medical Officer Review—TTS Fentanyl."* May 16, 1990. Acquired_Actavis_01096391. Available at: https://no -more-tears.org/Wright-1990.pdf; Wright, Curtis. Medical Officer Review: TTS Fentanyl. Volume 4 - Safety. May 12, 1990. JAN-MS-00552015. Available at: https://no-more-tears.org/Wright-1990B.pdf.

230 **She wrote a letter:** Schilling, Donna. Letter to Senator Connie Mack. September 14, 1993. JAN-MS-02908681. Available at: https://no-more-tears.org/Schilling -1993.pdf.

230 **Kessler responded forcefully:** Wright, Curtis. Memo to L. Katz et al. December 22, 1993. JAN-MS-02908571. Available at: https://no-more-tears.org /Wright-1993.pdf.

230 **In a press release:** American Association for Justice. "FDA Warns Health Professionals about Painkiller's Dangers." March 1, 1994. Available at: https://no -more-tears.org/ Duragesic-1994.pdf.

231 **in the last days of 1995:** Egilman et al. *"The Marketing of OxyContin."*

231 **Coming right out of the gate:** Van Zee, Art. "The Promotion and Marketing of OxyContin: Commercial Triumph, Public Health Tragedy." *American Journal of Public Health* 99, no. 2, February 2009: 221–27. Available at: https://no -more-tears.org/Van-Zee-2009.pdf.

231 **once they're physically addicted:** Centers for Disease Control and Prevention. "Patients' Frequently Asked Questions." 2021. Available at: https://no -more-tears.org/CDC-FAQ.pdf.

231 **"Purdue had a brilliant":** *State of Oklahoma v. Johnson & Johnson et al.* Trial transcript. May 28, 2019. Available at: https://no-more-tears.org/Oklahoma-05-28.pdf.

232 **The American Pain Society:** Committee on Homeland Security and Governmental Affairs, U.S. Senate. *Fueling an Epidemic. Minority Staff Report,* February 13, 2018. Available at: https://no-more-tears.org/HSGAC-2018.pdf.

232 **In late 1996:** The American Academy of Pain Medicine and the American Pain Society. "The Use of Opioids for the Treatment of Chronic Pain." Consensus statement. Approved June 29 and August 20, 1996. Available at: https://no -more-tears.org/APS-1997.pdf.

233 **"Our objective is to":** Janssen Pharmaceuticals. "Duragesic Transdermal System." Marketing plan, 2002. JAN-MS-00310227. Available at: https://no -more-tears.org/Janssen-2002.pdf.

233 **To do so:** Janssen Pharmaceuticals. "Duragesic: Positioning Evolution Overview." June 1, 2002. JAN-MS-00309606. Available at: https://no-more-tears .org/JAN-MS-00309606.pdf.

233 **In a March 1998:** Sherman, Stephen W. Letter to Jacqueline Brown, subject: "NDA 19-813. Duragesic (Fentanyl Transdermal System) MACMIS File ID #6194." March 5, 1998. JAN-MS-03090752. Available at: https://no-more -tears.org/Sherman-1998.pdf.

234 **J & J was so enamored:** Janssen Pharmaceuticals. "Project Pearl Internal Discussion Guide." JAN-MS-01051777. Available at: https://no-more-tears.org /ProjectPearl.pdf.

234 **The idea was that:** Grissinger, Michael. Email to Louis Ferrari and Barry Fitzsimons, subject: "Pearl." August 8, 2000. JAN-MS-00456650. Available at: https://no-more-tears.org/Grissinger-2000.pdf; Janssen Pharmaceuticals. "Project Pearl: Project Pearl Call Plan, Joint JNJ/Purdue." August 28, 2000. JAN-MS-00456655. Available at: https://no-more-tears.org/Janssen-2000b.pdf.

234 **Then, in February 2001:** Meier, Barry. *Pain Killer: A "Wonder" Drug's Trail of Addiction and Death.* Rodale Books, 2001.

CHAPTER 29: OPIUM BLOSSOMS IN TASMANIA

235 **One answer for:** Thomas, Katie, and Tiffany Hsu. "Johnson & Johnson's Brand Falters over Its Role in the Opioid Crisis." *The New York Times,* August 17, 2019. Available at: https://no-more-tears.org/Thomas-2019.pdf.

235 **In Tasmania, Glaxo discovered:** Fist, A. J. "The Tasmanian Poppy Industry: A Case Study of the Application of Science and Technology." Tasmanian Alkaloids Pty Ltd, 2001. Available at: https://no-more-tears.org/Fist-2001.pdf.

236 **In 1975, Abbott Laboratories:** Fist, *"The Tasmanian Poppy Industry."*

236 **As sales of the combined:** Bernstein, Lenny. *"Spotlight Shifts to Johnson & Johnson as First Major Opioid Trial Nears in Oklahoma."* *The Washington Post,* May 4, 2019. Available at: https://no-more-tears.org/Bernstein-2019.pdf.

236 **the amount of land:** International Narcotics Control Board. *Report of the International Narcotics Control Board for 1993.* Published by the United Nations, December 1993. Available at: https://no-more-tears.org/INCB-1994.pdf.

236 **But in 1994:** Kindergan, Michael B. "Letter to Ed Miglarese." October 15, 1998. PDD1701649792. Available at: https://no-more-tears.org/Kindergan -1998.pdf; Fist, A. J. "The Tasmanian Poppy Industry: A Case Study of the Application of Science and Technology." Tasmanian Alkaloids Pty Ltd, 2001. Available at: https://no-more-tears.org/Fist-2001.pdf.

238 **Tasmanian acreage planted:** Safi, Michael. "Tasmania's Grip on Opium Poppy Industry Weakens As Plant Moves North." *The Guardian,* October 21, 2014. Available at: https://no-more-tears.org/Safi-2014.pdf.

238 **One company accountant:** Whoriskey, Peter. "How Johnson & Johnson Companies Used a 'Super Poppy' to Make Narcotics for America's Most Abused Opioid Pills." *The Washington Post,* March 26, 2020. Available at: https://no-more-tears.org/Whoriskey-2020.pdf.

238 **Johnson & Johnson became:** *State of Oklahoma v. Johnson & Johnson et al.* Trial transcript. June 26, 2019. Available at: https://no-more-tears.org /Oklahoma-06-26.pdf.

238 **In a letter:** Kindergan, October 15, 1998, letter to Ed Miglarese.

238 **In one letter:** Friedman, Michael. Memo to Mortimer D. Sackler, Raymond R. Sackler, and Richard S. Sackler, subject: "Sales/Marketing/Licensing & Business Development Quarterly Report." October 13, 1999. PDD1701815348. Available at: https://no-more-tears.org/Friedman-1999.pdf.

238 **Two months later:** Janssen Pharmaceuticals. Supply agreement between PF Laboratories and NORAMCO. December 9, 1998. PPLP004491016. Available at: https://no-more-tears.org/Janssen-1998.pdf.

CHAPTER 30: LESS PRONE TO ABUSE

240 **This was the beginning:** Pochna, Peter. "New Drug of Choice Sweeps State: Painkiller OxyContin." *Portland Press Herald,* July 30, 2000.

240 **And then in February 2001:** Meier, Barry. *Pain Killer: A "Wonder" Drug's Trail of Addiction and Death.* Rodale Books, 2001.

241 **And a big reason:** Kessler, David. *"Expert Report."* December 18, 2019. Available at: https://no-more-tears.org/Kessler-2019.pdf.

241 **The reason J & J could:** Statement of Charges and Notice of Hearing (to Johnson and Johnson et al.). September 8, 2020. Available at: https://no-more-tears.org/Puvalowski-2000.pdf.

241 **As OxyContin abuse soared:** Keefe, Patrick Radden. *Empire of Pain: The Secret History of the Sackler Dynasty.* Doubleday, 2021.

241 **But DAWN had:** Gourlay, Douglas L., Howard E. Heit, and Yale H. Caplan. *Urine Drug Testing Clinical Practice.* May 31, 2015. Available at: https://no-more-tears.org/Gourlay-2015.pdf.

Here is an exchange between Brad Beckworth, an attorney for Oklahoma, and Kimberly Deem-Eshleman, a Johnson & Johnson executive.

BECKWORTH: Let's go to the next one. July 29, 2003. This is Page 15, Line 216. Holly Abraham, Oklahoma City. He uses Oxy and MS Contin. Now, let's stop there. Oxy and MS Contin were Purdue drugs, correct?

DEEM-ESHLEMAN: Yes.

Q: And by 2003, MS Contin was also a generic. Did you know that?

A: I believe so, yes.

Q: Okay. Now, in 2003, this says: Went over Allan study to show that Duragesic offers better patient functionality as well as pain control, right?

A: I see that, yes.

Q: And that's going about the efficacy of the drug, right?

A: Well, that's talking to functionality.

Q: Now, next it says: Told me about pain conference he attended. And speaker said patients are putting Duragesic in mouths to get high. Asked if they mentioned abuse of other medicine. Do you see that?

A: I see that, yes.

Q: And he said yes, right?

A: Yes.

Q: So specifically, there's a doctor asking about abuse of Duragesic and other pain meds, right?

A: Well, he stated it.

Q: And then your rep says: Went over DAWN data, right?

A: It says that, yes.

242 **Johnson & Johnson's own Chronic:** Janssen Pharmaceuticals. "Executive Summary: Chronic Pain Scientific Advisory Board." November 30, 2001. JAN-MS-00481055. Available at: https://no-more-tears.org/Janssen-2001.pdf.

242 **Every Duragesic business plan:** Janssen Pharmaceuticals. "Duragesic Fentanyl Transdermal System: 2003 Business & Tactical Plan Highlights." July 30, 2002. JAN-MS-03861460. Available at: https://no-more-tears.org/Janssen-2002c.pdf.

242 **A study by:** ZS Associates. "Duragesic PhysPulse Brand Monitoring and

Performance Enhancement Study: Summary of Wave 1 Results." September 16, 2003. JAN-TX-00387684. Available at: https://no-more-tears.org/ZS-Associates-2003.pdf.

242 **Sales aids provided to reps:** Janssen Pharmaceuticals. Duragesic package insert outline. 2001. JAN-MS-00785617. Available at: https://no-more-tears.org/Janssen-2001b.pdf.

242 **At trial in Oklahoma in 2019:** *State of Oklahoma v. Johnson & Johnson et al.* Trial transcript. May 31, 2019. Available at: https://no-more-tears.org/Oklahoma-05-31.pdf.

243 **The firm added that:** McKinsey & Company. *Duragesic Disease Modeling Workshop 2 Takeaways.* 2003. Available at: https://no-more-tears.org/McKinsey-2003.pdf.

243 **One 2000 memo:** Janssen Pharmaceuticals. Memo to Duragesic Sales Force. 2000. JAN-MS-00311782. Available at: https://no-more-tears.org/Janssen-2000d.pdf.

243 **Four doctors wrote:** Chupa, Kathleen. "Ortho Biotech POA III Presentation." 2000. JAN-MS-00790294. Available at: https://no-more-tears.org/Chupa-2000.pdf.

243 **In doing so:** Hoffman, Jan. "Johnson & Johnson Ordered to Pay $572 Million in Landmark Opioid Trial." *The New York Times,* August 26, 2019. Available at: https://no-more-tears.org/Hoffman-2019.pdf.

244 **Purdue Pharma managed to:** Noah, Lars. "Product Hopping 2.0: Getting the FDA to Yank Your Original License Beats Stacking Patents." *Marquette Intellectual Property Law Review* 19, no. 2, June 2015: 162–79. Available at: https://no-more-tears.org/Noah-2015.pdf.

244 **First, Johnson & Johnson sued:** Bloomberg News. "Mylan Loses Suit on Generic Pain Patch." *The New York Times,* March 24, 2004. Available at: https://no-more-tears.org/Bloomberg-News-2004.pdf.

245 **The company created ads:** Janssen Pharmaceuticals. "Duragesic Business Update." January 21, 2004. JAN-MS-02396626. Available at: https://no-more-tears.org/Janssen-2004.pdf.

245 **J & J put together a list:** Janssen Pharmaceuticals. "Script #3: Public Safety." 2004. JAN-MS-00724815. Available at: https://no-more-tears.org/Janssen-2004b.pdf.

246 **On November 12, 2004:** Rinne, Susan P. "Citizen Petition." November 12, 2004. JAN-MS-00386726. Available at: https://no-more-tears.org/Rinne-2004.pdf.

246 **To prepare for the launch:** Janssen-Cilag. *An Assessment of the Potential for Prescription Analgesic Abuse, Misuse and Diversion in Europe.* Report prepared for the proposed European Launch of Durogesic D-Trans Matrix Delivery System. October 2003. JAN-MS-01200052. Available at: https://no-more-tears.org/Janssen-2003.pdf.

246 **In early 2008:** Fields, Ellen W. "Center for Drug Evaluation and Research Application Number: 19-813/S0442009: Cross Discipline Team Leader Review." July 29, 2009. Available at: https://no-more-tears.org/Fields-2009.pdf.

246 **So, pulling a 180:** Abeysinghe, Harindra. Letter to Bob A. Rappaport, subject: "NDA 19-813." January 30, 2009. JAN-MS-04230555. Available at: https://no-more-tears.org/Abeysinghe-2009.pdf.

CHAPTER 31: EVOLVE THE VALUE DISCUSSION

247 **When Purdue Pharma:** Meier, Barry. "In Guilty Plea, OxyContin Maker to Pay $600 Million." *The New York Times,* May 10, 2007. Available at: https://no-more-tears.org/Meier-2007.pdf.

248 **To sell the pill:** Janssen Pharmaceuticals. "Cycle 2 Update: Video Walk-Through." June 6, 2012. JAN-MS-00774016. Available at: https://no-more-tears.org/Janssen-2012b.pdf.

248 **The one-two punch:** Janssen Pharmaceuticals. "Duragesic: 2001 Business Plan." August 2000. JAN-MS-00618253. Available at: https://no-more-tears.org/Duragesic-2000.pdf.

248 **"Evolve the value discussion":** Janssen Pharmaceuticals. "Nucynta (tapentadol): IR & ER 2010 Business Plan." July 21, 2009. JAN-MS-00331802. Available at: https://no-more-tears.org/Janssen-2009b.pdf.

248 **The FDA made clear:** Love, Lori A. Letter to Bob Rappaport, subject: "Tapentadol HCl (NDA 22-304)." November 4, 2008. Available at: https://no-more-tears.org/Love-2008.pdf.

248 **"The controlled release properties":** Kilgore Elizabeth. "Clinical Review." Application 200-533, Tapentadol Extended-Release. February 28, 2011. Available at: https://no-more-tears.org/Kilgore-2011.pdf.

249 **Per usual, J & J's:** Janssen Pharmaceuticals. "Tapentadol Global Commercial Team." April 15, 2008. JAN-MS-05471184. Available at: https://no-more-tears.org/Janssen-2008.pdf.

249 **On August 26, 2011:** Fienkeng, Mathilda. Letter to Roxanne O. McGregor-Beck. Subject: "NDA # 022304." August 26, 2011. Available at: https://no-more-tears.org/Fienkeng-2011.pdf.

249 **Specifically, it implies:** Janssen Pharmaceuticals. "Nucynta Speaker Training." October 10, 2012. JAN-MS-00027221. Available at: https://no-more-tears.org/Janssen-2012.pdf; Global Pharmaceuticals Pricing Committee, Janssen Pharmaceuticals. "Tapentadol IR: US Launch Price and Policy." February 11, 2009. JAN-MS-01137972. Available at: https://no-more-tears.org/Janssen-2009c.pdf.

249 **The record of:** *State of Oklahoma v. Johnson & Johnson et al.* Trial transcript. May 31, 2019. Available at: https://no-more-tears.org/Oklahoma-20190531.pdf.

Q: By the way, how come after 2008, 2009, you stopped using texts? You've referenced next calls. Why did you-all just stop doing this?

A: Because the reps are very busy, and we just streamlined situations so there's drop-downs now.

Q: Didn't have anything to do with the fact that Purdue got charged with a federal crime and pled guilty to it for things that were recorded in their call notes?

A: I'm not aware of that.

Q: I mean, you just got busier, that's why?

A: That's what I understand.

249 **Sales reps still sent:** Ellis, Randy. "Drug Company Rep Describes Oklahoma Doctor As Promising Opioid Sales Target in an Email." *The Oklahoman,* June 1, 2019. Available at: https://no-more-tears.org/Ellis-2019.pdf.

250 **A slide routinely included:** Janssen Pharmaceuticals. *Finding Relief: Pain*

Management for Older Adults. Conrad & Associates LLC, 2009. Available at: https://no-more-tears.org/Janssen-2009d.pdf.

250 **By 2010, according to the CDC:** Centers for Disease Control and Prevention. "Vital Signs: Overdoses of Prescription Opioid Pain Relievers: United States, 1999–2008." Morbidity and Mortality Weekly Report. CDC.gov, November 4, 2011. 1487-1492. Available at: https://no-more-tears.org/CDC-2011.pdf.

250 **Fifteen years into:** Manchikanti, Laxmaiah, and Angelie Singh. "Therapeutic Opioids: A Ten-Year Perspective on the Complexities and Complications of the Escalating Use, Abuse, and Nonmedical Use of Opioids." *Pain Physician* 11, no. 2, March 2008: S63–S88.

250 **One such plan:** Janssen Pharmaceuticals. "Number of Stakeholders That Influence Pain Prescribing Is Becoming More Complex." 2008. Available at: https://no-more-tears.org/Janssen-2008b.png.

251 **But Andrew Kolodny:** *State of Oklahoma v. Johnson & Johnson et al.* Trial transcript. June 17, 2019. Available at: https://no-more-tears.org/Oklahoma-06-17.pdf.

251 **A former FDA commissioner:** Johnson & Johnson. "Former FDA Commissioner, Dr. Mark B. McClellan, to Join Johnson & Johnson Board of Directors." JnJ.com, April 14, 2013.

CHAPTER 32: THE PILL AND THE PATCH

253 **In 1995, J & J:** Associated Press. "Ortho Fined $7.5 Million in Retin-A Case." *The New York Times,* April 18, 1995. Available at: https://no-more-tears.org/AP-1995.pdf.

254 **The birth control pill:** Harris, Gardiner. "It Started More Than One Revolution." *The New York Times,* May 3, 2010. Available at: https://no-more-tears.org/Harris-2010.pdf.

254 **The horrors of thalidomide:** Timmermans, Stefan, and Valerie Leiter. "The Redemption of Thalidomide: Standardizing the Risk of Birth Defects." *Social Studies of Science* 30, no. 1, February 2000: 41–71. Available at: https://no-more-tears.org/Timmermans-2000.pdf.

255 **Four years later:** Bloomberg News. "Johnson Seeks to Halt Generic Contraceptive." *The New York Times,* October 7, 2003. Available at: https://no-more-tears.org/Bloomberg-News-2003.pdf.

255 **The new patch:** Abraham, Yvonne. "No Patch for Deepest Cut." *The Boston Globe,* October 21, 2009. Available at: https://no-more-tears.org/Abraham-2009.pdf.

255 **Instead of a daily pill:** Watkins, Elizabeth Siegel. "How the Pill Became a Lifestyle Drug: The Pharmaceutical Industry and Birth Control in the United States Since 1960." *American Journal of Public Health* 102, no. 8, August 2012: 1462–72. Available at: https://no-more-tears.org/Watkins-2012.pdf.

255 **To see how Ortho Evra:** Yu, Eunice, and Sidney M. Wolfe. "Petition to Ban Ethinyl Estradiol/Norelgestromin (Ortho-Evra)." *Public Citizen,* May 8, 2008. Available at: https://no-more-tears.org/PublicCitizen-Petition.pdf.

256 **Patch patients on average:** Snell, Teddye. "With So Many Choices, It's Some-

times Difficult to Find the 'Perfect' Contraceptive." CNHI News Service, November 17, 2005. Available at: https://no-more-tears.org/Snell-2005.pdf.

256 **In fact, because up to half:** Harris, Gardiner, and Alex Berensen. "Drugmakers Near Old Goal: A Legal Shield." *The New York Times,* April 6, 2008. Available at: https://no-more-tears.org/Harris-2008a.pdf.

257 **On November 1, 2001:** Gardiner and Berensen, *"Drugmakers Near Old Goal."*

257 **The company scientists in charge:** Harris, Gardiner, and Alex Berensen. "Johnson & Johnson Seeks to Put Blame on Regulators." *The New York Times,* April 6, 2008. Available at: https://no-more-tears.org/Harris-2008d.pdf.

257 **And when J & J sent:** Zieman, Miriam, et al. "Contraceptive Efficacy and Cycle Control with the Ortho Evra/Evra Transdermal System: The Analysis of Pooled Data." *Fertil Steril* 77, no. 2, supplement 2, February 2002: S13–8.

258 **regulators in New Zealand:** Lane, Justinian. "Dr. Suzanne Parisian's Expert Report in an Ortho Evra Lawsuit." *Dangerous Drugs & Medical Devices,* July 22, 2009. Available at: https://no-more-tears.org/Parisian-2009.pdf.

258 **Sales took off:** Altomari, Alfred, et al. United States Securities and Exchange Commission Form 10-K: Agile Therapeutics Inc. March 12, 2019. Available at: https://no-more-tears.org/Agile-10K.pdf.

258 **Soon, the FDA started:** Mendoza, Martha. "Birth Control Patch Appears Riskier Than Pill; FDA Cites Safety." *Los Angeles Times,* July 17, 2005.

259 **A study later:** Galzote, Rosanna, et al. "Transdermal Delivery of Combined Hormonal Contraception: A Review of the Current Literature." *International Journal of Women's Health* 9, 2017: 315–21. Available at: https://no-more-tears.org/Galzote-2017.pdf.

259 **Called NED-1:** Lane, *"Dr. Suzanne Parisian's Expert Report."*

260 **On May 19, 2004:** Abaray Janet. Memorandum of Law in Support of Plaintiffs' Motion for Partial Summary Judgment on Defendants Affirmative Defenses Numbers 1, 2, 3, 4, 5, 6, 7, 8, 13, 14, 15, 16, 17, 18, 20 and 27. 2007.

261 **In November 2005:** Wooltorton, Eric. "The Evra (Ethinyl Estradiol/Norelgestromin) Contraceptive Patch: Estrogen Exposure Concerns." *Canadian Medical Association Journal* 174, no. 2, January 17, 2006: 164–65. Available at: https://no-more-tears.org/Wooltorton-2006.pdf.

261 **There were 10 million:** Wolfe, Sidney. "Testimony Before Drug Safety and Risk Management/Reproductive Health Drugs Advisory Committees." December 9, 2011. Available at: https://no-more-tears.org/Wolfe-2011.pdf.

262 **The company waited:** "Contraceptive Patch May Raise Blood Clot Risk." Reuters, August 10, 2007. Available at: https://no-more-tears.org/ReutersHealth-2007.pdf.

262 **At an FDA advisory committee meeting:** U.S. Food and Drug Administration, Office of Surveillance and Epidemiology. ARIA Insufficiency Memo. January 13, 2020. Available at: https://no-more-tears.org/FDA-2020.pdf.

CHAPTER 33: THE FDA GOES LOOKING FOR A SAVIOR

265 **Then came the Dalkon Shield:** Mastroianni, Jr., Luigi. "Products Liability and Contraceptive Development." In *Developing New Contraceptives: Obstacles*

and Opportunities, edited by Luigi Mastroianni, Peter J. Donaldson, and Thomas T. Kane. National Academy Press, 1990.

265 **While the FDA put:** O'Reilly, James. "Left to Our Own Devices, What Did We Get Wrong? The Medical Device Amendments of 1976 As Seen from the Insider's View." *Food and Drug Law Journal* 74, no. 1, 2019. 110–27.

266 **Losing patience:** U.S. Food and Drug Administration. "A History of Medical Device Regulation & Oversight in the United States." FDA.gov. Available at: https://no-more-tears.org/FDA-2019.pdf.

266 **To win approval:** Ardaugh, Brent M., Stephen E. Graves, and Rida E. Redberg. "The 510(k) Ancestry of a Metal-on-Metal Hip Implant." *The New England Journal of Medicine* 362, no. 2, January 2013: 97–100.

267 **AdvaMed responded:** Arke, Jane. "FDA Misses Deadline to File Financials for Review." Mesh News Desk, February 24, 2012. Available at: https://no-more-tears.org/Arke-2012.pdf.

267 **FDA's funding-vulnerable:** Llamas, Michelle. "Food and Drug Administration (FDA)." *Drugwatch.* Available at: https://no-more-tears.org/Llamas-PDUFA.pdf.

268 **"As you may have":** Baylor-Henry, Minnie. Email to William Hubbard, subject: "Alex Gorsky." April 4, 2012. Available at: https://no-more-tears.org/FDA-2011b.pdf.

CHAPTER 34: TWO TERRIBLE DILEMMAS

270 **The problem on this Friday:** Goldsmith Andrew. Email to Leanne Turner and Frank Chan, subject: "36mm MoM Friction?" November 10, 2000. DEPUY018132701. Available at: https://no-more-tears.org/Goldsmith-2000.pdf.

271 **For ten months:** Hastings, Cheryl. K00288 Product: Pinnacle Metal-on-Metal Acetabular Cup Liners. 2000. Available at: https://no-more-tears.org/Hastings-2000.pdf.

271 **Worse, any implant:** *Andrews v. DePuy Orthopaedics, Inc.* Trial transcript. November 7, 2016. Available at: https://no-more-tears.org/Andrews-20161107.pdf.

271 **Clinical testing would:** *Andrews v. DePuy Orthopaedics, Inc.* Trial transcript. October 11, 2016. Available at: https://no-more-tears.org/Andrews-20161011.pdf.

LANIER: So let's start out this morning with a pretty simple question, I hope: Why didn't you test the Pinnacle metal-on-metal in people before selling it on the mass market?

EKDAHL: Number of reasons.

Q: Okay. Let's list them.

A: Okay. So, first of all, the— the— there were predicate devices, Ultima and one-piece metal-on-metal that we were comfortable with.

Q: Wait a minute. So the first reason is y'all were comfortable with other devices?

A: Our own predicate devices.

Q: Comfortable with other ones. These are different ones?

A: They're the predicate devices.

Q: Excuse me. These are different devices, right?

A: There are some differences, yes.

Q: Okay. So you were comfortable with different devices. So you didn't feel like you needed to test this one?

A: Devices—

Q: Okay. What were the other reasons you didn't test it before you sold it?

A: There were other metal-on-metal devices in the market that had been performing well.

Q: Okay. So—

A: —in particular—

Q: I didn't mean to interrupt you. I apologize. So because your competitors could make them that work well, you assumed yours would. Is that what I'm hearing?

A: No. I'm saying that there were other devices that worked well that we had tested as well—

Q: Wait. Wait. Wait though. You said Sulzer and I thought you said competitive devices. In other words, your competitors had devices on the market, and you assumed that you could make one that would work as good as theirs. Is that what I'm hearing?

A: Sulzer had a metal-on-metal device—

Q: You're talking about the Metasul?

J & J LAWYER: I don't think he was finished with his answer.

LANIER: I didn't mean to interrupt. Are you talking about Metasul?

EKDAHL: I'm talking about Metasul as a metal-on-metal that was available.

Q: With a poly liner between the metal cup and metal liner?

A: Yes.

Q: So competitors had a product on the market, and you assumed yours would work as well as theirs?

A: Correct.

Q: And did competitors have a 36-millimeter on the market?

A: I believe— I'm going from memory, so forgive me. I believe Biomet had a 36- or 38-millimeter device—

Q: But this—

A: —approved.

Q: But the Sulzer— Look, we'll talk about the competitors in more detail in a minute.

A: Okay.

Q: But just right now let's make a little note on this extra page I'm using. The Sulzer Metasul that you're saying worked well had a— was a different device that had a poly insert in between the cup and liner, right?

A: That's correct.

Q: And it was 28 millimeters. It wasn't the large one that y'all were trying to sell, was it?

A: I believe it was 28 and 32.

Q: And y'all were looking to sell 36, weren't you?

A: Well, we had 28 and 36.

Q: 36 was your principal seller. That was your big market?

A: It was the one mostly prescribed, yes.

Q: Okay. So competitors had some, and so you didn't feel like you needed to test yours because the competitors were selling theirs so surely they had tested theirs?

A: I'm giving you all of the information here.

Q: Yeah. Any other reasons y'all didn't test it?

A: We had significant bench testing, our own wear simulator testing that—

Q: Right. But that's not in people.

A: No. That's correct.

Q: That's not going to tell you what the result of the debris and ions are in people, is it?

A: No. But it's going to help you understand the amount of wear that may or may not be generated.

Q: No question about that. I'm asking about the effects in people. You understand that— that's the concern in the trial, right?

A: I understand.

Q: In other words, your concern is not when you put this in a machine and you do a back and forth same process a million times how much is left in the liquid of the debris; our concern is what effect does the debris and ions have in people when people have it in them. You understand?

A: No, I understand.

Q: All right. So that's my question, is: Why didn't you test it in people? The simulator is not going to give you any results of what the metal ions can do in people, right?

A: That's correct.

Q: Okay.

A: But it's part of the body of evidence that I'm using— I'm answering your question.

Q: Okay. The simulator showed debris. What else? Any other reasons that y'all did not test it in people before you sold it?

A: The— I'm sorry. I'm again going from memory here. I think— The other piece I think that it's important to understand is this is exactly the same process as polyethylene-on-metal—or sorry—the metal-on-polyethylene, the Marathon product.

Q: Wait. You're saying you didn't test the Pinnacle metal-on-metal because you don't test any of your products on people; is that what I'm hearing?

A: No. I'm saying that would be another example— I'm saying that we went through the same process for metal-on-metal as metal-on-poly.

Q: All right. The fourth reason is y'all just don't test any of your products in people?

A: And then I think the final piece is that this is a process that's used for essentially all devices. I guess what I'm saying is we followed the industry norm of testing devices with our predicate devices, looking what our competitors had, using simulator data. We followed that with Marathon. And then overarching all of that, that is industry norm.

Q: Okay. I'm trying to figure out have you just bled through two of them in one or do I need to write them both down? Are you saying that y'all didn't test your other devices either? You didn't test your Marathon so why should you test metal-on-metal? That was a reason? Y'all just don't test your products before you sell them?

A: No.

Q: I mean, should I write that down, we don't test our plastic either? Do you want me to write that down as one of the reasons y'all didn't test it?

A: I'm just saying we didn't test the plastic either.

Q: All right. So don't test a lot of stuff.

A: I wouldn't characterize it like that.

Q: Well, I mean, you had Marathon in multiple sizes. I'm assuming you're saying you didn't test any of that. Am I right?

A: We tested it. We tested it in simulators, we tested it—

Q: In people.

A: So let's— That's correct. We— we did not test it in people.

Q: Okay.

A: But we tested.

Q: And then the fifth reason was you didn't think anybody else tests it. Nobody tests.

A: I'm just saying there is an industry norm around using all of these various tests in predicate devices for new products.

Q: In other words, you're saying nobody tests. Do you really want to say that under oath that nobody tests their products other than—

A: I didn't say.

Q: Okay.

A: You said that. I didn't say that.

Q: All right. Good. Let's cross that out then. Let's don't say nobody tests. Now, don't test a lot of stuff.

A: I disagree with that because we do test.

Q: In people. We're talking about in people. See, I've underlined "in people." That's the only thing I'm asking you.

A: A lot of our products aren't tested in people.

Q: People. Well, then we need to keep that on there. You don't test a lot of your stuff. You just said, "A lot of our products aren't tested in people." So we're going to keep that now, right?

A: In people.

Q: Okay. You understand, I've written this down so we can all see it together. Do you understand I'm asking you why you didn't test it in people? That's the only thing we're concerned about right here. All right?

A: I understand.

Q: So you don't test a lot of your stuff in people, right?

A: That's correct.

Q: All right. Now, simulator showed debris. Competitors had some metal-on-metal products. Of course, all metal-on-metal is not the same, right?

A: That's correct.

Q: All right. We know that all metal-on-metal— In fact, your company made a big deal out of this, telling the world this. All metal-on-metal is not the same, right?

A: That's correct.

Q: In fact, one reason y'all sold your ASR XL here in the U.S. without testing it on people is because you were comfortable with the Pinnacle. And you said ASR and Pinnacle are the same thing, right? For safety and efficacy?

A: I'm not sure. Did I say that? I didn't say that.

Q: Well, the company said that. The company swore to the FDA that ASR had the same safety and efficacy as Pinnacle.

A: I'm not sure what we say.

Q: All right. Well, let's do it this way. Can I suggest to you that maybe you've left out the real reason why? The real reason why is it's all about money?

A: I disagree with your statement, so—

Q: It would have cost y'all money to test and it would have cost you profits and market share to take the time to test the Pinnacle metal-on-metal in people. True?

A: I disagree with you.

Q: Okay. We're going to go through that, and we're going to look at it together then. By the way, to test that— Let me ask you this question: What was the downside to testing it in people? Let's— let's weigh the downside. Can you tell that to the jury, please?

A: I'm not sure what we would have learned.

Q: Okay. So one downside is you don't know that— you don't know the answer to the testing before you test it. Don't know answer before you test it. But that's not a downside. That's why you test it, isn't it? Can you answer that question I just asked, sir?

A: I'm sorry. Can you ask it again?

Q: Yeah. Your suggested answer number one is you don't know the answer that testing might show before you test it. In other words, I don't know what it would have shown. Isn't that why you test something, because you don't know the answer?

A: No, I'm— I'm saying, Mr. Lanier, I don't know what testing we could have done and what it would have shown. I don't— I'm not an expert in that. I don't know how to answer the question, to be candid.

Q: But, sir, if you don't know what the testing will show, you don't know the results of the testing, that's a reason to do the tests, isn't it?

A: I don't even know how to answer that. I apologize.

Q: That's okay. Can you think of any other downside to testing other than you wouldn't know what the testing would be or would show?

A: Off the top of my head I don't know how to answer the question. I apologize.

Q: Well, there are other reasons— a downside to testing. One is you'll lose market share because you've got competitors that are beating you out there. Right?

A: I don't think so, no.

Q: You don't think you would lose market share?

A: No.

Q: And you would lose profits that come from that selling?

A: I disagree.

271 **So the company faced:** *Andrews v. DePuy Orthopaedics, Inc.* Trial transcript. November 3, 2016. Available at: https://no-more-tears.org/Andrews-20161103.pdf.

LANIER: So y'all changed the clearance and didn't tell the truth to the FDA. Correct?

TURNER: No.

Q: Ma'am, y'all changed the clearance?

A: We did change the clearance.

Q: You changed the clearance in the countdown, didn't you?

A: We changed the clearance.

Q: And you didn't tell the FDA you changed the clearance, did you?

A: We told them we had the same effective radius.

LANIER: Objection, nonresponsive.

JUDGE: Sustained.

LANIER: Ma'am, do you know the difference between "clearance" and "effective radius"?

TURNER: Yes.

Q: Answer my question about the clearance then. Okay? And don't pivot to the effective radius.

A: I'm just trying to tell the whole truth here. I'm sorry.

Q: Okay. Well, the whole truth starts with answering the question, ma'am, so answer the question. Do you need Pam to read it back?

A: Did we mention the clearance? No, we did not mention a change in the clearance, if that was the question.

Q: Yes, ma'am. Because the jury got to hear from you and Mr. Quattlebaum talking about your submission to the FDA. Do you remember that?

A: Yes.

Q: And you never showed 'em the chart that y'all gave to the FDA, did you?

A: I don't remember if we showed the chart or not.

Q: Because there was a chart, wasn't there?

A: Yes. The chart I referenced.

Q: Defendant's Exhibit 467. This is what you gave to the FDA, isn't it?

A: Yes.

Q: The FDA has a device description, and it's got articulation requirements. Do you see that?

A: Yes.

Q: And we've got a column here for the 28-millimeter and we've got a column here for the 36-millimeter. Correct?

A: Yes.

Q: So we can see the 28-millimeter, 40 to 80 microns clearance. Do you see that?

A: Yes.

Q: And this is what you swore to or verified to the FDA.

A: It was part of a document, yes, an affidavit that I signed, yes.

Q: And then for the 36-millimeter you swore to the answer being the same, even though the truth of the matter is it wasn't. Correct?

A: Based on the date of that document, that is the correct information. The wrong table with the date of the 13th was not submitted.

LANIER: Objection, nonresponsive.

JUDGE: Sustained.

LANIER: Ask the witness be instructed to answer, please, Your Honor.

JUDGE: Answer the question, please, ma'am.

TURNER: I'm sorry, can you please repeat the question?

LANIER: Yes, ma'am. What you gave to the FDA was false?

A: Inconsistent. This table is incorrect information.

Q: That's what—

A: Yes.

Q: "False," you know what it means. Ma'am—

A: Yes.

Q: —do you know what false means?

A: Yes.

Q: It means not true; incorrect; or wrong, is the primary meaning. Do you see that?

A: Yes.

Q: So this was false by the primary meaning of the word, wasn't it?

A: That is, yes.

Q: So you gave false information to the FDA.

272 **Hip and knee replacements:** Bucholz, Robert W. "Indications, Techniques and Results of Total Hip Replacement in the United States." *Revista Médica Clínica Las Condes* 25, no. 5, September 2014: 756–59. Available at: https://no-more-tears.org/Bucholz-2014.pdf.

272 **In 1998, Johnson & Johnson:** Winslow, Ron. "Johnson & Johnson Agrees to Buy DePuy for $3.5 Billion." *The Wall Street Journal,* July 22, 1998. Available at: https://no-more-tears.org/Winslow-1998.pdf.

272 **With J & J's financial muscle:** Wentworth, Steve. Memo to "File," subject: "FDA Telecom for the One-Piece MOM Hip IDE." March 2, 1999. DEPUY081804758. Available at: https://no-more-tears.org/Wentworth-1999.pdf.

272 **Manufacturers started making:** Powers, Cara C., et al. "A Comparison of a Second- and a Third-Generation Modular Cup Design: Is New Improved?" *Journal of Arthroplasty* 25, no. 4, June 2010: 514–21.

272 **in the early 1960s:** Learmonth, Ian D. "The Rise and Fall of Large Bone Metal-on-Metal Hip Prostheses." *South African Orthopaedic Journal* 13, no. 3, Spring 2014: 21–27. Available at: https://no-more-tears.org/Learmonth-2014.pdf.

272 **Friction between the cup:** Munemoto, Mitsuru, et al. "The Pathology of Failed Mckee-Farrar Implants: Correlation with Modern Metal-on-Metal-Implant Failure." *Journal of Material Science: Material Medicine* 28, no 5, article 66, May 2017. Available at: https://no-more-tears.org/Munemoto-2017.pdf.

273 **Despite this disaster:** DePuy Synthes. "Project Title: Metal on Metal." Octo-

ber 10, 1994. DEPUY063303840. Available at: https://no-more-tears.org/DePuy
-1994.pdf.

273 **a 1995 internal memo:** Isaac, Graham. "End Game: The Failure of Total Hip
Replacement." 1995. DEPUY050669539. Available at: https://no-more-tears
.org/Isaac-1995.pdf.

273 **But incremental changes:** DePuy Synthes. "Project Approval Form; Project
Title: Alternate Bearing Project." February 12, 1995. DEPUY063303838. Available at: https://no-more-tears.org/DePuy-1995.pdf.

273 **On Monday, November 13:** Hastings, Cheryl. *K00288 Product.*

274 **For two months:** Johnson, Janet. Email to Leanne Turner, subject: "FW: Ulta-
met." September 14, 2001. DEPUY018128995. Available at: https://no-more
-tears.org/Johnson-2001.pdf.

274 **On December 2, 2004:** DePuy Synthes. K040627: DePuy ASR Modular Acetabular Cup System. 2004. Available at: https://no-more-tears.org/DePuy
-2004.pdf.

274 **This time, the company:** Hastings, Cheryl. Email to Pam Plouhar, subject:
"Regulatory Concerns." September 10, 2004. DEPUY-R-006793071. Available
at: https://no-more-tears.org/Hastings-2004.pdf.

274 **On May 23, 2005:** Heck, Natalie. Letter to the FDA, subject: "510(k): Premarket Notification." July 29, 2005. DEPUY011611588. Available at: https://no
-more-tears.org/Depuy-2005.pdf.

275 **A later FDA review:** Dover, Carl. "GMB Warsaw FDA 483 Update." September 19, 2011. DEPUY033707544. Available at: https://no-more-tears.org
/DePuy-2011.pdf.

275 **A later FDA review:** DePuy Synthes. "Risk Management Audit: Summary of
Findings." 2008. DEPUY013595955. Available at: https://no-more-tears.org
/DePuy-2008.pdf.

275 **These problems led to:** DePuy Synthes. "The US JTE Complaint Crisis."
2008. DEPUY011029636. Available at: https://no-more-tears.org/DePuy
-2008b.pdf.

276 **During an October 2016:** *Andrews v. DePuy Orthopaedics, Inc.* Trial transcript.
October 25, 2016. Available at: https://no-more-tears.org/Andrews-20161025
.pdf.

LANIER: Well, option 1 was "Continually grow the complaint department to
match the upward trend." Y'all did not choose option 1, and you never grew
the complaint department out of this, did you?

PLOUHAR: I— I would— I think I disagree.

Q: You think you did?

A: I think I— I disagree, yes.

Q: Are you suggesting that the two Kelley temps were the growth of the
department, complaint department, not adequately resourced? Use of Kelley
temps in permanent roles.

A: That's what the document says. I think that was a statement of what the
current state of the department was.

Q: So option 2, you don't think y'all chose. Ma'am, isn't it appalling that
y'all would even put down as an option to retrain the sales force not to report
every revision? Isn't that appalling?

A: It's an option. I think that we were trying to identify what the options were.

Q: Ma'am, that's like, "I'm going to have trouble paying my bills this month, all right, let me look at the options. One option is I can rob a bank." I mean, who sits there and looks at those options? There's some things that should be off the table, right?

A: I would agree, but I don't think that— I think that they were just putting what the options were.

CHAPTER 35: GOD, NAZIS, AND HIP IMPLANTS

277 **J & J / DePuy paid an $84.7 million fine:** Steffen, Joan E., et al. "Grave Fraudulence in Medical Device Research: A Narrative Review of the PIN Seeding Study for the Pinnacle Hip System." *Accountability in Research* 25, no. 1, 2018: 37–66. Available at: https://no-more-tears.org/Steffen-2017.pdf.

278 **PIN was conceived by:** DePuy Synthes. "Hip Business Unit Annual CRC Review Agenda." May 12, 2006. DEPUY046258123. Available at: https://no -more-tears.org/DePuy-2006.pdf.

278 **email dated June 5, 2000:** Schnieders, Barry. Email to Alan Cornell et al., subject: "Pinnacle Clinical Research Strategy." June 5, 2000. DEPUY048359419. Available at: https://no-more-tears.org/Schnieders-2000.pdf.

279 **Another company document:** DePuy Synthes. "10 Commandments of GCP for the Investigator." DEPUY047572074. Available at: https://no-more-tears .org/DEPUY047572074.pdf.

279 **So J & J referenced both Nazis:** DePuy Synthes. "Cross-Sectional, Multi-Center Evaluation of 8-Year Metal Ion Trends for Pinnacle MoM System used in Primary Total Hip Arthroplasty." November 21, 2014. DEPUY091757626. Available at: https://no-more-tears.org/DePuy-2014.pdf.

279 **Not one PIN patient:** *Andrews v. DePuy Orthopaedics, Inc.* Trial transcript. October 17, 2016. Available at: https://no-more-tears.org/Aoki-20161017.pdf.

279 **Four study sites never:** Steffen et al., *"Grave Fraudulence in Medical Device Research."*

279 **Someone crossed out the name:** DePuy Synthes. "Release of Medical Records: Pinnacle Study." August 29, 2001. DEPUY090308452. Available at: https://no-more-tears.org/DePuy-2001.pdf.

279 **J & J / DePuy started becoming more insistent:** Chan, Amy. Letter to Terry Jo Bala, subject: "Pinnacle Study Folders." June 15, 2001. DEPUY048357086. Available at: https://no-more-tears.org/Chan-2001b.pdf.

279 **One is the arrival:** *Andrews v. DePuy Orthopaedics, Inc.* Trial transcript. October 20, 2016. Available at: https://no-more-tears.org/Aoki-20161020.pdf.

280 **"The Board was primarily":** Mayo Clinic. "Multicenter, Prospective, Clinical Evaluation of Pinnacle Acetabular Implants in Total Hip Arthroplasty." May 3, 2002. Available at: https://no-more-tears.org/Mayo-Clinic-2002.pdf.

280 **they're dropping like flies!:** Chan, Amy. Email to John Reviere and Debbie Miller, subject: "More $$$." May 22, 2002. DEPUY045590629. Available at: https://no-more-tears.org/Chan-2002.pdf.

280 **The IRB at Baptist:** Joyce, Michael. Letter to Dr. Steven Lancaster, subject: "IRC #05-52, DePuy, 'Multi-Center, Prospective, Clinical Evaluation of Pinnacle Acetabular Implants in Total Hip Arthroplasty.'" September 14, 2005. Available at: https://no-more-tears.org/Joyce-2005.pdf.

281 **Lancaster told the Baptist:** Lancaster, Steven. Letter to Michael Joyce, subject: "IRC #05-52 DePuy, 'Multicenter, Prospective, Clinical Evaluation of Pinnacle Acetabular Implants and Total Hip Arthroplasty.'" September 20, 2005. DEPUY048360927. Available at: https://no-more-tears.org/Lancaster-2005.pdf.

281 **But in an email:** Lancaster, Steven. Email to Marilyn Cassell, subject: "Re: Conversation w/ Dr. Joyce." October 26, 2005. DEPUY048360797. Available at: https://no-more-tears.org/Lancaster-2005b.pdf.

281 **Lancaster subsequently admitted:** Lancaster, Steven. Videotaped deposition of Steven Lancaster. August 13, 2015. Available at: https://no-more-tears.org/Lancaster-2015.pdf.

281 **Having gathered the results: :** DePuy Synthes, *"Midterm Survival of the Pinnacle Multi-Liner."*

281 **The poster made five false claims:** DePuy Synthes. Midterm Survival of the Pinnacle Multi-Liner—Acetabular Cup in a Prospective Multi-Center Study. 2007. DEPUY006791359. Available at: https://no-more-tears.org/DePuy-2007.pdf.

282 **In sworn testimony:** Steffen et al., *"Grave Fraudulence in Medical Device Research."*

282 **In trial testimony:** *Andrews v. DePuy Orthopaedics, Inc.* Trial transcript. October 17, 2016. Available at: https://no-more-tears.org/Aoki-20161017.pdf.

LANIER: You're saying that the doctor sat on it and didn't give the information to the company. Is that what you're saying?

PLOUHAR: We did not have the case report forms.

Q: I'm sorry, ma'am, is that what you're saying?

A: I'm saying that they were not reported to the company.

Q: You understand some of these doctors that y'all claim wrote this paper (indicating) are the same doctors that you're saying sat on the information and didn't give it to you.

A: I'm saying that we did not have all the case report forms.

LANIER: Objection, nonresponsive.

JUDGE: Sustained.

PLOUHAR: We had not received the case report forms from the sites.

LANIER: Ma'am, that still wasn't my question. I said you understand the doctors that you say wrote this paper are some of the very doctors that you're now saying they never told us about the data.

A: I'd have to look in detail at the case reports. I don't know which surgeons submitted the case report forms. I know—

Q: Dr. Barrett was one of them?

A: Yes. Dr. Barrett was one.

Q: So Dr. Barrett himself, if he truly wrote this paper, you sure would think he doesn't have the excuse of saying, well, I didn't know that I'd revised that hip?

A: I don't know. You would have to talk to Dr. Barrett.

Q: I mean, but you're sitting here telling— By the way, you won't agree this was ghostwritten, even though y'all ghostwrote it?

A: It was not ghostwritten.

Q: Yeah. You think Dr. Barrett actually wrote this paper?

A: He participated in it.

Q: He didn't write a word of this paper, did he?

A: He participated in it.

Q: By participated, you're telling us he hid his revisions from you?

A: No.

Q: Did y'all know about his revisions?

A: We knew that he had a case that had been revised for infection.

Q: Did y'all know about the other revisions, or did your investigators hide 'em from you?

A: I don't think that they were hiding them from us. Sometimes it just takes time to get data.

CHAPTER 36: NEVER STOP MOVING

285 **Titled "Never Stop Moving":** Tandy, Marlene K. Letter to Christine Haas, subject: "Never Stop Moving—Advertisement: OTC Medical Device Advertising." July 23, 2008. DEPUY094109770. Available at: https://no-more-tears .org/Tandy-2008.pdf.

285 **"Thanks to his DePuy Hip replacements":** Berman, Paul. Email to DePuy Office Managers, et al., subject: "DePuy Print Ads." October 17, 2008. DEPUY000481474. Available at: https://no-more-tears.org/Berman-2008.pdf.

285 **The TV ads were complemented:** DePuy Synthes. "Never Stop Moving: 2008 Direct-to-consumer Campaign." 2008. DCMED000057585. Available at: https://no-more-tears.org/DePuy-2008c.pdf.

286 **By then, Pinnacle had already:** Ekdahl, Andrew. Email to Paul Berman, subject: "RE: Summit $100 Million and Summit/Pinnacle $1 Billion." October 13, 2007. DEPUY000458100. Available at: https://no-more-tears.org/Ekdahl -2007.pdf.

286 **In March 2008:** Pandit, H., et al. "Pseudotumours Associated with Metal-on-Metal Hip Resurfacings." *The Journal of Bone and Joint Surgery,* British vol. 90, no. 7, July 2008: 847–51. Available at: https://no-more-tears.org/Pandit-2008.pdf.

286 **In July, surgeons:** Donell, S. T., et al. "Early Failure of the Ultima Metal-on-Metal Total Hip Replacement in the Presence of Normal Plain Radiographs." *The Journal of Bone and Joint Surgery,* British vol. 92, no. 11, November 2010: 1501–08.

287 **In September, the Hip Society:** Rhee, Michael. Email to Paul Berman, subject: "Hip Society Meeting Update w/T Schmalzried." September 26, 2008. DEPUY003502811. Available at: https://no-more-tears.org/Rhee-2008.pdf.

287 **There was also:** Schmalzried, Thomas. Email to Michael Rhee, subject: "Update." September 4, 2008. DEPUY000487131. Available at: https://no-more -tears.org/Schmalzried-2008.pdf.

288 **Internally, this was:** Berman, Paul. Email to Derek Edgar, subject: "Re: DePuy

Revision Hips." April 1, 2009. MICA000023458. Available at: https://no-more
-tears.org/Berman-2009.pdf.

288 **The company got to profit:** *Andrews v. DePuy Orthopaedics, Inc.* Trial transcript. October 11, 2016. Available at: https://no-more-tears.org/Andrews
-20161011.pdf.

LANIER: If I buy a, I don't know, if I buy an iPhone and it doesn't work or a
Galaxy phone and it catches on fire and I take it back and they swap it for one
that works, y'all don't swap it for one that works, y'all sell 'em another one,
don't you?

A: Yes.

Q: So everyone that has the metal-on-metal revision just needs a new one
just buys it from you. That's the system you've got, right?

A: I disagree. They could buy it from everybody. They could buy all the
parts.

Q: Sir, you know there's a lot involved in cutting out this cup?

A: Yes.

Q: This cup's got this real weird-looking rough stuff on the back because it
truly grows straight into the bone, doesn't it?

A: Yeah. The bone grows into it.

Q: So surgeons don't take these things out lightly. That involves destroying
bone and doing a whole lot of work, right?

A: Correct.

Q: But y'all have come up with a system where the surgeon doesn't have to
take it out. He just pops out the metal liner, pops off the metal ball, puts on a
new ball, puts in a poly liner, and life goes on.

A: Yeah. Modularity is in demand from surgeons.

288 **Half of the company's hips revenues:** Berman, Paul. Email to Steve Corbett,
subject: "RE: aSphere Prioritization." August 20, 2008. DEPUY000491418.
Available at: https://no-more-tears.org/Berman-2008b.pdf.

289 **After the second meeting:** Johnson & Johnson. "ASR XL Situation Assessment: 2nd Meeting." 2010. DEPUY009975544. Available at: https://no-more
-tears.org/JJ-ASRXL.pdf.

289 **Dr. Jack Irving:** Irving, John. Email to Philipkar@aol.com, Dom Dinardo,
and Paul Berman, subject: "MOM." June 23, 2010. DEPUY000551879. Available at: https://no-more-tears.org/Irving-2010.pdf.

289 **Since he had been:** Irving, John. Letter to Paul Berman. 2010. p.
DEPUY063019852. Available at: https://no-more-tears.org/Irving-2010B.pdf.

290 **"They tried to suggest ideas":** *Andrews v. DePuy Orthopaedics, Inc.* Trial transcript. October 12, 2016. Available at: https://no-more-tears.org/Andrews
-20161012.pdf.

290 **Several weeks before:** *Medical Device Business Services, Inc. v. United States.*
Respondents' brief in opposition to petition for writ of certiorari. March 9,
2018. No 17-11082018. Available at: https://no-more-tears.org/Starr-2018.pdf.

291 **Several months later:** U.S. Food and Drug Administration. Hearing before
the of the Center for Devices and Radiological Health Medical Devices Advisory Committee, Orthopaedic and Rehabilitation Devices Panel. June 27,
2012. Available at: https://no-more-tears.org/FDA-2012.pdf.

292 **Australian health authorities:** de Steiger, Richard N., *et al.* "Five-Year Results of the ASR XL Acetabular System and the ASR Hip Resurfacing System: An Analysis from the Australian Orthopaedic Association National Joint Replacement Registry." *Journal of Bone and Joint Surgery,* American vol. 93, no. 24, December 2021: 2287–93.

292 **J & J / DePuy stopped selling Pinnacle:** Meier, Barry. "J.&J. Unit Phasing Out All-Metal Hip Devices." *The New York Times,* May 16, 2013. Available at: https://no-more-tears.org/Meier-2013.pdf.

292 **for $2.5 billion:** Rockoff, Jonathan D. "J&J to Pay at Least $2.5 Billion in Hip Settlement." *The Wall Street Journal,* November 19, 2013. Available at: https://no-more-tears.org/Rockoff-2013.pdf.

CHAPTER 37: A CURE FOR SAG

293 **Jill Mesigian was:** Fair, Matt. "J&J Hit with $80M Verdict in Philly Mesh Case." *Law360,* May 17, 2019. Available at: https://no-more-tears.org/Fair-2019.pdf.

293 **"I feel like I'm being ripped apart":** *Mesigian v. Ethicon, Inc.* Trial transcript. May 1, 2019. Available at: https://no-more-tears.org/Mesigian-20190501.pdf.

294 **Bladders often press against:** Cardozo, Linda, and David Staskin, eds. *Textbook of Female Urology and Urogynecology, Fourth Edition.* Two-volume set. CRC Press, 2016.

294 **This is called pelvic:** Yukhananov, Anna, and Randsell Pierson. "J & J to Stop Selling Controversial Vaginal Implants." Reuters, June 6, 2012. Available at: https://no-more-tears.org/Yukhananov-2012.pdf.

295 **The first pelvic mesh:** Llamas, Michelle. "Transvaginal Mesh Recalls & Discontinued Products." *Drugwatch.* 2020. Available at: https://no-more-tears.org/Llamas-2020.pdf.

295 **Among the largest manufacturers:** *Hrymoc v. Ethicon, Inc.* Decision on appeal. March 2, 2021. Available at: https://no-more-tears.org/Sabatino-2021.pdf.

297 **Citing Klinge's and others':** Akre, Jane. "Day 11: Linda Gross v Ethicon: Medical Director Signs Off on Prolift." Mesh News Desk, January 26, 2013. Available at: https://no-more-tears.org/Akre-2013.pdf.

297 **In 2002, the same:** *State of West Virginia v. Johnson & Johnson et al.* Complaint. Available at: https://no-more-tears.org/WestVirginiaComplaint.pdf.

298 **So the company hired:** *Hrymoc v. Ethicon, Inc.* Decision on appeal. March 2, 2021. Available at: https://no-more-tears.org/Sabatino-2021.pdf.

298 **email dated July 19, 2003:** *Gross v. Genecare.* Decision on appeal. March 29, 2016. Available at: https://no-more-tears.org/Gross-Gynecare.pdf.

299 **That same month:** Milani, Rodolfo, et al. "Functional and Anatomical Outcome of Anterior and Posterior Vaginal Prolapse Repair with Prolene Mesh." *BJOG* 112, January 2005: 107–111. Available at: https://no-more-tears.org/Milani-2005.pdf.

299 **The French team:** *Gross v. Genecare.* Decision on appeal. March 29, 2016. Available at: https://no-more-tears.org/Gross-Gynecare.pdf.

299 **"Early clinical experience":** Huntley, Alyssa. "J & J Faces Yet Another Mar-

keting Suit, This Time from the State of Kentucky." *Fierce Biotech,* August 17, 2016. Available at: https://no-more-tears.org/Huntley-2016.pdf.

300 **Scott Ciarrocca, a top:** Cowen, Richard. "Pelvic Mesh Case Gets Technical in Bergen Courtroom." NorthJersey.com, 2017. Available at: https://no-more-tears.org/Cowen-2017.pdf.

300 **"I would like that":** *California v. Johnson & Johnson, Inc. et al.* Statement of decision. May 24, 2016. Available at: https://no-more-tears.org/Sturgeon-2016.pdf.

302 **St. Hilaire responded:** Arke, Jane. "Grey Haze over Lake of the Ozarks as Prolift Pelvic Mesh Death Case Begins." Mesh News Desk, January 7, 2015. Available at: https://no-more-tears.org/Arke-2015.pdf.

304 **Several months after:** Caquant, Fréderic, et al. "Safety of Trans Vaginal Mesh Procedure: Retrospective Study of 684 Patients." *Journal of Obstetrics and Gynaecology Research* 34, no. 4, August 2008: 449–56.

CHAPTER 38: "USUALLY MINOR AND WELL MANAGEABLE"

305 **But in July 2011:** Anger, Jennifer T., and Karyn S. Eilber. *The Use of Robotic Technology in Female Pelvic Floor Reconstruction.* Springer, 2017.

305 **The trial was halted:** Iglesia, Cheryl B., et al. "Vaginal Mesh for Prolapse: A Randomized Controlled Trial." *Obstetrics & Gynecology* 116, no. 2, part 1, August 2010: 293–303.

306 **In 2010, at least:** Llamas, Michelle. "Transvaginal Mesh Verdicts and Settlements." *Drugwatch,* 2021. Available at: https://no-more-tears.org/Llamas-2021.pdf.

306 **In August 2011:** Carome, Michael, et al. "Petition to Ban Surgical Mesh for Transvaginal Repair of Pelvic Organ Prolapse." *Public Citizen,* August 25, 2011. Available at: https://no-more-tears.org/Carome-2011.pdf.

307 **In January 2012:** Sarvestani, Arezu. "FDA Probes JNJ, Bard and Others on Transvaginal Mesh Risks." *MassDevice,* January 5, 2012. Available at: https://no-more-tears.org/Sarvestani-2012.pdf.

308 **In 2018, the Australian:** Commonwealth of Australia Senate, Community Affairs References Committee. Transvaginal Mesh Implants and Related Matters. August 3, 2017. Available at: https://no-more-tears.org/Australia-2017.pdf.

308 **In 2007, J & J:** Steffen, Joan E., et al. "Grave Fraudulence in Medical Device Research: A Narrative Review of the PIN Seeding Study for the Pinnacle Hip System." *Accountability in Research* 25, no. 1, 2018: 37–66. Available at: https://no-more-tears.org/Steffen-2017.pdf.

CHAPTER 39: A RARE SHOT AT REDEMPTION

314 **"Good afternoon, everyone":** "Biden Holds White House Event with Vaccine Makers Johnson & Johnson and Merck." Transcript. March 10, 2021. Available at: https://no-more-tears.org/Gorsky-2021.pdf.

315 **On August 26, 2019:** *State of Oklahoma v. Johnson & Johnson et al.* Judgment

after non-jury trial. Available at: https://no-more-tears.org/Oklahoma-2019.pdf.

317 **"I want to thank":** The White House. "Remarks by President Biden at Event with the CEOs of Johnson & Johnson and Merck." Whitehouse.gov, March 10, 2021. Available at: https://no-more-tears.org/Biden-2021.pdf.

317 **Of the company's seven:** Brill, Steven. *America's Most Admired Lawbreaker.* Chapter 10: "Chess, at $1,000 an Hour." *The Huffington Post,* Fall 2015.

318 **Another huge seller in 2003:** MassDevice. "Drug-Eluting Stent Sales Down 31 Percent at Johnson & Johnson." *The Massachusetts Medical Devices Journal,* January 25, 2011. Available at: https://no-more-tears.org/MassDevice-2011.pdf.

318 **Yet another problematic drug:** Terhune, Chad, and Robin Respaut. "As Red Flags Multiplied, Johnson & Johnson Kept Quiet on Popular Diabetes Drug." Reuters, December 8, 2021. Available at: https://no-more-tears.org/Terhune-2021b.pdf; Respaut, Robin, Chad Terhune, and Deborah J. Nelson. "Drug-makers Pushed Aggressive Diabetes Therapy. Patients Paid the Price." Reuters, November 4, 2021. Available at: https://no-more-tears.org/Respaut-2021.pdf.

318 **In March 2014:** Terhune, Chad, and Robert Respaut. "J & J Kept Quiet on Popular Diabetes Drug as Red Flags Multiplied." Reuters, December 8, 2021. Available at: https://no-more-tears.org/Terhune-2021.pdf.

318 **Ketoacidosis and related reactions:** Lieberman, Trudy. "This Powerful Series on Diabetes from Reuters Lays Bare Our Health System's Gravest Faults." USC Annenberg Center for Health Journalism, December 13, 2021. Available at: https://no-more-tears.org/Lieberman-2021.pdf.

318 **But managers decided against:** Terhune, Chad, and Robert Respaut. "J&J Kept Quiet on Popular Diabetes Drug as Red Flags Multiplied." Reuters, December 8, 2021. Available at: https://no-more-tears.org/Terhune-2021.pdf.

318 **The next year:** Compton, Kristin. "Invokana Amputation." *Drugwatch,* 2021. Available at: https://no-more-tears.org/Compton-2021.pdf.

319 **Again and again and again:** Terhune, Chad, and Robert Respaut. "J&J Kept Quiet on Popular Diabetes Drug as Red Flags Multiplied." Reuters, December 8, 2021. Available at: https://no-more-tears.org/Terhune-2021.pdf.

320 **On January 10, 2020:** Zimmer, Carl. "Inside Johnson & Johnson's Nonstop Hunt for a Coronavirus Vaccine." *The New York Times,* July 17, 2020. Available at: https://no-more-tears.org/Zimmer-2020.pdf.

323 **J & J was so confident:** Herper, Matthew. "The Tragedy of Johnson & Johnson's Covid Vaccine." STAT, December 17, 2021. Available at: https://no-more-tears.org/Herper-2021.pdf.

323 **The most concerning:** Gresele, Paolo, et al. "Interactions of Adenoviruses with Platelets and Coagulation and the Vaccine-Induced Immune Thrombotic Thrombocytopenia Syndrome." *Haematologica* 106, no. 12, December 2021: 3034–45.

324 **So, in April 2020:** Hamby, Chris. "U.S. Authorities Seek Documents from Troubled Covid Vaccine Manufacturer." *The New York Times,* July 30, 2021. Available at: https://no-more-tears.org/Hamby-2021.pdf.

325 **Audits and investigations:** LaFraniere, Sharon, and Noah Weiland. "The F.D.A. Tells Johnson & Johnson That About 60 Million Doses Made at a Troubled Plant Cannot Be Used." *The New York Times,* July 12, 2021. Available at: https://no-more-tears.org/LaFraniere-2021b.pdf.

325 **Johnson & Johnson's auditors identified:** Rowland, Christopher. "Johnson & Johnson Documented Contamination Risks at Baltimore Plant Months Before Vaccine Was Ruined." *The Washington Post,* May 19, 2021. Available at: https://no-more-tears.org/Rowland-2021.pdf.

325 **Among them: "The site":** LaFraniere, Sharon, Sheryl Gay Stolberg, and Chris Hamby. "Federal Inspectors Fear More Vaccines Were Exposed to Contamination." *The New York Times,* May 12, 2021. Available at: https://no-more-tears.org/LaFraniere-2021.pdf.

327 **As the talks were underway:** Stolberg, Sheryl, Chris Hamby, and Sharon LaFraniere. "Emergent Hid Evidence of Covid Vaccine Problems at Plant, Report Says." *The New York Times,* May 10, 2022. Available at: https://no-more-tears.org/Stolberg-2022.pdf.

328 **California officials announced:** LaFraniere Sharon, Noah Weiland, and Jennifer Steinhauer. "Plunging Johnson & Johnson Vaccine Supply Dents State Inoculation Efforts." *The New York Times,* April 20, 2021. Available at: https://no-more-tears.org/LaFraniere-2021d.pdf.

328 **Two weeks later:** LaFraniere, Sharon, and Noah Weiland. "F.D.A. Attaches Warning of Rare Nerve Syndrome to Johnson & Johnson Vaccine." *The New York Times,* August 25, 2021. Available at: https://no-more-tears.org/LaFraniere-2021c.pdf.

328 **the Centers for Disease Control and Prevention:** Erman, Michael. "CDC Recommends Moderna, Pfizer COVID-19 Vaccines Over J&J's." Reuters, December 16, 2021. Available at: https://no-more-tears.org/Erman-2021.pdf.

331 **Gorsky and his predecessor:** Johnson & Johnson. *2002 Annual Report: Delivering in the Promise of Technology.* 2003. Available at: https://no-more-tears.org/JJ-2002.pdf.

331 **The paper lauded:** Rockoff, Jonathan D. "J & J's Gorsky to Leave as CEO, Duato to Take Helm." *The Wall Street Journal,* August 19, 2021. Available at: https://no-more-tears.org/Rockoff-2021.pdf.

332 **On November 12, 2021:** "Johnson & Johnson Chairman & CEO Alex Gorsky Speaks with CNBC's 'Squawk Box' Today." Unofficial transcript. CNBC, November 12, 2021. Available at: https://no-more-tears.org/CNBC-2021.pdf.

332 **Iconic products like:** Robbins, Rebecca, and Michael J. de la Merced. "Johnson & Johnson, Iconic Company Under Pressure, Plans to Split in Two." *The New York Times,* November 12, 2021. Available at: https://no-more-tears.org/Robbins-2021.pdf.

332 **But that was just:** Randles, Jonathan. "Judge Backs J & J Talc Bankruptcy, Keeping Cancer Lawsuits Frozen." *The Wall Street Journal,* February 25, 2022. Available at: https://no-more-tears.org/Randles-2022.pdf.

332 **A complete consumer spin-off:** *Hill v. Johnson & Johnson et al.* Shareholder derivative complaint. January 23, 2020. Available at: https://no-more-tears.org/Hill-2020.pdf.

333 **On May 4, 2023:** Constantino, Annika Kim. "J & J's Consumer-Health Spinoff Kenvue Jumps 22% in Public Market Debut." CNBC, May 4, 2023. Available at: https://no-more-tears.org/CNBC-2023.pdf.

334 **Its budget largely underwritten:** Hilzenrath, David Z. "Drug Money: FDA Depends on Industry Funding; Money Comes with 'Strings Attached.'" Proj-

ect on Government Oversight, December 1, 2016. Available at: https://no
-more-tears.org/Hilzenrath-2016.pdf.

334 **"You know, if you listen":** *Rankin et al. v. Janssen Pharmaceutica et al.* Trial
transcript. September 6, 2001. Available at: https://no-more-tears.org/Propulsid
-20010906.pdf.

334 **But Propulsid could:** American Association for Justice. *They Knew and Failed
To . . . : True Stories of Corporations That Knew Their Products Were Dangerous,
Sometimes Deadly.* Report 2014. Available at: https://no-more-tears.org/AAJ.pdf.

335 **The drug was especially:** Harris, Gardiner, and Eric Koli. "Lucrative Drug,
Danger Signals and the F.D.A." *The New York Times,* June 10, 2005. Available
at: https://no-more-tears.org/Harris-2005.pdf.

335 **J & J nonetheless quietly:** Saul, Stephanie. "Senators Ask Drug Giant to Explain Grants to Doctors." *The New York Times,* July 6, 2005. Available at:
https://no-more-tears.org/Saul-2005.pdf.

335 **the most troubling document:** Harris, Gardiner, and Eric Koli. "Lucrative
Drug, Danger Signals and the F.D.A." *The New York Times,* June 10, 2005.
Available at: https://no-more-tears.org/Harris-2005.pdf.

335 **As one baby after another died:** Sukkari, Sana R., and Larry D. Sasich. "Cisapride and Patient Information Leaflets." *Canadian Medical Association Journal*
164, no. 9, May 2001: 1276–68. Available at: https://no-more-tears.org/Sukkari
-2001.pdf; Associated Press. "FDA Issues Heartburn Drug Warning for Propulsid."
1998; "FDA Tells Doctors to Use Heartburn Drug As Last Resort." *British Medical
Journal* 320, no. 7231, February 2000: 336. Available at: https://no-more-tears.org/
BMJ-2000.pdf; Kaufman, Marc. "Heartburn Drug Linked to 70 Deaths: FDA
Warning Outlines Dangers of Propulsid." *The Washington Post,* January 25, 2000.
Available at: https://no-more-tears.org/Kaufman-2000.pdf; Neergaard, Lauran.
"Is Propulsid Safe for Babies?" Associated Press. February 7, 2000.

335 **J & J finally withdrew Propulsid:** Harris, Gardiner, and Eric Koli. "Lucrative
Drug, Danger Signals and the F.D.A." *The New York Times,* June 10, 2005.
Available at: https://no-more-tears.org/Harris-2005.pdf.

336 **This false mythology:** *Janssen Pharmaceuticals, Inc. v. A.Y. et al.* Petition for
writ of certiorari. January 29, 2021. Available at: https://no-more-tears.org
/Risperdal-Petition.pdf.

336 **FDA regulations:** Vladeck, David C. "The Difficult Case of Direct-to-Consumer
Drug Advertising." *Loyola of Los Angeles Law Review* 41, no. 1, September 2007:
259–95. Available at: https://no-more-tears.org/Vladeck-2007.pdf.

337 **In the summer of 2005:** Government Accountability Office. *Prescription
Drugs: Improvements Needed in FDA's Oversight of Direct-to-Consumer Advertising.* November 2006. Available at: https://no-more-tears.org/GAO-2007.pdf.

337 **But for doctors:** Smalley, Walter, et al. "Contraindicated Use of Cisapride:
Impact of Food and Drug Administration Regulatory Action." *JAMA* 284,
no. 23, December 2000: 3036–39. Available at: https://no-more-tears.org
/Smalley-2000.pdf.

337 **Dr. Kevin K. Howe:** *Andrews v. DePuy Orthopaedics, Inc.* Trial transcript. November 2, 2016. Available at: https://no-more-tears.org/Andrews-20161102.pdf.

337 **Prescriptions of newly introduced medicines:** Häuser, Winifred, et al. "Is
Europe Also Facing an Opioid Crisis? A Survey of European Pain Federation

Chapters." *European Journal of Pain* 25, no. 8, September 2021: 1760–69. Available at: https://no-more-tears.org/Hauser-2020.pdf.

337 **And since patent terms:** Kliff, Sarah. "The True Story of America's Sky-High Prescription Drug Prices." *Vox,* May 10, 2018. Available at: https://no-more-tears.org/Kliff-2018.pdf.

337 **Despite surveys that:** Erman, Michael. J&J Raises U.S. Prices on Around Two Dozen Drugs." Reuters, January 11, 2019. Available at: https://no-more-tears.org/Erman-2019.pdf.

338 **"FDA Loves Kids":** Miller, Henry I. "FDA Loves Kids So Much, It'll Make You Sick." *The Wall Street Journal,* August 18, 1997. Available at: https://no-more-tears.org/Miller-1997.pdf.

339 **"The FDA Is Out":** Miller, Henry. "The FDA Is out of Control and a Danger to the Public." *The Wall Street Journal,* December 28, 2010. Available at: https://no-more-tears.org/Miller-2010.pdf.

339 **the FDA adopted REMS:** *State of Minnesota vs. McKinsey & Company, Inc.* Complaint. February 4, 2021. Available at: https://no-more-tears.org/Ellison-2021.pdf.

339 **This was demonstrated:** Rappaport, Bob A. Letter to Janssen Pharmaceuticals Inc., subject: "Supplement Approval." 2017. Available at: https://no-more-tears.org/Rappaport-2017.pdf.

339 **So the FDA created:** Office of the Inspector General, Department of Health and Human Services. *FDA's Risk Evaluation and Mitigation Strategies: Uncertain Effectiveness in Addressing the Opioid Crisis.* September 20, 2020. OEI-01-17-005102020. Available at: https://no-more-tears.org/OIG-2020.pdf.

339 **The pages' decades-long:** Editorial Board. "FDA to Patients: Drop Dead." *The Wall Street Journal,* September 24, 2002. Available at: https://no-more-tears.org/The-Editorial-Board-2002.pdf.

340 **Under the headline:** Eckholm, Erik. "U.S. Meat Farmers Brace for Limits on Antibiotics." *The New York Times,* September 20, 2010. Available at: https://no-more-tears.org/Eckholm-2010.pdf.

340 **The new guidelines didn't:** Harris, Gardiner. "Antibiotics in Animals Need Limits, F.D.A. Says." *The New York Times,* June 28, 2010. Available at: https://no-more-tears.org/Harris-2010b.pdf.

341 **Already facing rising costs:** Wouters, Olivier J. "Lobbying Expenditures and Campaign Contributions by the Pharmaceutical and Health Product Industry in the United States, 1999–2018." *JAMA Internal Medicine* 180, no. 5, May 1, 2020: 688–97. Available at: https://no-more-tears.org/Wouters-2020.pdf.

341 **Another example came:** Sharp, Jonathan. "FDA's 'Closer to Zero' Plan Fails to Adequately Address Toxic Heavy Metals in Baby Food." *Food Safety News,* September 3, 2022. Available at: https://no-more-tears.org/FSN-2022.pdf.

342 **From 1991 through 2015:** Almashat, Sammy, Sidney M. Wolfe, and Michael Carome. "Twenty-Five Years of Pharmaceutical Industry Criminal and Civil Penalties: 1991 Through 2015." *Public Citizen,* March 16, 2016. Available at: https://no-more-tears.org/Almashat-2016.pdf.

343 **But despite its widely acknowledged role:** Kaplan, Sheila. "Who Will Be the Next F.D.A. Chief?" *The New York Times,* February 20, 2021. Available at: https://no-more-tears.org/Kaplan-2021.pdf.

343 **In the immediate aftermath:** Vaughan, Diane. *The Challenger Launch Deci-*

sion: Risky Technology, Culture, and Deviance at NASA. University of Chicago Press, 1997.

344 **Documents suggest that:** Munro, R. *"Cyprus Ore Reserve Evaluation Prelimi-nary Summary."* 1991. IMERYS416192. Available at: https://no-more-tears.org /IMERYS416192.pdf.

345 **Sometime in the 1980s:** Denton, R. Memo to W. Ashton and D. Jones, sub-ject: "Trip Report Talc Validation Team Meeting—November 10, 1993, Wind-sor, Vermont." November 23, 1993. JNJ000240739. Available at: https:// no-more-tears.org/Denton-1993.pdf.

345 **The company's stable:** Cirillo, Marco. "Johnson & Johnson Equity." Presenta-tion. 1996. Available at: https://no-more-tears.org/Cirillo-1996.pdf.

345 **Protecting that franchise:** Costello, Daniel. "Senators Cromote Amgen's Claim with Medicare." *Los Angeles Times,* September 6, 2007. Available at: https://no-more-tears.org/Costello-2007.pdf.

346 **The company conducted:** Armstrong, Sharon. *The Essential Performance Re-view Handbook: A Quick and Handy Resource for Any Manager or HR Profes-sional (The Essential Handbook).* Weiser, 2010.

347 **"You agree that":** Plaintiffs v. Janssen Pharmaceutical, Inc. et al. Plaintiffs' re-sponse to defendants' motion to preclude notices to attend addressed to Dr. Danielle Coppola and Dr. Gahan Pandina. March 2, 2020. Available at: https:// no-more-tears.org/Itkin-2020.pdf.

A: It's a very general statement, but they should abide by the regulations and rules.

Q: Sir, this is a simple— I promise you, it's not a trick question. Drug com-panies should be honest with the public, right?

A: Again, honesty is a very broad term. I would say they should abide by the regulations and rules.

Q: Okay. That's— In fact, I am going to write that one down so I remember it. 'Honesty is a broad term.'

. . .

Q: These numbers are not in the letter to the editor, are they, Dr. Coppola?

A: No, it—

Q: They are not, correct?

A: Dr. Bilker didn't for whatever reason put them in the letter.

Q: We have in the letter— and maybe we can put these side by side. I don't know if it will work side by side, but you and I can agree that those results did not make it into the letter to the world to see, correct?

A: Correct.

Q: They were not provided to the Food and Drug Administration, true?

A: Correct.

Q: They have not been provided as far as you know to Dr. Findling and Dr. Daneman?

A: I have no idea. I assume that Dr. Bilker shared all of this information.

Q: They have not been provided to the journal, correct?

A: No.

Q: Right here in this book, what we are seeing are different numbers than what were in the published paper, correct?

A: Yes.

Q: Do you remember way back when we started your discussion when we discussed lying? About scientific misconduct? We talked about a drug company should avoid scientific misconduct, correct?

A: Correct.

Q: You told us that was a 10, correct?

A: Yes.

Q: One of the things that was included in scientific misconduct was hiding data, correct?

A: Yes, and I— I never saw— I don't know what this data—

Q: Let's be real clear, right? The reason for this whole letter to the editor besides litigation is because Table 21 was never turned over way back when in 2003, correct?

A: No.

Q: Table 21 was never part of the original analysis, correct? It's not in the original Findling article?

A: It's not in the original Findling article.

Q: Okay. Daneman, we see multiple emails, and others, that were upset about, at least from their perspective, not being provided with Table 21, correct?

A: Yes, I think we've established that.

Q: We talked about when it was time to get this letter to the editor done, to get it sent out, especially send it to the FDA, err on the side of over-inclusion, right? Be transparent? We talked about that just a few minutes ago, right?

A: Yes.

Q: And here we are looking at data or were looking at data a moment ago that was never included in the published results, correct?

A: Yes.

Q: We saw emails about "Refute Table 21." Do you remember that?

A: Yes.

Q: We talked about the way to refute Table 21 is to make the significance go away, do you remember that?

A: Yes.

Q: Hiding data is not an acceptable way to refute Table 21, is it, ma'am?

A: No.

Q: Ma'am, I started your cross examination by asking you two simple questions. I'm going to try it one more time. In the course of all we've gone through over the last couple days, have you seen any conduct by Janssen that you feel is the type of conduct that should be deterred?

A: No.

348 **In 2012, J & J won:** Walker, Joseph, and Nathalie Tadina. "J & J Tuberculosis Drug Gets Fast-Track Clearance." *The Wall Street Journal,* January 2, 2013.

350 **In just one example:** Thomas, Katie. "Novartis Hid Manipulated Data While Seeking Approval for $2.1 Million Treatment." *The New York Times,* August 6, 2019.

Index

About the Author

GARDINER HARRIS is a consultant living in Southern California. From 2003 until 2019, he worked at *The New York Times* serving as an international diplomacy, White House, South Asia, public health, and pharmaceutical reporter. His stories in South Asia about air pollution led to profound changes to ameliorate the problem, and his pieces on sanitation helped inspire the government to build more than one million toilets. While he covered public health, his pieces led to legislation mandating public disclosures of drug company payments to doctors and inspired scores of drug withdrawals. Before joining the *Times,* he was a reporter for *The Wall Street Journal,* covering the pharmaceutical industry. His investigations there led to what was then the largest fine in the history of the Securities and Exchange Commission and criminal charges against top executives. Previously, he was the Appalachian reporter for the *Courier Journal* of Louisville, Kentucky. In 1999, he won the Worth Bingham Prize for investigative journalism and the George Polk Award for environmental reporting after revealing that coal companies deliberately and illegally exposed miners to toxic levels of coal dust. Among those coal companies was one once run by Kentucky's sitting governor at the time. His novel, *Hazard,* draws on his experience investigating these conditions. As a police reporter in Louisville, his investigation led to criminal charges being filed against a chief of police.